ASPEN PUBLISHERS

Sweet on Construction Industry Contracts: Major AIA Documents

Fifth Edition

by Jonathan Sweet

Sweet on Construction Industry Contracts: Major AIA Documents, Fifth Edition, is a comprehensive guide to AIA contract preparation, interpretation, and litigation. It contains everything you need to know, providing up-to-date information on enforcement and conduct of arbitration proceedings; clauses limiting design professional liability; indemnity and payment issues; jobsite safety; and analysis of all the relevant case law.

Highlights of the 2011 Supplement

The following developments and issues are included in the 2011 Supplement:

- Summaries of key provisions of the *ConsensusDocs,* a competitor to the AIA Documents, sponsored by many of the trade organizations that formerly endorsed AIA Documents
- Project Representative/CM liability, role
- Independent contractor vs. employee status
- Alternative Disputes Resolution
- Licensing
- California Right to Repair Act (SB 800)
- Equitable and contractual Indemnity
- Owner liability to subcontractors
- Jobsite safety responsibility
- Owner duty to provide financial information
- Mechanic's liens
- Subcontractor involvement, licensing
- Termination for cause, convenience
- Economic Loss rule

Wolters Kluwer
Law & Business

- Arbitration
- Bond claims
- Waiver of subrogation
- Admissibility of expert evidence
- Attorneys' fees recovery
- Change orders
- Owner termination of contractor for cause
- Payment clauses
- Architect standard of care
- Period of limitations

The Table of Cases, Table of AIA Documents, and Index have been updated to reflect all the changes to the text.

11/11

For questions concerning this shipment, billing, or other customer service matters, call our Customer Service Department at 1-800-234-1660.

For toll-free ordering, please call 1-800-638-8437.

ASPEN PUBLISHERS

SWEET ON CONSTRUCTION INDUSTRY CONTRACTS
MAJOR AIA DOCUMENTS

Fifth Edition

VOLUMES 1 AND 2

2011 Cumulative Supplement

JONATHAN J. SWEET
Law Offices of Jonathan J. Sweet
Los Gatos, California

This supplement supersedes all previous supplements.

Wolters Kluwer
Law & Business

Published by Wolters Kluwer Law & Business in New York.

Wolters Kluwer Law & Business serves customers worldwide with CCH, Aspen Publishers and Kluwer Law International products.

ISBN: 978-1-4548-0178-8

Printed in the United States of America

1 2 3 4 5 6 7 8 9 0

SUSTAINABLE FORESTRY INITIATIVE
Certified Chain of Custody
Promoting Sustainable Forestry
www.sfiprogram.org
SFI-00756

About Wolters Kluwer Law & Business

Wolters Kluwer Law & Business is a leading global provider of intelligent information and digital solutions for legal and business professionals in key specialty areas, and respected educational resources for professors and law students. Wolters Kluwer Law & Business connects legal and business professionals as well as those in the education market with timely, specialized authoritative content and information-enabled solutions to support success through productivity, accuracy and mobility.

Serving customers worldwide, Wolters Kluwer Law & Business products include those under the Aspen Publishers, CCH, Kluwer Law International, Loislaw, Best Case, ftwilliam.com and MediRegs family of products.

CCH products have been a trusted resource since 1913, and are highly regarded resources for legal, securities, antitrust and trade regulation, government contracting, banking, pension, payroll, employment and labor, and healthcare reimbursement and compliance professionals.

Aspen Publishers products provide essential information to attorneys, business professionals and law students. Written by preeminent authorities, the product line offers analytical and practical information in a range of specialty practice areas from securities law and intellectual property to mergers and acquisitions and pension/benefits. Aspen's trusted legal education resources provide professors and students with high-quality, up-to-date and effective resources for successful instruction and study in all areas of the law.

Kluwer Law International products provide the global business community with reliable international legal information in English. Legal practitioners, corporate counsel and business executives around the world rely on Kluwer Law journals, looseleafs, books, and electronic products for comprehensive information in many areas of international legal practice.

Loislaw is a comprehensive online legal research product providing legal content to law firm practitioners of various specializations. Loislaw provides attorneys with the ability to quickly and efficiently find the necessary legal information they need, when and where they need it, by facilitating access to primary law as well as state-specific law, records, forms and treatises.

Best Case Solutions is the leading bankruptcy software product to the bankruptcy industry. It provides software and workflow tools to flawlessly streamline petition preparation and the electronic filing process, while timely incorporating ever-changing court requirements.

ftwilliam.com offers employee benefits professionals the highest quality plan documents (retirement, welfare and non-qualified) and government forms (5500/PBGC, 1099 and IRS) software at highly competitive prices.

MediRegs products provide integrated health care compliance content and software solutions for professionals in healthcare, higher education and life sciences, including professionals in accounting, law and consulting.

Wolters Kluwer Law & Business, a division of Wolters Kluwer, is headquartered in New York. Wolters Kluwer is a market-leading global information services company focused on professionals.

WOLTERS KLUWER LAW & BUSINESS SUPPLEMENT NOTICE

This product is updated on a periodic basis with supplements to reflect important changes in the subject matter. If you have purchased this product directly from Wolters Kluwer Law & Business, we have already recorded your subscription for the update service.

If, however, you purchased this product from a bookstore and wish to receive future updates and revised or related volumes billed separately with a 30-day examination review, please contact our Customer Service Department at 1-800-234-1660 or send your name, company name (if applicable), address, and the title of the product to:

Wolters Kluwer Law & Business
Distribution Center
7201 McKinney Circle
Frederick, MD 21704

Important Contact Information

- To order any title, go to *www.aspenpublishers.com* or call 1-800-638-8437.
- To reinstate your manual update service, call 1-800-638-8437.
- To contact Customer Service, e-mail *customer.service@wolterskluwer.com*, call 1-800-234-1660, fax 1-800-901-9075, or mail correspondence to: Order Department—Aspen Publishers, Wolters Kluwer Law & Business, PO Box 990, Frederick, MD 21705.
- To review your account history or pay an invoice online, visit *www.aspenpublishers.com/payinvoices.*

Wolters Kluwer
Law & Business

To Lesly Sweet Miller (1932-2011), my mother and dedicated good-humored editor and friend.

CONTENTS

PREFACE

The *ConsensusDOCS* were recently issued as competitors to the AIA documents. The creators of the *ConsensusDOCS* claim that they are fair documents, reached through consensus with many diverse construction groups representing owners, contractors, and subcontractors. Trade organizations such as the Association of General Contractors (AGC), the Association of Specialty Contractors (ASC) and the American Subcontractors Association (ASA) formerly endorsed AIA documents. Now, those organizations no longer endorse the AIA documents, and have endorsed the *ConsensusDOCS*.

This supplement includes comparisons of key provisions of the *ConsensusDOCS* to AIA contract provisions, and describes how use of the *ConsensusDOCS* may shift risk and change roles of key project participants.

This supplement includes cases on project representative/CM liability, independent contractor vs. employee status, Alternative Disputes Resolution, licensing issues, California Right to Repair Act (SB 800), equitable and contractual indemnity issues, owner liability to subcontractors, jobsite safety responsibility, owner duty to provide financial information, mechanic's lien issues, licensing, termination for cause, termination for convenience, indemnity by subcontractors, insurance coverage, primary and excess, bond coverage, surety duties, arbitration waiver, jurisdiction, finality, and attorneys' fee recovery.

I appreciate the proofreading, editing, and style changes Lesly Miller, Esq., provided to this work. She has helped me to reduce complex ideas and issues to more comprehensible material.

I extend gratitude to my wife, Pamella Passaro, for recognizing the importance of my work on this supplement, and to my son, Misha Sweet.

As always, I appreciate any comments or suggestions from readers on particular topics or areas that should be addressed in future editions or supplements.

Los Gatos, California
August 2011

JONATHAN J. SWEET
Law Offices of Jonathan J. Sweet

VOLUME 1

Chapter 1

AIA DOCUMENT SYSTEMS

§ 1.04 PROCESS

Page 9, add at end of section:

Since the new ConsensusDOCS have been issued, articles have been published describing how these documents differ from other construction documents, including the AIA documents. The Construction Lawyer, published by the American Bar Association (ABA), included in its Winter 2009 edition a number of articles on the topic. In one of these, *Advantages of the ConsensusDOCS Construction Contracts*, Larry D. Harris and Brian M. Perlberg (Harris and Perlberg) describe the ConsensusDOCS as "contract documents based on best practices and proper risk allocation, for the benefit of organization members and the construction industry at large." *Advantages of the ConsensusDOCS Construction Contracts*, by Larry D. Harris and Brian M. Perlberg, The Construction Lawyer, Vol. 29, Number 1, Winter 2009.

Harris and Perlberg point out that many perceive the AIA documents to have been written by architects for architects. In the past, the AIA fought the perception of bias, receiving endorsements from the Association of General Contractors (AGC) and from the American Subcontractors' Association (ASA). However, the current AIA 2007 documents are not endorsed by these trade organizations. These organizations did endorse the ConsensusDOCS. Harris and Perlberg state that there is a need for documents other than the AIA documents, for those trade organizations which previously endorsed the ConsensusDOCS. Harris and Perlberg state that the drafting mandate for the ConsensusDOCS was to develop documents which represent the best interests of the project, rather than those of a single party. They claim that fair and balanced contracts encourage buy-ins from all parties, and they should attract the best contractors at their best prices by avoiding unnecessary risk contingencies. Harris and Perlberg say that the ConsensusDOCS provide commonsense solutions that could only be achieved by drawing upon all segments of the construction process for input.

Harris and Perlberg claim the ConsensusDOCS provide a more balanced approach to the ownership of design documents, a more comprehensive and practical approach to Building Information Modeling (BIM), and that the ConsensusDOCS represent significant improvements from "competing families of form contract documents."

Steven G.M. Stein and Ronald O. Wietecha, in their article, *A Comparison of ConsensusDOCS to the AIA Form Construction Contract Documents,* The Construction Lawyer, Vol. 29, Number 1, Winter 2009, define the primary philosophical difference between the AIA documents and the ConsensusDOCS as being that ConsensusDOCS provide for an immensely diminished role for the architect in project execution. The authors state that under the ConsensusDOCS, the architect has very few formal responsibilities and he is conceived of more as the owner's consultant rather than as the integral project administrator and facilitator described in the AIA documents. ConsensusDOCS 200, the Standard Agreement and General Conditions Between Owner and Contractor contains no provision similar to the Article 4, entitled "Architect," of A201-2007. Under ConsensusDOCS 200, the owner and contractor communicate directly, not through the architect. ConsensusDOCS 200 only calls for the contractor to communicate with the architect "if directed." ConsensusDOCS 200 Para. 3.14.1.

Stein and Wietecha state that the ConsensusDOCS differ from the AIA documents in that under the ConsensusDOCS most of the responsibilities of the architect during the construction phase shift to the owner, with the assistance and recommendations of the architect. ConsensusDOCS 200 Para. 3.2.8. Under the ConsensusDOCS, the architect does not occupy the role of arbiter and Initial Decision Maker (IDM). The parties under the ConsensusDOCS have the option of selecting a third-party mitigation facilitator at the time of signing the contract, or the option of retaining all contractual and project-related interpretations and determinations equally between the owner and the contractor.

Stein and Wietecha state that the changes which put more responsibility on owners for tasks performed under the AIA documents by the architect will be particularly noticeable on design-build projects. Under ConsensusDOCS 200 Para. 4.7, the owner must provide a representative, who is presumably to manage all of the communications. Under A201-2007 these communications are made through the architect. Also, under ConsensusDOCS 200, the owner must make almost all the decisions that under A201 would be made by the architect. A201-2007 Sec. 4.2.6, ConsensusDOCS 200 Para. 9.3.4, Para. 9.6.1, Para. 9.8.1, Para. 3.7.1.

Stein and Wietecha address the question of whether the ConsensusDOCS are pro-contractor. Under ConsensusDOCS 200 Para. 13.1, the owner can only assign the construction contract to a lender as long as the assignment is no less favorable to the contractor. Under A201-2007 Sec. 13.2.2, the owner's right to assign the construction contract is absolute. Under ConsensusDOCS 200 Para. 11.3.4, the owner who terminates the contractor for default may take over the contractor's materials, equipment, and tools. However, the ConsensusDOCS 200 clause requires the owner to return those items to the contractor in good condition once the work is completed. A201-2007 contains no such owner obligation. Stein and Weitecha point out that under ConsensusDOCS 200 Para. 6.3.1, the contractor is entitled to an extension of time for any delay beyond the control of the contractor. A201-2007 Sec. 8.3.1 limits the causes for delay that give rise to an extension of time to those listed.

§ 1.05 LANGUAGE SELECTION: AIA DRAFTING PRINCIPLES

Page 12, add at end of section:

Steven G.M. Stein and Ronald O. Wietecha state in their article, *A Comparison of ConsensusDOCS to the AIA Form Construction Contract Documents,* The Construction Lawyer, Vol. 29, Number 1, Winter 2009, that the value of the ConsensusDOCS as compared to the AIA documents depends on the specific circumstances of the project. Stein and Wietecha state that the need for new documents springs from the belief that the AIA documents do not represent a fair allocation of risk. However, the authors also state use of this new set of construction contract documents may lead to confusion, as both sets of documents can be used for the same projects. The authors state that unsophisticated users of form construction documents may not realize that the AIA and ConsensusDOCS are not necessarily compatible.

Stein and Wietecha address the assertion that the ConsensusDOCS are based on a consensus of designers, owners, contractors, and surety. The ConsensusDOCS are endorsed by 21 organizations, some of which formerly endorsed the AIA documents. However, the Engineers Joint Contract Documents Committee (EJCDC) has not endorsed the ConsensusDOCS. Also, the AIA did not participate in discussions regarding the ConsensusDOCS, nor did the AIA endorse the documents. Stein and Wietecha comment in their article that they believe that there is a question as to whether a consensus is achievable in an industry in which project participants have strikingly adverse interests.

The authors state that, at best, an organization's documents can reflect compromise among the various industry participants that will have inherent underlying dissatisfactions for each of the participants. Stein and Wietecha also note that the AIA documents contain a review and revision process, which is not part of the ConsensusDOCS development process.

Stein and Wietecha define the primary philosophical difference between the AIA documents and the ConsensusDOCS as being that the ConsensusDOCS provide for an immensely diminished role for the architect in project execution. The authors state that under the ConsensusDOCS, the architect has very few formal responsibilities, and he is conceived of more as the owner's consultant rather than as the integral project administrator and facilitator established in the AIA documents. ConsensusDOCS 200, the Standard Agreement and General Conditions Between Owner and Contractor contains no provision similar to the Article 4, entitled "Architect," of A201-2007. Under ConsensusDOCS 200, the owner and contractor communicate directly, not through the architect. ConsensusDOCS 200 only calls for the contractor to communicate with the architect "if directed." ConsensusDOCS 200 Para. 3.14.1.

Stein and Wietecha state that the ConsensusDOCS differ from the AIA documents in that under the ConsensusDOCS most of the responsibilities of the architect during the construction phase shift to the owner, with the assistance and recommendations of the architect. ConsensusDOCS 200 Para. 3.2.8. Under the ConsensusDOCS, the architect does not occupy the role of arbiter and Initial

Decision Maker (IDM). The parties under the ConsensusDOCS have the option of selecting a third-party mitigation facilitator at the time of signing the contract, or the option of retaining all contractual and project-related interpretations and determinations equally between the owner and the contractor.

Stein and Wietecha state that the changes which put more responsibility on owners for tasks performed under the AIA documents by the architect will be particularly noticeable on design-build projects. Under ConsensusDOCS 200 Para. 4.7, the owner must provide a representative, who is presumably to manage all of the communications. Under A201-2007 these communications are made through the architect. Also, under ConsensusDOCS 200, the owner must make almost all the decisions that under A201 would be made by the architect. A201-2007 Sec. 4.2.6, ConsensusDOCS 200 Para. 9.3.4, Para. 9.6.1, Para. 9.8.1, Para. 3.7.1.

In *Advantages of the ConsensusDOCS Construction Contracts*, by Larry D. Harris and Brian M. Perlberg, The Construction Lawyer, Vol. 29, Number 1, Winter 2009, Harris and Perlberg claim the ConsensusDOCS provide a more balanced approach to the use of ownership of design documents, a more comprehensive and practical approach to Building Information Modeling (BIM), and that the ConsensusDOCS represent significant improvements from "competing families of form contract documents."

CHAPTER 2

SHOULD YOU USE AN AIA DOCUMENT?

§ 2.04 QUALITY AND CHARACTER

Page 25, add after second full paragraph:

Since the new ConsensusDOCS (ConsensusDOCS) have been issued, articles have been published describing how these documents differ from other construction documents, including the AIA documents. The Construction Lawyer, published by the American Bar Association (ABA), included in its Winter 2009 edition a number of these articles. In one of these, *Advantages of the ConsensusDOCS Construction Contracts*, Larry D. Harris and Brian M. Perlberg describe the ConsensusDOCS as "contract documents based on best practices and proper risk allocation, for the benefit of organization members and the construction industry at large." *Advantages of the ConsensusDOCS Construction Contracts*, by Larry D. Harris and Brian M. Perlberg (Harris and Perlberg), The Construction Lawyer, Vol. 29, Number 1, Winter 2009.

Harris and Perlberg point out that many perceive the AIA documents as written by architects for architects. In the past, the AIA fought the perception of bias, receiving endorsements from the Association of General Contractors (AGC), and from the American Subcontractors' Association (ASA). However, the AIA 2007 documents, the current set of documents, are not endorsed by these trade organizations. These organizations did endorse the ConsensusDOCS. Harris and Perlberg state that there is a need for documents other than the AIA documents, based on the trade organizations which endorsed the ConsensusDOCS. Harris and Perlberg stated that the drafting mandate for the ConsensusDOCS was to develop documents which represent the best interests of the project, rather than those of a single party. They claim that fair and balanced contracts encourage buy-ins from all parties, and they should attract the best contractors at their best prices by avoiding unnecessary risk contingencies. Harris and Perlberg state that the ConsensusDOCS provide commonsense solutions that could only be achieved by drawing upon all segments of the construction process for genuine input.

CHAPTER 3
JUDICIAL ATTITUDE TOWARD AIA DOCUMENTS

§ 3.02 VARIABLES

[A] Construction Services Contracts vs. Design Services Contracts

Page 29, add at end of subsection:

Since the new ConsensusDOCS have been issued, numerous articles have been published describing how these documents differ from other construction documents, including the AIA documents. The Construction Lawyer, published by the American Bar Association (ABA), included in its Winter 2009 edition a number of these articles. In one of these, *Advantages of the ConsensusDOCS Construction Contracts*, Larry D. Harris and Brian M. Perlberg describe the ConsensusDOCS as "contract documents based on best practices and proper risk allocation, for the benefit of organization members and the construction industry at large." *Advantages of the ConsensusDOCS Construction Contracts*, by Larry D. Harris and Brian M. Perlberg (Harris and Perlberg), The Construction Lawyer, Vol. 29, Number 1, Winter 2009.

Harris and Perlberg point out that many perceive the AIA documents as written by architects for architects. In the past, the AIA fought the perception of bias, receiving endorsements from the Association of General Contractors (AGC), and from the American Subcontractors' Association (ASA). However, the AIA 2007 documents, the current set of documents, are not endorsed by these trade organizations. These organizations did endorse the ConsensusDOCS. Harris and Perlberg state that there is a need for documents other than the AIA documents, based on the trade organizations which endorsed the ConsensusDOCS. Harris and Perlberg stated that the drafting mandate for the ConsensusDOCS was to develop documents which represent the best interests of the project, rather than those of a single party. They claim that fair and balanced contracts encourage buy-ins from all parties, and they should attract the best contractors at their best prices by avoiding unnecessary risk contingencies. Harris and Perlberg state that the ConsensusDOCS provide commonsense solutions that could only be achieved by drawing upon all segments of the construction process for genuine input.

CHAPTER 5

ARCHITECTURAL SERVICES

§ 5.02 RANGE OF SERVICES: FINANCES, PERMITS, RENOVATION, AND DESIGN-ONLY

Page 83, add after third full paragraph after the text "occurred many years before":

Courts continue to grapple with whether to apply the economic loss rule to bar claims for those lacking privity. In *Flagstaff Affordable Housing Limited Partnership v. Design Alliance, Inc.*,[7.1] a property owner filed a complaint against an architect, alleging breach of contract and professional negligence. The superior court granted the architect's motion to dismiss. The court of appeals[7.2] reversed and remanded, and the architect appealed.

In *Flagstaff*, the Arizona Supreme Court held that the "economic loss doctrine" barred the plaintiffs, in certain circumstances, from recovering economic damages in tort. The court had previously applied the doctrine only to products liability claims. In this case, the Arizona Supreme Court held that it would apply the doctrine in a construction defect case and held that a property owner was limited to its contractual remedies when an architect's negligent design caused economic loss but no physical injury to persons or other property.

In 1995, Flagstaff Affordable Housing Limited Partnership ("Owner") contracted with Design Alliance, Inc. ("Architect") for the design of eight apartment buildings and a community center (the "apartments"). To qualify as a low income housing project, the apartments had to comply with the federal Fair Housing Act's accessibility guidelines. The owner separately contracted with Butte Construction Company ("Contractor") for the construction of the apartments, which were completed in 1996.

In 2004, the U.S. Department of Housing and Urban Development (HUD) filed a complaint against the owner, alleging that the apartments violated the accessibility guidelines. After settling with HUD, the owner, in 2006, sued the architect and the contractor, alleging they had breached their respective contracts and acted negligently. The contractor was later dismissed from the action.

The architect moved to dismiss the complaint under Rule 12(b)(6). The architect argued that the contract claim was barred by the statute of repose in Ariz. Rev. Stat. § 12-552, which provided that no action based in contract may be brought against a person who "furnishes the design . . . of an improvement to real

---

[7.1] 223 P.3d 664 (Ariz. 2010).

[7.2] 221 Ariz. 433, 212 P.3d 125 (2009).

property more than eight years after substantial completion of the improvement." The architect argued that the negligence claim should be dismissed based on *Carstens v. City of Phoenix*,[7.3] which held that the economic loss doctrine precluded tort recovery of economic losses in the "construction defect setting."

The owner voluntarily dismissed the contract claim, but argued that the economic loss doctrine did not bar the claim for professional negligence. The owner did not dispute that it sought recovery only for economic losses, and acknowledged that *Carstens* applied the doctrine in a construction defect case. The owner argued, however, that a claim for "professional negligence" was based on the special relationship between architects and their clients, and, therefore, it was excepted from the economic loss doctrine. The superior court dismissed the complaint.

The court of appeals reversed, holding that the economic loss doctrine did not bar negligence claims against design professionals.[7.4] The court acknowledged that prior Arizona cases, such as *Carstens*, applied the doctrine to cases involving construction defects. Distinguishing *Carstens*, the appellate court stated that this case did not involve construction defects, but an architect's alleged negligent design. The appellate court concluded that the economic loss doctrine should not apply, because the owner's claim was based in tort, not contract, and reflected the special duties imposed on architects by law.

On appeal to the Arizona Supreme Court, the architect argued that the superior court properly dismissed the complaint, because the owner alleged only economic loss, and that the economic loss doctrine applied in construction cases and precluded tort recovery by parties not in privity for such losses absent personal injury or damage to other property. The architect also argued that the doctrine should apply to claims against not only contractors, but also architects and other design professionals. The state supreme court stated that it had not addressed the economic loss doctrine since its 1984 decision in *Salt River Project Agricultural Improvement and Power District v. Westinghouse Electric Corp.*[7.5] In the absence of other decisions by the Arizona Supreme Court, the court of appeals and the federal courts had reached conflicting conclusions regarding the application of the doctrine under Arizona law.[7.6]

"Economic loss" refers to pecuniary or commercial damage, including any decreased value or repair costs for a product or property that is itself the subject

---

[7.3] 206 Ariz. 123, 125, 75 P.3d 1081, 1084 (Ct. App. 2003).

[7.4] Flagstaff Affordable Hous. Ltd. P'ship v. Design Alliance, Inc., 221 Ariz. 433, 212 P.3d 125 (Ct. App. 2009).

[7.5] 143 Ariz. 368, 694 P.2d 198 (1984).

[7.6] *Compare* Apollo Group, Inc. v. Avnet, Inc., 58 F.3d 477, 480 (9th Cir. 1995) (stating that *Salt River* reflected that Arizona applied the economic loss rule "broadly") *with* Evans v. Singer, 518 F. Supp. 2d 1134, 1142-45 (D. Ariz. 2007) (stating *Salt River* "provided anything but" a broad reading of the rule); *compare also Carstens*, 206 Ariz. at 128 ¶ 21, 75 P.3d at 1086 (arguing that *Salt River* supported applying doctrine to bar homeowners' claim for economic losses from construction defects) *with* Valley Forge Ins. Co. v. Sam's Plumbing, LLC, 220 Ariz. 512, 515-16 ¶¶ 11-12, 207 P.3d 765, 768-69 (Ct. App. 2009) (arguing that *Carstens* misconstrued *Salt River*).

of a contract between the plaintiff and defendant, and consequential damages such as lost profits.[7.7]

Some courts have stated that the economic loss doctrine "bars a party from recovering economic damages in tort unless accompanied by physical harm."[7.8] The *Flagstaff* court stated that this formulation of the doctrine was overly broad. In many contexts, tort recovery is available for solely pecuniary losses.[7.9] Describing the doctrine in this way conflates two distinct issues: (1) whether a contracting party should be limited to its contract remedies for purely economic loss; and (2) whether a plaintiff may assert tort claims for economic damages against a defendant absent any contract between the parties. The *Flagstaff* court held that the economic loss doctrine was best directed to the first of these issues, and used the phrase to refer to a common law rule limiting a contracting party to contractual remedies for the recovery of economic losses unaccompanied by physical injury to persons or other property.

In *Salt River*, an electric utility company asserted contract and tort claims against the seller of a control device that had allegedly malfunctioned and damaged the utility's turbine unit. In that case, the Arizona Supreme Court held that the utility could not recover in contract, because the seller had, consistent with the Uniform Commercial Code, disclaimed certain warranties and otherwise limited its liability.[7.10] The court, however, rejected the seller's argument that the contractual provisions also precluded a tort claim for strict products liability.[7.11] In the context of an alleged product defect, the *Salt River* court considered whether a plaintiff could seek tort recovery for economic losses related to the defendant's contractual performance. In resolving this question, the court noted the distinct policies served by tort and contract law. Strict liability promotes product safety and spreads the costs of accidents. Contract law, in contrast, seeks to preserve freedom of contract and to promote the free flow of commerce.[7.12] These goals are best served by allowing the parties to specify the consequences of a breach of their agreement. Accordingly, "[w]hen a defect renders a product substandard or unable to perform the functions for which it was manufactured, the purchaser's remedy for disappointed commercial expectations is through contract law." [7.13]

The *Salt River* court acknowledged that most courts had held that economic loss resulting from a product defect (including damage to the product itself) was not recoverable in tort absent accompanying physical damage to other property or

---

[7.7] *See Salt River*, 143 Ariz. at 379-80, 694 P.2d at 209-10.

[7.8] *Carstens*, 206 Ariz. at 125 ¶ 10, 75 P.3d at 1083.

[7.9] *See* Giles v. Gen. Motors Acceptance Corp., 494 F.3d 865, 875 (9th Cir. 2007) (noting that "[t]ort law has traditionally protected individuals from a host of wrongs that cause only monetary damage"); *Evans*, 518 F. Supp. 2d at 1139.

[7.10] 143 Ariz. at 374, 694 P.2d at 204.

[7.11] *Id.* at 375, 381, 694 P.2d at 205, 211.

[7.12] *Id.* at 376, 694 P.2d at 205-06.

[7.13] *Id.*

personal injury.[7.14] That court, however, expressly declined to follow that majority rule and, instead, embraced a narrower, case-specific approach:

> Where economic loss, in the form of repair costs, diminished value, or lost profits, is the plaintiff's only loss, the policies of the law generally will be best served by leaving the parties to their commercial remedies. Where economic loss is accompanied by physical damage to person or other property, however, the parties' interests generally will be realized best by the imposition of strict tort liability. If the only loss is non-accidental and to the product itself, or is of a consequential nature, the remedies available under the UCC will govern and strict liability and other tort theories will be unavailable.[7.15]

Under *Salt River*, the economic nature of the loss was only one factor in a three-part test to determine whether tort remedies would be available. The court also had to consider whether the defect was "unreasonably dangerous" and whether the loss occurred in a "sudden, accidental manner."[7.16] When these factors are present, *Salt River* allowed a plaintiff to recover in tort for purely economic loss.[7.17]

Thus, in the products liability context, *Salt River* declined to categorically bar tort recovery of economic losses. The court reasoned that, "[e]ach case must be examined to determine whether the facts preponderate in favor of the application of tort law or commercial law exclusively or a combination of the two."[7.18] Applying a narrow version of economic loss doctrine, *Salt River* held that the commercial purchaser in that case could assert a products liability claim against a commercial seller for economic losses for which the contract disclaimed liability.

The *Flagstaff* case involved alleged defects in a building rather than a defective product. Many other courts, and the parties here, assumed that Arizona law also applied the economic loss doctrine to construction defect cases. The only opinion cited by the Arizona Supreme Court for this proposition, however, is *Woodward v. Chirco Construction Co.*,[7.19] which was decided a few months before *Salt River*. *Woodward*, however, concerned the limitations period for contract actions for breach of implied warranty, not the preclusion of tort claims. In that case, a couple contracted with a builder for the construction and purchase of a residence.[7.20] After the closing, the soil subsided and caused extensive damage to the home. The homeowners sued the builder alleging both negligence for failing to conduct a soil study and breach of the implied warranty of workmanlike performance and habitability. The trial court dismissed the negligence claim for lack of proof of the relevant standard of care. It also dismissed the

---

[7.14] *Id.* at 379, 694 P.2d at 209.

[7.15] *Id.* at 379-80, 694 P.2d at 209-10.

[7.16] *Id.* at 379, 694 P.2d at 209.

[7.17] *Id.* at 380-81, 694 P.2d at 210-11 (applying factors and holding utility could seek tort recovery of damage to turbine unit even if it was not a loss to "other property").

[7.18] *Id.* at 380, 694 P.2d at 210.

[7.19] 141 Ariz. 514, 687 P.2d 1269 (1984).

[7.20] *Id.* at 515, 687 P.2d at 1270.

warranty claim as barred by the statute of limitations. The court of appeals affirmed the dismissal of the negligence claim but reversed the dismissal of the contract claim, holding that the six-year limitations period in Ariz. Rev. Stat. § 12-548 applied.

The builder in *Woodward* petitioned for review, arguing that breach of an implied warranty was actionable only in tort, which, generally, had a two-year limitations period.[7.21] Rejecting this argument, the Arizona Supreme Court agreed with other jurisdictions holding that a home purchaser could sue both in contract for breach of the implied warranty and in tort for the builder's breach of the common law duty of care.

The court stated:

> For example, if a fireplace collapses, the purchaser can sue in contract for the cost of remedying the structural defects and sue in tort for damage to personal property or personal injury caused by the collapse. Each claim will stand or fall on its own; a distinct statute of limitation applies to each.[7.22]

Although some courts have construed this language as approving the economic loss doctrine, the *Woodward* court was not asked to address the doctrine and did not discuss it. Moreover, when later applying the economic loss doctrine in *Salt River*, the Arizona Supreme Court did not mention *Woodward*. The *Woodward* court stated that it agreed with *Cosmopolitan Homes, Inc. v. Weller*,[7.23] which allowed a subsequent purchaser to assert negligence claims against a contractor for residential construction defects.[7.24] *Cosmopolitan Homes* rejected the argument that claims for recovery of economic loss sound exclusively in contract.[7.25]

Woodward did not resolve whether the economic loss doctrine should apply to construction defects. Although several opinions by the court of appeals concluded that the doctrine applied, those cases relied heavily on an interpretation of *Woodward* that the Arizona Supreme Court in *Flagstaff* rejected.[7.26]

To determine whether the doctrine should apply, the *Flagstaff* court stated that it was required to consider the underlying policies of tort and contract law in the construction setting.[7.27] The *Flagstaff* court stated that the contract law policy of upholding the expectations of the parties had as much, if not greater, force in construction defect cases as in product defect cases. Construction-related contracts often are negotiated between the parties on a project-specific basis and have detailed provisions allocating risks of loss and specifying remedies. In this

---

[7.21] *Id.*

[7.22] *Id.* at 516, 687 P.2d at 1271.

[7.23] 663 P.2d 1041 (Colo. 1983).

[7.24] *Woodward*, 141 Ariz. at 516, 687 P.2d at 1271.

[7.25] 663 P.2d at 1044-45.

[7.26] *See, e.g.*, *Carstens*, 206 Ariz. at 126 ¶¶ 11-12, 75 P.3d at 1084; Colberg v. Rellinger, 160 Ariz. 42, 44, 770 P.2d 346, 348 (1988); Nastri v. Wood Bros. Homes, Inc., 142 Ariz. 439, 444-45, 690 P.2d 158, 163-64 (1984).

[7.27] *Cf. Salt River*, 143 Ariz. at 376, 694 P.2d at 206 (stating that purposes of tort and contract law should determine which law applies in products liability cases).

context, allowing tort claims posed a danger of undermining the policy concerns of contract law. Contract law sought to encourage parties to order their prospective relationships, including the allocation of risk of future losses and the identification of remedies, and to enforce any resulting agreement consistent with the parties' expectations.[7.28]

In construction defect cases involving only pecuniary losses related to the building that is the subject of the parties' contract, the *Flagstaff* court stated that there were no strong policy reasons to impose common law tort liability in addition to contractual remedies. When a construction defect caused only damage to the building itself or other economic loss, common law contract remedies provided an adequate remedy, because they allowed recovery of the costs of remedying the defects[7.29] and other damages reasonably foreseeable to the parties upon entering the contract.[7.30]

The *Flagstaff* court went on to note that policies of accident deterrence and loss-spreading also did not require allowing tort recovery in addition to contractual remedies for economic loss from construction defects. The court stated these considerations had less force when parties to a site-specific construction contract have allocated the risk of loss and identified remedies for nonperformance.[7.31] Moreover, although a homeowner's purchase of a mass-produced home might, in some ways, be analogous to a consumer's purchase of a product, even in such a situation there would be less reason to preserve tort remedies for purely economic loss. Arizona law allowed home purchasers to bring contract claims for breach of the implied warranty of good workmanship and habitability, even if they were not in privity with the builder.[7.32]

The *Flagstaff* court concluded that in a construction defect case, "the policies of the law generally will be best served by leaving the parties to their commercial remedies" when a contracting party has incurred only "economic loss, in the form of repair costs, diminished value, or lost profits."[7.33] The court applied the economic loss doctrine and held that a contracting party was limited to its contractual remedies for purely economic loss from construction defects.

In the construction context, the economic loss doctrine respected the expectations of the parties when, as often will be true, they have expressly addressed liability and remedies in their contract. Thus, the parties can contractually agree to preserve tort remedies for solely economic loss, just as they may

---

[7.28] *See, e.g.*, Berschauer/Phillips Constr. Co. v. Seattle Sch. Dist. No. 1, 124 Wash. 2d 816, 881 P.2d 986, 993 (1994).

[7.29] *See Woodward*, 141 Ariz. at 516, 687 P.2d at 1271.

[7.30] *See* Higgins v. Ariz. Sav. & Loan Ass'n, 90 Ariz. 55, 63-64, 365 P.2d 476, 482-83 (1961) (adopting rule of Hadley v. Baxendale, 9 Exch. 341, 156 Eng. Rep. 145 (1854), for identifying damages recoverable in contract).

[7.31] *Cf. Salt River*, 143 Ariz. at 376, 694 P.2d at 206 (noting that contract law policy "is best served" by allowing "parties to limit the redress of a purchaser who fails to receive the quality of product he expected").

[7.32] *See* Richards v. Powercraft Homes, Inc., 139 Ariz. 242, 245, 678 P.2d 427, 430 (1984).

[7.33] *Salt River*, 143 Ariz. at 379, 694 P.2d at 209.

otherwise specify remedies that modify common law recovery.[7.34] On the other hand, if the parties do not provide otherwise in their contract, they will be limited to contractual remedies for any loss of the bargain resulting from construction defects that did not cause personal injury or damage to other property.

Applying the economic loss doctrine to construction cases also required the court to discuss two other aspects of the *Salt River* decision. First, *Salt River* identified certain requirements for the waiver of tort remedies, which is a separate question from whether the economic loss doctrine applied.[7.35] *Salt River*'s requirements for an effective waiver did not determine whether a party was limited to contractual remedies for purely economic losses resulting from construction defects. Instead, a party was so limited unless the parties provided in their contract for tort remedies.

Salt River also outlined a three-factor test for determining, on a case-specific basis, whether to apply the economic loss doctrine to claims involving a defective product. This approach allowed tort recovery for purely economic losses if they resulted from an "accident" that posed unreasonable risks of harm to other property or persons.[7.36] This minority view has been criticized as being too unpredictable and allowing noncontractual recovery when a purchaser has only been deprived of the benefit of the bargain.[7.37]

Whatever the wisdom of continuing to apply *Salt River*'s three-factor test in products liability cases, the *Flagstaff* court declined to extend that test to construction defect cases. The economic loss doctrine was held to appropriately apply in this context, because construction contracts typically are negotiated on a project-specific basis, and the parties should be encouraged to prospectively allocate risk and identify remedies within their agreements. The court noted that these goals would be undermined by an approach that allowed extra-contractual recovery for economic loss based not on the agreement itself, but instead on a court's *post hoc* determination that a construction defect posed risks of other loss or was somehow accidental in nature.[7.38]

The *Flagstaff* court adopted a version of the economic loss doctrine and held that a plaintiff who contracts for construction may not recover in tort for purely economic loss, unless the contract otherwise provides. The doctrine does not bar tort recovery when economic loss is accompanied by physical injury to persons or other property.

[7.34] *See* Green v. Snodgrass, 79 Ariz. 319, 322, 289 P.2d 191, 192 (1955) (noting that contract will control when it specifies remedies in event of breach).

[7.35] *See* 143 Ariz. at 375, 385, 694 P.2d at 205, 215.

[7.36] *See Salt River*, 143 Ariz. at 380-81, 694 P.2d at 210-11.

[7.37] *See* East River S.S. Corp. v. Transamerica Delaval, Inc., 476 U.S. 858, 869-70, 106 S. Ct. 2295, 90 L. Ed. 2d 865 (1986) (refusing to apply *Salt River*-type approach to products liability claim under admiralty law).

[7.38] *Cf.* Lincoln Gen. Ins. Co. v. Detroit Diesel Corp., 293 S.W.3d 487, 492-93 (Tenn. 2009) (noting similar concerns in adopting *East River*'s majority approach in products liability); Restatement (Third) of Torts: Products Liability § 21 & cmt. d (1998) (adopting *East River* approach).

The owner also argued that the economic loss doctrine should not apply to professional negligence claims based on an architect's design. The owner argued that applying the economic loss doctrine would conflict with *Donnelly Constr. Co. v. Oberg/Hunt/Gilleland*,[7.39] In *Donnelly*, a contractor relied on an architect's plans to prepare a bid for improvements to a school complex. After starting work, the contractor found the plans were in error, which increased the contractor's construction costs. The contractor later sued the architect to recover the increased costs, asserting claims for negligence, negligent misrepresentation, and breach of implied warranty. The architect argued that, because it had not entered into a contract with the contractor, it owed it no duty and could not be liable on any of the claims.

The *Donnelly* court held that lack of privity did not bar the claims.[7.40] With regard to the negligence claim, the *Donnelly* court noted that "[d]esign professionals have a duty to use ordinary skill, care, and diligence in rendering their professional services," and that "an action in negligence may be maintained upon the plaintiff's showing that the defendant owed a duty to him, that the duty was breached, and that the breach proximately caused an injury which resulted in actual damages."[7.41] The court further explained, "[w]e only hold here that design professionals are liable for foreseeable injuries to foreseeable victims which proximately result from their negligent performance of their professional services."[7.42]

Donnelly held that a contractor stated a valid claim for negligence to recover economic losses based on an architect's allegedly defective design. The architect did not argue that the contractor should be limited to its contractual remedies for economic loss. Instead, the architect argued that the absence of a contract precluded all liability. Without discussing the economic loss doctrine, *Donnelly* correctly implied that it would not apply to negligence claims by a plaintiff who had no contractual relationship with the defendant.

Although some courts have applied the doctrine in that context,[7.43] the *Flagstaff* court declined to do so. The principal function of the economic loss doctrine, in that court's view, was to encourage private ordering of economic relationships and to uphold the expectations of the parties by limiting a plaintiff to contractual remedies for loss of the benefit of the bargain. These concerns are not implicated when the plaintiff lacks privity and cannot pursue contractual remedies.[7.44]

[7.39] 139 Ariz. 184, 677 P.2d 1292 (1984).

[7.40] *Id.* at 187-89, 677 P.2d at 1295-97.

[7.41] *Id.* at 187, 677 P.2d at 1295.

[7.42] *Id.* at 188, 677 P.2d at 1296.

[7.43] *See, e.g.*, *Carstens*, 206 Ariz. at 127 ¶ 17, 75 P.3d at 1085; Davencourt at Pilgrims Landing Homeowners Ass'n v. Davencourt at Pilgrims Landing, LC, 221 P.3d 234, 243 (Utah 2009).

[7.44] *See* Vincent R. Johnson, *The Boundary-Line Function of the Economic Loss Rule*, 66 Wash. & Lee L. Rev. 523, 556 (2009) (concluding that when "established tort principles entitle a third party to protection under tort law for economic loss, an agreement to which the third party never assented should not be permitted to vitiate his or her right to tort remedies").

Rather than rely on the economic loss doctrine to preclude tort claims by noncontracting parties, the *Flagstaff* court stated that courts should, instead, focus on whether the applicable substantive law allowed liability in the particular context. For example, whether a noncontracting party may recover economic losses for a defendant's negligent misrepresentation should depend on whether the elements of that tort are satisfied, including whether the plaintiff is within the limited class of persons to whom the defendant owes a duty.[7.45]

The owner in *Flagstaff* also argued that the economic loss doctrine should not apply, because the architect breached duties imposed by law. Although architects have common-law duties of care, this case illustrates that it is often difficult to draw bright lines between obligations imposed by law and those arising from contract. The architect's duties with regard to the owner's project existed only because of the contract between the parties. Architectural contracts generally include compliance with applicable building codes and other legal design requirements as an implied term.[7.46]

The *Flagstaff* owner alleged that the architect designed a building that did not conform to certain requirements of the federal Fair Housing Act; and that this conduct both breached the architect's contractual obligations and constituted professional negligence. The court rejected the owner's attempts to label claims by distinguishing between contractual and extra-contractual duties as an unduly formalistic approach to determining if the plaintiffs, like the owner, should be limited to their contractual remedies for economic loss.

The court stated that the professional status of architects should not determine whether the economic loss doctrine applied in this context. The purposes of the doctrine were served by applying it to contracts entered by architects and design professionals, as other courts have recognized.[7.47] The fact that an architect, as a professional, had legally imposed duties of care did not displace the general policy concerns that parties to construction-related contracts should structure their relationships by prospectively allocating the risks of loss and identifying remedies.

The owner further contended that applying the economic loss doctrine to architects would be contrary to public policy, because it would reduce their incentives to properly design buildings. Limiting the parties to their contractual remedies for economic losses related to design defects did not, however, eliminate incentives for due care. The court stated that the doctrine, instead, limited a party to contractual remedies when the injury was solely economic (including damage to the property that is the subject of the contract), but allowed tort recovery if there was also physical injury to persons or other property. This was no more contrary

[7.45] *Cf. Donnelly*, 139 Ariz. at 189, 677 P.2d at 1297 (recognizing that defendants may be liable for pecuniary losses incurred by certain third parties based on defendant's negligent misrepresentations); Restatement (Second) of Torts § 552 (1977) (same).

[7.46] *See* Howard v. Usiak, 172 Vt. 227, 775 A.2d 909, 916 (2001).

[7.47] *See, e.g.*, Terracon Consultants W., Inc. v. Mandalay Resort Group, 206 P.3d 81, 83, 89 (Nev. 2009) (applying economic loss doctrine to negligence claims against design professionals).

to public policy than were contractual provisions limiting a design professional's liability to the amount of fees received.[7.48]

The owner in *Flagstaff* maintained that architects should be treated differently than contractors for purposes of the economic loss doctrine, based on Arizona statutes that regulate architects in order to protect the public. Contractors and architects are governed by different statutory requirements and administrative regulations.[7.49] These differences, however, did not preclude applying the economic loss doctrine to claims against architects.

The *Flagstaff* court held that more relevant here were Arizona statutes governing actions involving construction defects. These statutes did not distinguish between contractors and architects, although they did draw distinctions that, in some ways, paralleled the economic loss doctrine. For example, the statute of repose in Ariz. Rev. Stat. § 12-552 generally provided that actions based in contract involving the design, engineering, or construction of improvements to real property had to be brought within eight years. The statute applied to architects as well as contractors, but like the economic loss doctrine, it did not apply to actions involving personal injury.[7.50]

Similarly, Ariz. Rev. Stat. § 12-1363 (Supp. 2009) did not distinguish between architects and contractors in requiring notice and an opportunity to repair before plaintiffs could bring certain actions related to the "design, construction, condition or sale" of a dwelling.[7.51] This statute, like the economic loss doctrine, did not apply to claims involving personal injury or damage to other property.[7.52] In light of these provisions, the *Flagstaff* court was not persuaded by the owner's arguments that Arizona statutes required distinguishing architects from contractors for purposes of the economic loss doctrine.

Finally, the *Flagstaff* owner argued that applying the economic loss doctrine to architects would imply that it also applied to other claims for professional negligence, such as claims for legal malpractice. The court stated that this argument was not compelling. Lawyers owed fiduciary duties to their clients and generally were barred from entering into agreements that prospectively limited their liability.[7.53]

[7.48] *Cf.* 1800 Ocotillo, LLC v. WLB Group, Inc., 219 Ariz. 200, 202-04 ¶¶ 9-21, 196 P.3d 222, 224-26 (2008) (rejecting argument that contractual liability limits in design professional contracts were contrary to public policy).

[7.49] *Compare* Ariz. Rev. Stat. §§ 32-1101-1107 (2008) (regulating contractors) *with* Ariz. Rev. Stat. §§ 32-101-112, 121-131, 141-152 (2008 & Supp. 2009) (regulating architects).

[7.50] Ariz. Rev. Stat. § 12-552(D).

[7.51] Ariz. Rev. Stat. § 12-1361(7) (Supp. 2009) (defining "seller" as any person engaged in the business of designing, constructing, or selling dwellings).

[7.52] *See* Ariz. Rev. Stat. § 12-1366(A)(2) & (4) (Supp. 2009); *cf.* Ariz. Rev. Stat. § 32-1159 (2008) (barring certain indemnity provisions in both construction contracts and contracts for architect-engineer professional services).

[7.53] *See* Ariz. R. Sup. Ct. 42, ER 1.8(h)(1); *Dobbs, supra*, at 727 (arguing that economic loss doctrine should not apply to claims against lawyers and fiduciaries, because "[w]hen you retain someone for the express purpose of being on your side, he cannot rightly contract to be your adversary instead or to be on your side but free to be negligent").

The *Flagstaff* court stated that it did not hold that the economic loss doctrine applied to architects because they were professionals, but, instead, because the policy concerns that justified applying the doctrine to construction defect cases did not justify distinguishing between contractors, on the one hand, and design professionals, including architects, on the other. The court's adoption of the economic loss doctrine in construction defect cases reflected its assessment of the relevant policy concerns in that context. The decision did not suggest that the doctrine should be applied with a broad brush in other circumstances.[7.54]

Because the court of appeals found the economic loss doctrine inapplicable to the owner's negligence claim against the architect, the Arizona Supreme Court in *Flagstaff* vacated the appellate court's opinion. In ruling on the motion to dismiss, the lower court did not apply the version of the economic loss doctrine the *Flagstaff* court adopted. The complaint referred to the owner's contract with the architect, but a copy of the contract was not attached and was not otherwise included in the record. Although it seemed unlikely that the contract would preserve tort remedies for purely economic loss, the *Flagstaff* court stated that it would not make assumptions about its provisions. Instead, it held that it was appropriate to reverse the judgment for the architect and to remand this case to the superior court for further proceedings.

The *Flagstaff* decision continues the trend among many courts to enforce the economic loss rule, limiting the remedies of claimants against those defendants with whom the claimants lack privity, when there is no personal injury or death.

§ 5.07 SITE SERVICES GENERALLY

[B] Project Representative

[1] Role of Project Representative

Page 122, add at end of subsection:

In *Fifth Day, LLC v. Bolotin*,[74.1] a management company brought an action against a project owner and its principals, seeking compensation allegedly due for construction management services rendered by Fifth Day, LLC on an industrial real estate development project. The trial court entered summary judgment for the owners, and the management company appealed. The appellate court reversed, holding that the plaintiff construction management company was not required to be licensed pursuant to California Contractors' State License Law.

In *Fifth Day, LLC*, the property management company (plaintiff) entered into an agreement with Industrial Real Estate Development Company (owner) to provide certain "industrial real estate development and construction project management" services with respect to real property located in Chino, California.

[7.54] *Cf.* Ellen M. Bublick, *Economic Torts: Gains in Understanding Losses*, 48 Ariz. L. Rev. 693, 701 (2006) (noting that not all economic loss cases invoked the same interests or called for the same treatment).

[74.1] 172 Cal. App. 4th 939, 91 Cal. Rptr. 3d 633 (2009), *review filed* (May 5, 2009).

Plaintiff sued the owner and its principals, Pacific Allied Industrial Corporation and James P. Bolotin (defendants), for compensation alleged to be due for services rendered by Fifth Day.

The trial court granted summary judgment in favor of the owners on the ground that Fifth Day was acting as a general building contractor and therefore was required to hold a license pursuant to California Business and Professions Code section 7026. Because Fifth Day had no such license, the trial court held that it was barred by section 7031, subdivision (a), from maintaining this action. On appeal, Fifth Day contended that:

1. it was not a contractor within the meaning of section 7026;
2. it was exempt from the license requirement because it was an owner of the property or a partner of the owner;
3. even if some of the services it rendered required a contractor's license, it nevertheless could be compensated for other services that did not require a license.

The California appellate court held that the plaintiff was not a contractor within the meaning of the licensing statute, and that its claims were not barred by section 7031, subdivision (a). The trial court's judgment in favor of the owners was reversed.

In 1999, owners owned 12.3 acres of land in Chino, California, adjacent to land owned by Chino Industrial Commons, LLC (CIC). Fifth Day's managing member was Kevin Knox. At Knox's urging, owners and CIC agreed to develop their properties jointly. The property was divided into three parcels designated Lots 19, 20, and 21. CIC entered into 52-year ground leases on the three lots. The ground lease for Lot 20 required CIC to construct a 55,000-square-foot building on the lot within two years of execution of the contract. Once the building had been completed, CIC was to assign its interest in Lot 20 back to owners, and owners were to convey to CIC a fee simple interest in Lots 19 and 21. No rent was payable by CIC under the ground leases for the first two years, but rent was payable thereafter.

CIC failed to construct the building on Lot 20 during the first two years of the lease term, and rent began to accrue under the ground leases at a rate of five cents per square foot, or approximately $24,000 per month. In February 2001, rather than pay the rent, CIC assigned the three ground leases, along with its obligation to construct the building, to Fifth Day. The development plan for the property was changed to a seven-building commercial office park. Lot 20 was redesignated as Lots 1 and 2, and Lots 19 and 21 were redesignated as Lots 3 through 7. Fifth Day undertook to construct two buildings totaling 55,000 square feet on Lots 1 and 2 (formerly Lot 20) in return for a fee simple interest in Lots 3 through 7 (formerly Lots 19 and 21). Fifth Day was responsible for financing the construction.

By early 2003, Fifth Day had not constructed the buildings and owed the owners $465,000 in back rent. Fifth Day negotiated with PCI to obtain financing for the construction. Under the agreement contemplated between Fifth Day and PCI, Fifth Day would assign the ground leases to PCI. PCI would finance the construction of the seven buildings, pay owners the accrued back rent, and pay Fifth Day $100,000. Fifth Day was to receive a "Project Incentive Fee," based on a 25 percent share of the profits from the sale of the development.

The owners refused to consent to the assignment of the ground leases contemplated in the PCI deal, and proposed, instead, to finance the construction on terms similar to the PCI deal, including reassignment of the ground leases back to owners. The owners proposed to increase Fifth Day's Project Incentive Fee to 34 percent of the profits. Knox stated in his declaration that Fifth Day "reluctantly" accepted owners' proposal because of the increased Project Incentive Fee.

This agreement was memorialized in a written document dated May 5, 2003 between Fifth Day and the owners entitled "Development Management Agreement For the Construction of The Campus at CIC" (the DMA). The owners were referred to as the "Owner" and Fifth Day as the "Development Manager."

The DMA recited that the owners wished to undertake the development of the entire property. To do so, "Owner desires to have Professional Development and Construction Management Services to assist the owner . . ." Fifth Day was "experienced in industrial real estate development and construction project management and is willing to provide to Owner these services."

Fifth Day was to be paid a fixed development fee of $100,000 as a nonrefundable advance against a Project Incentive Fee of 34 percent of a defined "Project Value." The DMA provided, "The Owner agrees that for purposes of this agreement, any and all lease rents accrued are included in the value of the Land Contribution and that the leases for Lots 19, 20 and 21 previously entered into are to be terminated as and by those Lease Terminations attached as Exhibit ." The DMA specified that Fifth Day was to perform the following duties "as Owner may specifically and expressly direct," listing many specific tasks to be done by Fifth Day.

In addition, Fifth Day warranted and represented that (1) it was "experienced, competent and qualified to perform the work contemplated by" the DMA, (2) it had and would maintain "sufficient facilities, expertise, staff, assets and other resources to perform its duties," (3) it held and would hold "all licenses, permits or other certifications necessary to perform its duties," and (4) owner would "have full knowledge and involvement in the Project."

In January 2004, Fifth Day entered into a construction contract with Fullmer Construction, and Fullmer agreed to complete specified work, including the construction of seven concrete tilt-up buildings on the property, for a fee of nearly $4.9 million. Knox, Fifth Day's principal, was designated in the contractor agreement as the owner's representative. As such, Knox represented the owners with respect to all aspects of the contractor agreement and the work. Fifth Day performed the services required of it under the DMA. Construction was completed, and certificates of occupancy for the project issued in December 2004. Fifth Day alleged that, between December 2004 and March 2005, owners sold three of the buildings. According to Knox, the owners paid Fifth Day in excess of $785,000 in Project Incentive Fees. Fifth Day alleged that the owner subsequently sold or leased the remaining four buildings, but refused to pay Fifth Day the additional Project Incentive Fees earned under the DMA. Fifth Day alleged that, as a result, owners owed Fifth Day approximately $1.8 million in additional Project Incentive Fees. Fifth Day sued the owners for breach of contract and on common counts for money had and received and for services rendered.

The trial court sustained the owners' demurrers to the original complaint with leave to amend on the ground that Fifth Day failed to allege that it was a licensed contractor and was therefore barred from bringing suit by section 7031. Fifth Day then filed a first amended complaint that (1) omitted the common count for services rendered, (2) recast Fifth Day's cause of action for breach of contract to allege the breach of a partnership agreement, and (3) sought the additional remedies of rescission and restitution. The owners again demurred on the ground that section 7031 barred Fifth Day's suit. This time, the trial court overruled the demurrer, concluding that Fifth Day had alleged facts that, if true, avoided the section 7031 bar.

The owners subsequently moved for summary judgment on the sole ground that section 7031 barred Fifth Day's suit. The trial court granted the motion, concluding that the undisputed facts established that Fifth Day was a contractor within the meaning of section 7026. Because Fifth Day was not licensed, its action was barred by section 7031. The trial court entered judgment in favor of owners. Fifth Day appealed.

The appellate court held that the central question was whether an entity which provides construction management services to a private owner is required to be licensed as a contractor. After a lengthy review of California licensing law, the *Fifth Day LLC* court concluded that plaintiff did not perform or agree to perform construction services. It hired a general contractor to do that work, Fullmer Construction. The appellate court noted that on public works projects, a construction manager must be either a licensed architect, engineer, or general contractor. Cal. Gov't Code § 4525. Because the legislature did not require that construction managers on private works be licensed, the court reversed the trial court's holding and held that Fifth Day did not need to be licensed.

[F] Inspection

Page 145, add after carryover paragraph:

In *Varisco v. Gateway Science & Eng'g, Inc.*,[130.1] a construction inspector brought an action against a construction company for tortious termination of employment contract in violation of public policy, breach of implied contract of continued employment, and breach of implied covenant of good faith and fair dealing. The trial court granted summary judgment for the company, and the inspector appealed. The appellate court affirmed the trial court, and held that the inspector was not an employee of the company and that he could not bring the causes of action alleged.

[130.1] Varisco v. Gateway Science & Eng'g, Inc., 166 Cal. App. 4th 1099, 83 Cal. Rptr. 3d 393 (2008).

Appellant Al Varisco sued respondent Gateway Science and Engineering for wrongful termination of employment and similar causes of action, all of which depended on the allegation that he had been Gateway's employee. Gateway moved for summary judgment on the ground that Varisco was not an employee, but an independent contractor. The trial court found for Gateway, and the appellate court affirmed. All the undisputed facts added up to an independent contractor relationship. A single clause in the parties' letter agreement, which allowed either party to terminate at will, did not transform that relationship into an employment relationship.

Gateway provided professional services such as project management, planning and design management, inspection, and quality assurance to the construction industry. Varisco was a construction inspector and had a Class-1 Inspector certification from the California Division of the State Architect (DSA). In early 2004, Varisco contacted Gateway, seeking work. Gateway then had a contract with the Los Angeles Unified School District (LAUSD), under which it was to provide certified project inspectors for projects then under construction.

Gateway responded to Varisco's call, and on January 30, 2004, Varisco and Gateway signed a letter agreement in which Varisco agreed to provide "DSA Inspection Services to the Los AngelesUnifiedSchool District (Client)" and Gateway agreed to pay him an hourly rate. Varisco provided inspection services on two Gateway-LAUSD projects. His relationship with Gateway ended in November 2004, when Gateway sent him a letter terminating the agreement, citing his refusal to sign a new contract or to provide various documents.

Varisco filed suit, bringing causes of action for tortious termination of employment contract in violation of public policy, breach of implied contract of continued employment, and breach of the implied covenant of good faith and fair dealing. Each cause of action alleged that Varisco was Gateway's employee. Gateway moved for summary judgment, contending that Varisco was an independent contractor, not an employee. The trial court found that Varisco had no evidence to dispute the assertion that he was an independent contractor pursuant to an at-will agreement, and granted the motion. On appeal, Varisco conceded that the causes of action were viable only if he was an employee, not an independent contractor.[130.2]

The appellate court stated that the question on appeal was whether the company met its burden of showing that an element of each cause of action, that Varisco was an employee, could not be established, under *Union Bank v. Superior Court*,[130.3] or whether, as Varisco contended, there was a triable issue of fact on the question of his employment status.

The *Varisco* court stated that control is the principal factor in determining whether an individual worker is an employee or an independent contractor. Citing *S.A. Gerrard Co. v. Industrial Accident Comm'n*,[130.4] the *Varisco* court stated that

---

[130.2] *See* Sistare-Meyer v. Young Men's Christian Ass'n, 58 Cal. App. 4th 10, 14, 67 Cal. Rptr. 2d 840 (1997).

[130.3] 31 Cal. App. 4th 573, 37 Cal. Rptr. 2d 653 (1995).

[130.4] 17 Cal. 2d 411, 413, 110 P.2d 377 (1941).

the most significant question was whether the person to whom the service is rendered has the right to control the manner and means of accomplishing the result desired. Other factors cited by the *Varisco* court included: (a) whether the one performing services is engaged in a distinct occupation or business; (b) the kind of occupation, with reference to whether, in the locality, the work is usually done under the direction of the principal or by a specialist without supervision; (c) the skill required in the particular occupation; (d) whether the principal or the worker supplies the instrumentalities, tools, and the place of work for the person doing the work; (e) the length of time for which the services are to be performed; (f) the method of payment, whether by the time or by the job; (g) whether or not the work is a part of the regular business of the principal; and (h) whether or not the parties believe they are creating the relationship of employer-employee.

According to the parties' written agreement, Varisco was compensated by Gateway at $75 per hour, with no benefits such as medical, dental, paid sick leave, vacation, and holidays. Gateway was to cover Varisco for professional and general liability insurance, and Varisco would be required to complete Gateway time sheets. The written agreement also stated that overtime did not apply, unless authorized by the school district. The *Varisco* court held that when Varisco signed the written agreement, he understood that he was entering into an independent contractor relationship and not an employment relationship, and he so testified at his deposition. He also testified that he did not work for Gateway, and that Gateway acted as his agent to connect him to the school district. Varisco stated that he did not, would not, and would never work for Gateway.

Varisco received a 1099 for his compensation from Gateway, and Gateway did not supply uniform, apparel, equipment, materials, or tools to Varisco. Varisco wore his own hardhat and work boots, which were mandatory apparel at the job site. Varisco used his own car for transportation to and from the job site, and was not reimbursed for mileage or gas. Varisco's work hours were established by the architect of record, not by Gateway. He went to the Gateway office twice a month to pick up his paycheck, and never at any other time. If he had to call in sick, he called the school district, not Gateway.

The *Varisco* court held that the undisputed facts established that Varisco was an independent contractor of Gateway, and not an employee. The court stated that the issue on appeal was the right to control the manner and means of accomplishing Varisco's work. The court held that Gateway had no such control, and no right to such control.

Varisco argued that some of the factors showed that he was an employee. He argued that construction inspection was a part of Gateway's business, and the fact that he was paid by the hour, not the project, indicated that he was an employee. The *Varisco* court pointed out that although an hourly rate suggested an employment relationship, independent contractors are commonly paid on that basis. The court stated that even if those two factors suggested an employment relationship, all of the factors, when weighed and considered as a whole, show that Varisco was not an employee. The appellate court affirmed the trial court's grant of the motion of Gateway for summary judgment because Varisco was not an employee of Gateway.

[H] Issuing Certificates

Page 147, add at end of fourth full paragraph:

Statute of limitations defenses may be available on claims against a general contractor. In *Ferrante Immobiliare, LLC v. Pace,*[136.1] a project owner brought an action alleging claims for negligence and breach of contract against an architect and an engineer. The defendant design professionals brought a third-party complaint against the general contractor on the project. The trial court (state supreme court) had granted in part the owner's motion to amend its complaint to add a third-party defendant general contractor as a party defendant, and the owner, and the contractor appealed.

The supreme court, appellate division, held that (1) the owner's negligence and breach of contract claims against the general contractor accrued at the latest as of the date of the execution of a settlement agreement; (2) the owner's filing of a supplemental summons and amended complaint did not toll the three-year statute of limitations for a negligence claim; and (3) the owner's breach of contract claim against the contractor was not precluded by the settlement agreement.

The appellate court affirmed in part, and dismissed in part and held that the project owner's breach of contract claim against the general contractor regarding allegedly defective items was not precluded by a settlement agreement, where the agreement expressly preserved owner's claims for negligence and breach of warranty or defects in connection with work included in the scope of the agreement. The plaintiffs argued that because Vanguard never substantially completed its work under the contract, the statute of limitations never commenced to run, and that the March 30, 2005 settlement agreement did not necessarily mark the accrual date of their negligence and breach of contract claims since neither a "Certificate of Substantial Performance" nor a final Certificate of Payment had ever been issued by the architect Pace as required by the original contract. The appellate court held that these arguments were without merit.

In their original complaint, in which the claims of negligence and breach of contract were only alleged against defendant-architect Pace, and defendant-engineer, Goldman Copeland Associates, and in which the general contractor, Vanguard, was not a named party, plaintiffs admitted that "[b]y late 2003, Vanguard completed the Project and the Firm moved into the remaining space at the Premises." In their proposed amended complaint, the plaintiffs sought to add breach of contract and negligence claims against Vanguard, the general contractor. The court pointed out that plaintiffs, for obvious reasons, omitted such allegation and alleged instead that "[b]y late 2003, the Firm moved into the remaining space at the Premises, while work on the HVAC, plumbing and electrical systems was ongoing," which work "was never substantially completed."

Article 14 of the standard AIA agreement with Vanguard, the general contractor, defined substantial completion as "the stage in the progress of the

[136.1] 68 A.D.3d 463, 891 N.Y.S.2d 27 (2009).

Work when the Work . . . is sufficiently complete in accordance with the Contract Documents so that the Owner can occupy or utilize the Work for its intended use." It further provided that final payment would be made after the architect issued a Certificate of Substantial Completion and a final Certificate for Payment which stated that it had determined to the best of its knowledge that the work had been completed in accordance with the terms and conditions of the contract. According to section 14.5.1 of the contract, the architect's final certificate for payment constituted a further representation that the conditions precedent to Vanguard's being entitled to final payment of the entire balance found to be due it have been fulfilled.

Although the March 30, 2005 settlement agreement did not state when Vanguard's obligations under the contract were to be deemed substantially (or entirely) complete, or that Vanguard was otherwise absolved from all of its remaining responsibilities under the contract, the settlement agreement stressed that Vanguard, which had already completed or abandoned the project, was to receive its final payment under the contract. The settlement agreement also did not indicate that Vanguard had any further obligations under the contract.

After the architect, Pace, advised plaintiffs on January 20, 2005 that Vanguard was unwilling to return to the work site to perform unspecified work, and that Pace would sign off on the project "when all the issues are resolved," plaintiffs and Vanguard bypassed the architect (whom plaintiffs later sued for breach of contract and negligent design and supervision) and entered into the March 30, 2005 settlement agreement in which they agreed that plaintiffs would pay Vanguard $13,500 "as final payment under the Agreement." In the agreement, plaintiffs stated that, as of that date, they were "unaware of any defects or negligence in connection with the Project," while they retained their rights, if any, with respect to any claims based upon any subsequently discovered defects in workmanship.

The statute of limitations on plaintiffs' negligence and breach of contract claims, which arguably accrued as early as late 2003, began to run, at the latest, on March 30, 2005, the date of execution of the owners' settlement agreement with Vanguard, which expressly provided that in consideration for the settlement plaintiffs would pay Vanguard the sum of $13,500 "as final payment under the Agreement."[136.2] The original agreement with Vanguard provided, in pertinent part, that "[f]inal payment, constituting the entire unpaid balance of the Contract Sum, shall be made by the Owner to the Contractor where [ ] the Contractor has fully performed the Contract." Since the parties charted their own course and agreed to dispense with the architect's approvals preliminary to final payment under the original contract, the court found that there was no need to determine whether Vanguard's work was "substantially complete" within the meaning of that agreement.

Although the motion court, in its July 2, 2008 order, found that the plaintiffs interposed their proposed negligence claim on March 25, 2008 when they filed

---

[136.2] *See* Amedeo Hotels Ltd. P'ship v. Zwicker Elec. Co., 291 A.D.2d 322, 323, 739 N.Y.S.2d 10 (2002).

their motion to amend the complaint, the plaintiffs' having filed a supplemental summons and amended complaint on March 25, 2008 did not toll the three-year statute of limitations for negligence claims, since they failed to secure leave of the court or a stipulation signed by counsel for the parties. *See* CPLR 1003. Plaintiffs did not seek leave to amend the complaint until April 7, 2008, when their order to show cause was signed. Although the motion court erroneously found that its prior order dismissing the third-party complaint, holding that the negligence claim was time barred, constituted the law of the case as to the plaintiffs, the plaintiffs' subsequent failure to timely move to amend their complaint rendered that issue academic. Since the order to show cause could not have been submitted prior to April 2, 2008, the date of its supporting affirmation and affidavit, there was no need to determine when it was actually submitted.

Contrary to the general contractor's contention, the plaintiffs' breach of contract claim was not precluded by the settlement agreement that removed 14 enumerated items from the scope of the parties' agreement (the "excluded work"). The owners expressly preserved their claims for negligence and breach of warranty or defects in connection with the "included work." To the extent the motion court's order could be read to limit the relevant language, the settlement agreement, which preserved all claims for "defects, including, but not limited to, latent defects, and warranties for work remaining in the scope of the work under the Agreement," was controlling and dispositive of the issue. Whether the items alleged to be defective fell within the category of "excluded work" or "included work" was a factual determination that could not be made on this record.

Finally, in view of the trial court's determination in its July 2, 2008 order that the owner's proposed negligence claim against Vanguard was untimely, albeit for the wrong reason, i.e., the law of the case, plaintiffs' appeal from the December 4, 2007 order, to the extent it granted Vanguard's motion to dismiss the third-party complaint on the ground that the negligence claim was untimely, was academic.

§ 5.09 PROFESSIONAL STANDARD: MEASUREMENT OF PERFORMANCE

Page 165, add at end of section:

Courts continue to grapple with whether to apply the economic loss rule to bar claims for those lacking privity. In *Flagstaff Affordable Housing Limited Partnership v. Design Alliance, Inc.*,[170] a property owner filed a complaint against an architect, alleging breach of contract and professional negligence. The superior court granted the architect's motion to dismiss. The court of appeals (221 Ariz. 433, 212 P.3d 125 (2009)) reversed and remanded, and the architect appealed.

In *Flagstaff*, the Arizona Supreme Court held that the "economic loss doctrine" barred plaintiffs, in certain circumstances, from recovering economic damages in tort. The court had previously applied the doctrine only to products

[170] 223 P.3d 664 (Ariz. 2010).

liability claims. The Arizona Supreme Court held that it would apply the doctrine in a construction defect case and held that a property owner was limited to its contractual remedies when an architect's negligent design caused economic loss but no physical injury to persons or other property.

In 1995, Flagstaff Affordable Housing Limited Partnership ("Owner") contracted with Design Alliance, Inc. ("Architect") for the design of eight apartment buildings and a community center (the "apartments"). To qualify as a low income housing project, the apartments had to comply with the federal Fair Housing Act's accessibility guidelines. The owner separately contracted with Butte Construction Company ("Contractor") for the construction of the apartments, which were completed in Flagstaff in 1996.

In 2004, HUD filed a complaint against the owner, alleging that the apartments violated the accessibility guidelines. After settling with HUD, the owner in 2006 sued the architect and the contractor, alleging they had breached their respective contracts and acted negligently. The contractor was later dismissed from the action.

The architect moved to dismiss the complaint under Rule 12(b)(6). The architect argued that the contract claim was barred by the statute of repose in Arizona Revised Statutes (A.R.S.) section 12-552, which provided that no action based in contract may be brought against a person who "furnishes the design . . . of an improvement to real property more than eight years after substantial completion of the improvement." The architect argued that the negligence claim should be dismissed based on *Carstens v. City of Phoenix*,[171] which held that the economic loss doctrine precluded tort recovery of economic losses in the "construction defect setting."

The owner voluntarily dismissed the contract claim, but argued that the economic loss doctrine did not bar the claim for professional negligence. The owner did not dispute that it sought recovery only for economic losses, and acknowledged that *Carstens* applied the doctrine in a construction defect case. The owner argued, however, that a claim for "professional negligence" was based on the special relationship between architects and their clients, and, therefore, it was excepted from the economic loss doctrine. The superior court dismissed the complaint.

The court of appeals reversed, holding that the economic loss doctrine did not bar negligence claims against design professionals.[172] The court acknowledged that prior Arizona cases, such as *Carstens*, applied the doctrine to cases involving construction defects.[173] Distinguishing *Carstens*, the appellate court stated that this case did not involve construction defects, but an architect's alleged negligent design. The appellate court concluded that the economic loss doctrine should not apply, because the owner's claim was based in tort, not contract, and reflected the special duties imposed on architects by law.

---

[171] 206 Ariz. 123, 125 ¶ 10, 75 P.3d 1081, 1084 (Ct. App. 2003).

[172] Flagstaff Affordable Hous. Ltd. P'ship v. Design Alliance, Inc., 221 Ariz. 433, 212 P.3d 125 (Ct. App. 2009).

[173] *Id.* at 436 ¶ 10, 212 P.3d at 125, 128.

On appeal to the Arizona Supreme Court, the architect argued that the superior court properly dismissed the complaint, because the owner alleged only economic loss, and the economic loss doctrine applied in construction cases and precluded tort recovery by parties not in privity for such losses absent personal injury or damage to other property. The architect also argued that the doctrine should apply to claims against not only contractors but also architects and other design professionals. The court stated that it had not addressed the economic loss doctrine since its decision in *Salt River Project Agricultural Improvement and Power District v. Westinghouse Electric Corp.*[174] In the absence of other decisions by the Arizona Supreme Court, the court noted that state appellate courts and the federal courts had reached conflicting conclusions regarding the application of the doctrine under Arizona law.[175]

"Economic loss" refers to pecuniary or commercial damage, including any decreased value or repair costs for a product or property that is itself the subject of a contract between the plaintiff and defendant, and consequential damages such as lost profits.[176]

Some courts have stated that the economic loss doctrine "bars a party from recovering economic damages in tort unless accompanied by physical harm."[177] The state supreme court in *Flagstaff* court stated that this formulation of the doctrine was overly broad. In many contexts, tort recovery is available for solely pecuniary losses.[178] Describing the doctrine in this way conflates two distinct issues: (1) whether a contracting party should be limited to its contract remedies for purely economic loss; and (2) whether a plaintiff may assert tort claims for economic damages against a defendant absent any contract between the parties. The *Flagstaff* court held that the economic loss doctrine was best directed to the first of these issues, and used the phrase to refer to a common law rule limiting a contracting party to contractual remedies for the recovery of economic losses unaccompanied by physical injury to persons or other property.

In *Salt River*, an electric utility company asserted contract and tort claims against the seller of a control device that had allegedly malfunctioned and damaged the utility's turbine unit. The Arizona Supreme Court held in *Salt River* that the utility could not recover in contract, because the seller had, consistent with the Uniform Commercial Code, disclaimed certain warranties and otherwise

---

[174] 143 Ariz. 368, 694 P.2d 198 (1984).

[175] *Compare* Apollo Group, Inc. v. Avnet, Inc., 58 F.3d 477, 480 (9th Cir. 1995) (stating that *Salt River* reflects that Arizona applies the economic loss rule "broadly") *with* Evans v. Singer, 518 F. Supp. 2d 1134, 1142-45 (D. Ariz. 2007) (stating *Salt River* "provided anything but" a broad reading of the rule); *compare also Carstens*, 206 Ariz. at 128 ¶ 21, 75 P.3d at 1086 (arguing that *Salt River* supports applying doctrine to bar homeowners' claim for economic losses from construction defects) *with* Valley Forge Ins. Co. v. Sam's Plumbing, LLC, 220 Ariz. 512, 515-16 ¶¶ 11-12, 207 P.3d 765, 768-69 (Ct. App. 2009) (arguing that *Carstens* misconstrued *Salt River*).

[176] *See Salt River*, 143 Ariz. at 379-80, 694 P.2d at 209-10.

[177] *Carstens*, 206 Ariz. at 125 ¶ 10, 75 P.3d at 1083.

[178] *See* Giles v. Gen. Motors Acceptance Corp., 494 F.3d 865, 875 (9th Cir. 2007) (noting that "[t]ort law has traditionally protected individuals from a host of wrongs that cause only monetary damage"); *Evans*, 518 F. Supp. 2d at 1139.

limited its liability.[179] The *Salt River* court, however, rejected the seller's argument that the contractual provisions also precluded a tort claim for strict products liability.[180]

In the context of an alleged product defect, *Salt River* considered whether a plaintiff could seek tort recovery for economic losses related to the defendant's contractual performance. In resolving this question, the court noted the distinct policies served by tort and contract law. Strict liability promotes product safety and spreads the costs of accidents.[181] Contract law, in contrast, seeks to preserve freedom of contract and to promote the free flow of commerce. These goals are best served by allowing the parties to specify the consequences of a breach of their agreement. Accordingly, "[w]hen a defect renders a product substandard or unable to perform the functions for which it was manufactured, the purchaser's remedy for disappointed commercial expectations is through contract law."

The *Salt River* court acknowledged that most courts had held that economic loss resulting from a product defect (including damage to the product itself) was not recoverable in tort absent accompanying physical damage to other property or personal injury.[182] The court, however, expressly declined to follow that majority rule and, instead, embraced a narrower, case-specific approach:

> Where economic loss, in the form of repair costs, diminished value, or lost profits, is the plaintiff's only loss, the policies of the law generally will be best served by leaving the parties to their commercial remedies. Where economic loss is accompanied by physical damage to person or other property, however, the parties' interests generally will be realized best by the imposition of strict tort liability. If the only loss is non-accidental and to the product itself, or is of a consequential nature, the remedies available under the UCC will govern and strict liability and other tort theories will be unavailable.[183]

Under *Salt River*, the economic nature of the loss is only one factor in a three-part test to determine whether tort remedies will be available. A court must also consider whether the defect was "unreasonably dangerous" and whether the loss occurred in a "sudden, accidental manner."[184] When these factors are present, *Salt River* allows a plaintiff to recover in tort for purely economic loss.[185]

Thus, in the products liability context, *Salt River* declined to categorically bar tort recovery of economic losses. Instead, the court reasoned that, "[e]ach case must be examined to determine whether the facts preponderate in favor of the application of tort law or commercial law exclusively or a combination of the two."[186] Applying a narrow version of economic loss doctrine, *Salt River* held that

---

[179] 143 Ariz. at 374, 694 P.2d at 204.

[180] 143 Ariz. at 375, 381, 694 P.2d at 205, 211.

[181] 143 Ariz. at 375-76, 694 P.2d at 205-06.

[182] 143 Ariz. at 379, 694 P.2d at 209.

[183] 143 Ariz. at 379-80, 694 P.2d at 209-10.

[184] 143 Ariz. at 379, 694 P.2d at 209.

[185] 143 Ariz. at 380-81, 694 P.2d at 210-11 (applying factors and holding utility could seek tort recovery of damage to turbine unit even if it was not a loss to "other property").

[186] 143 Ariz. at 380, 694 P.2d at 210.

the commercial purchaser in that case could assert a products liability claim against a commercial seller for economic losses for which the contract disclaimed liability.

The *Flagstaff* case involved alleged defects in a building, rather than a defective product. Many other courts, and the parties here, assumed that Arizona law also applied the economic loss doctrine to construction defect cases. Nevertheless, the only opinion by the Arizona Supreme Court cited for this proposition is *Woodward v. Chirco Construction Co.*[187] case decided a few months before *Salt River*. *Woodward*, however, concerned the limitations period for contract actions for breach of implied warranty, not the preclusion of tort claims. In that case, a couple contracted with a builder for the construction and purchase of a residence.[188] After the closing, the soil subsided and caused extensive damage to the home. The homeowners sued the builder alleging both negligence for failing to conduct a soil study and breach of the implied warranty of workmanlike performance and habitability. The trial court dismissed the negligence claim for lack of proof of the relevant standard of care. It also dismissed the warranty claim as barred by the statute of limitations. The court of appeals affirmed the dismissal of the negligence claim but reversed the dismissal of the contract claim, holding that the six-year limitations period in A.R.S. § 12-548 applied.

The builder in *Woodward* petitioned for review, arguing that breach of an implied warranty was actionable only in tort, which generally had a two-year limitations period. Rejecting this argument, the Arizona Supreme Court agreed with other jurisdictions holding that a home purchaser may sue both in contract for breach of the implied warranty and in tort for the builder's breach of the common law duty of care. The court stated:

> For example, if a fireplace collapses, the purchaser can sue in contract for the cost of remedying the structural defects and sue in tort for damage to personal property or personal injury caused by the collapse. Each claim will stand or fall on its own; a distinct statute of limitation applies to each.[189]

Although some courts have construed this language as approving the economic loss doctrine, the *Woodward* court was not asked to address the doctrine and did never discuss it. Moreover, when later applying the economic loss doctrine in *Salt River*, the Arizona Supreme Court did not mention *Woodward*.

The *Woodward* court stated that it agreed with *Cosmopolitan Homes, Inc. v. Weller*,[190] which allowed a subsequent purchaser to assert negligence claims against a contractor for residential construction defects.[191] *Cosmopolitan Homes*

---

[187] 141 Ariz. 514, 687 P.2d 1269 (1984).

[188] 141 Ariz. at 515, 687 P.2d at 1270.

[189] 141 Ariz. at 516, 687 P.2d at 1271.

[190] 663 P.2d 1041 (Colo. 1983).

[191] *Woodward*, 141 Ariz. 514, 516, 687 P.2d 1269, 1271.

rejected the argument that claims for recovery of economic loss sounded exclusively in contract.[192]

Woodward did not resolve whether the economic loss doctrine should apply to construction defects. Although several opinions by the court of appeals have concluded that the doctrine applied, those cases relied heavily on an interpretation of *Woodward* that the Arizona Supreme Court in *Flagstaff* rejected.[193]

To determine whether the doctrine should apply in this case, the *Flagstaff* court stated that it was required to consider the underlying policies of tort and contract law in the construction setting.[194] The *Flagstaff* court stated that the contract law policy of upholding the expectations of the parties had as much, if not greater, force in construction defect cases as in product defect cases. Construction-related contracts often were negotiated between the parties on a project-specific basis and had detailed provisions allocating risks of loss and specifying remedies. In this context, allowing tort claims posed a danger of undermining the policy concerns of contract law. Contract law sought to encourage parties to order their prospective relationships, including the allocation of risk of future losses and the identification of remedies, and to enforce any resulting agreement consistent with the parties' expectations.[195]

In construction defect cases involving only pecuniary losses related to the building that is the subject of the parties' contract, the *Flagstaff* court stated that there were no strong policy reasons to impose common law tort liability in addition to contractual remedies. When a construction defect caused only damage to the building itself or other economic loss, common law contract remedies provided an adequate remedy because they allowed recovery of the costs of remedying the defects, and other damages reasonably foreseeable to the parties upon entering the contract.[196]

The *Flagstaff* court went on to note that policies of accident deterrence and loss-spreading also did not require allowing tort recovery in addition to contractual remedies for economic loss from construction defects. The court stated these considerations have less force when parties to a site-specific construction contract have allocated the risk of loss and identified remedies for nonperformance.[197] Moreover, although a homeowner's purchase of a mass-produced home might in some ways be analogous to a consumer's purchase of a product, even in such a

[192] 663 P.2d at 1044-45.

[193] *See, e.g.*, *Carstens*, 206 Ariz. at 126 ¶¶ 11-12, 75 P.3d at 1084; Colberg v. Rellinger, 160 Ariz. 42, 44, 770 P.2d 346, 348 (Ct. App. 1988); Nastri v. Wood Bros. Homes, Inc., 142 Ariz. 439, 444-45, 690 P.2d 158, 163-64 (Ct. App. 1984).

[194] *Cf. Salt River*, 143 Ariz. at 376, 694 P.2d at 206 (stating that purposes of tort and contract law should determine which law applies in products liability cases).

[195] *See, e.g.*, Berschauer/Phillips Constr. Co. v. Seattle Sch. Dist. No. 1, 124 Wash. 2d 816, 881 P.2d 986, 993 (1994).

[196] *See* Higgins v. Ariz. Sav. & Loan Ass'n, 90 Ariz. 55, 63-64, 365 P.2d 476, 482-83 (1961) (adopting rule of *Hadley v. Baxendale*, 9 Exch. 341, 156 Eng. Rep. 145 (1854), for identifying damages recoverable in contract).

[197] *Cf. Salt River*, 143 Ariz. at 376, 694 P.2d at 206 (noting that contract law policy "is best served" by allowing "parties to limit the redress of a purchaser who fails to receive the quality of product he expected").

situation there would be less reason to preserve tort remedies for purely economic loss. Arizona law allows home purchasers to bring contract claims for breach of the implied warranty of good workmanship and habitability, even if they are not in privity with the builder.[198]

The *Flagstaff* court concluded that in construction defect cases, "the policies of the law generally will be best served by leaving the parties to their commercial remedies" when a contracting party has incurred only "economic loss, in the form of repair costs, diminished value, or lost profits."[199] The *Flagstaff* court applied the economic loss doctrine and held that a contracting party was limited to its contractual remedies for purely economic loss from construction defects.

In the construction context, the economic loss doctrine respects the expectations of the parties when, as often will be true, they have expressly addressed liability and remedies in their contract. Thus, the parties can contractually agree to preserve tort remedies for solely economic loss, just as they may otherwise specify remedies that modify common law recovery.[200] But if the parties do not provide otherwise in their contract, they will be limited to contractual remedies for any loss of the bargain resulting from construction defects that do not cause personal injury or damage to other property.

In *Flagstaff*, applying the economic loss doctrine to construction cases also required the court to discuss two other aspects of the *Salt River* decision. First, *Salt River* identified certain requirements for the waiver of tort remedies, which is a separate question from whether the economic loss doctrine applies.[201] *Salt River*'s requirements for an effective waiver do not determine whether a party is limited to contractual remedies for purely economic losses resulting from construction defects. Instead, a party will be so limited unless the parties have provided in their contract for tort remedies.

Salt River also outlined a three-factor test for determining, on a case-specific basis, whether to apply the economic loss doctrine to claims involving a defective product. This approach allowed tort recovery for purely economic losses if they resulted from an "accident" that poses unreasonable risks of harm to other property or persons.[202] This minority view has been criticized as being too unpredictable and allowing noncontractual recovery when a purchaser has only been deprived of the benefit of the bargain.[203]

Whatever the wisdom of continuing to apply *Salt River*'s three-factor test in products liability cases, the *Flagstaff* court declined to extend it to construction defect cases. The economic loss doctrine was held to appropriately apply in this

---

[198] *See* Richards v. Powercraft Homes, Inc., 139 Ariz. 242, 245, 678 P.2d 427, 430 (1984).

[199] *Salt River*, 143 Ariz. at 379, 694 P.2d at 209.

[200] *See* Green v. Snodgrass, 79 Ariz. 319, 322, 289 P.2d 191, 192 (1955) (noting that contract will control when it specifies remedies in event of breach).

[201] *See* 143 Ariz. at 375, 385, 694 P.2d at 205, 215.

[202] *See Salt River*, 143 Ariz. at 380-81, 694 P.2d at 210-11.

[203] *See* East River S.S. Corp. v. Transamerica Delaval, Inc., 476 U.S. 858, 869-70, 106 S. Ct. 2295, 90 L. Ed. 2d 865 (1986) (refusing to apply a *Salt River*-type approach to products liability claim under admiralty law).

context, because construction contracts typically are negotiated on a project-specific basis, and the parties should be encouraged to prospectively allocate risk and identify remedies within their agreements. The court noted that these goals would be undermined by an approach that allowed extra-contractual recovery for economic loss based not on the agreement itself, but instead on a court's *post hoc* determination that a construction defect posed risks of other loss or was somehow accidental in nature.[204]

The *Flagstaff* court adopted a version of the economic loss doctrine and held that a plaintiff who contracts for construction cannot recover in tort for purely economic loss, unless the contract otherwise provides. The doctrine did not bar tort recovery when economic loss was accompanied by physical injury to persons or other property. The owner argued that the economic loss doctrine should not apply to professional negligence claims based on an architect's design.

The owner in *Flagstaff* argued that applying the economic loss doctrine would conflict with *Donnelly Construction Co. v. Oberg/Hunt/Gilleland*.[205] In *Donnelly*, a contractor relied on an architect's plans to prepare a bid for improvements to a school complex.[206] After starting work, the contractor found the plans were in error, which increased the contractor's construction costs.[207] The contractor later sued the architect to recover the increased costs, asserting claims for negligence, negligent misrepresentation, and breach of implied warranty.[208] The architect argued that, because it had not entered into a contract with the contractor, it owed it no duty and could not be liable on any of the claims.[209]

The *Donnelly* court held that lack of privity did not bar the claims.[210] With regard to the negligence claim, the *Donnelly* court noted that "[d]esign professionals have a duty to use ordinary skill, care, and diligence in rendering their professional services," and that "an action in negligence may be maintained upon the plaintiff's showing that the defendant owed a duty to him, that the duty was breached, and that the breach proximately caused an injury which resulted in actual damages."[211] The *Donnelly* court further explained, "[w]e only hold here that design professionals are liable for foreseeable injuries to foreseeable victims which proximately result from their negligent performance of their professional services."[212]

Donnelly held that a contractor had stated a valid claim for negligence to recover economic losses based on an architect's allegedly defective design. The

[204] *Cf.* Lincoln Gen. Ins. Co. v. Detroit Diesel Corp., 293 S.W.3d 487, 492-93 (Tenn. 2009) (noting similar concerns in adopting *East River*'s majority approach in products liability); Restatement (Third) of Torts: Products Liability § 21 & cmt. d (1998) (adopting *East River* approach).

[205] 139 Ariz. 184, 677 P.2d 1292 (1984).

[206] 139 Ariz. at 185, 677 P.2d at 1293.

[207] 139 Ariz. at 185-86, 677 P.2d at 1293-94.

[208] 139 Ariz. at 186, 677 P.2d at 1294.

[209] 139 Ariz. at 187, 677 P.2d at 1295.

[210] 139 Ariz. at 187-89, 677 P.2d at 1295-97.

[211] 139 Ariz. at 187, 677 P.2d at 1295.

[212] 139 Ariz. at 188, 677 P.2d at 1296.

architect did not argue that the contractor should be limited to its contractual remedies for economic loss; instead, the architect argued that the absence of a contract precluded all liability. Without discussing the economic loss doctrine, *Donnelly* correctly implied that it would not apply to negligence claims by a plaintiff who has no contractual relationship with the defendant.

Although some courts have applied the doctrine in that context,[213] the *Flagstaff* court declined to do so. The principal function of the economic loss doctrine, in that court's view, was to encourage private ordering of economic relationships and to uphold the expectations of the parties by limiting a plaintiff to contractual remedies for loss of the benefit of the bargain. These concerns are not implicated when the plaintiff lacks privity and cannot pursue contractual remedies.[214]

Rather than rely on the economic loss doctrine to preclude tort claims by noncontracting parties, the *Flagstaff* court stated that courts should instead focus on whether the applicable substantive law allows liability in the particular context. For example, whether a noncontracting party may recover economic losses for a defendant's negligent misrepresentation should depend on whether the elements of that tort are satisfied, including whether the plaintiff is within the limited class of persons to whom the defendant owes a duty.[215]

The owner in *Flagstaff* also argued that the economic loss doctrine should not apply, because the architect breached duties imposed by law. Although architects have common-law duties of care, this case illustrates that it is often difficult to draw bright lines between obligations imposed by law and those arising from contract. The architect's duties with regard to the owner's project existed only because of the contract between the parties. Architectural contracts generally include compliance with applicable building codes and other legal design requirements as an implied term.[216]

The *Flagstaff* owner alleged that the architect designed a building that did not conform to certain requirements of the federal Fair Housing Act; the complaint alleged that this conduct both breached the architect's contractual obligations and constituted professional negligence. The *Flagstaff* court rejected attempts to label claims by distinguishing between contractual and extra-contractual duties in an unduly formalistic approach to determining if plaintiffs like the owner should be limited to their contractual remedies for economic loss.

The *Flagstaff* court stated that the professional status of architects should not determine whether the economic loss doctrine applies in this context. The

---

[213] *See, e.g.*, *Carstens*, 206 Ariz. at 127 ¶ 17, 75 P.3d at 1085; Davencourt at Pilgrims Landing Homeowners Ass'n v. Davencourt at Pilgrims Landing, LC, 221 P.3d 234, 243 (Utah 2009).

[214] *See* Vincent R. Johnson, *The Boundary-Line Function of the Economic Loss Rule*, 66 Wash. & Lee L. Rev. 523, 556 (2009) (concluding that when "established tort principles entitle a third party to protection under tort law for economic loss, an agreement to which the third party never assented should not be permitted to vitiate his or her right to tort remedies").

[215] *Cf. Donnelly*, 139 Ariz. at 189, 677 P.2d at 1297 (recognizing that defendants may be liable for pecuniary losses incurred by certain third parties based on defendant's negligent misrepresentations); Restatement (Second) of Torts § 552 (1977) (same).

[216] *See* Howard v. Usiak, 172 Vt. 227, 775 A.2d 909, 916 (2001).

purposes of the doctrine are served by applying it to contracts entered by architects and design professionals, as other courts have recognized.[217] The fact that an architect, as a professional, has legally imposed duties of care does not displace the general policy concerns that parties to construction-related contracts should structure their relationships by prospectively allocating the risks of loss and identifying remedies.

The owner further contended that applying the economic loss doctrine to architects would be contrary to public policy, because it would reduce their incentives to properly design buildings. Limiting the parties to their contractual remedies for economic losses related to design defects does not, however, eliminate incentives for due care. The doctrine instead limits a party to contractual remedies when the injury is solely economic (including damage to the property that is the subject of the contract), but allows tort recovery if there is also physical injury to persons or other property. This is no more contrary to public policy than are contractual provisions limiting a design professional's liability to the amount of fees received.[218]

In a related argument, the owner in *Flagstaff* maintained that architects should be treated differently than contractors for purposes of the economic loss doctrine, because Arizona statutes regulate architects in order to protect the public. Contractors and architects are governed by different statutory requirements and administrative regulations.[219] But this does not preclude applying the economic loss doctrine to claims against architects.

The *Flagstaff* court held that more relevant here were Arizona statutes governing actions involving construction defects. These statutes did not distinguish between contractors and architects, although they did draw distinctions that, in some ways, paralleled the economic loss doctrine. For example, the statute of repose in Ariz. Rev. Stat. § 12-552 generally provided that actions based in contract involving the design, engineering, or construction of improvements to real property had to be brought within eight years. The statute applied to architects as well as contractors, but like the economic loss doctrine, it did not apply to actions involving personal injury. *Id.* § 12-552(D).

Similarly, Ariz. Rev. Stat. § 12-1363 (Supp.2009) did not distinguish between architects and contractors in requiring notice and an opportunity to repair before plaintiffs could bring certain actions related to the "design, construction, condition or sale" of a dwelling.[220] This statute, like the economic loss doctrine,

---

[217] *See, e.g.*, Terracon Consultants W., Inc. v. Mandalay Resort Group, 206 P.3d 81, 83, 89 (Nev. 2009) (applying economic loss doctrine to negligence claims against design professionals).

[218] *Cf.* 1800 Ocotillo, LLC v. WLB Group, Inc., 219 Ariz. 200, 202-04 ¶¶ 9-21, 196 P.3d 222, 224-26 (2008) (rejecting argument that contractual liability limits in design professional contracts are contrary to public policy).

[219] *Compare* Ariz. Rev. Stat. §§ 32-1101-1107 (2008) (regulating contractors) *with* Ariz. Rev. Stat. §§ 32-101-112, 121-131, 141-152 (2008 & Supp. 2009) (regulating architects).

[220] Ariz. Rev. Stat. § 12-1361(7) (Supp. 2009) (defining "seller" as any person engaged in the business of designing, constructing, or selling dwellings).

did not apply to claims involving personal injury or damage to other property.[221] In light of these provisions, the *Flagstaff* court was not persuaded by the owner's arguments that Arizona statutes required distinguishing architects from contractors for purposes of the economic loss doctrine.

Finally, the *Flagstaff* owner argued that applying the economic loss doctrine to architects would imply that it also applied to other claims for professional negligence, such as claims for legal malpractice. The court stated that this argument was not compelling. Lawyers owed fiduciary duties to their clients and generally were barred from entering agreements that prospectively limited their liability.[222]

The *Flagstaff* court stated that it did not hold that the economic loss doctrine applied to architects because they were professionals, but, instead, because the policy concerns that justified applying the doctrine to construction defect cases did not justify distinguishing between contractors, on the one hand, and design professionals, including architects, on the other. The court's adoption of the economic loss doctrine in construction defect cases reflected its assessment of the relevant policy concerns in that context. The decision did not suggest that the doctrine should be applied with a broad brush in other circumstances.[223]

Because the court of appeals found the economic loss doctrine inapplicable to the owner's negligence claim against the architect, the Arizona Supreme Court in *Flagstaff* vacated the appellate court's opinion. In ruling on the motion to dismiss, the lower court did not apply the version of the economic loss doctrine the *Flagstaff* court adopted. The complaint referred to the owner's contract with the architect, but a copy of the contract was not attached and was not otherwise included in the record. Although it seemed unlikely that the contract would preserve tort remedies for purely economic loss, the *Flagstaff* court stated that it would not make assumptions about its provisions. Instead, it held that it was appropriate to reverse the judgment for the architect and to remand this case to the superior court for further proceedings.

The *Flagstaff* decision continues the trend among many courts to enforce the economic loss rule, limiting the remedies of claimants against those defendants with whom the claimants lack privity, when there is no personal injury or death.

In a case involving a claim against an architect, a court found that the architect's failure to visit the site to verify conditions was not below the standard of care, based on the language of the AIA documents used in the transaction and based on the failure by the plaintiff's expert to prove what the standard of care was

---

[221] *See* Ariz. Rev. Stat. § 12-1366(A)(2) & (4) (Supp. 2009); *cf.* Ariz. Rev. Stat. § 32-1159 (2008) (barring certain indemnity provisions in both construction contracts and contracts for architect-engineer professional services).

[222] *See* Ariz. R. Sup. Ct. 42, ER 1.8(h)(1); *Dobbs*, *supra*, at 727 (arguing that economic loss doctrine should not apply to claims against lawyers and fiduciaries, because "[w]hen you retain someone for the express purpose of being on your side, he cannot rightly contract to be your adversary instead or to be on your side but free to be negligent").

[223] *Cf.* Ellen M. Bublick, *Economic Torts: Gains in Understanding Losses*, 48 Ariz. L. Rev. 693, 701 (2006) (noting that not all economic loss cases invoked the same interests or called for the same treatment).

or that the architect had violated that standard. In *Taylor v. DeLosso*,[223.1] a business owner sued architects and a surveyor to recover costs arising from site plan's mislocation of a tree. The superior court entered judgment on a jury verdict and an award against the architects, and on a verdict in favor of the surveyor. The appellate division, however, reversed that decision and held that: (1) the owner's expert's testimony that architect should have visited the property to confirm location of tree included on survey was a net opinion, and (2) the architect owed no duty to the owner to visit the property to confirm the tree's location. The appellate court, therefore, reversed and remanded for the entry of a judgment of dismissal in favor of the architects.

After the plaintiff purchased a structure for the purpose of operating a beauty salon and guesthouse, she contracted with a professional land surveyor to prepare a survey of the property for submission to the city zoning board for a special reasons variance and site plan waiver in order to utilize the structure as a beauty shop. The survey located a 30-inch diameter maple tree on the site. The survey, dated February 12, 1985, was submitted to the zoning board, which denied the plaintiff's request for a site plan waiver.

The plaintiff then hired architects to prepare a full site plan. DeLosso, an employee of the architects, prepared a site plan dated February 10, 1986. He testified that he relied on the survey prepared by the land surveyor "as the basis" for the site plan, because it contained all of the information required by the city. Specifically, DeLosso relied on the survey for the outline of the lot and location of physical features, including the maple tree.

The plaintiff's application for a special reasons variance was reconsidered, and it was, subsequently, approved. DeLosso, who had since been hired by DECO, another architect firm, appeared before the zoning board at the plaintiff's request, and the zoning board granted site plan approval, based on the plan.

Afterward, at the plaintiff's request, DeLosso revised the site plan to include a proposed deck, a parking and lighting plan, and a handicap ramp. Pursuant to a November 28, 1990 written agreement between the plaintiff and DECO, DeLosso's new employer, the plaintiff sent DeLosso the site plan as per her agreement to "furnish a legal description and certified land survey of the site, . . . and complete data pertaining to existing buildings, other improvements and trees . . ." According to DeLosso, he did not use a land survey in preparing the revised site plan, nor did he personally inspect the property. DeLosso completed the revised DECO site plan on April 16, 1991, certifying that he had supervised the preparation of the site plan and that all dimensions and information set forth thereon were correct. The Planning Board approved the DECO site plan on September 4, 1991.

The plaintiff's contractor started construction of the structure's alterations and revisions to the site layout in December 1991. The contractor, however, was forced to stop construction after determining that the 30-inch diameter maple tree

[223.1] 319 N.J. Super. 174, 725 A.2d 51 (1999).

was actually located in the proposed driveway area, rather than as shown on the DECO site plan. The plaintiff was advised by the city that she needed a new site plan.

In December 1991, the plaintiff hired Joseph Courter, a new architect, to prepare a new plan. The plaintiff gave Courter the 1985 survey and DECO's 1991 revised site plan. Based on these documents and an inspection of the site, Courter determined that the plans had mislocated the maple tree. After concluding that the original survey and the DECO site plan situated the tree between 11 and 14 feet from where it actually stood, Courter prepared a new site plan, which the Planning Board approved on July 29, 1992.

Courter charged the plaintiff $5,814 for his services in connection with preparation of the revised site plan. According to the plaintiff, she was unable to open her shop until October 1992, and she suffered approximately $12,128 in lost earnings, because she was not able to hire a second stylist. Moreover, she paid $1,625 to her contractor after construction was interrupted for reviewing site plans with zoning officers and appearing before the Board to obtain the new site plan approval.

Courter, who the plaintiff called as her expert witness, testified that "[i]n working in a small parking lot where there's a 30 inch diameter tree in the proximity, I would think it would be prudent to determine the location of that tree, fairly accurately." Courter concluded that DeLosso's failure to accurately denote the 30-inch diameter tree violated that standard of practice. He also opined that "a prudent architect would go to the site and make sure that he knows where that tree is, because all his work is going to revolve around that tree." Courter also testified that the original 1985 survey was prepared for a special reasons variance and site plan waiver. Therefore, there was no need to include vegetation in the survey, and, thus, the surveyor's mislocation of the maple tree had no impact on the validity of the survey. According to Courter, unless specifically requested to do so, land surveyors do not indicate vegetation on a survey.

The architects, DeLosso and DECO, moved for dismissal of the complaint for lack of sufficient expert testimony evidence. They argued that Courter's testimony was a "net opinion" since he made no reference to any recognized standard, written or oral, requiring an architect to make a site inspection prior to preparation of a site plan. The trial judge, however, denied the motion citing Courter's testimony that a reasonably prudent professional would either order a survey when confronted with the situation here, or would look to the site himself to determine whether or not the tree was properly placed. The trial judge, however, granted the land surveyor's motion for involuntary dismissal. Citing Courter's testimony that the land surveyor, Kemp, was not required to denote vegetation on the survey, the judge concluded that there would be "no basis on which this jury could conclude at least as to the plaintiff's claim, that Mr. Kemp was negligent."

In reversing the lower court as to the architects' motion to dismiss, the appellate court concluded that the plaintiff failed to introduce expert testimony to prove what the standard of care was or that the architect had violated that standard. Because this was a professional negligence case, the standard of care had to be established by expert testimony. Specifically, the plaintiff had to produce expert testimony upon which the jury could find that the consensus of the particular profession recognized the existence of the standard defined by the expert. It was insufficient for the plaintiff's expert simply to follow slavishly an "accepted practice" formula. There had to be some evidential support offered by the expert establishing the existence of the standard. A standard that was personal to the expert was equivalent to a net opinion.[223.2]

The crux of Courter's testimony was that DeLosso deviated from accepted standards of architectural practice by failing to make a site inspection of plaintiff's property to verify the location of the 30-inch diameter maple tree when he prepared the April 16, 1991 DECO site plan. Courter testified that when a plan involved a small site, a "prudent architect would go to the site and make sure that he knows where that tree is, because all his work is going to revolve around that tree."

> The problem is that Courter presented no authority supporting his opinion. No reference was made to any written document, or even unwritten custom or practice indicating that the consensus of the architectural community recognizes a duty to make a site inspection for "small sites." Courter simply explained: "I'm just using—I think general care in doing a small parking lot—I mean, I wasn't at the time referring to standards in my mind. I was referring to just the general care shown on a small project."

There was no standard that on a small site, an architect had to verify the survey. Ultimately, Courter acknowledged that it was his personal opinion that "it would be [a] prudent approach" to make such a site inspection.

The court next discussed Courter's reference to various administrative rules regulating an architect's preparation of site plans. The first, N.J.A.C. 13:27-6.5(a), provided that: "[t]he architect in responsible charge shall sign, date and seal all original tracings of construction drawings and the title page of the specifications prepared by the architect or under his or her supervision on the original tracing." The court disagreed with the expert who testified that by signing the April 16, 1991 DECO plan, DeLosso and DECO became "responsible" for its accuracy.

First, that rule referred to "construction drawings." It was, therefore, unclear whether the rule applied to site plans at all. Second, even assuming that DeLosso and DECO were "responsible" for the accuracy of the site plan, the rule did not state that an architect had to make a site inspection, or could not transfer site information provided by a licensed surveyor onto the site plan. In fact, another regulation, N.J.A.C. 13:27-7.2(a)1, provided that existing conditions and physical features of the site denoted on a survey "may be transferred to the site plan if duly noted as to the date of the survey, by whom, and for whom." DeLosso "transferred" the physical features of the site depicted on the original land survey to the site plan and from that site plan to the DECO plan, dated April 16, 1991. Although the DECO site plan did not "duly" note the land survey, the court found

---

[223.2] *Citing* Crespo v. McCartin, 244 N.J.Super. 413, 422-23, 582 A.2d 1011 (App. Div. 1990).

that it could not be seriously argued that technical error was a proximate cause of the plaintiff's damages. The plaintiff's expert, Courter, himself acknowledged that he transferred physical features depicted on that original survey to his own site plan that he prepared for the plaintiff, and he did not denote that fact on the plan as required by the rule.

More importantly, the expert admitted during cross-examination that an architect was not required to check the accuracy of a survey given to him by a client, and was entitled to rely on the survey in preparing a site plan. In fact, the contract between the plaintiff and DECO addressed this point as follows:

> 1. The Owner shall furnish a legal description and certified land survey of the site, giving as applicable, grades and lines of streets, alleys, pavements and adjoining property; right-of-way, restrictions, easements, encroachments, zoning, deed restrictions, [boundaries] and contours of the site; locations, dimensions and complete data pertaining to existing buildings, other improvements and trees; and full information concerning available service and utility lines both public and private, above and below grade including inverts and depths.
>
> . . .
>
> 5. The services, information, surveys and reports required by Paragraphs 1 through 4 inclusive shall be furnished at the Owner's expense and the Architect shall be entitled to rely upon the accuracy and completeness thereof.

This language generally tracked Form B-141 of the AmericanInstitute of Architects Standard Form Agreement (SFA), which provided that a site survey was to be furnished by the owner,[223.3] and that "the Architect shall be entitled to rely upon the accuracy and completeness thereof."[223.4]

The plaintiff's expert agreed that Form B-141 of the SFA set forth the applicable standard defining the conditions of an architect's services to a client. Thus, he essentially agreed that, pursuant to Form B141, the architect had the right to rely on a survey furnished by the client. He also acknowledged that the B141 standard made no exception for "smaller sites," such as the plaintiff's lot.

The court also discounted the expert's testimony that the "reliance" referred to by Form B-141 meant such features as metes and bounds, dimensions of buildings and utilities, features required by law to be depicted on a survey, and

---

[223.3] AIA Document B141, paragraph 4.5, stated that "[t]he Owner shall furnish surveys describing physical characteristics, legal limitations and utility locations for the site of the Project, and a written legal description of the site. The surveys and legal information shall include, as applicable, . . . locations, dimensions and necessary data pertaining to existing buildings, other improvements and trees; and information concerning available utility services and lines, both public and private, above and below grade."

[223.4] AIA Document B141, paragraph 4.9, provided that "[t]he Owner shall furnish surveys describing physical characteristics, legal limitations and utility locations for the site of the Project, and a written legal description of the site. The surveys and legal information shall include, as applicable, . . . locations, dimensions and necessary data pertaining to existing buildings, other improvements and trees; and information concerning available utility services and lines, both public and private, above and below grade."

that "normally" a survey "would not show vegetation," including trees. Whether or not this assertion was correct, the survey in question did in fact depict the mislocated 30-inch diameter tree and, in accordance with Form B141, the defendants were entitled to rely on that depiction.

Finally, the court rejected the plaintiff's argument that DeLosso testified that he did not rely on the original 1985 survey when preparing the DECO April 16, 1991 site plan. Although DeLosso did not refer to the survey in preparing the DECO revisions, he testified that he relied on it "as a basis" for the site plan, including the location of the 30-inch diameter maple tree. In addition, he relied on that site plan when he prepared the revised site plan. In short, the original 1985 survey was the genesis of the mislocation of the 30-inch diameter tree, and the defendants relied on that survey by their reliance on the site plan.

In sum, the appellate court concluded that the "reliance" provisions in Form B141 of the SFA, and in the written agreement between the plaintiff and DECO, gave the defendants an unqualified right to rely on both the 1985 land survey and the full site plan in preparing their April 16, 1991 revisions. It also nullified the plaintiff's expert's (Courter's) unsupported conclusion that the defendant had a duty to make a site inspection to check the accuracy of the physical features contained in the 1985 land survey. The court, therefore, concluded that Courter's testimony constituted a net opinion, and the defendants were entitled to a judgment of dismissal as a matter of law.

Certain jurisdictions require a plaintiff suing a design professional such an architect or surveyor to obtain a certificate of merit prior to filing suit. In *Highland Lakes Country Club and Community Association, v. Nicastro*,[224] a country club filed a boundary suit against property owners, and the owners brought a third-party complaint against their surveyors. The surveyors moved to dismiss the suit for failure of plaintiffs to comply with an affidavit of merit statute. The trial court denied the dismissal motion. The surveyors appealed, but the appellate court affirmed the trial court's decision, as modified.[225]

The trial court held that in light of the "entire controversy" doctrine, it was appropriate for landowners to bring third-party claims against surveyors, as opposed to deferring those claims until conclusion of a boundary suit, and the appellate court affirmed that decision. The state supreme court affirmed the appellate division's judgment substantially for the reasons expressed in the thorough and thoughtful opinion by the trial court. The panel correctly embraced and applied the principles powerfully presented in *Diocese of Metuchen v. Prisco & Edwards, AIA*,[226] concluding that "application of [the Affidavit of Merit Statute, *N.J.S.A.* 2A:53A-26 to -29] would be inconsistent with its overall purposes under the present circumstances of this case."

In addition to the authority cited by the trial court, the appellate court pointed out that third-party defendants, Suburban Consulting Engineers, Inc. and Martin

---

[224] 201 N.J. 123, 988 A.2d 90 (2009).

[225] HighlandLakes Country Club & Cmty. Ass'n v. Nicastro, 406 N.J. Super. 145, 966 A.2d 1102 (Ct. App. Div. 2009).

[226] 374 N.J. Super. 409, 864 A.2d 1168 (Ct. App. Div. 2005).

Sikorski, P.L.S., suggested that the better route in this case would have been for the defendants, the third-party plaintiffs Frank W. and Lisa Ann Nicastro, to have deferred any claim against the third-party defendants until the conclusion of the action between plaintiff Highland Lakes Country Club and Community Association and the Nicastros. That suggestion was rejected by the court, as it ignored the entire controversy doctrine. That doctrine "embodies the principle that the adjudication of a legal controversy should occur in one litigation in only one court; accordingly, all parties involved in a litigation should at the very least present in that proceeding all of their claims and defenses that are related to the underlying controversy."[227] In its application, the entire controversy doctrine required the court to consider fairness to the parties. The boundaries of the entire controversy doctrine were held not to be limitless. It remains an equitable doctrine whose application is left to judicial discretion, based on the factual circumstances of individual cases.

This decision is consistent with the general theory that a plaintiff should bring all claims regarding a particular transaction into one forum for one resolution, to serve the goals of judicial economy and fairness to all parties.

It may not be obvious in a particular case when the cause of action for a claim accrues and when the statute of limitations provides the defendants with a viable defense. In *Ferrante Immobiliare, LLC v. Pace*,[228] a project owner brought an action alleging claims for negligence and breach of contract against an architect and an engineer. The defendant design professionals brought a third-party complaint against the general contractor on the project. The trial court (state supreme court), granted in part the owner's motion to amend its complaint to add a third-party defendant general contractor as a party defendant, and the owner, and the contractor appealed.

The state supreme court, appellate division, held that (1) the owner's negligence and breach of contract claims against the general contractor accrued at the latest as of the date of the execution of a settlement agreement; (2) the owner's filing of a supplemental summons and amended complaint did not toll the three-year statute of limitations for a negligence claim; and (3) the owner's breach of contract claim against the contractor was not precluded by the settlement agreement.

The appellate court affirmed in part, and dismissed in part and held that the project owner's breach of contract claim against the general contractor regarding allegedly defective items was not precluded by a settlement agreement, where the agreement expressly preserved owner's claims for negligence and breach of warranty or defects in connection with work included in the scope of the agreement. The plaintiffs argued that because Vanguard never substantially completed its work under the contract, the statute of limitations never commenced

---

[227] Cogdell v. Hosp. Ctr. at Orange, 116 N.J. 7, 15, 560 A.2d 1169 (1989). "[T]he purposes of the doctrine include the needs of economy and the avoidance of waste, efficiency and the reduction of delay, fairness to parties, and the need for complete and final disposition through the avoidance of 'piecemeal decisions.' "

[228] 68 A.D.3d 463, 891 N.Y.S.2d 27 (2009).

to run, and that the March 30, 2005 settlement agreement did not necessarily mark the accrual date of their negligence and breach of contract claims since neither a "Certificate of Substantial Performance" nor a final Certificate of Payment had ever been issued by the architect Pace as required by the original contract. The appellate court held that these arguments were without merit.

In their original complaint, in which the claims of negligence and breach of contract were only alleged against defendant-architect Pace, and defendant-engineer, Goldman Copeland Associates, and in which the general contractor, Vanguard, was not a named party, plaintiffs admitted that "[b]y late 2003, Vanguard completed the Project and the Firm moved into the remaining space at the Premises." In their proposed amended complaint, the plaintiffs sought to add breach of contract and negligence claims against Vanguard, the general contractor. The court pointed out that plaintiffs, for obvious reasons, omitted such allegation and alleged instead that "[b]y late 2003, the Firm moved into the remaining space at the Premises, while work on the HVAC, plumbing and electrical systems was ongoing," which work "was never substantially completed."

Article 14 of the standard AIA agreement with Vanguard, the general contractor, defined substantial completion as "the stage in the progress of the Work when the Work . . . is sufficiently complete in accordance with the Contract Documents so that the Owner can occupy or utilize the Work for its intended use." It further provided that final payment would be made after the architect issued a Certificate of Substantial Completion and a final Certificate for Payment which stated that it had determined to the best of its knowledge that the work had been completed in accordance with the terms and conditions of the contract. According to section 14.5.1 of the contract, the architect's final certificate for payment constituted a further representation that the conditions precedent to Vanguard's being entitled to final payment of the entire balance found to be due it have been fulfilled.

Although the March 30, 2005 settlement agreement did not state when Vanguard's obligations under the contract were to be deemed substantially (or entirely) complete, or that Vanguard was otherwise absolved from all of its remaining responsibilities under the contract, the settlement agreement stressed that Vanguard, which had already completed or abandoned the project, was to receive its final payment under the contract. The settlement agreement also did not indicate that Vanguard had any further obligations under the contract.

After the architect, Pace, advised the plaintiffs on January 20, 2005 that Vanguard was unwilling to return to the work site to perform unspecified work, and that Pace would sign off on the project "when all the issues are resolved," plaintiffs and Vanguard bypassed the architect (whom plaintiffs later sued for breach of contract and negligent design and supervision) and entered into the March 30, 2005 settlement agreement in which they agreed that plaintiffs would pay Vanguard $13,500 "as final payment under the Agreement." In the agreement, plaintiffs stated that, as of that date, they were "unaware of any defects or negligence in connection with the Project," while they retained their rights, if any, with respect to any claims based upon any subsequently discovered defects in workmanship.

The statute of limitations on plaintiffs' negligence and breach of contract claims, which arguably accrued as early as late 2003, began to run, at the latest, on March 30, 2005, the date of execution of the owners' settlement agreement with Vanguard, which expressly provided that in consideration for the settlement plaintiffs would pay Vanguard the sum of $13,500 "as final payment under the Agreement."[229] The original agreement with Vanguard provided, in pertinent part, that "[f]inal payment, constituting the entire unpaid balance of the Contract Sum, shall be made by the Owner to the Contractor where [ ] the Contractor has fully performed the Contract." Since the parties charted their own course and agreed to dispense with the architect's approvals preliminary to final payment under the original contract, the court found that there was no need to determine whether Vanguard's work was "substantially complete" within the meaning of that agreement.

Although the motion court, in its July 2, 2008 order, found that the plaintiffs interposed their proposed negligence claim on March 25, 2008 when they filed their motion to amend the complaint, the plaintiffs' having filed a supplemental summons and amended complaint on March 25, 2008 did not toll the three-year statute of limitations for negligence claims, since they failed to secure leave of the court or a stipulation signed by counsel for the parties.[230] Plaintiffs did not seek leave to amend the complaint until April 7, 2008, when their order to show cause was signed. Although the motion court erroneously found that its prior order dismissing the third-party complaint, holding that the negligence claim was time barred, constituted the law of the case as to the plaintiffs, the plaintiffs' subsequent failure to timely move to amend their complaint rendered that issue academic. Since the order to show cause could not have been submitted prior to April 2, 2008, the date of its supporting affirmation and affidavit, there was no need to determine when it was actually submitted.

Contrary to the general contractor's contention, the plaintiffs' breach of contract claim was not precluded by the settlement agreement, that removed 14 enumerated items from the scope of the parties' agreement (the "excluded work"). The owners expressly preserved the owners' claims for negligence and breach of warranty or defects in connection with the "included work." To the extent the motion court's order could be read to limit the relevant language, the settlement agreement, which preserved all claims for "defects, including, but not limited to, latent defects, and warranties for work remaining in the scope of the work under the Agreement," was controlling and dispositive of the issue. Whether the items alleged to be defective fell within the category of "excluded work" or "included work" was a factual determination that could not be made on this record.

Finally, in view of the trial court's determination in its July 2, 2008 order that the owner's proposed negligence claim against Vanguard was untimely, albeit for the wrong reason, i.e., the law of the case, the plaintiffs' appeal from the

---

[229] *See* Amedeo Hotels Ltd. P'ship v. Zwicker Elec. Co., 291 A.D.2d 322, 323, 739 N.Y.S.2d 10 (2002).

[230] *See* CPLR 1003.

December 4, 2007 order, to the extent it granted Vanguard's motion to dismiss the third-party complaint on the ground that the negligence claim was untimely, was academic.

Although a settlement agreement may be drafted and agreed to at the end of a long mediation or settlement conference, care must be taken in reviewing the agreement to ensure the terms are consistent with the parties' intent, and do not waive reserved claims.

CHAPTER 6

COMPENSATION AND OTHER OWNER OBLIGATIONS

§ 6.04 EQUITABLE ADJUSTMENTS

Page 183, add at end of section:

In *Advantages of the ConsensusDOCS Construction Contracts*, by Larry D. Harris and Brian M. Perlberg, The Construction Lawyer, Vol. 29, Number 1, Winter 2009, the authors discuss consequential damages. The ConsensusDOCS provide for a limited waiver of consequential damages. The documents call for the owner to promptly delineate liquidated damage, and to identify items specifically excluded from the waiver of consequential damages under the documents. Harris and Perlberg claim that this sharing of information concerning the downside risk of failures of performance provides the financial incentives to achieve proper performance.

Chapter 7

OWNERSHIP OF DOCUMENTS/ INTELLECTUAL PROPERTY

§ 7.02 THE ISSUES

Page 207, add at end of section:

In *Advantages of the ConsensusDOCS Construction Contracts*, by Larry D. Harris and Brian M. Perlberg, The Construction Lawyer, Vol. 29, Number 1, Winter 2009, the authors describe how ownership and future use of design documents is handled. The ConsensusDOCS require the parties to discuss issues regarding ownership and use of design documents before a dispute arises. The ConsensusDOCS give the parties a vehicle to use design plans for what Harris and Perlberg call "just compensation." Harris and Perlberg call this approach "more project-friendly in instances when a design professional is no longer actively involved in a renovation, or has been terminated for cause of convenience." If an owner wants a copyright transfer, the parties negotiate a fair price for the transfer. ConsensusDOCS 240, Para. 10.1. AIA documents explicitly recognize that the contractor does not have an ownership interest in the documents, while the ConsensusDOCS do so implicitly. The ConsensusDOCS provide that the owner is to provide appropriate documents to the contractor to enable the contractor to perform its work. ConsensusDOCS 200m, Para. 2.3.

CHAPTER 8

ARBITRATION

§ 8.01 DISPUTE RESOLUTION ALTERNATIVES

Page 230, add after third full paragraph:

In *Advantages of the ConsensusDOCS Construction Contracts*, by Larry D. Harris and Brian M. Perlberg, The Construction Lawyer, Vol. 29, Number 1, Winter 2009, Harris and Perlberg describe how claim resolution is handled differently. Under the ConsensusDOCS, the parties initially meet and discuss the issues at the project level. If that is not successful, then parties raise discussion of the issues to the senior management level. If issues are still unresolved, the parties may utilize a project-neutral or dispute review board to issue non-binding findings to help resolve claims. The next step for dispute resolution is to proceed to mediation under the American Arbitration Association (AAA) Rules. If still unresolved, disputes go to binding dispute resolution. The forum to be used is selected by the parties, checking a box on the forms for either litigation or arbitration. If arbitration is chosen, the AAA rules in effect at the time the claim is presented apply, rather than the rules in effect at the time the contract was signed.

CHAPTER 9

PLANNING OVERVIEW: SELECTION OF DOCUMENTS

§ 9.05 CONSTRUCTION MANAGER

Page 250, add at end of section:

In *Fifth Day, LLC v. Colotin,*[12.1] a management company brought an action against a project owner and its principals, seeking compensation allegedly due for construction management services rendered by Fifth Day, LLC on an industrial real estate development project. The trial court entered summary judgment for the owners, and the management company appealed. The appellate court reversed, holding that the plaintiff construction management company was not required to be licensed pursuant under California Contractors' State License Law.

In *The Fifth Day, LLC*, the plaintiff property management company (plaintiff) entered into an agreement with Industrial Real Estate Development Company (owner) to provide certain "industrial real estate development and construction project management" services with respect to real property located in Chino, California. Plaintiff sued the owner and its principals, Pacific Allied Industrial Corporation and James P. Bolotin, for compensation alleged to be due for services rendered by Fifth Day.

The trial court granted summary judgment in favor of the owners on the ground that Fifth Day was acting as a general building contractor and therefore was required to hold a license pursuant to California Business and Professions Code Section 7026. Because Fifth Day had no such license, it was barred by Section 7031, subdivision (a), from maintaining this action. On appeal, Fifth Day contended that:

1. it was not a contractor within the meaning of Section 7026;
2. it was exempt from the license requirement because it was an owner of the property or a partner of the owner;
3. even if some of the services it rendered required a contractor's license, it nevertheless could be compensated for other services that did not require a license.

The appellate court held that the plaintiff was not a contractor within the meaning of the licensing statute, and that its claims were not barred by Section 7031, subdivision (a). The trial court's judgment was reversed.

[12.1] 172 Cal. App. 4th 939, 91 Cal. Rptr. 3d 633 (2009), *review filed* (May 5, 2009).

In 1999, the owners owned 12.3 acres of land in Chino, California, adjacent to land owned by Chino Industrial Commons, LLC (CIC). Fifth Day's managing member was Kevin Knox. At Knox's urging, owners and CIC agreed to develop their properties jointly. The property was divided into three parcels designated Lots 19, 20, and 21. CIC entered into 52-year ground leases on the three lots. The ground lease for Lot 20 required CIC to construct a 55,000-square-foot building on the lot within the first two years. Once the building had been completed, CIC was to assign its interest in Lot 20 back to the owners, and the owners were to convey to CIC a fee simple interest in Lots 19 and 21. No rent was payable by CIC under the ground leases for the first two years, but rent was payable thereafter.

CIC failed to construct the building on Lot 20 during the first two years of the lease term, and rent began to accrue under the ground leases at a rate of five cents per square foot, or approximately $24,000 per month. In February 2001, rather than pay the rent, CIC assigned the three ground leases, along with its obligation to construct the building, to Fifth Day. The development plan for the property was changed to a seven-building commercial office park. Lot 20 was redesignated as Lots 1 and 2, and Lots 19 and 21 were redesignated as Lots 3 through 7. Fifth Day undertook to construct two buildings totaling 55,000 square feet on Lots 1 and 2 (formerly Lot 20) in return for a fee simple interest in Lots 3 through 7 (formerly Lots 19 and 21). Fifth Day was responsible for financing the construction.

By early 2003, Fifth Day had not constructed the buildings and owed the owners $465,000 in back rent. Fifth Day negotiated with PCI to obtain financing for the construction. Under the agreement contemplated between Fifth Day and PCI, Fifth Day would assign the ground leases to PCI. PCI would finance the construction of the seven buildings, pay the owners the accrued back rent, and pay Fifth Day $100,000. The plaintiff was to receive a "Project Incentive Fee," based on a 25 percent share of the profits from the sale of the development.

The owners refused to consent to the assignment of the ground leases contemplated in the PCI deal, and proposed, instead, to finance the construction on terms similar to the PCI deal, including reassignment of the ground leases back to the owners. The owners proposed to increase Fifth Day's Project Incentive Fee to 34 percent of the profits. Knox stated in his declaration that Fifth Day "reluctantly" accepted the owners' proposal because of the increased Project Incentive Fee.

This agreement was memorialized in a written document dated May 5, 2003 between Fifth Day and the owners entitled "Development Management Agreement For the Construction of The Campus at CIC" (the "DMA"). Fifth Day is referred to as the "Development Manager."

The DMA recited that the owners wished to undertake the development of the entire property. To do so, "Owner desires to have Professional Development and Construction Management Services to assist the owner. . . ." Fifth Day was "experienced in industrial real estate development and construction project management and is willing to provide to Owner these services."

Fifth Day was to be paid a fixed development fee of $100,000 as a nonrefundable advance against a Project Incentive Fee of 34 percent of a defined

"Project Value." The DMA provided, "The Owner agrees that for purposes of this agreement, any and all lease rents accrued are included in the value of the Land Contribution and that the leases for Lots 19, 20 and 21 previously entered into are to be terminated as and by those Lease Terminations attached as Exhibit __." The DMA specified that Fifth Day was to perform the following duties "as Owner may specifically and expressly direct," listing many specific tasks to be done by Fifth Day.

In addition, Fifth Day warranted and represented that (1) it was "experienced, competent and qualified to perform the work contemplated by" the DMA, (2) it had and would maintain "sufficient facilities, expertise, staff, assets and other resources to perform its duties," (3) it held and would hold "all licenses, permits or other certifications necessary to perform its duties," and (4) the owner would "have full knowledge and involvement in the Project."

In January 2004, Fifth Day entered into a construction contract with Fullmer Construction, and Fullmer agreed to complete specified work, including the construction of seven concrete tilt-up buildings on the property, for a fee of nearly $4.9 million. Knox, Fifth Day's principal, was designated in the contractor agreement as the owner's representative. As such, Knox represented the owner with respect to all aspects of the contractor agreement and the work. Fifth Day performed the services required of it under the DMA. Construction was completed, and certificates of occupancy for the project issued in December 2004. Fifth Day alleged that, between December 2004 and March 2005, the owners sold three of the buildings. According to Knox, the owners paid Fifth Day in excess of $785,000 in Project Incentive Fees. Fifth Day alleged that the owners subsequently sold or leased the remaining four buildings, but refused to pay Fifth Day the additional Project Incentive Fees earned under the DMA. Fifth Day alleged that, as a result, the owners owed Fifth Day approximately $1.8 million in additional Project Incentive Fees. Fifth Day sued the owners for breach of contract and on common counts for money had and received and for services rendered.

The trial court sustained the owners' demurrers to the original complaint with leave to amend on the ground that Fifth Day failed to allege that it was a licensed contractor and was therefore barred from bringing suit by Section 7031. Fifth Day then filed a first amended complaint that (1) omitted the common count for services rendered, (2) recast Fifth Day's cause of action for breach of contract to allege the breach of a partnership agreement, and (3) sought the additional remedies of rescission and restitution. The owners again demurred on the ground that Section 7031 barred Fifth Day's suit. This time, the trial court overruled the demurrer, concluding that Fifth Day had alleged facts that, if true, avoided the Section 7031 bar.

The owners subsequently moved for summary judgment on the sole ground that Section 7031 barred Fifth Day's suit. The trial court granted the motion, concluding that the undisputed facts established that Fifth Day was a contractor within the meaning of Section 7026. Because Fifth Day was not licensed, its action was barred by Section 7031. The trial court entered judgment in favor of the owners. Fifth Day appealed.

The California appellate court held that the central question was whether an entity which provides construction management services to a private owner is required to be licensed as a contractor. After a lengthy review of California licensing law, the *Fifth Day LLC* court concluded that plaintiff did not perform or agree to perform construction services. It hired a general contractor to do that work, Fullmer Construction. The appellate court noted that on public works projects, a construction manager must be either a licensed architect, engineer, or general contractor.[12.2] Because the legislature did not require that construction managers on private works be licensed, the court reversed the trial court's holding and held that Fifth Day did not need to be licensed.

§ 9.10 CONTRACTOR'S LICENSING ISSUES

Page 283, add at end of section 9.10:

When a contractor is unlicensed or has a license lapse, many jurisdictions, including California, allow owners the extreme remedy of denying any recovery for work performed or even that the contractor be required to return all money paid by the owner, regardless of the value of the work provided by the unlicensed contractor. In *Alatriste v. Cesar's Exterior Designs, Inc.*,[60] a homeowner brought an action against a contractor to recover compensation paid for a project begun while the contractor was unlicensed. The appellate court affirmed the trial court's grant of summary judgment for the homeowner. The court held that:

1. defenses of unjust enrichment, estoppel, or unclean hands did not bar the homeowner's claim;
2. the contractor was not entitled to offset for work after contractor obtained license;
3. the contractor was not entitled to offset for materials; and
4. the defense of fraud did not bar the homeowner's claim.

In the case, Esaul Alatriste hired Cesar's Exterior Designs, Inc. (Cesar's Designs) to perform landscaping work at his home. After working for about five months, Cesar's Designs terminated its services when Alatriste refused to continue to pay for work performed. By that time, Alatriste had paid Cesar's Designs $57,500. Alatriste then brought an action against Cesar's Designs alleging fraud, negligent misrepresentation, and unfair competition, and also sought to recover the total amount paid ($57,500) under Business and Professions Code § 7031, because Cesar's Designs was unlicensed when it began the work. Specifically, Section 7031, allowed a party to recover "all compensation paid to [an] unlicensed contractor." Alatriste successfully moved for summary adjudication on this claim. After Alatriste dismissed his remaining claims, the court entered judgment in Alatriste's favor on the Section 7031(b) claim for $57,500, plus interest and costs.

[12.2] Cal. Gov't Code § 4525.

[60] 183 Cal. App. 4th 656, 108 Cal. Rptr. 3d 277 (2010).

Although Cesar's Designs conceded that it was unlicensed when it began the landscape work, it, nevertheless, contended that the trial court erred in granting summary adjudication, because it presented facts supporting its defenses and/or offsets to Alatriste's Section 7031(b) claim. The appellate court found this contention without merit. It held that the proffered facts did not support a viable defense or offset to Alatriste's reimbursement claim under Section 7031(b), and the appellate court affirmed the trial court's grant of summary judgment.

In support of his claim, Alatriste presented evidence that the parties signed a contract on December 1, 2006, in which Alatriste agreed to pay $91,900 in four installments for the landscape work. This evidence showed that Cesar's Designs began work on December 11 and left the project five months later on May 26, 2007. Alatriste also submitted documents from the state licensing board showing Cesar's Designs did not have a landscaping contractor's license until April 5, 2007, and had never before been licensed. Alatriste said he paid a total of $57,500 to Cesar's Designs.

Cesar's Designs submitted a declaration of its president (Cesar Hernandez), who stated he had known Alatriste for 12 years and:

> At the time we were negotiating the contract, [Alatriste] understood that neither I nor my company had a California contractor's license. At that time, my son, Cesar Hernandez Jr., was studying for, and was scheduled to take, the California contractor's license exam. My company was going to operate under my son's license. [¶] . . . Between September and November of 2006, I informed [Alatriste] on at least three (3) occasions that my son was scheduled to take the California contractor's license exam at the end of 2006 or early 2007. [Alatriste] understood that my company did not yet have a license during this time. [¶] . . . Knowing that [Cesar's Designs] did not yet have a license at the time, [Alatriste] nonetheless asked [Cesar's Designs] to perform the landscaping work at his new home.

Hernandez also explained the circumstances under which his company became licensed:

> "On January 23, 2007, before any significant work had been performed at [Alatriste's] home, my son tested for his California contractor's license. On that same day, we found out my son passed the test. . . . [¶] . . .Two (2) months later, in March of 2007, not having received any word regarding the issuance of the license, I contacted the State Contractor's License Board . . . [and] was informed the Board was unable to issue a license because it allegedly never received a $150 processing and license fee when the application was submitted in January. Immediately, I resubmitted the paperwork and the $150 fee." Hernandez said his son was then issued the license on April 5, 2007. Hernandez stated that at least once during the construction period, he "discussed with [Alatriste] the fact that [Cesar's Designs] was awaiting the issuance of a license."

Hernandez also asserted that Alatriste never expressed any dissatisfaction with the work performed during the project, and the sole reason Alatriste stopped paying for the work was because Alatriste was having financial problems. In this respect, Hernandez said: "[Alatriste] continually reminded me that we were 'good friends' and [Alatriste] would come up with the money soon. [Cesar's Designs] attempted to accommodate the situation by extending the time for payments, but eventually had to cease work due to [Alatriste's] failure to make payments."

Hernandez said that when Cesar's Designs left the site, Alatriste still owed $15,648.55 for work performed. With respect to Cesar's Designs' offset claims, Hernandez said: "Of the amount paid by [Alatriste] to Cesar's Designs, $11,968 was for labor and materials provided while Cesar's Designs had a California contractor's license[,] [¶] [and] . . . $20,045.16 was for materials used and incorporated into the project."

In reply, Alatriste denied that he knew that Cesar's Designs was not licensed during the project, but argued that even if he knew, knowledge by the consumer was not a bar to recovery under Section 7031(b). Alatriste also stated that in May 2007, he experienced "serious problems with Cesar's performing substandard, shoddy work on my residence," and identified numerous specific defects. Alatriste said he informed Hernandez and his son of those problems.

After a hearing, the trial court granted summary adjudication on Alatriste's statutory reimbursement claim. The trial court found that Alatriste proved he was entitled to full reimbursement, and rejected Cesar's Designs' defenses. Specifically, the court ruled that a plaintiff's prior knowledge of a defendant's unlicensed status did not bar recovery under Section 7031(b), and that Cesar's Designs did not establish a substantial compliance defense under the statute. Alatriste then dismissed all remaining causes of actions and defendants. The court entered a final judgment against Cesar's Designs for $57,500 plus interest for a total amount of $66,762.25.

In affirming the lower court's judgment, the appellate court stated that it presumed the legislature meant what it said, and the plain meaning of the statute governed.[61] Where the terms of the statute provide no definitive answer, courts may resort to extrinsic sources, including the ostensible objects to be achieved and the legislative history.

The shield portion of the statute, denying an unlicensed contractor recovery, has been a longstanding part of the statute. In 2001, the Legislature amended Section 7031 to add a sword remedy. This sword remedy, contained in Section 7031(b), currently reads:

> Except as provided in subdivision (e), a person who utilizes the services of an unlicensed contractor may bring an action in any court of competent jurisdiction in this state to recover all compensation paid to the unlicensed contractor for performance of any act or contract.

By adding this remedy, the legislature sought to further Section 7031(a)'s policy of deterring violations of licensing requirements by "allow[ing] persons who

[61] San Diego County Employees Retirement Ass'n v. County of San Diego, 151 Cal. App. 4th 1163, 1174, 60 Cal. Rptr. 3d 601 (2007).

utilize unlicensed contractors to recover compensation paid to the contractor for performing unlicensed work."[62]

A legislative committee analysis stated the measure was enacted in response to *Cooper v. Westbrook Torrey Hills, LP*,[63] in which the court referred to Section 7031(a), which, at that time, prohibited an unlicensed contractor from recovering fees, but did not require any refund of compensation already paid to the contractor. The court in *Alatriste* determined that Section 7031(a) was intended to clearly state that those using the services of unlicensed contractors were entitled to bring an action for recovery of compensation paid.[64]

On this record, Alatriste met his summary adjudication burden of showing that pursuant to Section 7031(b)'s sword provision, he was entitled to a full reimbursement of the amounts paid to Cesar's Designs when he presented evidence that the work performed required a landscape contractor's license, but Cesar's Designs did not have this license when it began the work. Further, Alatriste's evidence showed he paid $57,500 to Cesar's Designs for the landscaping work and materials. The burden, thus, shifted to Cesar's Designs to show a triable issue of fact as to Alatriste's entitlement to the $57,500. Cesar's Designs contends it met this burden by presenting evidence that Alatriste knew Cesar's Designs was unlicensed, but, nonetheless, retained its services and benefited from the work. He argued this evidence supported its defenses of fraud, unjust enrichment, estoppel, and unclean hands. Cesar's Designs alternatively argued that it was entitled to an offset, because: (1) a portion of Alatriste's payment was for work after Cesar's Designs became licensed; and (2) a portion of Alatriste's payment to Cesar's Designs was for materials (rather than labor). The appellate court found those contentions to be without merit.

Section 7031(b) does not specifically state whether a plaintiff's prior knowledge of the defendant's unlicensed status is relevant to a plaintiff's recovery. Because the statute is ambiguous on this point, the appellate court stated that it could look to other indicia of intent, including legislative history and other related statutes. These materials unequivocally showed that in enacting Section 7031(b), the legislature specifically intended to permit full recovery even if the hiring party had actual knowledge the contractor was unlicensed.

Section 7031(a) has long been interpreted to allow a homeowner to apply the shield to any recovery despite the homeowner's knowledge of a contractor's unlicensed status.[65] The legislature enacted Section 7031(b) to ensure that the same penalties applied for an unlicensed contractor regardless whether the contractor was the plaintiff or the defendant. The appellate court inferred that the legislature intended that a moving party's knowledge would not affect his or her right to reimbursement under Section 7031(b).

---

[62] White v. Cridlebaugh, 178 Cal. App. 4th 506, 519, 100 Cal. Rptr. 3d 434 (2009).

[63] 81 Cal. App. 4th 1294, 97 Cal. Rptr. 2d 742 (2000).

[64] *Citing White*, 178 Cal. App. 4th 506, 519, 100 Cal. Rptr. 3d 434, *quoting* Assem. Com. on Judiciary, Analysis of Assem. Bill No. 678 (2001-2002 Reg. Sess.) as introduced Feb. 22, 2001, pp. 2-3.

[65] Hydrotech Systems Ltd. v. Oasis Water Park, 52 Cal. 3d 988, 997, 277 Cal. Rptr. 517, 803 P.2d 370 (1991).

The court pointed out that the knowledge issue was specifically addressed in the legislative history materials.[66] An earlier version of the bill enacting Section 7031(b) had provided that reimbursement would not be permitted "when the person who used the services of an unlicensed contractor knew that the contractor was unlicensed prior to the time that any payments are made."[67] This provision was initially included because of a concern that the bill would be "unfair" to a contractor who fully performed the contract and would "unjustly enrich" the hiring party.[68]

However, the senate later deleted this language "in order to more strongly encourage contractors to become licensed."[69]

An earlier legislative committee analysis quoted the bill sponsor explaining that:

> In AB No. 678, the question has been raised as to whether a person for whom work was performed by an unlicensed contractor would be entitled to recover compensation paid the unlicensed contractor if the person receiving the services knew the contractor was unlicensed. By a parity of reasoning from the state of the law respecting Section 7031(a), knowledge of the status of an unlicensed contractor is irrelevant to the recovery of compensation from the unlicensed contractor. California courts have unmistakably ruled that in any action by an unlicensed contractor to recover for the value of a contractor's services . . . , the unlicensed contractor cannot recover money even if the person for whom the work was performed knew the contractor was unlicensed. [Citations.] [¶] AB No. 678 constitutes an additional and consistent legislative determination that such deterrence can best be realized by compelling violators to return all compensation received from providing their unlicensed services . . . . That policy is furthered in AB No. 678 by specifically recognizing the capacity of an owner to recover money already paid an unlicensed contractor, even if the person knew the contractor was unlicensed.[70]

The Assembly Judiciary Committee analysis further noted that recovery would be allowed even if the unlicensed contractor argued that the person seeking reimbursement had "unclean hands" based on his or her prior knowledge of the unlicensed status.[71] Under Section 7031(b), a party is entitled to reimbursement for amounts paid to an unlicensed contractor even if the party knew the contractor was unlicensed. The appellate court rejected Cesar's Designs' contention that its

[66] *See White*, 178 Cal. App. 4th 506, 519, 100 Cal. Rptr. 3d 434.

[67] Sen. Com. on Bus. & Prof. Analysis of Assem. Bill No. 678, as amended May 1, 2001.

[68] *See* Assem. Com. on Judiciary, Analysis of Assem. Bill No. 678 (2001-2002 Reg. Sess.) as introduced Feb. 22, 2001, p. 4.

[69] Assem. Com. on Jud., Bill Analysis on Concurrence in Sen. Amendments of Assem. Bill No. 678, as amended July 3, 2001.

[70] Assem. Com. on Judiciary, Analysis of Assem. Bill No. 678 (2001-2002 Reg. Sess.), as introduced Feb. 22, 2001, p. 3.

[71] *Id.* at 4.

equitable defenses (unclean hands, estoppel, unjust enrichment) were viable, based on the evidence of Alatriste's prior knowledge of its unlicensed contractor status.

The court next rejected Cesar's Designs contention that the lower court erred in granting summary adjudication on the entire claimed amount ($57,500) based on its argument that $11,968 of this amount reflected payment for work after Cesar's Designs obtained a California landscape contractor's license. This contention is without merit. Section 7031(b) provided a reimbursement right for *all* amounts paid to an unlicensed contractor if the contractor was unlicensed *at any time during the performance*, unless the statutory substantial compliance rules were met. In this case, there was no showing the substantial compliance rules were satisfied.

Courts interpreting Section 7031(a) have long held that a contractor "is ineligible to recover any compensation under the terms of that statute, if, at any time during performance of an agreement for contractor services, he or she was not duly licensed." In addition, a California appellate court recently applied this same rule in an action for reimbursement brought under Section 7031(b).[72]

As noted, the legislature enacted Section 7031(b) to disapprove of the decisions recognizing a distinction between a contractor's affirmative and defensive (offset) claims, and to ensure that the rules pertaining to an unlicensed contractor's compensation rights were consistent, regardless whether the contractor was suing or the contractor was being sued.[73]

When the legislature enacted Section 7031(b), courts had long held that a contractor was not entitled to any compensation for any work performed unless the contractor was licensed during the entire project (absent a showing of statutory substantial compliance).[74] The legislature was presumed to be aware of existing laws and judicial decisions interpreting those laws when it enacts legislation.[75] Accordingly, if the legislature had intended a different result in Section 7031(b) with respect to whether a contractor could offset a recovery for work performed with a license, it would have said so. Instead, that section broadly reads that "a person who utilizes the services of an unlicensed contractor may bring an action . . . to recover all compensation paid to the unlicensed contractor for performance of any act or contract."

Cesar's Designs argued that the legislature must have intended a different result in Section 7031(b), because it used different language in the two subdivisions. Specifically, Section 7031(a) states a contractor may not bring an action for compensation unless the contractor alleges that he or she was a "duly licensed contractor at all times during the performance of that act or contract," whereas the legislature did not use this "at all times" phrase in Section 7031(b). The court was not persuaded by this argument.

---

[72] Goldstein v. Barak Constr., 164 Cal. App. 4th 845, 79 Cal. Rptr. 3d 603 (2008).

[73] *See White*, 178 Cal. App. 4th 506, 519-20, 100 Cal. Rptr. 3d 434.

[74] MW Erectors, Inc. v. Niederhauser, 36 Cal. 4th 412, 425, 30 Cal. Rptr. 3d 755, 115 P.3d 41 (2005).

[75] Voss v. Superior Court, 46 Cal. App. 4th 900, 925, 54 Cal. Rptr. 2d 225 (1996).

The court held that the fact that the legislature used different language in the two subdivisions did not mean the legislature intended a different result. While a court could reasonably infer from the legislature's use of different language in statutory provisions to conclude that the legislature intended a different meaning in each statute,[76] this rule was not to be applied rigidly and without considering the entire context of the legislation. In this case, the legislature included the phrase "at all times" in Section 7031(a) to clarify the pleading and proof requirement for a contractor to recover on an affirmative claim against a party utilizing its services. With respect to Section 7031(b), the legislature addressed the hiring party's right to recover compensation paid to an unlicensed contractor. In this situation, there was no need for the legislature to require the plaintiff to allege when the contractor was unlicensed or that the contractor was unlicensed "at all times."

The statutory language providing that the party was entitled to recover "all compensation paid to the unlicensed contractor for performance of any act or contract" was sufficient to reflect the legislative intent to permit full reimbursement regardless of a contractor's subsequent license status (Section 7031(b)).

In amending Section 7031 two years after enacting Section 7031(b), the legislature expressed an understanding that: (1) without a substantial compliance defense a contractor would be required to disgorge all of its compensation even if it was unlicensed for only one day of the work; and (2) the legislature had been unwilling to establish an exception that would allow reimbursement only for the period of time when a contractor was unlicensed. Although a legislative expression of a prior intent was not binding upon the courts, the expression was a relevant factor in the analysis. Additionally, at the same time it added the substantial compliance defense to Section 7031(b), the legislature reconfirmed that the defense was inapplicable if the contractor had never been licensed.

The appellate court held that this legislative history, together with the broad statutory language and the circumstances showing that the legislature intended that Section 7031(b) be a mirror image of Section 7031(a), convinced the court that Section 7031(b) did not permit an offset for work performed after a license was obtained, unless the statutory substantial compliance rule applied (Section 7031(e)). The appellate court held that the substantial compliance rule did not apply in this case.

Cesar's Designs argued at length that because the sword provision (Section 7031(b)) created more opportunities for a homeowner to take unfair advantage of an unlicensed contractor than the shield provision (Section 7031(a)), the provisions should be interpreted differently on the issue of whether partial recovery would be allowed if the contractor became licensed during the performance of the work. Cesar's Designs was essentially asking this court to evaluate the wisdom of the legislature's policy determination. However, the court's function was to ascertain and give effect to legislative intent, and "not to determine whether the

---

[76] Singh v. Superior Court, 140 Cal. App. 4th 387, 399, 44 Cal. Rptr. 3d 348 (2006).

Legislature's policy choices were right or wrong."[77] The court, however, ruled that it could not evaluate the desirability of the policies embodied in legislation.

The *Alatriste* court next ruled that the lower court did not err in applying Section 7031(b) to allow Alatriste to obtain reimbursement for amounts paid for materials used in the project ($20,045.16). The *White* court rejected the identical argument.[78] Construing Section 7031(b)'s language, the *White* court stated that "the authorization of recovery of 'all compensation paid to the unlicensed contractor for performance of any act or contract' means that unlicensed contractors are required to return all compensation received without reductions or offsets for the value of material or services provided." The court reasoned that this "interpretation . . . is consistent with the usual meaning of the word 'all,' which signifies the whole number and does not admit of an exception or exclusion not specified."

The *Alatriste* court agreed with this analysis and reached the same result. In support of a contrary argument, Cesar's Designs cited only one decision.[79] That decision, however, predated Section 7031(b) and was not helpful. Cesar's Designs contended that allowing Alatriste to obtain reimbursement for materials that remain in his possession was unfair and "serves no purpose other than punishment." As noted, the legislative committee reports showed that, in enacting Section 7031(b), the legislature was specifically aware that permitting reimbursement could result in harsh and unfair results to an individual contractor and could result in unjust enrichment to a homeowner. The legislature, nonetheless, decided that the rule was essential to effectuate the important public policy of deterring licensing violations and ensuring that all contractors were licensed.

Next, the court rejected Cesar's Designs contention that fraud was a valid defense to a Section 7031(b) action. However, the only facts presented by Cesar's Designs in support of its fraud claim were that Alatriste knew it was unlicensed when Alatriste retained Cesar's Designs to perform the work, and knew that the company president's son was in the process of obtaining a license. The appellate court noted that the legislature specifically intended to permit recovery by a party even if the party had knowledge of an unlicensed status.

The fraud defense was unsupported on this record. Similarly, the appellate court rejected Cesar's Designs' argument that it should be entitled to defend the action on the basis that Alatriste obtained benefits from his landscaping work. As with Section 7031(a), Section 7031(b) did not permit a contractor to assert legal or equitable defenses even if the facts showed the hiring party knowingly and substantially benefited from the work.

The *Alatriste* court upheld the trial court's grant of summary judgment and refused to allow the contractor any offsets to the Section 7031 disgorgement claim by the homeowner.

---

[77] County of Orange v. Superior Court, 155 Cal. App. 4th 1253, 1262, 66 Cal. Rptr. 3d 689 (2007).

[78] *White*, 178 Cal. App. 4th at 520-21, 100 Cal. Rptr. 3d at 434.

[79] Harrison v. Shamalian, 110 Cal. App. 2d 500, 243 P.2d 82 (1952).

Attorneys representing contractors in California need to ensure, prior to filing suit, that the contractor was properly licensed at all times during the project. In addition, prior to bringing the matter to trial, the attorney representing the contractor needs to provide at trial, as proof of proper history of licensing, a certified copy of the license history from the Contractors State Licensing Board. Failure to prove licensing by the prescribed method is the equivalent of the contractor being unlicensed, with claim being barred and the contractor being exposed to a claim for disgorgement of all money received from the owner.

In *MW Erectors, Inc. v. Niederhauser Ornamental and Metal Works Co.*,[80] a subcontractor brought an action for breach of contract against a contractor for work performed on structural steel and ornamental metals work contracts as part of a hotel project. The trial court granted summary judgment in the contractor's favor. The subcontractor appealed. The court of appeal reversed, and the contractor sought review.

The California Supreme Court held the following: (1) the doctrine of judicial estoppel was inapplicable; (2) the California statute that barred suit by unlicensed contractors from recovering payment when they are unlicensed at any time during the project prevented the subcontractor from recovering for work done prior to the time its license was issued; (3) the statutory exception for substantial compliance with licensing requirements was not available to the subcontractor under the facts of this case; and (4) the subcontractor was not barred from recovering for work solely because it was unlicensed at the time it executed the contract.

In *MW Erectors*, the California Supreme Court summarized the public policy rationale for license laws such as California Business and Professions Code Section 7031. The court stated that the purpose of such laws is to protect the public. Section 7031 provides that regardless of the merits of a claim by an unpaid contractor, the contractor may not maintain any action, legal or equitable, to recover compensation for the performance of any act or contract unless the contractor was duly licensed at all times during the performance of the act or contract.

The *MW Erectors* court noted that earlier case law had softened the severity of this scheme, by allowing contractors, though technically unlicensed at the time of performance, to show they had substantially complied with licensing requirements. However, the law states that the judicial doctrine of substantial compliance shall not apply unless the contractor had been duly licensed as a contractor in California prior to performance of the act or contract for which the license was required.[81]

In *MW Erectors*, Disney Corporation hired Turner Construction as a general contractor. Turner hired Niederhauser to perform steel specialty work. Niederhauser hired MW Erectors to perform certain aspects of the structural and ornamental steel work on the project. MW began the work under a structural steel subcontract on approximately December 3, 1999, but it did not obtain a C-51

[80] 36 Cal. 4th 412, 115 P.3d 41, 30 Cal. Rptr. 3d 755 (2005).

[81] Cal. Bus. & Prof. Code § 7031.

structural steel license until December 21, 1999. Work by MW under a second subcontract with Niederhauser began in early January 2000.

Due to payment disputes, MW sued Niederhauser and Niederhauser's payment bonds for $955,553 for work under the structural steel subcontract, and for $366,694 under the ornamental subcontract. Niederhauser moved for summary judgment, alleging that the MW claim was barred by Section 7031(a) since MW was not properly licensed at all times during the performance of its contracts. Niederhauser also argued that MW could not demonstrate substantial compliance with Section 7031 because MW had never held a California contractor's license before beginning work under the contracts in December 1999.

In opposing the summary judgment motion, MW admitted that the C-51 license was not technically in place when MW began work on the structural contract, and admitted that it never obtained a C-23 (ornamental steel) license. MW asserted that there were triable issues that it was in substantial compliance with C-51 license requirements, and that no C-23 license was required. The trial court granted summary judgment to Niederhauser, and dismissed MW's action. MW appealed, arguing (1) it had shown substantial compliance with the C-51 license requirement, (2) it did not need a C-23 license, and (3) that Niederhauser was judicially estopped from questioning MW's licensure.

The California Court of Appeal reversed. It held that the subcontracts were not void at the outset, despite MW's lack of a license when the subcontracts were executed. Instead, MW's right to recover depended on its licensure during performance of the contracts. The court of appeal held that MW could not recover for the work it performed before it obtained either a C-51 or C-23 license. However, Section 7031 allowed MW to obtain compensation for acts it performed under the structural and ornamental subcontracts after the necessary license was in place. Although MW never obtained a C-23 license, it raised a triable issue of fact that the C-51 license was sufficient.

The California Supreme Court affirmed the court of appeal in part, and reversed in part. Niederhauser did not raise the C-23 license issue on appeal before the California Supreme Court, so the court did not address it in its opinion.

MW argued that Niederhauser was judicially estopped from raising the estoppel issue because it claimed that Niederhauser had asserted in its lawsuit against Disney, the owner, that MW was licensed, and that Niederhauser could not now use the opposite argument to defeat the MW claim. The California Supreme Court precluded MW using judicial estoppel. It held that the courts may not resort to equitable considerations in defiance of the legislative determination represented by Section 7031 on the importance of deterring unlicensed persons from engaging in the contracting business. This legislative policy outweighs any harshness between the parties.

The *MW* Court declined to follow what it called the court of appeal's "strained construction" of the statute's language in considering the time of lack of licensure as being during any "act or contract." The *MW* Court held that the plausible meaning of the words "act or contract" is that the legislature did not intend to require contractors to perform exclusively by formal contract, but to deter them from offering or performing unlicensed services for pay. The *MW*

Court summarized some of the case history on the substantial compliance doctrine, and the harshness of the bar presented by Section 7031. Despite arguments raised by MW about the problems presented by strict construction of Section 7031, the MW Court held that the purpose of the statute was served by such strict construction, encouraging careful adherence to the licensing laws, and deterring persons from offering or providing unlicensed contractor services for pay.

The *MW* Court held that the subcontractor had not met the substantial compliance test as to the C-51 license requirement because MW never held a license prior to beginning its work under the structural steel subcontract. It stated that the doctrine of substantial compliance was intended to cover an intended licensee whose license lapses due to inadvertence, such as failing to renew the license on time, and who then has a brief period in which it is unlicensed. The *MW* Court reviewed the statutory history of Section 7031 to support the theory that a lapsed licensee is treated differently than one that was never licensed before beginning work or executing a contract. Because MW could not establish that it was licensed at all times, or that it held a valid license prior to beginning performance, the *MW* Court reversed the court of appeal, and denied MW recovery of any money under the structural steel subcontract. The California Supreme Court held that summary judgment by the trial court was proper.

The *MW* Court reviewed the argument that the subcontractor was licensed at all times during performance of the ornamental steel work, the second subcontract. The *MW* Court referred to the statutory purpose of Section 7031, which is to protect the public from incompetence and dishonesty in those who provide building and construction services, and to provide minimal assurance that all persons offering such services have the requisite skill and character. Holding that Section 7031 and other California licensing laws did not automatically void the MW subcontract for the ornamental steel portion of the work, the *MW* Court held that MW was not barred from recovering compensation for its work on the sole ground that it was unlicensed when it executed the agreement.

In *Wright v. Issak*,[82] a California appellate court held that a contractor's underreporting of payroll resulted in automatic suspension of his license. This precluded his action against homeowners, because he was not licensed at all times as required by California Business and Professions Code Section 7031. The appellate court upheld the trial court's decision denying any recovery to the contractor.

In *Wright*, the contractor sued homeowners for $11,000. The homeowners' primary defense was that the contractor was not a licensed contractor, and that Section 7031 provided that an unlicensed contractor may not sue for unpaid work that requires a license. After a court trial, the trial court found for the defendants, and awarded the homeowners approximately $27,000 in reimbursement, and $10,000 in punitive damages. The trial court later added $90,000 of contractual attorneys' fees to the award, and $7,000 in costs. On appeal, Wright argued that

---

[82] 149 Cal. App. 4th 1116, 58 Cal. Rptr. 3d 1149 (2007), *as modified* (May 10 and May 22, 2007).

the trial court finding was erroneous as a matter of law by finding that he had been an unlicensed contractor. The appellate court affirmed the trial court's decision in its entirety.

The contractor worked on the defendants' home for a four-month period during 2004. In June 2004, the contractor paid a crew of 3-5 employees approximately $15,000 for approximately 4,000 man hours. State Compensation Fund workers compensation records showed that from November 2003 to August 2004 the contractor reported, under penalty of perjury, a payroll of $312 while having an actual payroll of $135,000. The State Compensation Fund records showed that the contractor reported zero or next to zero payroll for every payroll period between his initial application for workers compensation insurance in May 2002, through the end of 2004. The contractor's underreporting was not inadvertent, and the court stated that the underreporting was the contractor's pattern and practice from the first moment he applied for workers compensation insurance.

The contract between the contractor and the homeowners provided for the homeowners to pay the contractor for labor and material costs, plus a 12 percent markup on costs for his overhead, and an 8 percent markup of the cost-plus-overhead amount for the contractor's profit. The amount for labor costs that the contractor reported to the homeowners and the amount that the homeowners actually paid to the contractor was twice the amount of costs that the contractor actually incurred.

The trial court found that the contractor was not a licensed contractor because his license had been automatically suspended by operation of California Business and Professions Code Section 7125.2 for failure to obtain and maintain workers compensation insurance.

On appeal, the contractor did not dispute that the work he was performing for the homeowners required a license. He also accepted that unless he was a duly licensed contractor, he could not sue the homeowners for money due because of his work, and that the homeowners could sue him for reimbursement of money paid for the unlicensed work. The contractor's dispute on appeal was the trial court's interpretation of Section 7125.2.

Section 7125.2 states:

> The failure of a licensee to obtain or maintain workers' compensation insurance coverage, if required under this chapter, shall result in the automatic suspension of the license by operation of law in accordance with the provisions of this section, but this suspension shall not affect, alter, or limit the status of the licensee as an employer for purposes of section 3716 of the Labor Code.
>
> (a) The license suspension imposed by this section is effective upon the earlier of either of the following:
>
> (1) On the date that the relevant workers' compensation insurance coverage lapses.
>
> (2) On the date that workers' compensation coverage is required to be obtained.

> (b) A licensee who is subject to suspension under paragraph (1) of subdivision (a) shall be provided a notice by the registrar [of contractors] that includes all of the following:
>
> > (1) The reason for the license suspension and the effective date.
> > (2) A statement informing the licensee that a pending suspension will be posted to the license record for not more than 45 days prior to the posting of any license suspension periods required under this article.
> > (3) The procedures required to reinstate the license.
>
> (c) Reinstatement may be made at any time following the suspension by showing proof of compliance as specified in sections 7125 and 7125.1.
> (d) In addition, with respect to an unlicensed individual acting in the capacity of a contractor who is not otherwise exempted from the provisions of this chapter, a citation may be issued by the registrar under section 7028.7 for failure to comply with this article and to maintain workers' compensation insurance. An opportunity for a hearing as specified in section 7028.10 will be granted if requested within 15 working days after service of the citation.

Section 7125.2 essentially provides that a contractor's license is automatically suspended as of the date the contractor was required to obtain workers compensation insurance but failed to do so. As applied to this case, because the contractor underreported his payroll, and did not obtain workers compensation insurance in 2004, the contractor's license was suspended before, during, and after he performed the work for the homeowners.

The contractor argued that he had a valid contractor's license despite his lack of workers compensation coverage because he never received the registrar's notice. The basis for the argument was that one portion of the statute states that the automatic suspension happens "in accordance with" [Section 7125.2] which includes the registrar's notice detailing the reasons for a pending suspension and the means for reinstatement.

The appellate court refused to accept his argument. The appellate court pointed out that if the failure to receive the registrar's notice overcame an automatic suspension, the contractor had the burden to prove his lack of notice. The trial was not reported, and the contractor's submittal to the appellate court was based on a clerk's transcript only. When an appeal is based on this type of record, the appellate court conclusively presumes the evidence was ample to support the trial court's finding. Therefore, the appellate court conclusively presumed that the contractor failed to carry his burden to prove lack of notice. In any case, the appellate court stated that this argument of the contractor failed on the merits as well. The case cited by the contractor analyzed an earlier version of Section 7125.2 which the court characterized as materially different. The current version of Section 7125.2 has two failure prongs: failure-to-obtain, and failure-to-maintain. Subdivision (a)(1) pertains to the failure-to-maintain prong by providing that the effective date is the date coverage lapses. Subdivision (a)(2) explicitly pertains to the failure-to-obtain prong by providing that the effective date is the date the coverage should have been obtained. A case about underreporting payroll is, by definition, a failure-to-obtain case rather than a failure-to-maintain case.

In affirming the trial court's decision to deprive the contractor of any recovery, and to award the homeowners reimbursement, attorneys' fees, and punitive damages, the *Wright* court cited *HydrotechSystems, Ltd. v. Oasis Waterpark* for language on the purpose of Section 7031:

> The purpose of the licensing law is to protect the public from incompetence and dishonesty in those who provide building and construction services. . . . The licensing requirements provide minimal assurance that all persons offering such services in California have the requisite skill and character, understand applicable local laws and codes, and know the rudiments of administering a contracting business. . . .section 7031 advances this purpose by withholding judicial aid from those who seek compensation for unlicensed contract work. The obvious statutory intent is to discourage persons who have failed to comply with the licensing law from offering or providing their unlicensed services for pay. Because of the strength and clarity of this policy, it is well settled that section 7031 applies despite injustice to the unlicensed contractor. 'Section 7031 represents a legislative determination that the importance of deterring unlicensed persons from engaging in the contracting business outweighs any harshness between the parties, and that such deterrence can best be realized by denying violators the right to maintain any action for compensation in the courts of this state.'[83]

In *Great West Contractors v. WSS Industrial Constr.*,[84] a corporate subcontractor brought an action against a general contractor to recover for work performed under a construction services agreement. The general contractor and its surety filed a motion for nonsuit due to subcontractor's improper licensing. The trial court denied the motion and entered judgment on a jury verdict for subcontractor. The appellate court held that:

1. the subcontractor's tasks of ordering anchor bolts and preparing shop drawings could not be segregated from the subcontract;
2. the subcontractor's tasks of ordering anchor bolts and preparing shop drawings were done "in performance of" the subcontract;
3. the subcontractor's act in drafting shop drawings was work performed under subcontract rather than a prefatory task;
4. the subcontractor was required to be licensed in order to order anchor bolts incorporated into construction or to coordinate and oversee steel galvanization;
5. the subcontractor did not substantially comply with the requirements of the Construction Services Licensing Law.

---

[83] Hydrotech Systems, Ltd. v. Oasis Waterpark, 52 Cal. 3d 988, 995, 277 Cal. Rptr. 517, 803 P.2d 370 (1991).

[84] 162 Cal. App. 4th 581, 76 Cal. Rptr. 3d 8 (2008).

The appellate court reversed the trial court's ruling, and remanded for further proceedings.

At trial, the general contractor and its surety moved for nonsuit arguing the subcontractor was barred by the Construction Services Licensing Law, Business and Professions Code Section 7000 *et seq.*, from maintaining any action for recovery because the subcontractor was not properly licensed at all times during its performance of the contract. The trial court disagreed. It concluded thecorporation's president held a valid individual contractor's license at all times and that, in any event, licensure was not required for tasks the corporation performed prior to obtaining its license. The court found "there was substantial compliance with the licensing [statute] during the contract and work was performed in good faith," and denied the motions for nonsuit. A jury found in favor of the subcontractor and awarded over $220,000 in damages, statutory penalties, and interest.

The appellate court concluded the trial court erred in denying nonsuit. With one exception, the CSLL forbids a contractor from recovery, in law or at equity, on an otherwise valid claim for performance of any service for which a license is required if the contractor was unlicensed at any time during performance of the work. In this case, the subcontractor was unlicensed during a period in which it performed services that could only be performed by a licensed contractor. The court held that the subcontractor was unable to meet the threshold requirement to invoke the statutory exception of substantial compliance with the CSLL, because it was never licensed as a state contractor prior to beginning performance. The appellate court reversed and remanded the matter for entry of judgment in favor of the general contractor and its surety.

The subcontractor in this case argued that it should be allowed to recover because it met the substantial compliance doctrine. The trend over the years has been to limit the substantial compliance doctrine. It only applies if all three requirements of subdivision (e) are met. The *Great West* court cited *Construction Financial v. Perlite Plastering*,[85] which reviews the legislative history of Section 7031. The verified complaint alleged on information and belief that Vaknin never went to the job site, negligently failed to supervise any of Barak's work, and was not a bona fide responsible managing officer of Barak but merely "rented" his license to Barak. Weisz claimed Barak performed "very little" work on respondents' project, primarily site preparation and demolition, prior to issuance of the license. He stated the "majority" of the work under the contract occurred after Barak had its license. He denied ever telling respondents he or Barak had a contractor's license, and he asserted the subject of licensing never came up in his discussions with respondents. Weisz contended on information and belief that respondents "knew" Barak did not have a contractor's license when they entered into the contract. He stated he advised respondents at the time of contracting that he would engage a licensed onsite project supervisor or manager, and Barak did in fact engage a bonded and licensed general building contractor other than Vaknin to oversee the project, both before and after Barak had secured its own license.

---

[85] 53 Cal. App. 4th 170, 61 Cal. Rptr. 2d 574 (1997).

After a hearing, the trial court granted respondents' application for a right to attach order and order for issuance of a writ of attachment solely against Barak in the amount of $385,388 upon the filing of a $10,000 undertaking. The appellate court held that a claim under California Contractors State License Law against an unlicensed contractor may form the basis for a right to attach order since an agreement for the performance of services lies at the heart of the claim.

The appellate court rejected the contractors' argument that there should have been an offset for work performed after Barak became licensed. California Business and Professions Code Section 7031 requires licensure at all times during the performance of any act or contract. Because contractors herein were not licensed at all times, they are not entitled to recover for work performed even after Barak obtained its license. The *Barak* court cited the legislative policy of the rule which includes the ideas that the contractor is to recover nothing even where the person for whom the work was performed has taken calculated advantage of the contractor's lack of license, since, according the court, it does not matter that the beneficiary of the contractor's labors knew the contractor was unlicensed. The *Barak* court held that the contractors were to recover nothing for their work on this project.

CHAPTER 10

PERFORMANCE DETERMINANTS

§ 10.07 SUMMARY OF CHANGES TO A201-2007

Page 330, add at end of section:

Since the new ConsensusDOCS have been issued, articles have been published describing how these documents differ from other construction documents, including the AIA documents. The Construction Lawyer, published by the American Bar Association, (ABA) included in its Winter 2009 edition a number of these articles. In one of these, *Advantages of the ConsensusDOCS Construction Contracts*, Larry D. Harris and Brian M. Perlberg (Harris and Perlberg) describe the ConsensusDOCS as "contract documents based on best practices and proper risk allocation, for the benefit of organization members and the construction industry at large."[90.1]

Harris and Perlberg point out that many perceive the AIA documents as written by architects for architects. In the past, the AIA fought the perception of bias, receiving endorsements from the Association of General Contractors (AGC), and from the American Subcontractors' Association (ASA). However, the AIA 2007 documents, the current set of documents, are not endorsed by these trade organizations. These organizations did endorse the ConsensusDOCS. Harris and Perlberg state that there is a need for documents other than the AIA documents, based on the trade organizations which endorsed the ConsensusDOCS. Harris and Perlberg stated that the drafting mandate for the ConsensusDOCS was to develop documents which represent the best interests of the project, rather than those of a single party. They claim that fair and balanced contracts encourage diverse buy-ins from all parties, and they should attract the best contractors at their best prices by avoiding unnecessary risk contingencies. Harris and Perlberg state that the ConsensusDOCS provide commonsense solutions that could only be achieved by drawing upon all segments of the construction process for genuine input.

Steven G.M. Stein and Ronald O. Wietecha, in their article, *A Comparison of ConsensusDOCS to the AIA Form Construction Contract Documents*,[90.2] define the primary philosophical difference between the AIA documents and the ConsensusDOCS as being that the ConsensusDOCS provide for an immensely diminished role for the architect in project execution. The authors state that, under

---

[90.1] Larry D. Harris & Brian M. Perlberg, *Advantages of the ConsensusDOCS Construction Contracts*, *The Construction Lawyer*, Vol. 29, No. 1, Winter 2009.

[90.2] Steven G.M. Stein & Ronald O. Wietecha, *A Comparison of ConsensusDOCS to the AIA Form Construction Contract Documents*, *The Construction Lawyer*, Vol. 29, No. 1, Winter 2009.

the ConsensusDOCS, the architect has very few formal responsibilities, and he is conceived of more as the owner's consultant rather than as the integral project administrator and facilitator established in the AIA documents. ConsensusDOCS 200, the Standard Agreement and General Conditions Between Owner and Contractor contains no provision similar to the Article 4, entitled "Architect," of A201-2007. Under ConsensusDOCS 200, the owner and contractor communicate directly, not through the architect. ConsensusDOCS 200 only calls for the contractor to communicate with the architect "if directed." ConsensusDOCS 200 Para. 3.14.1.

Stein and Wietecha state that the ConsensusDOCS differ from the AIA documents in that under the ConsensusDOCS most of the responsibilities of the architect during the construction phase shift to the owner, with the assistance and recommendations of the architect. ConsensusDOCS 200 Para. 3.2.8. Under the ConsensusDOCS, the architect does not occupy the role of arbiter and Initial Decision Maker (IDM). The parties under the ConsensusDOCS have the option of selecting a third-party mitigation facilitator at the time of signing the contract, or the option of retaining all contractual and project-related interpretations and determinations equally between the owner and the contractor.

Stein and Wietecha state that the changes which put more responsibility on owners for tasks performed under the AIA documents by the architect will be particularly noticeable on design-build projects. Under ConsensusDOCS 200 Para. 4.7, the owner must provide a representative, who is presumably to manage all of the communications. Under A201-2007, these communications are made through the architect. Also, under ConsensusDOCS 200, the owner must make almost all the decisions that under A201 would be made by the architect.[90.3]

Stein and Wietecha address the question of whether the ConsensusDOCS are pro-contractor. Under ConsensusDOCS 200 Para. 13.1, the owner can only assign the construction contract to a lender as long as the assignment is no less favorable to the contractor. Under A201-2007 Sec. 13.2.2, the owner's right to assign the construction contract is absolute. Under ConsensusDOCS 200 Para. 11.3.4, the owner who terminates the contractor for default may take over the contractor's materials, equipment, and tools. However, the ConsensusDOCS 200 clause requires the owner to return those items to the contractor in good condition once the work is completed. A201-2007 contains no such owner obligation. Stein and Weitecha point out that under ConsensusDOCS 200 Para. 6.3.1 the contractor is entitled to an extension of time for any delay beyond the control of the contractor. A201-2007 Sec. 8.3.1 limits the causes for delay that give rise to an extension of time to those listed.

[90.3] A201-2007 Sec. 4.2.6, ConsensusDOCS 200 Para. 9.3.4, Para. 9.6.1, Para. 9.8.1, Para. 3.7.1.

CHAPTER 11

CHANGES

§ 11.04 A201 (1987): CHANGE ORDERS (CONSTRUCTION CHANGE DIRECTIVES)

[A] Scope: Cardinal Change

Page 366, add at end of section:

Owner-ordered work creates problems regarding whether additional compensation is allowed to the contractor if it appears the owner has changed the original scope of work. In *Pulver Roofing Co., Inc. v SBLM Architects, P.C.*,[33.1] a contractor contracted to install a roof on a school in accordance with plans provided by an architect and subsequently agreed pursuant to a settlement agreement to perform remedial work in exchange for payment from an escrow account. The School District was dissatisfied with the roof, and the court held that the contractor stated a valid quantum meruit claim by alleging that the owner had requested that it perform additional work outside the scope of remedial work set forth in a settlement agreement. The contractor allegedly performed work at the owner's behest, pursuant to an express promise that it would be paid, and the contractor was entitled to recover the reasonable value of its work whether or not the owner in any economic sense benefitted from the contractor's work. The court held that the quantum meruit claim was not precluded by existence of settlement agreement, since there was a bona fide dispute whether additional work was outside the scope of the settlement agreement.

By agreeing with the contractor that the amended complaint stated a valid quantum meruit claim, the court reversed the lower court's dismissal of the contractor's quantum meruit claim. The elements of such a claim are the performance of services in good faith, the acceptance of the services by the party for whom they were rendered, the expectation of compensation for those services, and a statement of the reasonable value of the services. Each of those elements was set forth in the amended complaint. The court concluded that the lower court erred in determining that the architect could not accept the contractor's additional work because that work was rendered for the benefit of the School District rather than the defendant architect. Although the lower court was correct that the work was in fact rendered for the benefit of the School District, the contractor was not required to establish that the architect received a benefit in order to recover in quantum meruit. Here, the contractor allegedly performed the work at the

[33.1] 65 A.D.3d 826, 884 N.Y.S.2d 802, *reh'g denied*, 67 A.D.3d 1459, 887 N.Y.S.2d 925 (2009).

architect's behest, pursuant to an express promise that it would be paid, and the contractor was, therefore, entitled to recover the reasonable value of its work whether or not the architect, in any economic sense, benefitted from the work.

The court held that the contractor's quantum meruit claim was not precluded by the existence of the settlement agreement. Although generally a contract covering a specified subject matter precludes recovery in quasi contract, the quantum meruit claim in this case could proceed, inasmuch as there was "a bona fide dispute" whether the additional work was outside the scope of the Settlement Agreement.

[F] Price and Time Adjustments

Page 375, add after second full paragraph:

The court in *Valenti v. Butcher*[52.1] reviewed various change orders entered into between the contractor and owners. At issue was which of the change orders were validly entered into by the parties and how much the contactor should be paid for the valid and completed change orders after the court held that the owners terminated the contract for cause. The court also discussed whether the owners could terminate the contract for cause and not pay the contractor for a change order when that change order was based upon errors the architect's plan, when the contractor did not comply with contractual obligations, which resulted in that change order.The contractor had argued that section 3.2.3 of AIA Document A201-1997 allowed him to recover for change orders that were premised on errors in the architect's blueprints. He argued that the owners had failed to show that the contractor recognized and knowingly failed to report any error. However, the trial court properly concluded that the contractor had failed to perform the obligations of sections 3.2.2 and 3.2.3, in that he had failed to review contract documents and take field measurements, resulting in various change orders.

In March 2007, Valenti, the contractor, and the Butchers, the owners, had entered into a contract to construct an addition and remodel their home for the stipulated sum of $225,940.00. The contract was embodied in a standard form agreement referred to as AIA Document A101-1997. The architect's design plans and specifications as well as blueprints were incorporated into the contract. The contract also adopted by reference AIA Document A201-1997. Upon receipt of a down payment of 18 percent of the stipulated sum ($40,669.20), began work on the project. Pursuant to the contract terms, the work was to be completed by August 31, 2007.

The owner also entered into a construction loan agreement with a bank. Because the contractor prepared a total of 16 change orders during the course of construction, the owner and bank did not close on the loan until four months after construction began. At the time of the construction loan closing, eight change orders, totaling $36,300.47, had been prepared and submitted to the bank as part of the loan amount. At the time of the closing, the owners had already paid the

[52.1] 2010 WL 1253094, 2010 Ind. App. Unpub. LEXIS 460 (Ind. Ct. App. Apr. 1, 2010).

contractor $82,169.20 (down payment of $40,669.20 and additional payments totaling $41,500). As part of the construction loan closing, the contractor received his first construction draw, totaling $46,328.63.

One of these change orders (for $11,000) involved extending the floor plan of the house by approximately six feet because of a problem the contractor encountered with a utility pole that was not included in the architect's plans but would inhibit access to the driveway if the addition to the home was built according to the original plans.

At that same time, the contractor had presented the owner with a policy statement that provided, "[i]t is the policy of The Mark of Quality Construction that all change orders shall be signed by the Owner and the Builder and paid before the work can commence." The owner signed the form but informed the contractor that he was not adhering to the policy.

Another change order was issued to remove the concrete floor that the contractor had already poured in the basement, because the basement ceiling height was merely six feet, seven inches instead of the eight-foot ceiling height as bid by the contractor. This change order (invoiced at $14,483), was precipitated in part by an error in the architect's blueprints and in part by the contractor's reliance on those blueprints and failure to do any field measurements prior to commencing the work.

By the end of August 2007, the scheduled end date of construction, the project was only 60 percent complete, and not all of the change order work had been done. At that time, the contractor submitted his request for his second construction draw, in which he included a request for payment of approximately $15,000 for a subcontractor. Although the contractor obtained the second construction draw, which totaled $28,899, he did not pay the subcontractor from that draw. As a result, the subcontractor filed a notice of mechanic's lien for $16,617.41 against the owners' property.

On October 8, 2007, the owner informed the contractor by letter that they were terminating the contract for cause and cited the contractor's failure to pay his subcontractor. By that point, the owners, through both direct payments and payments via construction draws, had paid the contractor $166,440.83.

On February 26, 2008, the contractor filed a complaint to foreclosure on the mechanic's lien, naming the owners and the bank as defendants. On April 21, 2008, the owners filed their answer and counterclaim, in which they sought damages for breach of contract, breach of warranties, negligence, and constructive fraud. The owners also filed a cross-claim against their bank.

The trial court found that the owners terminated the contract for cause, because the contractor failed to pay the subcontractor, failed to carefully study the contract documents and take field measurements prior to beginning portions of construction, and failed to timely complete the project. The trial court determined that the contractor was not entitled to payment on all the change orders, because the policy statement was not an amendment to the contract and was not binding on the owners. The trial court determined the change orders were controlled by the contract and incorporated contract documents, which did not require advanced payments and required change orders to be in writing, signed by the parties, and had to identify the change in work and any change in the contract sum and contract time.

The trial court found that the contractor failed to comply with the contractual requirements for many of the change orders and found that the contractor was entitled to payment on allowed change orders for a total of $30,291.73.

When assessing the amount due to the parties at the termination of the contract, the trial court determined that the contractor was entitled to 60 percent of the original contract price, or $135,564,based on his completion of 60 percent of the project plus $30,291.73 for allowed change orders, resulting in $165,855.73 due to the contractor. However, because the owners had already paid $166,440.83, the trial court determined that the contractor owed the owners $585.10. Additionally, the trial court found that the owners' estimate of the cost of completion included upgraded costs not included in the original contract and determined that the owners had only proved damages of $10,000, not $30,000 as the owners had argued. Thus, the trial court entered judgment in favor of the Butchers, the owners, and against Valenti, the contractor, in the amount of $10,585.10.

The appellate court affirmed the trial judge's verdict. It disagreed that there was no evidence to support the trial court's determination that Valenti breached the contract and that it was instead the owners who breached the contract. Thus, the trial court did not err in determining that the owners terminated the contract for cause, because the contractor failed to pay the subcontractor, failed to carefully study the contract documents and take field measurements, and failed to timely complete the project.

The contract between the contractor and the owners, specifically, AIA Document A201-1997, which was adopted as part of the contract, provided that the owners could terminate the contract for cause if, among other reasons, the contractor "fails to make payment to Subcontractors for materials or labor in accordance with the respective agreements between the Contractor and Subcontractors" and "otherwise is guilty of substantial breach of a provision of the Contract Documents." Additionally, section 3.2.1 of AIA Document A201-1997 provided, in relevant part:

> Since the Contract Documents are complementary, before starting each portion of the Work, the Contractor shall carefully study and compare the various Drawings and other Contract Documents relative to that part of the Work, as well as the information furnished by the Owner ..., shall take field measurements of any existing conditions related to that portion of the Work [,] and shall observe any conditions at the site affecting it.

Evidence was presented that the contractor's failure to review the contract documents and take field measurements resulted in various change orders, that the construction project was only 60 percent complete by the contractual end date of August 31, 2007, and that the contractor did not pay his subcontractor from his second contract draw despite the fact his submission for payment included a request for payment for the subcontractor. Thus, the trial court did not err by determining the owners terminated the contract for cause based on the contractor's breach. The contractor's argument that it was the owners and not he who breached the contract amounted to nothing more than a request for the court to reweigh the evidence, which the appellate court refused to do.

Next, the appellate court held that the trial court did not err by selectively reducing or excluding the amounts Valenti, the contractor, could recover on certain change orders. Specifically, the trial court did not err in awarding varying sums based on the level of responsibility chargeable to the contractor.

Section 7.2.1 of AIA Document A201-1997 provided that a change order must be signed by the owner and contractor and must state their agreement upon the "change in the Work; the amount of the adjustment, if any, in the Contract Sum; and the extent of the adjustment, if any, in the Contract Time." At trial, the trial court considered the testimony of the contractor, the owner, a city building inspector, and an expert architect with regard to the appropriateness, normal costs, and fault associated with the 16 different change orders. The trial court, after reviewing each of the change orders, found that the contractor failed to comply with the contract provision for change orders, and he failed to comply with contractual requirements such as reviewing the blueprints and taking field measurements prior to starting a portion of the work.

The trial court also determined that the contractor was not entitled to recover payment for change orders that were not completed, were not signed by the owners, were the result of the contractor's error, or were excessive. In the end, the trial court concluded that the contractor was entitled to $30,291.73 for change orders.

When arguing that the trial court erred by reducing or prohibiting payment on change orders based on his errors, the contractor cited to one sentence in section 3.2.3 of AIA Document A201-1997, which provided:

> The Contractor shall not be liable to the Owner or Architect for damages resulting from errors, inconsistencies or omissions in the Contract Documents for differences between field measurements or conditions and the Contract Documents unless the Contractor recognized such error, inconsistency, omission or difference and knowingly failed to report it to the Architect.

The contractor had argued that the owners failed to show that he recognized and knowingly failed to report any error, and he contended that the trial court should have allowed him to recover for change orders that were premised on errors in the architect's blueprints. Here, the trial court acknowledged that some of the change orders were precipitated by underlying errors in the blueprints but still concluded that the contractor could not recover the full amount of the change order, because he failed to comply with some of the contractual provisions, such as sections 3.2.1 and 3.2.2 of AIA Document A201-1997. Furthermore, the preceding sentence of section 3.2.3 cited by the contractor provided, "[i]f the Contractor fails to perform the obligations of Subparagraphs 3.2.1 and 3.2.2, the Contractor shall pay such costs and damages to the Owner as would have been avoided if the Contractor had performed such obligations." The trial court found that the contractor had failed to comply with these obligations, and the contractor did not specifically challenge those findings on appeal. Because Valenti's failure to review contract documents and take field measurements resulted in various change orders and because he failed to comply with the contractual requirements for change orders, the appellate court held that the trial court did not err by reducing or prohibiting payment on certain change orders.

Next, the court held that there was evidence to support the trial court's determination that the owners were entitled to $10,000 in damages for the cost of completion of the contract. Section 14.2.4 of AIA Document A201-1997, which addressed payment when an owner terminated a contract for cause, provided:

> If the unpaid balance of the Contract Sum exceeds costs of finishing the Work, including compensation for the Architect's *services* and expenses made necessary thereby, and other damages incurred by the Owner and not expressly waived, such excess shall be paid to the Contractor. If such costs and damages exceed the unpaid balance, the Contractor shall pay the difference to the Owner. The amount to be paid to the Contractor or Owner, as the case may be, shall be certified by the Architect, upon application, and this obligation for payment shall survive termination of the Contract.

Here, the original contract was $225,940, the trial court allowed the contractor to recover $30,291.73 for change orders, and the owners paid the contactor $166,440.83. At trial, the Butchers sought $30,000 in damages and presented evidence that the cost to complete the project was $117,874.00. The trial court found that the owners' estimate of the cost of completion included upgraded costs not included in the original contract and, therefore, determined that the owners had only proven damages of $10,000. Although the trial court did not set forth its exact calculation to arrive at the $10,000 amount for the cost of completion, there was evidence that supported the trial court's determination that the Butchers were entitled to $10,000 in damages for the cost of completion of the contract. Accordingly, the appellate court declined the contactor's invitation to reweigh the evidence in regard to the damages amount.

The court also rejected the owners' appeal on the amount of damages. Thus, the trial court did not err in entering judgment in the amount of $10,585.10. The owners had contended that the trial court's calculation that they were owed $508.10 for overpayment was based on the trial court's finding that the contractor was owed $35,406.56 for change order work. They further reasoned that if the trial court had used the proper amount due to the contractor for change orders, or $30,291.73, then they would be owed $5,114.83. The appellate court held, however, that despite the trial court's reference to the $35,406.56 amount, the trial court used the $30,291.73 amount, not the $35,406.56 amount, when calculating the amounts due as part of the judgment. Accordingly, the appellate court affirmed the trial court, and found that the Butchers' cross-appeal issue was without merit.

CHAPTER 12

DEFECTS

§ 12.02 INSPECTIONS AND TESTS

Page 399, add after third full paragraph on the page:

A trial court admitting or barring expert testimony of a party can make a huge difference in the outcome of a case. In *Stonehill-PRM WC L.L.P v. Chasco Constructors, Limited, L.L.P.*,[7.1] appellant Stonehill-PRM WC I, L.P., ("Stonehill") appealed the district court's judgment in favor of appellees Chasco Constructors, Ltd., L.L.P. ("Chasco") and Safeco Insurance Company of America ("Safeco"). Stonehill contended that the district court erred when it determined the measure of damages, when it excluded testimony from two of Stonehill's experts and one of its owners as to the value of the proposed construction, when it excluded evidence of the cost to complete the construction project, and when it refused to admit an alleged copy of the contract between the parties. The appellate court affirmed the district court's judgment, concluding that the district court did not err in determining the measure of damages, and that any error in the challenged evidentiary rulings was not reversible error.

In the summer of 2005, Stonehill hired Page Southerland Page Architects and Engineers ("PSP") to design a student housing facility (the "Project") for property that Stonehill owned in Austin, Texas. In approximately September 2005, Stonehill began negotiations with Chasco for Chasco to be the contractor for the project. The proposed scope of work included demolishing the existing structure on the property. Chasco provided several different budgets to Stonehill including a line-item budget of $16,638,030 in December 2005. The December 2005 budget was based upon design and development drawings that PSP issued in October 2005. PSP also issued permit plans for the project on February 6, 2006, and an "Addendum # 1" to the permit plans in March 2006.

Stonehill and Chasco executed a "Standard Form of Agreement Between Owner and Contractor, dated February 22, 2006 (the "Contract"). The standard form, titled "AIA Document A111-1997," is a form agreement from the American Institute of Architects and reflects the parties' modifications to the standard form. Section 15.1.2 of this document incorporates the standard form "AIA Document A201-1997, as modified" as the agreed "[g]eneral [c]onditions" of the contract. The contract provided that Chasco would be paid its costs for performing the work plus a fee with a guaranteed maximum price ("GMP"). Neither party produced an original of the contract, and the parties disagreed as to whether the contract

[7.1] 2009 Tex. App. LEXIS 1019, 2009 WL 349136 (Tex. App.-Austin 2009).

contained a GMP addendum and, if so, whether the GMP addendum actually contained a guaranteed maximum price. Stonehill contended that the contract contained a GMP addendum with a GMP of $16,638,030, the amount Chasco provided as the budget in December 2005.

Chasco contended that, at the time the parties executed the contract, the contract did not contain a GMP addendum and that Chasco had not completed the bidding process from the permit plans to provide final cost numbers. Based on a subsequent request from Stonehill's lender that was financing the project, two GMP addenda were prepared. According to Chasco, both addenda contained a GMP of $16,638,030 that was not final, and a sentence that the GMP "will be modified upon verification of pricing of City of Austin permit plans dated February 6, 2006."

Article 5 of the contract set forth the "basis for payment." Section 5.2.1, as modified by the parties, stated:

> The sum of the Cost of the Work and the Contractor's Fee is guaranteed by the Contractor not to exceed ($), (*see GMP addendum*) subject to additions and deductions by Change Order as provided in the Contract Documents. Such maximum sum is referred to in the Contract Documents as the Guaranteed Maximum Price.

In March 2006, Safeco issued a performance and payment bond on the project for $16,638,030, and Chasco began the demolition work on the existing structure. On April 4, 2006, Chasco notified Stonehill that construction costs based on the completion of the bidding process from the permit plans were $30,250,000. Thereafter, Chasco sent notice to Stonehill that "[b]ased upon verification of pricing of the City of Austin permit plans and specifications dated February 6, 2006 and Addendum # 1 dated March 9, 2006 along with our Final GMP budget and qualifications dated April 4, 2006," Chasco needed a written change order modifying the initial GMP to the "Final GMP budget" of $30,250,000 to "begin construction of the new structure." Stonehill would not agree to a GMP of $30,250,000, and Chasco did not begin construction.

In May 2006, Stonehill sent written notice to Safeco and Chasco that it was "formally" terminating Chasco's right to complete the project and declaring a "Contractor Default" as a result of Chasco's failure to perform its obligations, including its failure to comply with performance for the agreed GMP. In July 2006, Stonehill filed suit alleging breach of the contract and the performance bond. Attached to Stonehill's original petition was a copy of the contract that contained the version of the GMP addendum titled "Guaranteed Maximum Price Addendum to Contract."

In July 2007, Stonehill filed a second amended petition alleging additional claims and attaching a different copy of the contract, one that contained the version of the addendum titled "West Campus Student Housing" with the date "December 20, 2005." In its second amended response to appellees' request for disclosure, Stonehill disclosed that it was seeking its "expectancy damages"—the difference between the value of the project had it been constructed in accordance with the plans and specifications, "calculated using appropriate rents, expenses and prevailing capitalization rates in Austin, Texas for similar apartment structures," and the costs that Stonehill avoided. Stonehill designated Greg Hallman, Ph.D., as its damages valuation expert, disclosing that he would testify "about the value of the building that is the subject matter of this lawsuit were it constructed pursuant to the parties' Construction Contract." It was Hallman's opinion that the value of the "resulting building" would have been in excess of $36,000,000.

After deposing Hallman, Chasco filed a motion to exclude Hallman as Stonehill's designated expert and his testimony on several grounds, alleging that he was not qualified, because he was not licensed by the Texas Appraiser Licensing and Certification Board ("TALCB"), because he lacked "sufficient knowledge, skill, experience, training, or education," and that his testimony was not reliable, because his "methodology, assumptions, and processes" were not accurate and did not comply with industry standards for appraising commercial real estate. Safeco joined Chasco's motion. After a hearing in September 2007, the district court excluded Hallman.

In September 2007, the district court also granted Safeco's first motion for summary judgment, in part. It granted the motion regarding the "current model of damages sought by [Stonehill] against Safeco" and found as a matter of law that Stonehill was only entitled to actual damages under the performance bond, that "[a]ctual damages can include expectancy damages for the breach of an express contract," and that the "legal measure of damages in this case for such actual damages cannot include, either directly or indirectly, possible future rental rates, occupancy rates or similarly speculative income projections."

The district court conditionally granted Stonehill's motion for a continuance from the October 2007 trial setting, continuing the trial setting to February 2008 and extending the parties' deadlines to designate "appraiser/damages experts" and to amend their pleadings and discovery responses "to conform to the revised damages testimony and methodology[ies]." Stonehill's new deadline to designate experts was October 15, 2007, and its deadline to amend its pleadings and discovery responses was December 28, 2007.

In its third amended response to request for disclosure that it served on December 28, 2007, Stonehill disclosed that its designated damages expert, Rudy R. Robinson, III, MAI, would testify "about the value of the building that is the subject matter of this lawsuit were it constructed according to the parties' Construction Contract." Stonehill did not amend the measure of damages that it was seeking, continuing to seek its "expectancy damages" based on the difference in value of the proposed building had it been built according to the plans and specifications and the costs that it avoided, but it amended the proposed building's value. In discovery, Stonehill stated that the building "would have a value in the range of $32,000,000 to $37,000,000, calculated using appropriate rents, expenses and prevailing capitalization rates in Austin, Texas for similar apartment structures and commonly understood appraisal methods and techniques for valuation of commercial property."

In January 2008, Chasco and Safeco filed a joint motion to exclude Robinson as Stonehill's designated expert and his testimony on several grounds, including that his testimony as to the market value of the proposed building was irrelevant. The district court granted their motion to exclude Robinson on February 8, 2008. Safeco also filed a second motion for summary judgment based on Stonehill's failure to revise its damages model against Safeco. On February 8, 2008, the district court granted this motion, and because the order disposed of all claims asserted against Safeco, entered judgment dismissing Safeco with prejudice.

On the same day, the district court granted a partial summary judgment in favor of Chasco on the proper measure of damages. The district court ruled:

> The Court declares that if, *and only if,* an enforceable contract exists between the parties:
>
> i) As a matter of law, the proper measure of [Stonehill's] damages under the alleged contract is the cost to complete construction of the project to the extent the costs of completing the construction of the project exceed those costs which would have been payable to [Chasco];
> ii) As a matter of law, Stonehill's damages may not include any consequential damages, including damages for rental expenses, losses of use, income, profit, financing, and business because they are prohibited by the alleged contract; and
> iii) As a matter of law, [Stonehill] contractually waived the "benefit of the bargain" (a/k/a "expectancy") damages it seeks in this lawsuit.

Meanwhile, on February 4, 2008, Stonehill served its fourth amended response to request for disclosure, disclosing for the first time that it sought costs to complete construction as an alternative measure of damages:

> Alternatively, Stonehill will seek damages for the difference between the costs to complete the Work of the Construction Contract and the costs payable to Chasco to complete the Work pursuant to the Construction Contract except for Chasco's default.

Stonehill did not disclose the amount of damages that it sought under its alternative measure of damages. Stonehill also amended its response as to Jim Brownlow, one of Stonehill's owners. Stonehill disclosed, for the first time, that Brownlow had knowledge of "what the construction costs would have been had Chasco performed the Construction Contract and the Facility." Chasco thereafter filed a motion to exclude this evidence for failing to timely respond. Chasco sought the exclusion of evidence of the cost to complete the Project, contending that Stonehill had not timely disclosed this alternative measure of damages in response to appellees' request for disclosure by the revised deadline of December 28, 2007. On February 12, 2008, the district court granted Chasco's motion and excluded Stonehill's fourth amended response to appellees' request for disclosure.

The jury trial occurred February 12 to 14, 2008. The primary disputed fact was whether the parties contractually had agreed to a GMP of $16,638,000. It was Stonehill's position that the parties had, and Chasco's position that they had not. Stonehill's witnesses included Brownlow, Michael Mace, PSP's senior vice president; and Brian Selbo, the project's development coordinator for Stonehill.

Brownlow testified concerning the background of the project, communications and negotiations between the parties, and the different GMP addenda. Mace testified concerning PSP's role in the project, the plans and drawings that PSP issued, and his opinion that Chasco had adequate information based on the October 2005 plans to submit a GMP. Selbo testified to his role with the project, Stonehill's receipt of three signed copies of the contract from Chasco, and Stonehill's unsuccessful search to find an original executed contract.

Stonehill also called Curtis Cline, Chasco's corporate representative, and Temple Aday, Chasco's president, as adverse witnesses. Cline testified to the negotiations between Chasco and Stonehill, the various budgets that Chasco prepared, the bidding process, the changes between the design and development plans and the permit plans and the effect of the changes on cost, the GMP addenda, and the final GMP of $30,250,000 that Chasco provided after the bidding process was completed. Aday testified that "it's practice in the construction industry" to attach a GMP addendum at a later date, that "it's customary in the construction field to sign a contract with the price to be determined at a later date," that the contract that he signed on behalf of Chasco did not have "any addendums attached," and that it was his understanding that "the addendum had not been established and would be established at a later date."

Through its witnesses, Stonehill attempted to admit the version of the contract that contained Chasco's December 2005 budget as the GMP addendum, but the district court sustained Chasco's objections and refused to admit it into evidence. No witness was able to testify to what had happened to the originals or to explain how or by whom the version that Stonehill was seeking to admit was pieced together during the litigation. Stonehill's version of the contract contained pages that had different Bates numbering identifiers. The district court admitted other versions of the contract, including the version that was attached to Stonehill's original petition.

After Stonehill rested, Chasco moved for a directed verdict on Stonehill's remaining claims for fraudulent inducement and breach of contract. The district court granted the motion, stating that there was no evidence of a "present intention not to perform" as to the fraudulent inducement claim and no evidence of damages as to the breach of contract claim. The district court entered a take-nothing judgment against Stonehill. Stonehill filed a motion for new trial, which motion the district court denied.

On appeal, Stonehill challenged the district court's determination of the proper measure of damages and its exclusion of evidence. In its first issue, Stonehill contended that the district court erred in ruling that Stonehill's measure of damages for breach of the contract was the cost to complete the project to the extent those costs exceeded the costs that would have been payable to Chasco. In its second issue, Stonehill contended that the district court erred in concluding that the consequential damages provision of the contract precluded use of an income stream to determine the value of the proposed building. In its third, fourth, and fifth issues, Stonehill contended that the district court improperly excluded the testimony of Brownlow and its experts Hallman and Robinson as to the value of the proposed building. In its sixth and seventh issues, Stonehill contended that the district court erred in sustaining Chasco's objections to evidence of cost to complete construction and in refusing to admit a copy of the contract.

Stonehill challenged the district court's ruling as to the proper measure of damages. The appellate court stated that whether the trial court erred in applying an improper measure of damages was a question of law subject to *de novo* review.[7.2]

The appellate court stated that the measure of damages in this case involved matters of contract construction. When a court concludes that contract language can be given a certain or definite legal meaning, then the language is not ambiguous, and the court will construe the contract as a matter of law. A court interprets a contract by ascertaining the true objective intentions of the parties, based on the contract language. Contract terms are given their plain, ordinary, and generally accepted meanings unless the contract itself shows them to be used in a technical or different sense. A court construes written instruments as a whole in an effort to harmonize and give effect to all the provisions of the instrument so that none will be rendered meaningless. No single provision taken alone will be given controlling effect; all the provisions must be considered with reference to the whole instrument.

Stonehill also challenged evidentiary rulings by the district court. The admission or exclusion of evidence was a matter within the trial court's discretion. A trial court abuses its discretion when it acts without reference to any guiding rules or principles. To reverse a judgment based on an error in the admission or exclusion of evidence, an appellate court must conclude that the error probably resulted in an improper judgment.[7.3] To make this determination, an appellate court reviews the entire record and usually requires the complaining party to demonstrate that the judgment turns on the particular evidence admitted or excluded.

In its first issue, Stonehill contended that the district court erred in concluding that Stonehill's measure of damages under the contract was its cost to complete the project to the extent those costs exceeded the costs that would have been payable to Chasco. Stonehill relied on Section 13.4.1 of the contract that provided that contractual "rights and remedies" were in addition to "rights and remedies otherwise imposed or available by law or in equity" to contend that Stonehill was entitled to damages under the "recognized legal standard when there has not been substantial performance, that is, the difference between the value of the building as constructed and its value had it been constructed in accordance with the Construction Contract." Stonehill also contended that Section 14.2.4 of the contract, which provided that Stonehill's measure of damages was its cost to complete the project that exceeded the costs that would have been payable to Safeco, only applied if Stonehill chose to complete the project. Appellees

---

[7.2] TA Operating Corp. v. Solar Applications Eng'g, Inc., 191 S.W.3d 173, 183 (Tex. Ct. App.-San Antonio 2005).

[7.3] Tex. R. App. P. 44 .1(a)(1).

responded that, assuming that the contract was valid and enforceable, the parties agreed to Stonehill's recoverable damages as stated in Section 14.2.4 of the contract.

The actual language of Sections 13.4.1 and 14.2.4. Sections 13.4.1 and 14.2.4 as modified by the parties read:

> §§ 13.4.1 Duties and obligations imposed by the Contract Documents and rights and remedies available thereunder shall be in addition to and not a limitation of duties, obligations, rights and remedies otherwise imposed or available by law or in equity or by any other agreement, and any such rights and remedies shall survive the acceptance of the Work and/or any termination of the Contract Documents.
>
> * * *
>
> §§ 14.2.4 To the extent the costs of completing Work, including, without limitation, compensation for additional professional services and expenses, exceed those costs which would have been payable to Contractor to complete the Work except for Contractor's default, Contractor shall pay the difference to Owner, and this obligation for payment shall survive termination of the Contract. Such costs incurred by Owner will be determined by the Owner and confirmed by the Architect.

The court concluded that the contract provisions at issue were unambiguous and could be interpreted as a matter of law. Based on the plain language of the contract provisions and the applicable common law measure of damages, the appellate court concluded that the district court did not err in determining the measure of damages. Where there has been a "complete failure of performance" to construct a building, the common law "recognized" measure of damages for breach of contract is the "excess of the reasonable and necessary cost of completion over and above the unpaid portion of the contract price."[7.4] The parties' agreed measure of damages in the contract was consistent with the common law measure of damages for a "complete failure of performance" to build a building.[7.5] The facts and circumstances in each breach of a building contract case determined whether the remedial cost or the difference in value was the proper measure of damages.

Stonehill's interpretation that Section 14.2.4 applied only if Stonehill had chosen to complete the project ignoring the section's plain language, as modified by the parties. The plain language did not condition Stonehill's recovery on a requirement that the project be completed, and courts routinely award costs to complete a construction contract without requiring that those costs be incurred. The parties could also agree contractually to the measure of damages in the event of a breach.

[7.4] Ashley v. Bizzell, 694 S.W.2d 349, 353 (Tex. App.-San Antonio 1985.), *quoting* Smith v. Kinslow, 598 S.W.2d 910, 913 (Tex. Civ. App.-Dallas 1980).

[7.5] *See Bizzell*, 694 S.W.2d at 353; *see also* Fidelity & Deposit Co. v. Stool, 607 S.W.2d 17, 21 (Tex. Civ. App.-Tyler 1980).

Stonehill's interpretation of Section 14.2.4 was not consistent with the contract as a whole. Section 14.2.4 is within Article 14 that is titled "Termination or Suspension of the Contract." Section 14.2 is titled "Termination by the Owner for Cause," and subsection 14.2.4 expressly addressed the owner's remedies when it has terminated for cause. The parties also agreed to waive consequential damages for breach of the contract by the other party. Stonehill expressly agreed to waive any damages that it incurred for "losses of use, income, [and] profit." Binding the parties to the contractually agreed measure of damages in the event Stonehill terminated for cause was consistent with Stonehill's waiver of the types of damages expressed in the consequential damages clause.

Section 4.3.10 of the contract addressed claims for consequential damages. It read in relevant part:

> §§ 4.3.10 Claims for Consequential Damages. The Contractor and Owner waive Claims against each other for consequential damages arising out of or relating to this Contract. This mutual waiver includes:
>
> 1. damages incurred by the Owner for rental expenses, for losses of use, income, profit, financing, business and reputation, and for loss of management or employee productivity or of the services of such persons; and
>
> 2. damages incurred by the Contractor for principal office expenses including the compensation of personnel stationed there, for losses of financing, business and reputation, and for loss of profit except anticipated profit arising directly from the Work.
>
> This mutual waiver was applicable, without limitation, to all consequential damages due to either party's termination in accordance with Article 14. . . .

The court rejected Stonehill's contention that, in any event, Section 13.4.1 provided Stonehill additional remedies, including expectancy damages based on the difference-in-value measure of damages. Stonehill relied on *Turner, Collie & Braden, Inc. v. Brookhollow, Inc.*,[7.6] to support its position. In *Turner*, the Texas Supreme Court addressed when the measure of damages for the breach of a construction contract were "remedial damages"—the cost to complete construction—as opposed to the "difference-in-value measure." At issue was a dispute between the contractor and the owner after the contractor completed the construction of a sewer line that the owner alleged was defective. In the context of defective work and economic efficiencies, the Texas Supreme Court explained that the difference-in-value measure was appropriate when the contractor had not substantially complied with the contract between the parties, and the remedial measure was appropriate when the contractor had substantially performed. In contrast, Chasco had not begun construction on the new building, and Stonehill did not allege defective work.

The district court did not err in its conclusions as to the contractual measure of damages. The parties' objective intent from the plain language of Section

[7.6] 642 S.W.2d 160 (Tex. 1982).

14.2.4 and the contract as a whole was to agree that Stonehill's measure of damages in the event Chasco defaulted was the cost to complete the project to the extent those costs exceeded the costs that would have been payable to Chasco. The appellate court overruled Stonehill's first issue.

In its second issue, Stonehill contended that the district court erred in ruling that the consequential damages section of the contract precluded the use of an income stream in determining the value of the proposed building. Because the appellate court concluded that the district court did not err in determining that the measure of damages was the cost to complete the project that exceeded the costs that would have been payable to Chasco, the value of the proposed building was not relevant to an issue of material fact.[7.7] Even if the district court erred in precluding the use of an income stream in determining the value of the proposed building, such error did not probably cause the rendition of an improper judgment. *See* Tex. R. App. P. 44.1(a). The appellate court overruled Stonehill's second issue.

In its third, fourth, and fifth issues, Stonehill contended that the district court erred in excluding testimony from its experts, Hallman and Robinson, and its owner, Brownlow, as to the value of the proposed building had it been completed in accordance with the plans and specifications. Since the district court did not err in determining that the measure of damages was the cost to complete the project that exceeded the costs payable to Chasco, evidence of the value of the proposed building was not relevant to an issue of material fact. *See* Tex. R. Evid. 401. Even if the district court erred in excluding testimony from these witnesses of the value of the proposed building, the exclusion of their testimony did not probably cause the rendition of an improper judgment.[7.8] The appellate court overruled Stonehill's third, fourth, and fifth issues.

In its sixth issue, Stonehill contended that, if its measure of damages was the cost to complete the project that exceeded the costs payable to Chasco, the district court should have allowed Stonehill to introduce evidence of costs. Stonehill contended that Robinson and Brownlow would have testified to the cost to complete the project and would have required a jury question on that issue. Appellees responded that the district court properly excluded evidence of the costs to complete the project, because Stonehill failed to timely designate this theory of damages. Stonehill did not dispute that it first disclosed that it would seek the cost to complete the project that exceeded the costs payable to Chasco as an alternative measure of damages in its fourth amended response to request for disclosure that it served on appellees on February 4, 2008, after the court-ordered deadline of December 28, 2007.

Texas Rule of Civil Procedure 193.6 provides for the exclusion of evidence that has not been timely disclosed and the exceptions to exclusion. Rule 193.6 provides that a party that fails to timely disclose evidence may not introduce the

[7.7] *See* Tex. R. Evid. 401.

[7.8] *See* Tex. R. App. P. 44.1(a).

evidence unless the party shows that there was good cause for the failure to disclose and that the failure does not unfairly surprise or unfairly prejudice the other party. Rule 193.6(b) and (c) place the burden on the party seeking to introduce the evidence and allows a trial court to continue a trial setting even if the party seeking to admit evidence fails to carry its burden.

The appellate court held that Stonehill failed to address its burden to show good cause for its failure to disclose that it was seeking its cost to complete the project as an alternative measure of damages. Stonehill did not seek a continuance or trial postponement to amend its discovery responses, or to allow Chasco to conduct discovery regarding the costs to complete the project. Stonehill filed suit in July 2006 and, after Stonehill's initial damages expert was excluded, the district court continued the trial setting and gave Stonehill additional time to designate a new damages expert and to amend its measure of damages, specifically extending the deadline to amend the parties' pleadings and discovery responses "to conform to the revised damages testimony and methodology[ies]." The contract also expressly addressed the measure of damages in the event Stonehill terminated for cause as the cost to complete the project to the extent those costs exceed the costs that would have been payable to Chasco. The appellate court held that trial court did not abuse its discretion in excluding evidence of the cost to complete the project for failure to timely disclose. The court overruled Stonehill's sixth issue.

In its seventh issue, Stonehill contended that the district court erred in refusing to admit its offered version of the contract even though it was properly authenticated and admissible. *See* Tex. R. Evid. 1003, 1004. Chasco objected that Stonehill's offered version was not an original and challenged its authenticity. Stonehill's version contained a different GMP addendum from the versions of the contract that were admitted into evidence, but the parties agreed that the contract contained the terms that were relevant to the challenged rulings on appeal. Even if the district court erred in excluding Stonehill's version of the contract, Stonehill failed to show how this exclusion probably caused the rendition of an improper judgment.[7.9] The appellate court overruled Stonehill's seventh issue.

Because the court concluded that the district court did not err in its conclusions as to the measure of damages under the contract and that any error by the district court in the challenged evidentiary rulings was not reversible error, the appellate court affirmed the district court's judgment.

The contract remedy accepted by a court can make a substantial difference in the outcome of a construction case, and the admissibility of expert theories or testimony may be crucial to support a damages theory. The AIA documents waiver of consequential damages continues to be a controversial portion of the documents, and may be the sole reason that parties refuse to use AIA documents.

[7.9] *See* Tex. R. App. P. 44.1(a).

§ 12.06 QUALITY OF WORKMANSHIP AND MATERIAL: WARRANTIES

[C] Remedies

Page 454, add at end of subsection:

In *Greystone Homes, Inc. v. Midtec, Inc.*,[125.1] a home builder brought an action against a manufacturer of plumbing fittings for negligence and equitable indemnity. The trial court granted summary judgment for the manufacturer, and the builder appealed. The California Court of Appeal held that:

1. The Right to Repair Act (RRA), (Cal. Civ. Code Sec. 895, *et. seq*., also referred to as SB 800) abrogated the economic loss rule in homeowners' actions against individual product manufacturers;
2. a builder may bring an equitable indemnity action under the RRA for reimbursement for a homeowner's economic losses;
3. RRA standards for plumbing systems apply to individual product manufacturers as well as to home builders;
4. a fact issue existed as to whether a manufacturer caused a violation of RRA standards;
5. a builder may not pursue a negligence per se action against an individual product manufacturer for violation of RRA standards; and
6. a builder had no special relationship with a manufacturer supporting recovery for economic losses.

The case was reversed and remanded to the trial court with directions.

In *Aas v. Superior Court*,[125.2] the California Supreme Court had concluded that a group of homeowners could not recover damages in negligence from the developer, contractor, or subcontractors who built their homes, for existing construction defects that had not yet caused either property damage or personal injury. In reaching this conclusion, the *Aas* court explained that while "tort law provides a remedy for construction defects that cause property damage or personal injury",[125.3] the "economic loss rule" precludes recovery for damages such as "the difference between price paid and value received, and deviations from standards of quality that have not resulted in property damage or personal injury."

In response to the holding in *Aas*, the California Legislature enacted Civil Code Section 895*et seq.* ("the Right to Repair Act" or "RRA"). The RRA establishes a set of building standards pertaining to new residential construction, and provides homeowners with a cause of action against, among others, builders and individual product manufacturers for violation of the standards (Secs. 896, 936). The RRA makes clear that upon a showing of violation of an applicable standard, a homeowner may recover economic losses from a builder without having to show that the violation caused property damage or personal injury

---

[125.1] 168 Cal. App. 4th 1194, 86 Cal. Rptr. 3d 196 (2008).

[125.2] 24 Cal. 4th 627, 636, 101 Cal. Rptr. 2d 718, 12 P.3d 1125 (2000).

[125.3] *Id.* at p. 635, 101 Cal. Rptr. 2d 718, 12 P.3d 1125

(Secs. 896, 942). In such an instance, the RRA abrogates the economic loss rule, thus legislatively superseding *Aas*.

In *Greystone*, Greystone Homes, Inc. (Greystone), a home builder, brought this action against Midtec, Inc. among others. In its complaint, Greystone alleged that various homeowners had made claims against Greystone for damage caused by plumbing fittings that Midtec manufactured, and that the fittings were defective within the meaning of the RRA. Greystone claimed that it had incurred costs to replace the defective fittings, and alleged claims including negligence and equitable indemnity causes of action against Midtec.

Midtec brought a motion for summary judgment and/or summary adjudication in which it claimed that Greystone could not recover for purely economic losses that it incurred in replacing the fittings. In opposition, Greystone claimed that the RRA abolished the economic loss rule under the circumstances of this case, and argued that both builders and individual product manufacturers are liable under the RRA for the costs of repairing construction defects. In reply, Midtec contended that the RRA did not apply to Greystone's action, and that the economic loss rule precluded Greystone from prevailing against Midtec on its claims.

The trial court granted Midtec's motion for summary judgment. The trial court acknowledged that the RRA provides an exception to the economic loss rule for actions brought under the RRA by homeowners. However, the court concluded that Greystone was not entitled to pursue the statutorily created cause of action because Greystone was not a homeowner. The court ruled that the economic loss rule bars Greystone from recovering against Midtec on Greystone's common law claims.

Greystone's appeal raised two questions of first impression concerning the RRA. The first question was whether a builder may recover for economic losses caused by a product manufacturer's violations of the RRA standards, through an equitable indemnity claim against the manufacturer. The second question was whether a builder may recover its economic losses from an individual product manufacturer through a direct negligence claim based on the product manufacturer's violation of the RRA standards. The appellate court concluded that a builder may recover from a product manufacturer for economic losses caused by the manufacturer's violation of the standards set forth in the RRA, through an equitable indemnity action, but that a builder may not recover for these losses through a direct negligence claim against the manufacturer. The court reversed the trial court's summary judgment and remanded the matter to the trial court with directions to consider Midtec's alternative motion for summary adjudication.

In late 2000 or early 2001, Radiant Technologies, Inc. (RTI), purchased plastic plumbing fittings from Midtec. RTI used the fittings as a component part in its Plum-Pex plumbing system. RTI distributed the Plum-Pex system to plumbing wholesalers, who in turn sold the system to plumbing subcontractors.

Greystone was a merchant home builder. Beginning in approximately 2003, Greystone developed and built a new home community in Chula Vista known as Willow Bend. Willow Bend is composed of 110 condominiums/townhouses, clustered in 17 buildings. Greystone's plumbing subcontractor, Production Plus

Plumbing, installed the RTI Plum-Pex system, which contained Midtec fittings, in 66 of the Willow Bend units, between 2003 and 2005.

The owners of some of the units that contained the Midtec fittings began to complain to Greystone about leaks in their plumbing systems. Twenty-two of the units experienced failures of Midtec fittings. In some instances, there were multiple failures in a single unit. The Midtec fittings failed primarily due to fatigue caused by a molding defect in the manufacturing process. Fittings continued to fail during Greystone's investigation of the homeowners' complaints. Water leaks associated with the fitting failures presented a health risk to homeowners.

There were a total of approximately 1,980 Midtec fittings in the 66 homes. Greystone determined that if it did not replace the Midtec fittings, it was highly probable that there would be additional failures. Greystone replaced all of the Midtec fittings, including those that had not yet actually failed. The total cost to replace all of the fittings was approximately $1,494,904.04. The cost for repairs related to fittings that had failed was approximately $106,000.

While Midtec had a contractual relationship with RTI, it did not have a contractual relationship with Greystone. Midtec did not provide a warranty to RTI for the fittings. The only warranty that was provided to either Greystone or to homeowners in the Willow Bend project that related to plumbing was RTI's warranty for the Plum-Pex system.

In May 2005, Greystone filed a complaint against RTI, RTI's insurance company, Zurich American Insurance Company (Zurich), and Midtec. As to Midtec, Greystone brought a claim for negligence, a separate claim for indemnity and contribution, and requested declaratory relief. Greystone subsequently reached a settlement with RTI. As part of the settlement, RTI paid Greystone $460,000, an amount that exceeded Greystone's costs to repair water damage caused by fittings that actually failed. In February 2007, the trial court found that Greystone and RTI had entered into the settlement in good faith. The court subsequently dismissed Greystone's complaint as to RTI and Zurich.

In April 2007, Midtec filed a motion for summary judgment or, in the alternative, for summary adjudication. In its motion, Midtec noted that pursuant to the economic loss rule, a plaintiff may not recover, in tort, economic losses caused by an allegedly defective product when those losses are unrelated to either property damage or bodily injury. Midtec argued that Greystone had already recovered all of its damages that were related to property damage caused by the allegedly defective fittings, through its settlement with RTI, and maintained that the economic loss rule precluded Greystone from recovering additional damages from Midtec related to the cost of replacing fittings that had not failed or caused property damage.

Greystone opposed the motion. In its opposition, Greystone argued that the RRA had entirely abrogated the economic loss rule in construction defect litigation. Specifically, Greystone argued that the RRA imposed "cost-of-repair liability upon builders and individual product manufacturers whose products are defective, even in the absence of any specific property damage or bodily injury." Greystone claimed that Midtec was thus liable to Greystone for Greystone's costs to replace all of the fittings, including those that had not yet caused property damage. Greystone noted that its total cost to repair all of the fittings was approximately $1.5 million, which far exceeded the $460,000 it received in its settlement with RTI.

In its reply to Greystone's opposition, Midtec argued that the RRA is "completely inapplicable to the circumstances of this case." Midtec maintained that only homeowners are authorized to bring an action pursuant to the RRA. Midtec also noted that Section 936 provides in part, "Nothing in this title modifies the law pertaining to joint and several liability for builders, general contractors, subcontractors, material suppliers, individual product manufacturer[s], and design professionals that contribute to any specific violation of this title." Based on this language, Midtec argued that "[S]ection 936 alone is dispositive of the issue that [S]ections 895 et seq. do not apply to this action between the developer and a component part manufacturer." In July 2007, the trial court held a hearing on Midtec's motion for summary judgment or summary adjudication. After oral argument, the trial court granted Midtec's motion for summary judgment. In granting the motion, the trial court reasoned in part:

> [Midtec] has met its initial burden of demonstrating each of the claims asserted by [Greystone] seeks to recover the economic losses associated with replacing defective plumbing fittings that had not yet failed, i.e. had not yet caused property damage. Per Separate Statement [of Facts] number 22, it is undisputed that the $460,000 settlement with [RTI] exceeds the cost of repairing the fittings that actually leaked prior to replacement. Therefore [Midtec] has met its burden of demonstrating that the economic loss rule bars any further recovery by [Greystone], and the burden shifts to [Greystone]. [Greystone's] only contention refuting defendant's position is that the enactment of Senate Bill 800 abolishes the economic loss rule. This contention lacks merit. Rather than abolish the economic loss rule completely, S.B. 800 created an exception to the rule where a homeowner or [homeowners'] association brings a claim to recover damages for enumerated construction defects. [(Secs. 895, subd. (f), 896, and 942).] Arguably, the defective fittings fall within the enumerated construction defects. [(See Secs. 896, subds. (a)(14), (15)].) However, [Greystone] is not a homeowner or [homeowners' association], and as a result is not entitled to pursue the statutorily created cause of action. [Greystone's] only recourse is a common law claim, and the economic loss rule applies to bar such common law claims. In addition, [Greystone] provides no evidence demonstrating its compliance with the procedural prerequisites of S.B. 800, i.e. a pre-lawsuit notice and opportunity to repair. [(§§§§ 910, 917, 930, subd. (b).)]

The trial court subsequently entered judgment in favor of Midtec. Greystone appealed.

Greystone argued that the trial court erred in granting summary judgment as a matter of law on the common law indemnity claim. The *Greystone* court cited a series of cases allowing for equitable indemnity where both joint tortfeasors are responsible for an indivisible injury, and stated that the right to indemnity is one manner in which joint tortfeasors may apportion joint and several liability.

However, the court stated that for such equitable indemnity to apply there must be some basis for tort liability against the proposed indemnitor.

The *Greystone* court cited *Aas v. Superior Court*,[125.4] for the proposition that for defective products and negligent services that have caused neither property damage nor personal injury, and have caused solely economic loss, the manufacturer is not liable to the homeowner. The California legislature enacted the RRA in response to *Aas*. The RRA sets standards for residential construction, and provides tort liability for entities which fail to meet the standards set forth in the RRA. The *Greystone* court reviewed the legislative history of the RRA, and held that the RRA abrogated the economic loss rule in actions brought under the RRA by homeowners against individual product manufacturers.

Midtec argued that the RRA preserved the economic loss rule for claims against product manufacturers that alleged a violation of the RRA standards. The *Greystone* court stated that to determine if this claim exists, the court must first determine whether the economic loss rule would preclude a homeowner from collecting damages from Midtec, since Greystone's ability to pursue an indemnity action against Midtec under the RRA is contingent upon Midtec and Greystone sharing a joint legal obligation to the homeowners for economic losses caused by violation of the RRA standards.

Section 896 provides that individual product manufacturers are liable to homeowners for violation of the RRA standards, and Sections 942 and 944 abrogate the economic loss rule and allow a homeowner to recover economic losses from a product manufacturer for a violation of the RRA standards which is caused by the manufacturer's negligence or breach of contract. Midtec argued that Greystone's equitable indemnity claim was barred because a product manufacturer was only liable to a homeowner for an unmet standard under the RRA if there is resulting damage to persons or property. Midtec claimed that since it was not obligated to the homeowners for economic losses under the RRA, there was no predicate tort upon which Greystone, as an indemnitee, may base its equitable indemnity claim. The appellate court refused to accept these arguments.

For the first time, on appeal, Midtec raised the argument that it was not an individual product manufacturer under Sections 896 and 936. The appellate court held that the failure to raise this argument either to the trial court or to the appellate court in a manner which would have allowed Greystone to respond to the argument caused Midtec to forfeit this argument. The appellate court held that Midtec was an "individual product manufacturer" as referred to in Sections 896 and 936 for the purposes of the appeal.

Although the *Greystone* court stated the rule that there was generally no duty to prevent economic loss to third parties in negligence actions at common law, the court found that the RRA had created such a duty. The *Greystone* court held that a more reasonable interpretation of Section 936 was that a product manufacturer was liable only where its negligent act or omission or a breach of contract caused a violation of the RRA standards. The court noted that although Section 942 adopted a strict liability standard by providing for liability without "showing

---

[125.4] 24 Cal. 4th 627, 101 Cal. Rptr. 2d 718, 12 P.3d 1125 (2000).

causation or damages," Section 945.5 established a series of statutory defenses that were consistent with the principles of comparative fault. The *Greystone* court rejected Midtec's assertion that if this court were to conclude that the economic loss rule does not bar Greystone's claims, that this would "expand the law of strict product liability beyond tolerable limits."

The *Greystone* court concluded that the RRA abrogated the economic loss rule in actions brought by homeowners against individual product manufacturers for a violation of the RRA standards based upon the manufacturer's negligence or breach of contract. The matter was remanded to the trial court with directions to deny Midtec's motion for summary judgment, and for the trial court to consider Greystone's procedural objections to Midtec's alternative motion for summary adjudication.

§ 12.07 GUARANTEE

[A] A201-2007: Correction of Work

Page 465, add at end of subsection:

Steven G.M. Stein and Ronald O. Wietecha, in their article, *A Comparison of ConsensusDOCS to the AIA Form Construction Contract Documents*,[144.1] point out that, under ConsensusDOCS 200 Para. 3.9.4, the owner must give the contractor the opportunity to correct work beyond the one-year-correction-of-work period, although the right is limited by the statute of limitations.

[144.1] Steven G.M. Stein & Ronald O. Wietecha, *A Comparison of ConsensusDOCS to the AIA Form Construction Contract Documents*, The Construction Lawyer, Vol. 29, No. 1, Winter 2009.

CHAPTER 14

SITE CONTROL AND RESPONSIBILITIES

§ 14.02 CONTRACTOR'S SITE AND OPERATIONAL CONTROL

Page 506, add after second full paragraph:

The issue of site control and supervision of the site, particularly as the supervision relates to safety, is heavily litigated. Not only do the AIA documents attempt to prevent an architect from being responsible for job safety, but the documents attempt to insulate the general contractor from liability for accidents. In *Santos v. Ashforth, Co.*,[31.1] a Connecticut superior court denied a motion for summary judgment on a project using AIA A401, the AIA form subcontract, where there was a material issue of fact whether the general contractor exercised control sufficiently over the subcontractor's work so as to be liable for a workplace injury of a subcontractor's employees. In *Santos*, the plaintiffs, Jose Santos and Oscar Pena, were injured during the course of their employment with the defendant, Jose Gomez , d/b/a Gola Roofing on November 9, 2000. On that date, Gola Roofing had hired the plaintiffs to apply roofing paper to the New CanaanTeenCenter, then under construction. Gola Roofing was hired the previous day (without a written contract or subcontract) by the roofing subcontractor, the defendant, Antonelli Roofing, to put up the roofing paper on an expedited schedule.

The plaintiffs both fell from the steeply pitched roof of the Teen Center when one or more roof brackets supporting the planks upon which they were standing collapsed, causing the planks and both plaintiffs, who were not wearing safety harnesses or any other restraining device, to fall approximately 27 feet to the edge of the roof where they hit the scaffolding which failed to stop their fall, and then fell about another 14½ feet from the eave onto a concrete slab. Both plaintiffs sustained personal injuries for which they claim moneyed damages from all defendants.

Count One of the amended complaint stated the negligence claim of the plaintiff, Jose Santos, against the general contractor (AP Construction, Inc.). Count Five stated the negligence claim of the plaintiff, Oscar Pena, against AP Construction. Count Four was derivative of Count One and stated the loss of consortium claim of the plaintiff, Lilliana Ruiz, the wife of Jose Santos. The negligence claims of the plaintiffs against AP Construction included allegations

---

[31.1] 2009 Conn. Super. LEXIS 353, 2009 WL 567208 (2009).

that it, as the general contractor at the job site, failed to exercise reasonable care in the selection of a roofing subcontractor; failed to provide a safe workplace; failed to implement and enforce rules for workplace safety; failed to require the roofing subcontractor to comply with the job site safety rules promulgated by AP Construction; failed to supervise and inspect the work of the roofing subcontractor; failed to comply or require the roofing subcontractor to comply with OSHA regulations including the OSHA "6 foot rule" for roofing work; and "failed, as controlling employer with general supervisory authority over the job site, to comply with all safety measures including all applicable laws, ordinances, rules, regulations and orders of public authorities for the safety of persons."

AP Construction submitted a motion for summary judgment to the trial court on December 17, 2007, in which it claimed that there was no triable issue of fact, and that the undisputed record showed that it was entitled to judgment as a matter of law in that: (1) since it did not hire, employ, control or supervise the injured workers, it owed no duty to the plaintiffs, and (2) there was no basis upon which a reasonable jury could conclude that AP Construction was negligent.

Both parties submitted extensive factual materials to the trial court, including excerpts from the depositions of AP Constriction job site supervisor, Thomas Coleman, Antonelli Roofing principal, John Antonelli, and Antonelli Roofing foreman Hector Comacho. In addition, the defendant, AP Construction, submitted the written subcontract (on the form of AIA Document A401) between AP Construction and Antonelli Roofing, and an affidavit of John E. Antonelli. The plaintiffs submitted copies of Thomas Coleman's job site notes, the OSHA investigative report, photographs of the accident site, photographs of the "Job Safety Rules" sign posted at the site by AP Construction, and a report and affidavit of its expert Dr. John Mroszczyk.

The primary issue was whether or not, or under what circumstances, a general contractor had a duty to protect and safeguard the subcontractors' employees. As to AP Construction, Gola Roofing (the employer of the injured plaintiffs) was an independent subcontractor of AP Construction's independent roofing subcontractor, Antonelli Roofing.

In Connecticut, as a general rule, "an employer is not liable for the negligence of its independent contractors." *Pelletier et al. v. Sordoni/Skansa Construction Co.* (*Pelletier II*).[31.2] The premise underlying this general rule is that "the assumption and exercise of control over the offending area is deemed to be in the independent contractor."[31.3]

The court in *Pelletier II* had overruled part of the court's earlier decision in *Pelletier et al. v. Sordoni/Skansa Construction Co.* (*Pelletier I*),[31.4] which had held that, as a matter of law, an employee of an independent contractor could never pursue a common-law negligence claim against another contractor, limiting a contractor's liability to only innocent third parties. *Pelletier II* held that an

[31.2] 264 Conn. 509, 517, 825 A.2d 72 (2003).

[31.3] Darling v. Burrone Bros., Inc., 162 Conn. 187, 196 (1972).

[31.4] 262 Conn. 372 (2003).

employee of a subcontractor was not restricted as a matter of law from pursuing a claim against a general contractor.

The *Pelletier II* court stressed, however, that in order to succeed on its claim, the plaintiff employee had to establish a basis for the contractor's liability under the case law—i.e., show that the facts fell within one of the exceptions to the general rule of nonliability of a general contractor. The court identified four such exceptions to the general rule: (1) the work contracted for was intrinsically dangerous; (2) the independent contractor hired was incompetent or untrustworthy; (3) the general contractor had a legal duty to see that the work was performed properly; and (4) the general contractor exercised control over the subcontractor.[31.5]

In this case, the defendant claimed that, as a matter of law, none of the *Pelletier II* exceptions applied to this case. In contrast, the plaintiffs claimed that there were genuine disputed issues of fact as to the application of all the *Pelletier II* exceptions. The court found that there were genuine disputed issues of fact as to the control issue, which prevented it from entering summary judgment in favor of AP Construction as a matter of law.

Pelletier II remanded the case for trial. The case was tried to a superior court jury on the negligence and loss of consortium counts (the very same counts outstanding against AP Construction in the case). Following a jury verdict for the plaintiffs which the trial court declined to set aside, both parties appealed and the case went to the Connecticut Supreme Court for a third time: *Pelletier et al. v. Sordoni/Skansa Construction Co.* (*Pelletier III*).[31.6] On the plaintiffs' cross appeal, one of the issues was the trial court's refusal to instruct the jury that Sordoni, the general contractor had a duty as the general contractor to exercise reasonable care with respect to any part of the work site or inspection process over which it retained control.

Pelletier involved a claim that the general contractor had a duty to inspect the weld which failed, permitting a steel beam to fall on the plaintiff, an employee of the structural steel subcontractor who had a contract obligation to inspect all welds. The court held that the general contractor was not in control of the fabrication and inspection of welds, because "a fair and reasonable person could reach but one conclusion as to who exercised control . . ." In reaching that position, the *Pelletier II* court relied on the fact that the contract documents required the subcontractor to fabricate and inspect the welds at its own shop, thus clearly demonstrating that the general contractor did not retain control over "the area or instrumentality" that caused the plaintiff harm.[31.7] "It [Sordoni] thus had no control over the shop in which the welds were fabricated or the manner in which the inspections were to be performed . . ." The court rejected the argument that an orientation and procedures manual that Sordoni provided to the subcontractor indicating that Sordoni would conduct its own weekly inspections to ensure compliance with its safety program was evidence of an exercise of control

[31.5] 264 Conn. 509, 591-692.

[31.6] 286 Conn. 563 (2008).

[31.7] 286 Conn. 563, 602.

by Sordoni. The manual was not a legally binding contract, but rather "an informational tool designed to educate the plaintiff in the protocols for the job site . . . [It was] strictly informational."[31.8]

In *Archambault v. Soneco/Northeastern, Inc.*,[31.9] the Connecticut Supreme Court addressed whether or not a general contractor had a nondelegable duty to the plaintiff subcontractor's employee to ensure a safe construction site, because the general contractor had allegedly exercised control over the excavation of trenches at the site. The court remanded the case for a new trial because of an error in ruling on evidence, but addressed the control issue because that issue "was likely to arise in the new trial,"[31.10] The *Archambault* court found that the trial court had improperly instructed the jury that the general contractor had such a nondelegable duty.

There was evidence that the contract between Konover (the general contractor) and Soneco (the excavation and site work subcontractor) obligated Soneco to comply with all applicable laws and regulatory safety rules (including OSHA regulations), and to observe and comply with the Safety Project Plan. Konover had provided Soneco with a copy of its construction safety manual. This gave Konover's site superintendents the power to conduct weekly job site safety meetings, conduct safety inspections, and to issue violation notices to subcontractors. Konover also published a safety manual for excavations. Konover superintendents were authorized to halt activities that could constitute a safety violation. The Konover site supervisor testified that he was in "overall control" of the 10-acre construction site. He also testified that "the buck stopped with Konover" on overall safety and "It was my job to make sure that the contractors did the best they could with regard to safety."[31.11] In finding that under these circumstances that the nondelegable duty instruction had been improper, the appellate court found that a reasonable person could reach but one conclusion: Soneco, and not Konover, was in control and was responsible for safety at the site. The court said: "Overall responsibility for safety on the work site, however, does not necessarily translate into a nondelegable duty."[31.12]

The appellate court found that Konover's safety manual was not the source of a contractual or legal duty to provide a safe work site but was merely an informational tool.

Although the safety manual described Konover's interest in providing safe conditions on the work site, it did not suggest that Konover would engage in daily supervision of its subcontractor's employees . . . Rather, the manual suggested that Konover would foster safety by developing site specific safety plans to identify potential hazards that might arise . . . *None of the safety concerns*

[31.8] *Id.*

[31.9] 287 Conn. 20, 946 A.2d 839 (2008).

[31.10] 287 Conn. 20, 41.

[31.11] 287 Conn. 20, 51.

[31.12] 287 Conn. 20, 54.

discussed in the manual involved control over the manner in which specific tasks would be performed by the subcontractor's employees.[31.13]

In *Santos*, in their post-*Pelletier III* and *Archambault* supplemental memoranda, AP Construction argued that it, like Konover, had only general overall supervision over safety at the Darien Teen Center work site, while the plaintiffs argued that there was evidence from which a reasonable juror could find that AP Construction went beyond the role of an overall supervisor and exercised control over the manner in which subcontractors performed their duties so as to ensure safety.

A juror could have concluded that the sign posted at the premises was more binding and obligatory than a mere "informational tool." For example, the sign stated:

> OSHA's 6-foot rule in proper fall protection *is to be utilized* as required.
>
> The following safety requirements are mandatory:
>
> Eye protection *must be worn* when using power tools . . .
>
> Gloves *must be* worn . . .
>
> Hard hats *must be worn* at all times . . .

Furthermore, Thomas Coleman testified at deposition that it was part of his job to "make sure that these rules were enforced," and that he had authority to stop work if he thought it was not being done in a safe manner. Yet, he testified that he saw the plaintiffs working on the roof (obviously more than six foot above ground) without wearing safety harnesses. There was also a notation in his job notes that, sometime prior to the date of the plaintiffs' fall, he: "[r]eviewed safety, parking and site storing requirements, w/ Panel Pro's foreman (Brian) . . . Warned Panel Pros that they *all* need to wear hart hats & [be] 'tied off.' They were tied off but not all wore hard hats. R. Marin gave out 2 for their use." This, at least suggested that AP Construction was passing out safety equipment to subcontractor employees and requiring that it be used, which could support a finding of control even under the *Pelletier III/Archambault* criteria.This was not a case where a reasonable juror could reach no conclusion other than that AP Construction was not in control of safety at the job site. There was a genuine issue of material fact that could not be decided by a motion for summary judgment. For the reasons stated, the trial court denied the motion for summary judgment.

In the context of a serious injury or death, the court may be motivated to spread the cost of the loss more broadly, increasing the chance that an owner or general contractor may be liable for such a loss.

Indemnity claims can also arise in the context of the control issue. Indemnity claims are made difficult because of the public policy considerations limiting enforcement and the complexity of the clauses themselves. In *Staub v. William H.*

[31.13] 287 Conn. 20, 55.

Lane, Inc.,[31.14] an employee of the subcontractor brought an action against a general contractor for negligence and brought claims under New York Labor Law. The parties had used the AIA A401 form subcontract. The general contractor sought third-party indemnification from the subcontractor for indemnification. The trial court had granted the general contractor partial summary judgment on its indemnification claim, and the subcontractor appealed.

The New York Supreme Court, Appellate Division held that a genuine issue of material fact precluded summary judgment on the indemnity claim, reversing the trial court's grant of summary judgment. The court held that there was a genuine issue of material fact as to whether the general contractor and its subcontractor agreed to be bound by the indemnification provision of the form contract incorporated by an unsigned, written proposal. Thus, an order of the supreme court was entered on November 20, 2007, partially granting the defendant's cross-motion for summary judgment seeking contractual indemnification from the third-party defendant.

In *Staub*, the plaintiff, an employee of the subcontractor third-party defendant, was injured while installing a steel beam on a building. He commenced the underlying action against the general contractor for the project, asserting causes of action sounding in negligence and Labor Law §§ 200(1), §§ 240(1) and §§241(6). Following a joinder of issue, the defendant commenced a third-party action seeking contractual indemnification from a third-party defendant based upon an unsigned, written proposal submitted by third-party defendant.

The proposal purported to incorporate the terms of AIA Document A401 into the quote, and was accepted by the defendant orally. The parties did not, however, sign a formal, written contract containing an express agreement to indemnify. AIA Form A401, which was not transmitted to defendant along with the proposal, contains the following indemnity provision:

> To the fullest extent permitted by law, the [s]ubcontractor shall indemnify and hold harmless the [o]wner, [c]ontractor . . . from and against claims, damages, losses and expenses, including but not limited to attorney's fees, arising out of or resulting from performance of the [s]ubcontractor's Work under this [s]ubcontract . . . but only to the extent caused by the negligent acts or omissions of the [s]ubcontractor . . .

The third-party defendant moved for summary judgment dismissing the third-party complaint in its entirety, and the defendant cross-moved for summary judgment on its indemnification claim. The New York Supreme Court denied the third-party defendant's motion, and it granted the defendant's cross-motion in part, directing that the defendant be granted conditional indemnification and defense by the third-party defendant in connection with the underlying action. The third-party defendant appealed, and the appellate court modified by denying defendant's cross-motion for summary judgment in its entirety.

[31.14] 58 A.D.3d 933, 870 N.Y.S.2d 630 (2009).

New York Workers' Compensation Law § 11 precludes third-party indemnification claims against employers unless the claim is "based upon a provision in a written contract entered into prior to the accident or occurrence by which the employer had expressly agreed to contribution to or indemnification of the claimant or person asserting the cause of action for the type of loss suffered."

Whether a written contract satisfies section 11 involves a two-part inquiry. First, the court considers whether the parties entered into a written contract containing an indemnity provision applicable to the site or job where the injury giving rise to the indemnity claim took place. Second, if so, the court examines whether the indemnity provision was sufficiently particular to meet the requirements of section 11.[31.15] The parties' dispute centered on whether the first prong of the two-part inquiry had been met.

A written agreement could be enforceable if "the course of conduct between [the parties], including their writings . . . was sufficient to spell out a binding contract, notwithstanding the failure of the parties to sign [an] integrated agreement."[31.16] Thus, the parties' course of conduct must be reviewed "to determine whether there was a meeting of the minds sufficient to give rise to an enforceable contract."[31.17]

In this case, the third-party defendant included a note on its written proposal. This was the only written document governing the work performed. This document purported to incorporate the terms of AIA Contract A401. A401 includes an indemnity provision running from the employer (third-party defendant) to the contractor (defendant), as noted above. Nevertheless, third-party defendant's president, Peter Browning, indicated that the parties never used a formal AIA Contract A401 in their prior agreements. The defendant generally submitted its own written contract after receiving proposals, and Browning expected and intended that practice to be followed on this occasion.

This testimony was consistent with a statement from the defendant's senior project manager that the formal subcontract that defendant typically used was not supplied in connection with the job at issue. The court noted that while Browning admitted during his deposition that formal subcontracts were not always used, and arguably stated that he intended AIA Contract A401, including the indemnification provision, to apply to this project, the record indicated that AIA Contract A401 was never provided to the defendant. Given the failure to provide the indemnification provision of AIA Contract A401 and the absence of any evidence that the parties agreed to that provision through either past practice or their course of conduct, the New York Supreme Court concluded that questions of fact existed

[31.15] Rodrigues v. N & S Bldg. Contractors, Inc., 5 N.Y.3d 427, 432, 839 N.E.2d 357, 805 N.Y.S.2d 299 (2005).

[31.16] Flores v. Lower E. Side Serv. Ctr., Inc., 4 N.Y.3d 363, 368, 828 N.E.2d 593, 795 N.Y.S.2d 491 (2005), *quoting* Brown Bros. Elec. Contractors v. Beam Constr. Corp., 41 N.Y.2d 397, 399, 361 N.E.2d 999, 393 N.Y.S.2d 350 (1977).

[31.17] Flores v. Lower E. Side Serv. Ctr., Inc., 4 N.Y.3d 363, 370, 828 N.E.2d 593, 795 N.Y.S.2d 491 (2005).

as to whether the parties agreed to be bound by the indemnification provisions of AIA Contract A401.[31.18]

In *Staub*, the New York court denied the defendant's cross-motion for summary judgment in its entirety, and it modified the trial court's order, with costs to third-party defendant, by reversing so much thereof as partially granted defendant's cross-motion for summary judgment.

Even if an indemnity clause is well-written and appears to be clear on its face, courts may be reluctant to enforce such clauses because of the risk-shifting they represent, often from a stronger party who imposes adhesive indemnity obligations on a weaker party.

Claims for injury are usually handled differently than claims for property damage. In *Spiegler v. Gerken Building Corp.*[31.18.1] an injured construction worker brought a personal injury action against a premises owner and a general contractor. The general contractor filed a third-party complaint against the subcontractor that employed the worker, asserting claims for common-law and contractual indemnification. The supreme court granted the subcontractor's motion for summary judgment dismissing indemnification claims. The subcontractor appealed.

The New York Supreme Court held that:(1) the workers' compensation statute barred the general contractor from asserting common-law indemnification claim against the subcontractor, and(2) factual issues precluded summary judgment for the subcontractor on the claim for contractual indemnification.The appellate court agreed with the trial court's ruling (the judgment was modified for unrelated reasons). The appellate court held that the general contractor could pursue a contractual indemnification claim against the subcontractor who employed the worker under Workers' Compensation Law § 11, because the subcontractor's purchase order left unresolved material issues of fact as to whether the parties intended the indemnification provision in the standard form agreement to be incorporated by reference into that purchase order.

The injured worker was allegedly injured when a length of pipe fell on him. He completed his workday, reported back to work the next day, and continued working for at least "a few months." He later claimed that the accident caused injury to his lumbar spine area, including disc bulges and herniations, as well as radiculopathy. He received workers' compensation for his medical expenses.

In the case, the subcontractor, the injured worker's employer, had moved for summary judgment dismissing the contractual indemnification cause of action on the ground that there was no agreement to indemnify, and dismissing the common-law indemnification cause of action on the ground that the worker had not sustained a "grave injury" within the meaning of Workers' Compensation Law § 11.

[31.18] *See* Mentesana v. Bernard Janowitz Constr. Corp., 36 A.D.3d 769, 771, 828 N.Y.S.2d 522 (2007); Gilbert v. Albany Med. Ctr., 21 A.D.3d 677, 678, 799 N.Y.S.2d 685 (2005); Miller v. Mott's Inc., 5 A.D.3d 1019, 1020, 773 N.Y.S.2d 727 (2004).

[31.18.1] 35 A.D.3d 715, 826 N.Y.S.2d 674 (2006).

The appellate court agreed with the subcontractor that the cause of action for common-law indemnity should have been dismissed. Employers such as the subcontractor who provide workers' compensation coverage are immune from tort liability except in a narrow class of cases in which the plaintiff has sustained a "grave injury." Under Workers' Compensation Law § 11, "grave injury" is "both narrowly and completely described" as "death, permanent and total loss of use or amputation of an arm, leg, hand or foot, loss of multiple fingers, loss of multiple toes, paraplegia, quadriplegia, total and permanent blindness, total and permanent deafness, loss of nose, loss of ear, permanent and severe facial disfigurement, loss of an index finger or an acquired injury to the brain caused by an external physical force resulting in permanent total disability." In this case, the worker, who was allegedly injured when pipe fell on him, completed his work day and continued working for at least "a few months." He later claimed that the accident caused injury to his lumbar spine area, including disc bulges and herniations, as well as radiculopathy, and he received workers' compensation for his medical expenses.

Because the worker's alleged injuries to his back, as described in his deposition testimony and as further amplified in his second supplemental verified bill of particulars, clearly did not fall within any of the enumerated categories, he did not sustain a "grave injury," and, therefore, the lessee of the premises was barred from asserting a common-law indemnification claim against the subcontractor.

The Workers' Compensation Law did not, however, preclude the lessee from pursuing a contractual indemnification claim against the subcontractor, provided that such claim was "based upon a provision in a written contract entered into prior to the accident or occurrence by which the employer had expressly agreed to contribution to or indemnification of the claimant or person asserting the cause of action for the type of loss suffered." Workers' Compensation Law § 11. In this case, the lessee and the subcontractor had executed a "Subcontractor Purchase Order," which provided that "[t]his document has been prepared to be used in conjunction with the AIA Document, A-401 Standard Form of Agreement between Contractor and Subcontract [sic] 1987 Edition." Although the purchase order itself contained no indemnification provision, the A401 Standard Form of Agreement referred to in the purchase order did contain such a provision. Thus, the court held that the subcontractor failed to establish its prima facie entitlement to judgment as a matter of law dismissing the contractual indemnification claim. Its submission left unresolved material issues of fact as to whether the parties to the purchase order intended the provisions of the A401 Standard Form of Agreement to be incorporated by reference into the purchase order.

In *Padilla v. Pomona College*,[31.19] another case that considered control over work site and the manner in which subcontractors performed their duties, after being injured during a dormitory remodeling project, an employee of a subcontractor brought an action against a college and a general contractor for negligence and premises liability. The trial court entered judgment for the defendants, and the employee appealed.

[31.19] 166 Cal. App. 4th 661, 82 Cal. Rptr. 3d 869 (2008), *review denied* (Dec. 10, 2008).

The appellate court affirmed the trial court. It held that (1) any control that the college and the general contractor retained over the pressurized pipe did not affirmatively contribute to the employee's injuries; (2) a California Occupational Safety and Health (Cal-OSHA) regulation requiring that water lines be protected from damage did not impose a nondelegable duty; (3) the failure of the college and the general contractor to take steps in regulation did not affirmatively contribute to injuries; (4) the college and the general contractor did not violate a duty under a regulation supporting per se liability; and (5) the college and the general contractor did not fail to disclose a hazardous condition.

In *Padilla*, the college hired a general contractor to remodel a dormitory on its college campus. The general contractor contracted with TEG/LVI, plaintiff's employer, for the demolition of water pipes in the basement of the dormitory. The water pressure to some of the pipes in the basement area was not shut off because the pipes were needed during the remodeling process.

During the demolition, plaintiff stood on a ladder to demolish an unpressurized cast-iron metal pipe. A portion of that pipe came loose and fell, striking a pressurized PVC pipe and breaking it. Plaintiff was knocked off his ladder by the gusher of water erupting from the broken PVC pipe and sustained serious physical injuries. The parties did not dispute that the PVC pipe was not to be demolished.

Plaintiff's complaint asserted two theories, negligence and premises liability. He alleged that defendants violated their common law and statutory duties to ensure that there was no water pressure in the pipes in the area plaintiff was working.

Defendants Pomona and the general contractor moved for summary judgment, contending they had no duty to plaintiff because they did not retain control over the details of the activities causing plaintiff's injuries and did not engage in any affirmative act that contributed to plaintiff's injuries. Further, they contended that plaintiff's claim was barred because his employer, TEG/LVI, knew or should have known of the danger presented by the PVC pipe.

Defendants presented evidence that it was TEG/LVI's contractual duty to demolish pipes, asbestos, lead, and drywall, and that TEG/LVI had agreed to protect items that remained in the employees' work area. Prior to the start of the project, the general contractor worked with TEG/LVI to ensure that TEG/LVI understood the scope of the demolition, including which pipes would remain and which would be demolished. Specifically, the architect's plans for the project showed that a PVC pipe would remain in the building during demolition, and it would remain pressurized to provide water for work on the project.

The general contractor retained co-defendant Deel Mechanical to prepare the plumbing system in the dormitory for demolition, and to ensure that those pipes that were not to be demolished were cut and capped. Deel marked the pipes to be removed, and redirected temporary piping on the outside of the building. The basement was barricaded to prevent access by Deel and other subcontractors. The trial court, in a separate summary judgment motion, found Deel "had no duty to prevent the injury that occurred to plaintiff." The trial court granted Deel's motion for summary judgment. Plaintiff did not appeal from judgment in favor of Deel.

At the time of the accident, plaintiff was using TEG/LVI's tools and equipment. He was directed in his work by his TEG/LVI supervisor, Armando Takata, who according to defendant's evidence, identified to plaintiff that the PVC pipe was one of the pipes that had been left pressurized. The moving papers provided evidence that Takata expressly advised plaintiff to avoid damaging the pressurized PVC pipe. TEG/LVI's standard demolition procedures for the type of pipe that plaintiff demolished required plaintiff and a nondelegable to use separate ladders, tie a rope around the midsection of the pipe to be demolished, break the pipe, and lower the pipe to the ground slowly. Plaintiff was not following this procedure at the time of the accident. Defendants, in particular Gordon & Williams, did not supervise plaintiff.

Plaintiff opposed the motion, contending that (1) the general contractor's failure to depressurize the pipe constituted negligence per se, a breach of its contractual duties, and was contrary to custom and practice; and (2) the general contractor's failure to depressurize the pipe affirmatively contributed to plaintiff's injury. Plaintiff specifically contended that the general contractor failed to follow Cal-OSHA regulations[31.20] which required utilities to be shut off, capped, or otherwise controlled during demolition, or protected if use was necessary. Plaintiff also contended the general contractor's contract with Pomona College specified that the general contractor was "responsible for initiating, maintaining and supervising all safety precautions and programs in connection with the performance of the Contract" and that the general contractor was to "take reasonable precautions for safety of, and shall provide reasonable protection to prevent damage, injury or loss to . . . employees on the Work and other persons who may be affected thereby." In addition, the general contractor was to "comply with applicable laws, ordinances, rules, regulations . . . bearing on safety of persons or property or their protection from damage, injury or loss" and designate a responsible person whose duty would be the prevention of accidents.

Hooker v. Department of Transportation,[31.21] provides the hirer can nonetheless be liable if its conduct affirmatively contributed to the injuries of the independent contractor's employees. Plaintiff herein argued that the defendants retained control over the worksite and failed to take the necessary precautions by depressurizing the pipe, thereby contributing to his injuries.

Specifically, plaintiff contended that TEG/LVI did not have control of the water pressure in the PVC pipe, and therefore could not shut it off. The general contractor could have shut the water off to the PVC pipe while the demolition was going on in the basement. Following the accident, the general contractor had difficulty shutting the water off, and after the accident, placed a ball valve over the pipe to protect it. The plans for the project only showed that the pipe was to "remain," not that it would be pressurized. The plaintiff's supervisor did not tell him how to do his job, or that the PVC pipe would remain pressurized. His supervisor only told him that pipes marked with red paint would not be demolished, not that they were pressurized. The pipes in the area where he worked

[31.20] Cal. Code Regs. tit. 8, §§ 1735, subd. (a).

[31.21] 27 Cal. 4th 198, 115 Cal. Rptr. 2d 853, 38 P.3d 1081 (2002).

were not marked with red paint. The supervisor demolished the sewer pipe the way he had been trained to do. Plaintiff proffered expert deposition testimony that the accident was the result of the general contractor's failure to comply with custom and practice by shutting off the water before demolition began, and that damage to the PVC pipe was foreseeable.

The trial court granted defendants' motion on the basis that defendants had fully delegated the task of providing a safe work environment to TEG/LVI. Defendants had not exercised any retained control in a manner that affirmatively contributed to plaintiff's injuries. The court found that Regulation 1735(a) did not impose a duty on defendants independent of the retained control theory of liability, because plaintiff did not establish that the regulation imposed a duty on defendants as opposed to TEG/LVI, or that it was in fact necessary to relocate or shut off the PVC pipe under the circumstances. The court also sustained defendants' objection to plaintiff's expert deposition testimony on the grounds that no foundation had been laid either for the expert's qualification as an expert or for his opinion.

Plaintiffs had contended that defendants, who retained control over the PVC pipe, should have depressurized, rearranged, or relocated the pipe before the project began, or at least temporarily, while demolition was taking place in the basement. The appellate court held that the plaintiff did not successfully establish that the defendants retained control over the PVC pipe or that defendants affirmatively contributed to the accident. The appellate court in *Padilla* reviewed a series of cases on exceptions to the peculiar risk doctrine, such as *Toland v. Sunland Housing Group, Inc.*,[31.22] and *Privette v. Superior Court.*[31.23] The *Padilla* court found that under the facts of this case, the plaintiff could not establish that Regulation Section 1735(a) imposed a nondelegable duty on defendants. The *Padilla* court also found that plaintiff could not use Regulation 1735(a) to establish negligence per se, or that defendants failed to disclose a known hazardous condition of the property. The *Padilla* court held that the hazardous condition asserted by the plaintiff was the pressurized PVC pipe. TEG/LVI, the plaintiff's employer, knew of the pipe and failed to take the necessary precautions to protect its employee from harm during the demolition process. Because there was no triable issue of fact, the appellate court upheld the trial court's granting defendants' motion for summary judgment.

§ 14.05 PROTECTION OF PERSONS AND PROPERTY

Page 538, add at end of section:

In *Jones v. DHR Cambridge Homes,*[97.01] a worker brought an action against a general contractor for injuries he sustained while working for a subcontractor who had contracted with a general contractor to perform carpentry work on a

---

[31.22] 18 Cal. 4th 253, 264, 74 Cal. Rptr. 2d 878, 955 (1998).

[31.23] 5 Cal. 4th 689, 21 Cal. Rptr. 2d 72, 854 P.2d 721 (1993).

[97.01] 381 Ill. App. 3d 18, 885 N.E.2d 330, 319 Ill. Dec. 59 (2008).

construction site. He was injured after walking out on a wooden sill plate that was mounted on a structural beam. The general contractor filed a third-party complaint against the worker's employer, seeking contribution under the Joint Tortfeasor Contribution Act. The trial court entered a directed verdict in favor of the employer on the contribution claim and entered judgment on a jury verdict in favor of worker.

The appellate court, however, reversed the directed verdict in favor of the subcontractor. The general contractor presented expert testimony that the subcontractor was responsible for the means and methods of performing work on a project and for providing a safe work place for the employee. Specifically, the court held:(1) the general contractor could rely on the evidence as a whole to establish its claim for contribution;(2) the issue of whether employer breached its duty to the worker was for the jury; (3) The steel contractor that was not a party to case was not to be included in calculation of fault for the purposes of determining comparative fault, joint and several liability and contribution; and (4) evidence of an absence of Occupational Safety and Health Administration (OSHA) violations was not supported by adequate foundation.

The plaintiff described the process of erecting first floor joists. The sill plates were affixed to the steel beams set in place and braced by the ironworkers. Sometimes, the carpenters had to move the steel slightly and rebrace it. There were several houses in the subdivision on which the plaintiff had to restraighten the bracing before the sill plates could be placed. The plaintiff reported the problem to his foreman. Even though the foreman testified that he reported the problem to the superintendent, the problem was not resolved before the accident.

The plaintiff was injured after he walked out on a wooden sill plate that was mounted on a structural steel beam to take measurements for the layout of the floor joists. The sill plate was approximately eight to nine feet off the ground and was wider than the steel beam. The "brace," which the plaintiff had secured the day before, ran perpendicular to the sill plate on which the plaintiff stood and spanned the distance between that sill plate and an adjacent sill plate and beam. In performing his measurement, the plaintiff placed his left foot upon the brace and leaned forward to obtain a measurement. The brace flipped up causing the plaintiff to fall forward into the basement area.

According to the plaintiff, he was never told he could not walk out on a sill plate on a steel beam. While he was trained not to walk on a brace, he was never told he could not place the weight of his foot on the brace. It was not unusual to put a foot on a brace.

The subcontract agreement between the general contractor and the subcontractor provided in pertinent part as follows:

> *Safety Precautions and Procedures*—The Subcontractor shall take all reasonable safety precautions with respect to the Work and shall comply with all safety measures required by Contractor and by all applicable laws, ordinances, rules, regulations and orders of any public authority for the safety of persons or property, including but not limited to the provisions of the Occupational Safety and Health Act,as amended from time to time and all regulations relating thereto.

And

> *Temporary Facilities and Services*—Subcontractor shall furnish all temporary offices, sheds and tool houses, equipment, power, water, temporary lights, hoistings, scaffolding, ladders, deckings, stagings, runways, and all other facilities required in connection with the Work.

The subcontract agreement also provided that "the latest edition of the General Conditions of the Contract for Construction, AIA Document A-201" was also made part of the subcontract agreement.

Throughout the trial, the plaintiff maintained and provided evidence that the general contractor was responsible for safety on the job and that they had employees in place to ensure the subcontractors complied with the general contractor's safety manual and guidelines. However, the general contractor's safety expert testified that the subcontractor, the plaintiff's employer, was responsible for the means and methods of performing the plaintiff's work and that the injury resulted from the plaintiff's work methods. The general contractor also claimed that even if it had maintained a supervisory role over safety, OSHA had never issued a citation for this type of incident, and, therefore, it could not be negligence. The trial court, however, barred all evidence of the lack of OSHA citations, which was upheld on appeal. Testimony that OSHA had never issued the general contractor a citation for a prior similar incident was based purely on the expert's own knowledge, and not based on anything of an official or definitive nature

The court summarized all of the testimony that the parties presented at trial. The general contractor's construction superintendent, whose job involved scheduling and sequencing the work of the various trades on the project and whose job was to ensure compliance with the general contractor's safety manual, testified that if he observed an OSHA violation or an unsafe practice on a construction site, he could stop it. OSHA required that residential construction workers have some type of fall protection if they were exposed to a six-foot or greater fall. A "controlled access zone" (CAZ) was used to control the environment for particular work. Other than "awareness," no other fall protection was in place, even though the witness was aware that the subcontractor's carpenters were working nine feet in the air on the sill plates. The construction superintendent did not think this was dangerous; it was a common practice and utilizing a CAZ complied with OSHA. While there were safer alternatives to walking the sills, he chose not to instruct the trades on how to perform their jobs. He also recalled that an employee of the subcontractor had alerted him to the problems with the steel.

The subcontractor's safety coordinator at the time of the plaintiff's accident described the plaintiff as a very qualified carpenter and not known to take any unnecessary risks. While working on the project, he observed the contractor's supervisors inspecting the work on the site. If the supervisors requested that a trade correct a problem, the trade would do so. Only the contractor had authority to change specifications, and no safety issue was ever raised about working off the sill plates. While it was safer to use a ladder, the job then took longer. Neither the contractor nor the subcontractor told the carpenters they could not use ladders. It was also the subcontractor's job to educate its employees, not the general contractor's.

The general contractor's regional director, whose job was to oversee the various projects and to supervise the superintendents, testified that the contractor's job was to ensure that the job was done according to specifications and that the subcontractors were in the right place. He also testified concerning the superintendents' job to enforce the safety manual. He acknowledged that the contractor did not tell its subcontractors how to do their jobs. He never told a carpentry contractor that the employees should not walk on a sill plate. He understood that activity was permitted by OSHA. Finally, he acknowledged that using a "controlled access zone" (CAZ) to control the environment for particular work did not protect against injuries sustained in falls.

A superintendent at the time of the plaintiff's accident, who was the highest ranked employee of the subcontractor on the site, stated that, at the weekly safety classes that the subcontractor's workers were required to attend, he was unaware of the contractor's instructing the plaintiff to walk on the sill plates. However, all of the means and methods of doing the work were the responsibility of the subcontractor, not the contractor. Thus, the subcontractor had supplied all the equipment. The subcontractor did not permit new carpenters on heights or dangerous areas initially. Finally, he testified that if the plaintiff stepped on a brace that was unsecured or possibly unsecured, he was not following the safety rules.

According to a self-employed construction safety expert, who had previously worked at OSHA, the plaintiff should have been provided fall protection suited to the job at hand, which, in this case, would have been ladders or sawhorses with planks. The regulations also required inspections. Although the subcontractor should have enforced the safety rules, it was the contractor's job to intervene and rectify the unsafe situation.

The subcontractor's foreman at the time of the accident, in addition to noting the plaintiff's complaint about the setting of the steel, also testified that one of his duties was to stop a subcontractor's work if it was not performed in accord with the general contractor's safety program. The foreman explained that the carpenters laying out the sill plates had no fall protection, other than the CAZ, which only warned of a fall hazard. Neither the subcontractor nor contractor provided the plaintiff with training regarding walking on the sill plates. Although walking on the sill plates did not violate the subcontractor's policies, the plaintiff also had the authority to stop work if he considered walking on the sill plate to be unsafe.

The general contractor's employee who prepared the contract with the subcontractor related that the contract did not instruct subcontractors how to do their work. After stating the requirement that the subcontractor perform its work in compliance with federal, state, and local laws and the minimum statutory health and safety requirements, the contract provided that each trade, and not the general contractor, was responsible for providing its own safety equipment. In addition, while the witness maintained that the general contractor did not really dictate the means and methods of doing the subcontractors' work, he testified the intention to bind the subcontractor and general contractor to the general conditions of AIA

Document A-201, even though that document was not physically included in the contract, and that document provided general conditions between the owner and the general contractor, while the specific contract involved a subcontractor and the general contractor. Sections 3.3.1 and 10.1.1 of the general conditions provided that the contractor, as the contractor, was solely responsible for and had control over the means and methods of the work and was responsible for safety in connection with the work. According to the witness, if the contractor did not want to undertake these obligations, it could have chosen not to incorporate them into its contract with the subcontractor.

The general contractor's construction safety expert explained that OSHA rules held an employee responsible for his actions, but these rules required that the employer furnish a working environment free from hazards likely to cause death or serious harm to the employees. Thus, in this case, the subcontractor, as the plaintiff's employer, had the obligation to provide a safe workplace. The direct employer was responsible for supplying safety equipment. There was no OSHA regulation that would require the general contractor to provide such equipment to someone it did not employ. According to the expert, the subcontractor was in direct, operative control over its employees and was responsible for defining the means and methods of performing the work, including the procedures and the safe way of doing them. Whether the measurement was done from a ladder or walking on the sill plate, it was a means or method of performing the work. There was no evidence that the general contractor had the same authority to control the means and methods. Therefore, no action on the part of the general contractor had anything to do with the plaintiff's accident. However, he acknowledged that at his deposition he had stated that had the steel been erected correctly, the accident could have been avoided and that the general contractor should have inspected the lot prior to allowing the subcontractor to work on it.

In its third-party complaint, the general contractor alleged that the subcontractor, the injured worker's employer, had a duty to exercise reasonable and ordinary care for the safety of the plaintiff and breached its duty to the plaintiff by committing negligence in a variety of ways. The court rejected the subcontractor's claim that the contractor did not present any evidence of the contractor's negligence, and it argued that the general contractor could not rely on the evidence introduced by the plaintiff. The court relied on a products liability case, *Frisch v. International Harvester Co.,*[97.02] which rejected that argument. The court in that case, held that once the plaintiff presented the elements of strict liability by competent evidence, it would be a waste of judicial resources to require the seller, who counterclaimed against the manufacturer in that case, to separately prove the elements of strict liability.

In the present case, on the one hand, the contractor argued that walking on the sill plates was not dangerous. On the other hand, it argued that if walking on the sills was dangerous, the subcontractor was responsible or at least partly responsible for the plaintiff's safety. The general contractor introduced evidence establishing the subcontractor's duty, but relied on the plaintiff's evidence to

[97.02] 33 Ill.App.3d 507, 338 N.E.2d 90 (1975).

establish that that subcontractor breached its duty to the plaintiff by allowing him to walk on the sills and that this breach resulted in the plaintiff's injury.

The court reversed the directed verdict for the subcontractor. The plaintiff was injured as the result of walking on a sill plate without fall protection. The responsibility for providing the fall protection was disputed at trial. The plaintiff presented evidence that the general contractor was responsible for all of the safety issues. However, the contractor presented the testimony of the safety expert who opined that the subcontractor was responsible for the means and methods of performing the work on the project and for providing a safe work place for the plaintiff. Thus, the trial court erred in directing a verdict in favor of the subcontractor, and the appellate court remanded the case for a new trial.

In *C.R. Pittman Construction Co. v. United States,*[97.03] a contractor sued the United States, seeking payment for equipment necessary for the performance of two contracts with Army Corps of Engineers to construct flood control project pumping stations, after equipment was damaged by flooding from Hurricane Katrina. The court of claims held that(1) the government was not contractually responsible for uninstalled, off-site, flood-damaged equipment, and (2) the parties' course of performance did not estop Corps from interpreting the contract to preclude compensation for equipment. The appellate court agreed that the government was not responsible for the flood-damaged equipment under the contracts.

This dispute arose after flooding from Hurricane Katrina damaged equipment that was necessary for the performance of two contracts between the contractor and the government. The contractor alleged that a clause in both contracts, specifically the damage to work clause, entitled the contractor to payment for the damaged equipment.

In 2000, the Army Corps of Engineers (the Corps) had awarded C.R. Pittman Construction Co. a fixed-price contract for the construction of a road pumping station. That contract included demolition and removal of the existing pump station, purchase of equipment and materials, and construction of a new pump station. Two years later, the Corps awarded the contractor a second fixed-price contract for the construction of a similar pumping station. That contract included the purchase of equipment and materials, and construction of a new pump station.

As required under the contracts, the contractor purchased the equipment and materials for the contracts, the Corps made progress payments to the plaintiff to purchase specified equipment, and the contractor stored certain equipment and materials at an agreed upon off-site storage area prior to construction and installation. The off-site equipment included generators, climber screen cleaners, and pumps. On August 29, 2005, Hurricane Katrina struck the New Orleans area, flooding the storage sites and damaging the off-site equipment. Both parties agreed that the flood damage to the off-site equipment would require total replacement or substantial refurbishment, prior to its installation.

On March 6 and 7, 2006, the Corps demanded that the contractor replace the damaged equipment. On July 11, 2006, the Corps advised the contractor that the

---

[97.03] 92 Fed. Cl. 20 (Fed.Cl.2010).

Corps had overpaid progress payments, because the damaged equipment's value no longer warranted the progress payments. In response to the government's assertion that the contractor had been overpaid, the contractor put the Corps on administrative notice that the damaged equipment fell under the scope of the damage to work clause as "part of the permanent work" and, therefore, the contracts placed responsibility for the damaged equipment on the Corps.

On April 6, 2007, the contracting officer issued two final decisions pertaining to each contract, ordering the contractor to return to the Corps a total of $2,340,109.53 in progress payments, which were earlier paid for the equipment. On May 3, 2007, the contractor filed suit against the Corps in the United States District Court for the Eastern District of Louisiana, pursuant to the Federal Tort Claims Act, for flood damage to property seeking supplemental jurisdiction or pendent jurisdiction for the Corps' breach of contract. On May 22, 2007, the contractor formally requested a deferment of collection for the contracting officer's order to return payment, in order to avoid financial hardship.

The contracting officer forwarded the contractor's deferment of collection request to the United States Attorney's Office. After an agreement was reached with the United States Attorney's Office deferring collection, the parties submitted a joint order to the district court. The district court issued an order recognizing the deferment of collection agreement, which "granted a deferment of collection of the claim at issue in this case during the pendency of the determination of [Plaintiff's] action against the Corps."

On October 26, 2007, the contracting officer informed the contractor that "all contract earnings that have been withheld prior to September 2007 would continue to be withheld until the resolution of [the matter in the District Court]." After the district court dismissed the matter without prejudice for jurisdictional reasons, the contractor re-filed its action and requested that the court recognize the deferment of collection agreement.

The contractor filed a summary judgment motion on the damage to work clause, arguing that the government was responsible for the damaged equipment. The contractor filed a second summary judgment motion on deferment of collection, in which the contractor argued that the Corps breached the agreement between the parties to defer collection of the amounts specified in the contracting officer's final decisions.

The government moved for partial summary judgment arguing that the contracts imposed responsibility on the contractor for the damaged materials at issue. The government also filed a motion to strike and its response to the plaintiff's deferment of collection claim.

The appellate court held that the responsibility for the cost of the damaged equipment rested upon its interpretation of the damage to work clause, and what was considered "part of the permanent work" under that clause. The plaintiff-contractor raised three arguments to support its claim that the defendant was responsible for the replacement costs of the damaged equipment. First, the plaintiff argued that, by definition and ordinary meaning, the damaged equipment stored off-site was "part of the permanent work" as described in the damage to work clause. Second, the contractor argued that various other clauses within the contracts would be superfluous if the damage to work clause excluded uninstalled equipment as "part of the permanent work." Third, the contractor claimed that the government's course of performance indicated that the damage to work clause applied to the damaged equipment in this case.

In response, the government asserted that: (1) the damage to work clause was not ambiguous; (2) the court should adhere to the ordinary and plain meaning of "part of the permanent work"; and (3) "part of the permanent work" did not include the flood-damaged equipment in this case. The government argued that the contractor did not establish a course of performance that was applicable to these facts.

The appellate court agreed with the government's arguments. First, it held that the ordinary meaning of the damage to work clause did not include the damaged off-site equipment, and, therefore, the government was not responsible for the flood damage to the uninstalled, off-site equipment. Thus, the contractor's claim under the contracts failed. The clause stated:

> The responsibility for damage to any *part of the permanent work* shall be as set forth in the . . . [Permits and Responsibilities Clause]. However, if, in the judgment of the Contracting Officer, any *part of the permanent work* performed by the Contractor is damaged by flood . . . [and] is not due to the failure of the Contractor to take reasonable precautions or to exercise sound engineering and construction practices . . . the Contractor shall make the repairs . . . and full compensation for such repairs will be made . . . as fixed and established in the contract.

The parties agreed that the Board for Contract Appeals had interpreted "permanent work" to be work that was the "chief purpose of the contract." In addition, the plaintiff provided that "permanent work" was "work performed by the contractor which would become a part of the completed project, as opposed to that of a temporary nature which would not become a part of the completed project." Therefore, the contractor contended that the off-site and uninstalled equipment, which would eventually become part of the final pumping station, should be covered under the damage to work clause allowing the contractor to recover the costs of replacing the damaged equipment. Thus, a temporary scaffolding would never be "part of the permanent work." Similarly, it is clear that a foundation, even before project completion, was "part of the permanent work."

The appellate court, however, rejected the contractor's argument. It agreed with the government's interpretation of "part of the permanent work." Applying its ordinary meaning, "part of the permanent work" could not include uninstalled, unincorporated equipment. The purpose of each contract was to construct a pumping station. Therefore, only the pumping stations qualified as "permanent work" under its ordinary meaning. The court found that according to the contractor's reasoning, any piece of equipment that would eventually become part of the final project would be considered "part of the permanent work," and there would be no logical way to draw a line between any bolt being manufactured at a factory and the final installed equipment. As applied to this case, equipment that was stored off-site and not yet incorporated into the final pumping station was not "part of the permanent work." Therefore, the court held that the ordinary meaning of "part of the permanent work" was a subdivision of the whole that was the chief purpose of the contract, and was incorporated into the final project at its ultimate location, and the contractor was responsible for the cost of the flood-damaged equipment.

The contractor argued in the alternative that, if the court were to agree with the government's interpretation of the damage to work clause, that interpretation would render four other provisions in the contracts superfluous. The appellate court disagreed. Although the appellate court had already held that the ordinary meaning of "part of the permanent work" clearly established responsibility on the part of the contractor, the appellate court addressed the four other contract provisions.

The contractor argued that if the appellate court were to accept the government's interpretation, the damage to work clause would be superfluous, because it would add nothing to the contractor's responsibility under the permits and responsibilities clause, which placed responsibility on the contractor for all materials delivered and work performed before completion and acceptance of the entire work. The contractor contended that the damage to work clause applied before final completion, since the clause had to apply to ongoing work so as to not repeat the permits and responsibilities clause.

The appellate court, however, agreed with the government that, pursuant to the permits and responsibilities clause and absent some exception like the damage to work clause, responsibility for damage to equipment lay with the contractor. Furthermore, it was irrelevant whether the damage to work clause applied before final completion, since completion was not the issue in the damage to work clause. Rather, at issue was whether the damaged equipment was "part of the permanent work." Thus, because the appellate court held that the damaged equipment was not "part of the permanent work, the contractor's argument that the damage to work clause applied to "ongoing work" was irrelevant. The damage to work clause shifted responsibility imposed by the permits and responsibilities clause from the contractor to the government when "permanent work" was damaged and before final acceptance. The damage to work clause was not superfluous, because it served as an exception to the permits and responsibilities clause in specific instances. In this case, it would have relieved the contractor from responsibility had the machinery been installed before the Hurricane. That would hardly be seen as "superfluous" by the contractor in that hypothetical case.

In addition, the contractor argued that, after the government made progress payments for the equipment identified in the fixed-price construction clause, title transferred from the contractor to the government, and the equipment became "part of the permanent work." The court, however, agreed with the government that the damage to work clause established that the government's progress payments under the fixed-price construction clause had no effect upon the contractor's responsibility for the purchased materials. The court reasoned that the contractor's interpretation of the fixed-price construction clause was not logical. It would make the other clauses superfluous, instead substituting personal property common law that would on a daily basis give a different answer as to responsibility depending on the flow of purchases and payment. This would replace the relatively straightforward approach that the contracts take. Even under such a regime, it was doubtful the contractor would prevail. The government's narrower interpretation was more accurate. There was nothing in the fixed-price construction clause to indicate that, once the government made progress payments for an item, it became "part of the permanent work" and that the government was responsible for its care.

The contractor further argued that the payment for materials stored off-site clause established that the parties understood that the off-site equipment was to be part of the permanent work, even though uninstalled. In pertinent part, that clause stated that payment for off-site materials would be limited to those that were "approved . . . and fabricated to the point where they are identifiable to an item of work required under the contract." Again, the court held that the damage to work clause did not support the contractor's conclusion, and that items that were "identifiable" as work required under the contract were not necessarily "part of the permanent work" for the purpose of responsibility for flood damage. The appellate court concluded that the concept of "identifiable" was only a payment mechanism. It was not intended to shift legal rights, other than to determine the progress payment schedule. According to the appellate court, the concept came from the Uniform Commercial Code, and dealt with the totally different commercial problem of specific performance by buyers, and also the bankruptcy problem.

The contractor argued that the off-site storage clause indicated that the parties recognized that certain component parts of the pumping station, which were ready to perform the functions of the final project, would be stored off-site and were "part of the permanent work." The court, however, held that the contractor's interpretation was unreasonable, because it would impose on the defendant the risk of loss for any item immediately upon completion of its manufacture, during transit, and while in storage prior to final installation. Such an interpretation would nullify the very meaning of the damage to work clause, thus rendering the government responsible for all component parts without regard to where the parts were when they were damaged. Therefore, the appellate court held that the parties' intent with regard to off-site storage was irrelevant to the definition of "part of the permanent work," since they were two separate issues. As a result, the appellate court held that the contractor's arguments, regarding the four other clauses, failed to show that the damage to work clause was superfluous in light of the other provisions.

Finally, the contractor contended that both parties were engaged in a course of performance that was contrary to the government's interpretation of the damage to work clause; therefore, the government should be estopped from advancing its interpretation. The appellate court, however, agreed with the government that none of the instances cited by the contractor established a course of performance contrary to the contractor's interpretation of the damage to work clause.

In general, course of performance evidence was relevant to contract interpretation only when the terms of the contract were ambiguous. Absent any ambiguity, the ordinary meaning controlled unless the parties intended otherwise and agreed upon it, either explicitly or implicitly.

In this case, the contractor argued that four specific instances established a course of performance contrary to the government's interpretation. First, the contractor stated that the government told the contractor's CEO, in a pre-construction meeting, that "in case of any flood events, the contractor will be protected for damage to the *ongoing* work by the Damage to Work Clause." Second, the contractor claimed that the government's past compensation for flood damage indicated that the government would compensate the contractor for the damaged equipment at issue. The past instances of flood damage were related to: (1) the hurricane; (2) various portions of work that were not permanently installed; and (3) clean-up expenses on the project site. Third, the contractor argued that on the government's other projects, which involved drainage improvement in the New Orleans area, the government compensated the contractor under the damage to work clause for damage done to portions of incomplete work, permanently installed work, and work that was affixed to the permanent work. Fourth, the contractor claimed that the government took possession of the damaged equipment and had been repairing it at the government's expense, instead of directing the contractor to do so.

First, the appellate court agreed with the government with regard to the pre-construction meeting, because the government could not be estopped, except by the conduct of a person with authority to bind the United States. Here, the contractor did not identify who had authority to bind the government with regard to the alleged modification, and the government argued that the meeting minutes referred to flood damage that was consistent with the language of the damage to work clause. Thus, the affidavit from the contractor's CEO, even when read in the light most favorable to the contractor, did not show that the government modified the clause.

Second, with regard to the past compensation for damage to uninstalled work, the appellate court agreed that the government only compensated the contractor for items damaged due to government-directed flooding. Here, unlike in the instance cited by the contractor, the damage to uninstalled equipment was not caused by the government's directed flooding, but by an act of God.

Third, the appellate court further agreed with the government with regard to other projects in the New Orleans area. Here, the contractor was never compensated under the damage to work clause for hurricane-caused flooding, which damaged items that were not "part of the permanent work." Instead, the government only compensated the contractor for damage caused by government-directed flooding. Finally, the appellate court agreed with the government that it never took possession of, or responsibility for, the damaged equipment. Any amount to be paid for the repair and replacement of the equipment was to be paid out of the original contract price.

It was clear to the appellate court that the other instances cited by the contractor were isolated instances and not inconsistent with the government's interpretation. Therefore, because course of performance evidence was only relevant to contract interpretation if the terms of the instrument were ambiguous, and because the ordinary meaning of the damage to work clause was clear and unambiguous, the contractor's course of performance arguments did not change the appellate court's holding.

Accordingly, the appellate court held that the damage to work clause in the contracts placed responsibility on the plaintiff-contractor for the damaged equipment.

When there is a workplace injury, the court closely examines control and supervision of the job site in order to equitably distribute the damages associated with an injury or death. In *McCarthy v. Turner Construction,*[97.1] the plaintiff, John McCarthy, a journeyman electrician, sought damages for injuries he sustained when he fell from a ladder while at a building work site in Times Square on March 2, 2005. McCarthy and his wife, who asserted derivative claims, sued two owners of the building, defendants Boston Properties, Inc. and Times Square Tower Associates, LLC (collectively, the owners), and the general contractor on the job, the defendant, John Gallin & Son, Inc. (Gallin). Gallin impleaded its subcontractor, Linear Technologies, Inc. (Linear), which impleaded its own subcontractor, Samuels Datacom, LLC (Samuels). Samuels was McCarthy's employer.

Following a bifurcated jury trial on the issue of negligence, and settlement of a jury trial on damages, the owners moved for judgment in their favor on their cross-claim for common-law indemnification against Gallin.

Non-party Ann Taylor, Inc. had hired Gallin as a construction manager, pursuant to a Standard Form of Agreement Between Owner and Construction Manager, AIA Document A121/Cmc and AGC Document 565 (1991) (Agreement). Section 3.3.1 of the General Conditions of the Contract for Construction to the Agreement (AIA Document A201-1987) stated:

> The Contractor [Gallin] shall supervise and direct the Work, using the Contractor's best skill and attention. The Contractor shall be solely responsible for and have control over construction means, methods, techniques, sequences and procedures for coordinating all portions of the Work under the Contract.

By decision and order dated May 16, 2007, the trial court granted, among other things, the plaintiffs' motion for summary judgment as to liability on their Labor Law §§ 240(1) claim against the owners. The trial court found that "Gallin had no supervisory authority over Samuels's work," and that "Gallin did not provide any tools or ladders to the subcontractors who worked at the site." The appellate division affirmed that decision.[97.2] Gallin did not direct McCarthy or his work. Gallin did not provide any ladders at the job site.

At a court conference with the parties' counsel on November 5, 2008, the parties agreed to separate trials of certain issues in this action. The first trial was on the specific issue whether the plaintiff, John McCarthy or his employer, Samuels, was negligent, and whether such negligence was a substantial factor in

[97.1] 24 Misc. 3d 1245(A), 2009 N.Y. Slip Op. 51889(U) (N.Y. Sup. Ct. 2009).

[97.2] McCarthy v. Turner Constr., Inc., 52 A.D.3d 333, 859 N.Y.S.2d 648 (1st Dep't 2008), *claim dismissed, motion denied,* 2009 N.Y. Misc. LEXIS 2289 (N.Y. Sup. Sept. 7, 2009).

causing the accident, so as to trigger Linear's duty to indemnify Gallin and the owners. The second trial focused on the plaintiffs' damages. The parties agreed that the trial court would determine the remaining indemnification issues on papers to be submitted.

It is undisputed that, at the first trial, the jury did not find that Samuels was negligent. The second trial was settled in open court for $1.6 million. The owners agreed to pay half of the settlement amount; Gallin contributed the other half. On the record, counsel to the owners stated, "At the present time there certainly is a common law indemnity claim that has been asserted by Boston Properties and Time Square Tower Associates that hasn't been disposed of."

The trial court noted:

> I don't think there's any doubt that Boston Properties and Times Square Associates asserted such a claim . . . But whether it has already been disposed, for example, as a result of the summary judgment decision which is law of the case and binding on everyone or whether otherwise anything said in this trial, it is premature to give you an advisory opinion on that now.
>
> So, I understand your reservation of rights, but that doesn't-that doesn't determine, and it shouldn't be viewed as an agreement by anybody that such rights currently exists. So, it's whatever rights, if any, that you are reserving, and you can bring an appropriate motion to get that determined should you not be able to work that out amicably together.

On appeal, the court rejected Gallin's argument on appeal that the motion was an untimely motion for summary judgment. The parties had agreed that, after the trials, the trial court would determine the remaining indemnification issues on papers submitted. Thus, the parties agreed, in effect, to a bench trial of the owners' indemnification claims against Gallin, to be decided on papers by motion. The trial court expressly permitted the instant motion on the day of the settlement in open court. The owners' motion was not one for summary judgment.

Contrary to Gallin's argument, the record did not support a finding that the owners waived their cross claim for indemnification against Gallin at the court conference. "A waiver is not created by negligence, oversight, or thoughtlessness, and cannot be inferred from 'mere silence.' Rather, there must be proof that there was a voluntary and intentional relinquishment of a known and otherwise enforceable right." Here, nothing in the transcript of the conference with the trial court on November 5, 2008 evinced an intent of Boston Properties LLC or Times Square Tower Associates, LLC to waive or discontinue their cross-claim for indemnification against Gallin. On the contrary, Boston Properties LLC and Times Square Tower Associates, LLC continued to insist that their indemnification claim remained even after they offered $800,000 to settle the action.

A party may settle and then seek indemnification from the party responsible for the wrongdoing as long as the settling party shows that it may not be held liable in any degree. However, the owners and Gallin disagreed as to the applicable standard for determining the party responsible for the wrongdoing.

The owners relied on *Rodriguez v. Metropolitan Life Insurance Co.*,[97.3] and its progeny, such as *Hernandez v. Two E. End Ave Apt. Corp.*[97.4] In *Rodriguez*, the Appellate Division, First Department stated, "a subcontractor may be obligated to indemnify under the common law upon proof that its actual negligence caused an accident, but it can also be held liable where it had the authority to direct, supervise and control the work giving rise to the injury."[97.5]

The owners contended that Gallin's contractual authority under its agreement with non-party, Ann Taylor Inc., to supervise and direct construction work was sufficient to establish that it had the "authority to direct, supervise and control the work giving rise to the injury" articulated in *Rodriguez* and *Hernandez*.

Gallin relied on cases holding that when an owner is held liable for injuries solely by virtue of the provisions of Labor Law §§ 240(1), despite its lack of supervision or control over the work being done or proof of actual negligence, the owner was entitled to indemnity from the party who was actually responsible for the supervision, direction and control of the work the plaintiff was performing at the time of injury.[97.6] To determine which standard should control, the appellate court returned to *Rodriguez*, which formulated the standard that differs from the cases that Gallin cited. *Rodriguez* cited *Terranova v. City of New York* for the proposition that a subcontractor is liable for common-law indemnification where "it had the authority to direct, supervise and control the work giving rise to the injury." In *Terranova*, the quote appears in its full context as follows:

> Labor Law §§ 240(1) imposes no liability on a subcontractor for job site injuries unless the subcontractor had **the authority to direct, supervise and control the work giving rise to the injury,** the burden being on the party asserting such liability, here the general contractor, "to present evidence of the particular defendant's supervision and control of the activity which resulted in [the] injury" [citation omitted]. Of course, a subcontractor can also be held liable upon proof that its actual negligence contributed to the accident.[97.7]

The court in *Terranova* discussed two bases for liability: (1) the liability of the subcontractor as agent under Labor Law §§ 240(1), which is grounded upon the authority to direct, supervise, and control the work[97.8] and (2) the subcontractor's liability under a theory of negligence. It would appear that *Rodriguez* quoted the language from *Terranova*, which set forth an agent's liability under Labor Law §§ 240(1), to formulate the subcontractor's liability for common-law indemnification. In doing so, *Rodriguez* held that a subcontractor liable under Labor Law §§ 240(1) was, therefore, liable for common-law indemnification to a

---

[97.3] 234 A.D.2d 156, 651 N.Y.S.2d 475 (1st Dep't 1996).

[97.4] 303 A.D.2d 556, 757 N.Y.S.2d 65 (2d Dep't 2003).

[97.5] *Rodriguez*, 234 A.D.2d at 156, *citing* Terranova v. City of New York, 197 A.D.2d 402, 602 N.Y.S.2d 830 (1st Dep't 1993).

[97.6] Carr v. Jacob Perl Assoc., 201 A.D.2d 296, 297, 607 N.Y.S.2d 301 (1st Dep't 1994); Cava Constr. Co., Inc. v. Gealtec Remodeling Corp., 58 A.D.3d 660, 661-62, 871 N.Y.S.2d 654 (2d Dep't 2009).

[97.7] *Terranova*, 197 A.D.2d at 402 (emphasis added indicating matter quoted in *Rodriguez*).

[97.8] Russin v. Louis N. Picciano & Son, 54 N.Y.2d 311, 318, 445 N.Y.S.2d 127 (1981).

party whose liability under the statute was only vicarious, i.e., the owner who neither controls nor directs the injured plaintiff's work.

In more recent decisions citing *Rodriguez,* the Appellate Division ruled that indemnification lies against the party that "had direct control over the work giving rise to the injury."[97.9] The court stated that it could not follow the cases cited by the owners. To establish entitlement to common-law indemnification against a party "actually responsible" for the plaintiff's work, the indemnitee must establish that the party "had direct control over the work giving rise to the injury." A contract for construction work with a general contractor or construction manager was not, in itself, sufficient to establish that the general contractor or construction manager actually supervised or had direct control over the injured plaintiff's work, when the general contractor or construction manager contracted the plaintiff's work to a subcontractor. Under those circumstances, it was not reasonable to infer that the general contractor or construction manager had direct control over the plaintiff's work.

Neither the general contractor's or construction manager's inspection privileges nor a general power of supervision over construction work is sufficient to establish actual supervision or direct control. Otherwise, every general contractor or construction manager would owe a common law duty to indemnify the owner, because inspection privileges and/or a general power to supervise are typical duties of a general contractor or a construction manager, as set forth in the construction contract.

The owners pointed to *Ortega v. Catamount Construction Corp.*,[97.10] where the appellate division affirmed the ruling of the lower court granting the owner summary judgment against the construction manager for common-law indemnity, even though the appellate court stated that there was no evidence that the construction manager had direct supervision over the injured plaintiff's work. The appellate court agreed with Gallin that *Ortega* should not be followed in light of the recent appellate cases.

In the prior decision and order dated May 7, 2007, the trial court had found that "Gallin had no supervisory authority over Samuels's work," and "Gallin did not provide any tools or ladders to the subcontractors who worked at the site." The appellate court made the same findings on this motion, based on Kondracki's deposition testimony. Gallin's contract with non-party, Ann Taylor, Inc., was not sufficient to establish that Gallin was a party that had direct control over the work giving rise to the injury. The trial court held that the testimony that Gallin walked the job site for dangerous conditions, or that Gallin had given instructions at safety meetings was insufficient to impose liability on Gallin. The owners were held not entitled to common-law indemnification against Gallin.

The appellate court found in favor of the defendant, Gallin. Gallin was granted a judgment dismissing the cross-claim of the defendants, Boston Properties, Inc. and Times Square Tower Associates, LLC.

[97.9] *See, e.g.*, Mejia v. Levenbaum, 57 A.D.3d 216, 393 N.Y.S.2d 1005 (1st Dep't 2008).

[97.10] 264 A.D.2d 323, 694 N.Y.S.2d 367 (1st Dep't 1999).

Contract review by an attorney for any party in construction should include particular attention to responsibility for workplace safety, and responsibility for the means and methods of construction to avoid unanticipated liability for personal injury or death, which occurs on a project.

The question who is responsible for workplace safety and control over construction means and methods may prevent a case from being decided by summary judgment. In *Santos v. Ashforth, Co.*,[97.11] a Connecticut superior court denied a motion for summary judgment on a project using AIA A401, the AIA form subcontract, where there was a material issue of fact whether the general contractor exercised control sufficiently over the subcontractor's work so as to be liable for a workplace injury of a subcontractor's employees. In *Santos*, the plaintiffs, Jose Santos and Oscar Pena, were injured during the course of their employment with the defendant, Jose Gomez , d/b/a Gola Roofing on November 9, 2000. On that date, Gola Roofing had hired the plaintiffs to apply roofing paper to the New CanaanTeenCenter, then under construction. Gola Roofing was hired the previous day (without a written contract or subcontract) by the roofing subcontractor, the defendant, Antonelli Roofing, to put up the roofing paper on an expedited schedule.

The plaintiffs both fell from the steeply pitched roof of the Teen Center when one or more roof brackets supporting the planks upon which they were standing collapsed, causing the planks and both plaintiffs, who were not wearing safety harnesses or any other restraining device, to fall approximately 27 feet to the edge of the roof where they hit the scaffolding which failed to stop their fall, and then fell about another 14½ feet from the eave onto a concrete slab. Both plaintiffs sustained personal injuries for which they claim moneyed damages from all defendants.

Count One of the amended complaint stated the negligence claim of the plaintiff, Jose Santos, against the general contractor (AP Construction, Inc.). Count Five stated the negligence claim of the plaintiff, Oscar Pena, against AP Construction. Count Four was derivative of Count One and stated the loss of consortium claim of the plaintiff, Lilliana Ruiz, the wife of Jose Santos. The negligence claims of the plaintiffs against AP Construction included allegations that it, as the general contractor at the job site, failed to exercise reasonable care in the selection of a roofing subcontractor; failed to provide a safe workplace; failed to implement and enforce rules for workplace safety; failed to require the roofing subcontractor to comply with the job site safety rules promulgated by AP Construction; failed to supervise and inspect the work of the roofing subcontractor; failed to comply or require the roofing subcontractor to comply with OSHA regulations including the OSHA "6 foot rule" for roofing work; and "failed, as controlling employer with general supervisory authority over the job site, to comply with all safety measures including all applicable laws, ordinances, rules, regulations and orders of public authorities for the safety of persons."

The defendant submitted a motion for summary judgment to the trial court on December 17, 2007, in which it claimed that there was no triable issue of

[97.11] 2009 Conn. Super. LEXIS 353, 2009 WL 567208 (2009).

fact, and that the undisputed record showed that it was entitled to judgment as a matter of law in that: (1) since it did not hire, employ, control or supervise the injured workers, it owed no duty to the plaintiffs, and (2) there was no basis upon which a reasonable jury could conclude that AP Construction was negligent.

Both parties submitted extensive factual materials to the trial court, including excerpts from the depositions of AP Construction job site supervisor, Thomas Coleman, Antonelli Roofing principal, John Antonelli, and Antonelli Roofing foreman Hector Comacho. In addition, the defendant, AP Construction, submitted the written subcontract (on the form of AIA Document A401) between AP Construction and Antonelli Roofing, and an affidavit of John E. Antonelli. The plaintiffs submitted copies of Thomas Coleman's job site notes, the OSHA investigative report, photographs of the accident site, photographs of the "Job Safety Rules" sign posted at the site by AP Construction, and a report and affidavit of its expert Dr. John Mroszczyk.

The primary issue was whether or not, or under what circumstances, a general contractor had a duty to protect and safeguard the subcontractors' employees. As to AP Construction, Gola Roofing (the employer of the injured plaintiffs) was an independent subcontractor of AP Construction's independent roofing subcontractor, Antonelli Roofing.

In Connecticut, as a general rule, "an employer is not liable for the negligence of its independent contractors." *Pelletier et al. v. Sordoni/Skansa Construction Co.* (*Pelletier II*).[97.12] The premise underlying this general rule that is that "the assumption and exercise of control over the offending area is deemed to be in the independent contractor."[97.13]

The court in *Pelletier II* overruled part of the court's earlier decision in *Pelletier et al. v. Sordoni/Skansa Construction Co.* (*Pelletier I*),[97.14] which had held that, as a matter of law, an employee of an independent contractor could never pursue a common-law negligence claim against another contractor, limiting a contractor's liability to only innocent third parties. *Pelletier II* held that an employee of a subcontractor was not restricted as a matter of law from pursuing a claim against a general contractor.

The *Pelletier II* court stressed, however, that in order to succeed on its claim, the plaintiff employee had to establish a basis for the contractor's liability under the case law—i.e., show that the facts fell within one of the exceptions to the general rule of nonliability of a general contractor. The court identified four such exceptions to the general rule: (1) the work contracted for was intrinsically dangerous; (2) the independent contractor hired was incompetent or untrustworthy; (3) the general contractor had a legal duty to see that the work was performed properly; and (4) the general contractor exercised control over the subcontractor. 264 Conn.at 591-692.

In this case, the defendant claimed that, as a matter of law, none of the *Pelletier II* exceptions applied to this case. In contrast, the plaintiffs claimed that

---

[97.12] 264 Conn. 509, 517, 825 A.2d 72 (2003).

[97.13] Darling v. Burrone Bros., Inc., 162 Conn. 187, 196 (1972).

[97.14] 262 Conn. 372 (2003).

there were genuine disputed issucs of fact as to the application of all the *Pelletier II* exceptions. The court found that there were genuine disputed issues of fact as to the control issue, which prevented it from entering summary judgment in favor of AP Construction as a matter of law.

Pelletier II remanded the case for trial. The case was tried to a jury in the superior court on the negligence and loss of consortium counts (the very same counts outstanding against AP Construction in the case). Following a jury verdict for the plaintiffs which the trial court declined to set aside, both parties appealed and the case went to the Connecticut Supreme Court for a third time (*Pelletier III*).[97.15] On the plaintiffs' cross appeal, one of the issues was the trial court's refusal to instruct the jury that Sordoni, the general contractor had a duty as the general contractor to exercise reasonable care with respect to any part of the work site or inspection process over which it retained control.

Pelletier involved a claim that the general contractor had a duty to inspect the weld which failed, permitting a steel beam to fall on the plaintiff, an employee of the structural steel subcontractor who had a contract obligation to inspect all welds. The court held that the general contractor was not in control of the fabrication and inspection of welds, because "a fair and reasonable person could reach but one conclusion as to who exercised control . . ." In reaching that position, the *Pelletier II* court relied on the fact that the contract documents required the subcontractor to fabricate and inspect the welds at its own shop, thus clearly demonstrating that the general contractor did not retain control over "the area or instrumentality" that caused the plaintiff harm.[97.16] "It [Sordoni] thus had no control over the shop in which the welds were fabricated or the manner in which the inspections were to be performed . . ." The court rejected the argument that an orientation and procedures manual that Sordoni provided to the subcontractor indicating that Sordoni would conduct its own weekly inspections to ensure compliance with its safety program was evidence of an exercise of control by Sordoni. The manual was not a legally binding contract, but rather "an informational tool designed to educate the plaintiff in the protocols for the job site . . . [It was] strictly informational."[97.17]

In *Archambault v. Soneco/Northeastern, Inc.*,[97.18] the Connecticut Supreme Court addressed whether or not a general contractor had a nondelegable duty to the plaintiff subcontractor's employee to ensure a safe construction site, because the general contractor had allegedly exercised control over the excavation of trenches at the site. The court remanded the case for a new trial because of an error in ruling on evidence, but addressed the control issue because that issue "was likely to arise in the new trial,"[97.19] The *Archambault*court found that the trial court had improperly instructed the jury that the general contractor had such a nondelegable duty.

[97.15] Pelletier et al. v. Sordoni/Skansa Constr. Co., 286 Conn. 563 (2008).

[97.16] 286 Conn. 563, 602.

[97.17] *Id.*

[97.18] 287 Conn. 20, 946 A.2d 839 (2008).

[97.19] 287 Conn. 20, 41.

There was evidence that the contract between Konover (the general contractor) and Soneco (the excavation and site work subcontractor) obligated Soneco to comply with all applicable laws and regulatory safety rules (including OSHA regulations), and to observe and comply with the Safety Project Plan. Konover had provided Soneco with a copy of its construction safety manual. This gave Konover's site superintendents the power to conduct weekly job site safety meetings, conduct safety inspections, and to issue violation notices to subcontractors. Konover also published a safety manual for excavations. Konover superintendents were authorized to halt activities that could constitute a safety violation. The Konover site supervisor testified that he was in "overall control" of the 10-acre construction site. He also testified that "the buck stopped with Konover" on overall safety and "It was my job to make sure that the contractors did the best they could with regard to safety."[97.20] In finding that under these circumstances that the nondelegable duty instruction had been improper, the appellate court found that a reasonable person could reach but one conclusion: Soneco, and not Konover, was in control and was responsible for safety at the site. The court said: "Overall responsibility for safety on the work site, however, does not necessarily translate into a nondelegable duty."[97.21]

The appellate court found that Konover's safety manual was not the source of a contractual or legal duty to provide a safe work site but was merely an informational tool.

> Although the safety manual described Konover's interest in providing safe conditions on the work site, it did not suggest that Konover would engage in daily supervision of its subcontractor's employees . . . Rather, the manual suggested that Konover would foster safety by developing site specific safety plans to identify potential hazards that might arise . . . *None of the safety concerns discussed in the manual involved control over the manner in which specific tasks would be performed by the subcontractor's employees.*[97.22]

In *Santos*, in their post-*Pelletier III* and *Archambault* supplemental memoranda, AP Construction argued that it, like Konover, had only general overall supervision over safety at the Darien Teen Center work site, while the plaintiffs argued that there was evidence from which a reasonable juror could find that AP Construction went beyond the role of an overall supervisor and exercised control over the manner in which subcontractors performed their duties so as to ensure safety.

A juror could have concluded that the sign posted at the premises was more binding and obligatory than a mere "informational tool." For example, the sign stated:

> OSHA's 6-foot rule in proper fall protection *is to be utilized* as required.
>
> The following safety requirements are mandatory:

[97.20] 287 Conn. 20, 51.

[97.21] 287 Conn. 20, 54.

[97.22] 287 Conn. 20, 55.

Eye protection *must be worn* when using power tools . . .

Gloves *must be* worn . . .

Hard hats *must be worn* at all times . . .

Furthermore, Thomas Coleman testified at deposition that it was part of his job to "make sure that these rules were enforced," and that he had authority to stop work if he thought it was not being done in a safe manner. Yet, he testified that he saw the plaintiffs working on the roof (obviously more than six feet above ground) without wearing safety harnesses. There was also a notation in his job notes that, sometime prior to the date of the plaintiffs' fall, he: "[r]eviewed safety, parking and site storing requirements, w/ Panel Pro's foreman (Brian) . . . Warned Panel Pros that they *all* need to wear hart hats & [be] 'tied off.' They were tied off but not all wore hard hats. R. Marin gave out 2 for their use." This, at least suggested that AP Construction was passing out safety equipment to subcontractor employees and requiring that it be used, which could support a finding of control even under the *Pelletier III/Archambault* criteria.

This was not a case where a reasonable juror could reach no conclusion other than that AP Construction was not in control of safety at the job site. That issue was a genuine issue of material fact which could not be decided by a motion for summary judgment. For the reasons herein stated trial court denied the motion for summary judgment.

In *Staub v. William H. Lane, Inc.*,[97.23] an employee of the subcontractor brought an action against a general contractor for negligence and brought claims under New York Labor Law. The parties had used the AIA A401 form subcontract. The general contractor sought third-party indemnification from the subcontractor for indemnification. The trial court had granted the general contractor partial summary judgment on its indemnification claim, and the subcontractor appealed.

The New York Supreme Court, Appellate Division held that a genuine issue of material fact precluded summary judgment on the indemnity claim, reversing the trial court's grant of summary judgment. The court held that there was a genuine issue of material fact as to whether the general contractor and its subcontractor agreed to be bound by the indemnification provision of the form contract incorporated by an unsigned, written proposal. Thus, an order of the supreme court was entered on November 20, 2007, partially granting the defendant's cross-motion for summary judgment seeking contractual indemnification from the third-party defendant.

In *Staub*, the plaintiff, an employee of subcontractor third-party defendant, was injured while installing a steel beam on a building in the village of Johnson City, BroomeCounty. He commenced the underlying action against the general contractor for the project, asserting causes of action sounding in negligence and Labor Law §§ 200(1), §§ 240(1) and §§ 241(6). Following a joinder of issue, the defendant commenced a third-party action seeking contractual indemnification

---

[97.23] 58 A.D.3d 933, 870 N.Y.S.2d 630 (2009).

from a third-party defendant based upon an unsigned, written proposal submitted by third-party defendant.

The proposal purported to incorporate the terms of AIA Document A401 into the quote, and was accepted by the defendant orally. The parties did not, however, sign a formal, written contract containing an express agreement to indemnify. AIA Form A401, which was not transmitted to defendant along with the proposal, contains the following indemnity provision:

> To the fullest extent permitted by law, the [s]ubcontractor shall indemnify and hold harmless the [o]wner, [c]ontractor . . . from and against claims, damages, losses and expenses, including but not limited to attorney's fees, arising out of or resulting from performance of the [s]ubcontractor's Work under this [s]ubcontract . . . but only to the extent caused by the negligent acts or omissions of the [s]ubcontractor . . .

The third-party defendant moved for summary judgment dismissing the third-party complaint in its entirety, and the defendant cross-moved for summary judgment on its indemnification claim. The New York Supreme Court denied the third-party defendant's motion, and it granted the defendant's cross-motion in part, directing that the defendant be granted conditional indemnification and defense by the third-party defendant in connection with the underlying action. The third-party defendant appealed, and the appellate court modified by denying defendant's cross-motion for summary judgment in its entirety.

New York Workers' Compensation Law §§ 11 precludes third-party indemnification claims against employers unless the claim is "based upon a provision in a written contract entered into prior to the accident or occurrence by which the employer had expressly agreed to contribution to or indemnification of the claimant or person asserting the cause of action for the type of loss suffered."

Whether a written contract satisfies section 11 involves a two-part inquiry. First, the court considers whether the parties entered into a written contract containing an indemnity provision applicable to the site or job where the injury giving rise to the indemnity claim took place. Second, if so, the court examines whether the indemnity provision was sufficiently particular to meet the requirements of section 11.[97.24] The parties' dispute centered on whether the first prong of the two-part inquiry had been met.

A written agreement could be enforceable if "the course of conduct between [the parties], including their writings . . . was sufficient to spell out a binding contract, notwithstanding the failure of the parties to sign [an] integrated agreement."[97.25] Thus, the parties' course of conduct must be reviewed "to

[97.24] Rodrigues v. N & S Bldg. Contractors, Inc., 5 N.Y.3d 427, 432, 839 N.E.2d 357, 805 N.Y.S.2d 299 (2005).

[97.25] Flores v. Lower E. Side Serv. Ctr., Inc., 4 N.Y.3d 363, 368, 828 N.E.2d 593, 795 N.Y.S.2d 491 (2005), *quoting* Brown Bros. Elec. Contractors v. Beam Constr. Corp., 41 N.Y.2d 397, 399, 361 N.E.2d 999, 393 N.Y.S.2d 350 (1977).

determine whether there was a meeting of the minds sufficient to give rise to an enforceable contract."[97.26]

In this case, the third-party defendant included a note on its written proposal. This was the only written document governing the work performed. This document purported to incorporate the terms of AIA Contract A401. A401 includes an indemnity provision running from the employer (third-party defendant) to the contractor (defendant), as noted above. Nevertheless, third-party defendant's president, Peter Browning, indicated that the parties never used a formal AIA Contract A401 in their prior agreements. The defendant generally submitted its own written contract after receiving proposals, and Browning expected and intended that practice to be followed on this occasion.

This testimony was consistent with a statement from the defendant's senior project manager that the formal subcontract that defendant typically used was not supplied in connection with the job at issue. The court noted that while Browning admitted during his deposition that formal subcontracts were not always used, and arguably stated that he intended AIA Contract A401, including the indemnification provision, to apply to this project, the record indicated that AIA Contract A401 was never provided to the defendant. Given the failure to provide the indemnification provision of AIA Contract A401 and the absence of any evidence that the parties agreed to that provision through either past practice or their course of conduct, the New York Supreme Court concluded that questions of fact existed as to whether the parties agreed to be bound by the indemnification provisions of AIA Contract A401.[97.27]

In *Staub*, the New York court denied the defendant's cross-motion for summary judgment in its entirety, and it modified the trial court's order, with costs to third-party defendant, by reversing so much thereof as partially granted defendant's cross-motion for summary judgment.

Contract review by an attorney for any party in construction should include particular attention to responsibility for workplace safety, and responsibility for the means and methods of construction to avoid unanticipated liability for personal injury or death which occurs on a project.

There can also be issue over who is an employee in the context of bringing an action against a contractor.

In *Varisco v. Gateway Science & Engineering, Inc.*,[97.28] a construction inspector brought an action against a construction company for tortious termination of employment contract in violation of public policy, breach of implied contract of continued employment, and breach of implied covenant of good faith and fair dealing. The trial court granted summary judgment for the company, and the inspector appealed. The appellate court affirmed the trial court, and held that

---

[97.26] Flores v. Lower E. Side Serv. Ctr., Inc., 4 N.Y.3d at 370, 828 N.E.2d 593, 795 N.Y.S.2d 491 (2005).

[97.27] *See* Mentesana v. Bernard Janowitz Constr. Corp., 36 A.D.3d 769, 771, 828 N.Y.S.2d 522 (2007); Gilbert v. Albany Med. Ctr., 21 A.D.3d 677, 678, 799 N.Y.S.2d 685 (2005); Miller v. Mott's Inc., 5 A.D.3d 1019, 1020, 773 N.Y.S.2d 727 (2004).

[97.28] 166 Cal. App. 4th 1099, 83 Cal. Rptr. 3d 393 (2008).

the inspector was not an employee of the company and thus, he could not bring the causes of action alleged.

Appellant Al Varisco sued respondent Gateway Science and Engineering for wrongful termination of employment and similar causes of action, all of which depended on the allegation that he had been Gateway's employee. Gateway moved for summary judgment on the ground that Varisco was not an employee, but an independent contractor. The trial court found for Gateway, and the appellate court affirmed. All the undisputed facts added up to an independent contractor relationship. A single clause in the parties' letter agreement, which allowed either party to terminate at will, did not transform that relationship into an employment relationship.

Gateway provided professional services, such as project management, planning and design management, inspection, and quality assurance to the construction industry. Varisco was a construction inspector and had a Class-1 Inspector certification from the California Division of the State Architect (DSA). In early 2004, Varisco contacted Gateway, seeking work. Gateway then had a contract with the Los Angeles Unified School District (LAUSD), under which it was to provide certified project inspectors for projects then under construction.

Gateway responded to Varisco's call, and on January 30, 2004, Varisco and Gateway signed a letter agreement in which Varisco agreed to provide "DSA Inspection Services to the Los AngelesUnifiedSchool District (Client)" and Gateway agreed to pay him an hourly rate. Varisco provided inspection services on two Gateway-LAUSD projects. His relationship with Gateway ended in November 2004, when Gateway sent him a letter terminating the agreement, citing his refusal to sign a new contract or to provide various documents.

Varisco filed suit, bringing causes of action for tortious termination of employment contract in violation of public policy, breach of implied contract of continued employment, and breach of the implied covenant of good faith and fair dealing. Each cause of action alleged that Varisco was Gateway's employee. Gateway moved for summary judgment, contending that Varisco was an independent contractor, not an employee. The trial court found that Varisco had no evidence to dispute the assertion that he was an independent contractor pursuant to an at-will agreement, and granted the motion. On appeal, Varisco conceded that the causes of action were viable only if he was an employee, not an independent contractor.[97.29]

The appellate court stated that the question on appeal was whether the company met its burden of showing that an element of each cause of action, that Varisco was an employee, could not be established, under *Union Bank v. Superior Court*,[97.30] or whether, as Varisco contended, there was a triable issue of fact on the question of his employment status.

The *Varisco* court stated that control is the principal factor in determining whether an individual worker is an employee or an independent contractor. Citing

---

[97.29] *See* Sistare-Meyer v. Young Men's Christian Ass'n, 58 Cal. App. 4th 10, 14, 67 Cal. Rptr. 2d 840 (1997).

[97.30] 31 Cal. App. 4th 573, 37 Cal. Rptr. 2d 653 (1995).

S.A. Gerrard Co. v. Industrial Accident Comm'n,[97.31] the *Varisco* court stated that the most significant question was whether the person to whom the service is rendered has the right to control the manner and means of accomplishing the result desired. Other factors cited by the *Varisco* court included: (a) whether the one performing services is engaged in a distinct occupation or business; (b) the kind of occupation, with reference to whether, in the locality, the work is usually done under the direction of the principal or by a specialist without supervision; (c) the skill required in the particular occupation; (d) whether the principal or the worker supplies the instrumentalities, tools, and the place of work for the person doing the work; (e) the length of time for which the services are to be performed; (f) the method of payment, whether by the time or by the job; (g) whether or not the work is a part of the regular business of the principal; and (h) whether or not the parties believe they are creating the relationship of employer-employee.

According to the parties' written agreement, Varisco was compensated by Gateway at $75 per hour, with no benefits such as medical, dental, paid sick leave, vacation, and holidays. Gateway was to cover Varisco for professional and general liability insurance, and Varisco would be required to complete Gateway time sheets. The written agreement also stated that overtime did not apply, unless authorized by the school district. The *Varisco* court held that when Varisco signed the written agreement, he understood that he was entering into an independent contractor relationship and not an employment relationship, and he so testified at his deposition. He also testified that he did not work for Gateway, and that Gateway acted as his agent to connect him to the school district. Varisco stated that he did not, would not, and would never work for Gateway.

Varisco received a 1099 for his compensation from Gateway, and Gateway did not supply uniform, apparel, equipment, materials, or tools to Varisco. Varisco wore his own hardhat and work boots, which were mandatory apparel at the job site. Varisco used his own car for transportation to and from the job site, and was not reimbursed for mileage or gas. Varisco's work hours were established by the architect of record, not by Gateway. He went to the Gateway office twice a month to pick up his paycheck, and never at any other time. If he had to call in sick, he called the school district, not Gateway.

The *Varisco* court held that the undisputed facts established that Varisco was an independent contractor of Gateway, and not an employee. The court stated that the issue on appeal was the right to control the manner and means of accomplishing Varisco's work. The court held that Gateway had no such control, and no right to such control.

Varisco argued that some of the factors showed that he was an employee. He argued that construction inspection was a part of Gateway's business, and the fact that he was paid by the hour, not the project, indicated that he was an employee. The *Varisco* court pointed out that although an hourly rate suggested an employment relationship, independent contractors are commonly paid on that basis. The court stated that even if those two factors suggested an employment relationship, all of the factors, when weighed and considered as a whole, show

[97.31] 17 Cal. 2d 411, 413, 110 P.2d 377 (1941).

that Varisco was not an employee. The appellate court affirmed the trial court's grant of the motion of Gateway for summary judgment because Varisco was not an employee of Gateway.

In *Chin v. Namvar*,[97.32] a painter who fell from a ladder while painting at a shopping center brought an action against those who hired him for unfair competition, Labor Code violations, wrongful termination, and negligence. The trial court entered judgment for defendants, finding the painter was not an employee. The painter appealed.

The appellate court held that (1) one who misrepresents himself as a licensed contractor is estopped from asserting that his unlicensed status makes him an employee; (2) the burden was on the defendants to show misrepresentation estopping the painter from claiming employee status; (3) the painter's misrepresentation estopped him from claiming employee status; and (4) the painter was an independent contractor, and could not sue on the causes of action asserted in the suit.

The plaintiff in this matter, Chin, was injured in May 2005 when he fell off a ladder while performing painting services at a shopping center. Although Chin at one time had been a licensed painting contractor, his license had expired in 2000, and he was not licensed at the time of injury. In January 2006, Chin and his wife filed a complaint naming as defendants the persons and entities who hired Chin to do painting work at the shopping center.

The gist of the complaint was that Chin was respondents' employee at the time he was injured, and was entitled to wages and other compensation owed him. Also, as an employee for whom his employer had no workers' compensation coverage, he was entitled to recover for negligence. Finally, he claimed he was wrongfully terminated. He claimed that respondents' assertion that Chin was an independent contractor, not an employee, was only an attempt to avoid complying with the wage and hour and insurance provisions of the Labor Code.

The trial court entered judgment against the Chins and in favor of respondents, finding that Chin was an independent contractor, not an employee. On appeal, the Chins' principal contentions were that the trial court erred by (1) ignoring Labor Code Section 2750.5 which created a rebuttable presumption that an unlicensed person who performs work requiring a license is an employee, not an independent contractor; (2) imposing on Chin the burden of proving that he was an employee; and (3) concluding that Chin was estopped to assert he was an employee. The appellate court affirmed the trial court's ruling granting summary judgment, finding Chin was an employee, not an independent contractor.

On appeal, the Chins also contended the trial court erred (1) in failing to find that respondents were joint employers; (2) in applying Business and Professions Code section 7031, which precludes unlicensed contractors from bringing an action for compensation for the performance of work that requires a contractor's license; and (3) in failing to enter judgment in Chin's favor on his unpaid wage and other claims. Since it was undisputed that Chin was performing work for

[97.32] 166 Cal. App. 4th 994, 2 Cal. WCC 1047, 83 Cal. Rptr. 3d 294 (2008).

which a license was required but was unlicensed, the trial court properly applied Business and Professions Code section 7031.[97.33]

The appellate court held that since Chin was estopped from denying that he was an independent contractor, the claims arising out his alleged status as an employee necessarily failed. The appellate court stated that it did not need to address the issue of whether respondents were joint employers.

Respondent employers had used Chin over a long period of years, and he had a contractor's license at the outset, but he had allowed it to lapse. Employers paid Chin as though he were an independent contractor, and believed he was a licensed contractor under California law.

Chin fell from a ladder and broke his leg while doing painting work at the shopping center. He filed this suit alleging various causes of action, all relying on the allegation that he was an employee of the respondents. Chin testified that the ladder from which he fell and the scaffolding onto which he fell were provided by Nadjat-Haiem. There was conflicting testimony about whether Chin provided any tools or materials for performance of the work.

Section 2750.5 establishes "a rebuttable presumption affecting the burden of proof that a worker performing services for which a [contractor's] license is required . . . is an employee rather than an independent contractor." Section 2750.5, subdivisions (a), (b), and (c), describes the proof that may satisfactorily rebut the presumption. The penultimate paragraph in section 2750.5 provides: "In addition to the factors contained in subdivisions (a), (b), and (c), any person performing any function or activity for which a [contractor's] license is required [ ] shall hold a valid contractor's license as a condition of having independent contractor status." In other words, under the statute, the presumption of employee status can be rebutted only as to persons who hold a valid contractor's license. The presumption cannot be rebutted as to persons who do not hold a valid contractor's license.

Section 2750.5 provides in part:

> Proof of independent contractor status includes satisfactory proof of these factors:
>
> (a) That the individual has the right to control and discretion as to the manner of performance of the contract for services in that the result of the work and not the means by which it is accomplished is the primary factor bargained for.
>
> (b) That the individual is customarily engaged in an independently established business.
>
> (c) . . . [T]he presence of cumulative factors such as substantial investment other than personal services in the business, holding out to be in business for oneself, bargaining for a contract to complete a specific project for compensation by project rather than by time, control over the time and place the work is performed, supplying the tools or instrumentalities used in the work . . . , hiring employees, performing work that is not ordinarily in the course of the principal's work, performing work that requires a particular

[97.33] *See* Fillmore v. Irvine, 146 Cal. App. 3d 649, 657, 194 Cal. Rptr. 319 (1983).

> skill, holding a license pursuant to the Business and Professions Code, the intent of the parties that the work relationship is of an independent contractor status, or that the relationship is not severable or terminable at will by the principal but gives rise to an action for breach of contract.

The appellate court held that there was no dispute that Chin was a licensed painting contractor doing business as KPC Painting when he first began work for Namvar in 1996. There was no dispute that Namvar, at the time he first hired Chin, discussed with Chin that the latter was licensed. There was also no dispute that Chin continued to provide painting services to Namvar on a number of different projects over the next several years. Namvar testified that he believed Chin would advise him of any license revocation, but Chin had said nothing.

Based on all the facts of this case, the appellate court affirmed the trial court's holding that Chin was an independent contractor, not an employee. He was not able to sue respondents on the theories alleged because he was not an employee.

In *Oceguera v. Cohen*,[97.34] plaintiff, Theresa Oceguera, appealed from a judgment after a trial in which she was awarded $11,255, based on her claims that defendants, David Cohen, Yossi Grimberg, and L.A.'s Best Home Improvement (the partnership), performed defective construction work on her home.

Ms. Oceguera contended the pretrial summary adjudication order in defendants' favor as to her second and sixth causes of action must be reversed, a contention with which the appellate court agreed. She also raised arguments concerning the trial. The appellate court rejected these contentions because she failed to provide the appellate court with a reporter's transcript or other suitable substitute of the trial proceedings. The appellate court remanded for a limited retrial on the second and sixth causes of action or other relevant proceedings. The appellate court concluded the conflicting evidence as to the partnership's license status on the date the contract was executed required them to provide a "verified certificate of license" within the meaning of California Business and Professions Code Section 7031, subdivision (d).

The complaint in *Oceguera*, filed on March 1, 2004, contained these allegations:

1. the partnership was a general partnership composed of Mr. Cohen and Mr. Grimberg;
2. the partnership recorded a fictitious business name statement on May 6, 2003;
3. on or about June 16, 2003, plaintiffs and the partnership entered into a written home improvement contract;
4. pursuant to the June 16, 2003 contract, defendants agreed to complete a remodel of plaintiffs' residence by July 20, 2003.

The complaint further alleged that defendants were unlicensed at the time of entering the contract, that defendants changed the terms of the costs from $36,800

[97.34] Not reported in Cal. Rptr. 3d, 2006 WL 2294593, nonpublished/noncitable (2006).

to $60,787 after the work began, and that defendants began performing the work without the necessary building permits, tools, or equipment and in an inferior, shabby, and substandard manner. When plaintiffs refused to pay the additional charges, defendants recorded a mechanic's lien on the property, and defendants left plaintiff's residence in an uninhabitable condition.

The partnership cross-complained against plaintiff, seeking damages for an alleged contract breach and restitution on various common counts. On November 22, 2004, defendants filed a summary judgment or adjudication motion on the ground that defendants were unlicensed. The contractors contended that the undisputed evidence established that they were in fact licensed, and the contractors argued that the intentional infliction of emotional distress claim failed for lack of extreme or outrageous conduct. Citing section 7068.2, the contractors argued that they were entitled to summary adjudication. Defendants asserted that the contract was entered into on June 16, 2003 and that the partnership was duly licensed until the board received the disassociation notice on July 30, 2003. The defendants relied primarily on Mr. Cohen's declaration. Mr. Cohen declared that, from January 2003 through July 2003, the partnership engaged in the construction business. The partnership had three partners: Arie Golan, Mr. Cohen, and Mr. Grimberg. Mr. Golan was the licensed partner and the responsible managing employee. In mid-July 2003, Mr. Golan signed and submitted a disassociation notice pursuant to section 7068.2 to the California State Contractor's License Board (the board). Exhibit A to Mr. Cohen's declaration showed the board received the disassociation notice on July 30, 2003. The partnership subsequently "obtained a continuance" which allowed it to complete projects that had been commenced prior to Mr. Golan's disassociation as permitted by section 7076, subdivision (c). Exhibit B to Mr. Cohen's declaration was the June 16, 2003, written home improvement contract between the partnership and Ms. Oceguera.

Ms. Oceguera's opposition to the motion for summary judgment asserted that the partnership was unlicensed when the June 16, 2003 contract was executed and throughout the time work was being performed on Ms. Oceguera's residence. Ms. Oceguera argued that defendants failed to meet their burden under section 7031, subdivision (d), of establishing licensure. She further argued that defendants failed to provide a certified copy of a license during the applicable period for the summary judgment motion hearing, and that the partnership was cancelled by operation of law on May 4, 2003 when Mr. Golan, the qualifying partner, executed a disassociation notice pursuant to section 7076, subdivision (c). Ms. Oceguera submitted one document which stated Mr. Golan disassociated himself from the partnership on May 4, 2003. Also, Ms. Oceguera submitted other documents which stated the disassociation occurred effective May 24, 2003. The owners submitted an unsigned letter dated August 7, 2003 from Linda Loudon in the License Modification Unit of the board stating that the partnership license No. 774744 was cancelled on May 24, 2003 due to Mr. Golan's disassociation. According to this letter, Mr. Golan's disassociation caused "the automatic cancellation" of the license. Ms. Loudon's letter also provided that the remaining partners were entitled to continue conducting business 1 year from the date of disassociation if a request for continuance was made in writing within 90 days of Mr. Golan's disassociation. The August 7, 2003 letter further stated that defendants could not act as a contractor for any new projects while conducting business under a continuance. (As noted, the home improvement contract was executed on June 16, 2003.)

Ms. Oceguera also produced a document file-stamped by the board dated July 15, 2003, entitled, "Application for Replacing the Qualifying Individual." The application stated that the exact date of Mr. Golan's disassociation was May 24, 2003. In addition, plaintiff produced evidence Mr. Golan's disassociation notice was filed with the board on July 30, 2003.

In reply, defendant contractors argued that section 7068.2 controlled the disposition of the case because it applied to partnerships expressly incorporating section 7068, subdivision (b)(2) which states in part, "If a copartnership or a limited partnership, it shall qualify by the appearance of a general partner or by the appearance of a responsible managing employee who is qualified for the same license classification as the classification being applied for." Defendants also argued there was no duty to provide a certified copy of the licensure history pursuant to section 7031, subdivision (d). According to defendants, this was because defendants were defending the action, not bringing a lawsuit under section 7031, subdivision (a).

The trial court subsequently entered a summary adjudication order as to the second and sixth causes of action based upon Mr. Cohen's declaration. The trial court concluded that, at all pertinent times, the partnership was duly licensed. In the trial court's view, Mr. Golan, "the licensed partner and the responsible managing employee, was associated with the partnership" until the board received the July 30, 2003 disassociation notice. The trial court based its decision on the following facts and conclusions: the board did not receive written notification of disassociation of the qualifying person under section 7068.2 until July 30, 2003. This was after the June 16, 2003 contract was signed. When the June 16, 2003 contract was signed, the partnership was licensed to act as a contractor.

The trial court rejected Ms. Oceguera's contention that section 7068.2 did not apply to partnerships. The court further rejected Ms. Oceguera's contention that the outcome of the motion was controlled by section 7076, subdivision (c) which states that a license is cancelled upon a disassociation of a partner. In this case disassociation occurred on May 24, 2003 when Mr. Golan signed the disassociation notice, rather than in July 2003 when the board received notification. The trial court ruled:

> First, [section] 7068.2 is applicable to partnerships. [Section] 7068, [subdivision](b)(2) provides: 'If a copartnership or a limited partnership, it shall qualify by the appearance of a general partner or by the appearance of a responsible managing employee who is qualified for the same license classification as the classification being applied for,' [Section] 7068's requirement concerning written notification applies to "[t]he person qualifying on behalf of an individual or firm under subdivision (a), (b), or (c) of Section 7068. . . ." Second, the case upon which plaintiff relied, *Swickheimer v. King, 22 Cal. App. 3d 220* (1971), supported the subcontractor defendant's position.

> In *Swickheimer,* the court did not discuss whether or not [section] 7068.2 applied to a partnership. It held that the defendant contractor, who was too ill to supervise job sites, was not required to notify the board of his disassociation pursuant to [the Business and Professions] Code due to his illness. As he continued to be connected with his employer, he was not disassociated so long as he did not file a Notice of Association with the board. In other words, as the Notice of Disassociation was not submitted to the board until July 2003, Mr. Golan remained the responsible managing employee and the partnership had the proper license. The trial court's written order made no reference to any evidentiary objections. On March 10, 2005, the trial court summarily denied Ms. Oceguera's amended mandate petition which challenged the trial court's order granting defendants' summary adjudication order as to the second and sixth causes of action.

The matter proceeded to trial on the remaining causes of action on March 29, 2005. The only plaintiff when the trial commenced was Ms. Oceguera. On August 9, 2005, the trial court entered judgment in Ms. Oceguera's favor in the amount of $11,255, finding that defendants breached the contract by not completing the work in a timely manner. The trial court adopted the amount testified to by Mr. Krastman. Mr. Guliex's report and estimate (Exhibit 15) was not received into evidence because it was not produced in a timely manner during discovery. Mr. Guliex testified that it would cost $35,353.67 to repair defects since everything had to be redone. However, on questioning by the court, he said that the cabinetry could be adjusted for $400.00. The plaintiff wanted it replaced and, in his opinion, replacement cost was $6,000.00-$7,000.00. The court adopted the testimony of Mr. Krastman as to the cost to complete the work rather than redo the work.

The trial court awarded nothing to the partnership on its cross-complaint. Ms. Oceguera's subsequent motion for a new trial and relief pursuant to Code of Civil Procedure section 473 was denied on September 20, 2005. On October 7, 2005, Ms. Oceguera filed a notice of appeal from the August 9, 2005 judgment and the February 7, 2005 order granting summary adjudication of the second and sixth causes of action.

Ms. Oceguera had provided a reporter's transcript of the February 4, 2005 summary adjudication and the September 20, 2005 new trial motion hearings. On February 2, 2006, the appellate court issued an order directing the parties to brief the issue of whether the plaintiff's failure to designate a reporter's transcript of the trial or to provide a suitable substitute warranted affirmance. The appellate court stated that it never presumes error, and a presumption of correctness must be accorded to the trial court's ruling. In the absence of a complete record, a reviewing court will not presume error. In numerous situations, appellate courts have refused to reach the merits of an appeal because no reporter's transcript of a pertinent proceeding or a suitable substitute was provided.

Ms. Oceguera argued the trial court erroneously ruled that the partnership was duly licensed when the contract was executed on June 16, 2003. Section 7031 provides:

> (a) Except as provided in subdivision (e), no person engaged in the business or acting in the capacity of a contractor, may bring or maintain any action, or recover in law or equity in any action, in any court of this state for the collection of compensation for the performance of any act or contract where a license is required by this chapter without alleging that he or she was a duly licensed contractor at all times during the performance of that act or contract, regardless of the merits of the cause of action brought by the person, except that this prohibition shall not apply to contractors who are each individually licensed under this chapter but who fail to comply with Section 7029(b); Except as provided in subdivision (e), a person who utilizes the services of an unlicensed contractor may bring an action in any court of competent jurisdiction in this state to recover all compensation paid to the unlicensed contractor for performance of any act or contract.
>
> . . .
>
> (d) If licensure or proper licensure is controverted, then proof of licensure pursuant to this section shall be made by production of a verified certificate of licensure from the Contractors' State License Board which establishes that the individual or entity bringing the action was duly licensed in the proper classification of contractors at all times during the performance of any act or contract covered by the action. Nothing in this subdivision shall require any person or entity controverting licensure or proper licensure to produce a verified certificate. When licensure or proper licensure is controverted, the burden of proof to establish licensure or proper licensure shall be on the licensee. . . .

In order to protect the public, section 7031 "imposes strict and harsh penalties" when a contractor performs work while unlicensed. In her second and sixth causes of action, Ms. Oceguera sought recovery of monies under section 7031, subdivision (b). She asserted the partnership was not duly licensed at all times during the performance of the contract. The controlling issue was when the partnership lost its licensure status. There was evidence the disassociation occurred on May 4 or 24, 2003. One board document stated the license was cancelled on May 24, 2003. The contract was signed on June 16, 2003. Further, there was evidence the disassociation notice was not filed with the board until July 30, 2003. There was controversy as to whether the partnership was licensed when the contract was signed on June 16, 2003.

Defendants argued that the partnership could enter into construction contracts until July 30, 2003, the date upon which the board received the dissociation notice. Defendants relied on section 7068.2, arguing that, under the plain language of section 7068.2, the partnership was duly licensed because Mr. Golan remained liable for all operations until the board received the disassociation notice. Defendants argued the partnership's license was valid pursuant to section 7076, subdivision (c): "Failure to notify the registrar of the disassociation or dissolution within 90 days shall cause the license to be canceled effective the date the written notification is received at the board's headquarters office." Ms. Oceguera countered that the disposition of this case was controlled by section 7076 subdivision (c) which provided:

> A partnership license shall be canceled upon the disassociation of a general partner or upon dissolution of the partnership. The disassociating partner or the remaining partner or partners shall notify the registrar in writing within 90 days of the disassociation of a general partner or dissolution of the partnership. Failure to notify the registrar of the disassociation or dissolution within 90 days shall cause the license to be canceled effective the date the written notification is received at the board's headquarters office. Failure to notify the registrar within 90 days of the disassociation or dissolution is grounds for disciplinary action. The remaining general partner or partners may request a continuance of the license to complete projects contracted for or in progress prior to the date of disassociation or dissolution for a reasonable length of time to be determined by rules of the board. The request for a continuance must be made in writing and received at the board's headquarters office within 90 days after the disassociation or dissolution. The remaining general partner or partners must apply for and obtain a new license to undertake new work and to continue contracting after the continuance expires.

Ms. Oceguera contended that, under the express language of section 7076, subdivision (c), the disassociation was effective on May 4 or 24, 2003, the date Mr. Golan executed the disassociation notice, not the date the board received the notice.

The appellate court found that a careful reading of these statutes showed they were not in conflict. Under section 7076, subdivision (c), a qualifying partner's disassociation results in a cancellation of its contractor's license. Section 7068.2 nevertheless provided that, when the disassociating partner leaves, the partnership has 90 days to notify the board in writing and to replace the qualifying partner by filing a new application. There was evidence of this. Mr. Golan executed a notice of disassociation in mid-May 2003.

A new application was submitted to the board in mid-July 2003 to replace Mr. Golan. The notice of disassociation was received by the board on July 30, 2003. The contract was entered into on June 16, 2003, which was within the 90-day period when defendants could apply to reinstate with a new qualifying person. Contractor defendants argued the trial court could have ruled they were duly licensed during the applicable time despite evidence the license was canceled as of May 4 or 24, 2003, before the June 16, 2003 contract was signed.

The appellate court agreed with the owner, Ms. Oceguera. The existence of this controversy required defendants to produce a verified certificate of licensure pursuant to section 7031, subdivision (d) which stated: "If licensure or proper licensure is controverted, then proof of licensure pursuant to this section shall be made by production of a verified certificate of licensure from the Contractor's State License Board which establishes that the individual or entity bringing the action was duly licensed in the proper classification of contractors at all times during the performance of any act or contract covered by the action. Nothing in this subdivision shall require any person or entity controverting licensure or proper licensure to produce a verified certificate." The statute further stated: "When licensure or proper licensure is controverted, the burden of proof to establish licensure or proper licensure shall be on the licensee." The licensure issue was controverted, as reflected in the pleadings, separate statements, and documents produced in connection with the summary judgment motion. By its express terms, section 7031, subdivision (d) required defendants to prove the existence of a proper license with a verified certificate of licensure from the board. No such proof was presented prior to entry of summary adjudication on this issue. As a matter of law, defendants failed to prove the partnership was duly licensed. [Sec. 7031, subd. (d)]

Defendant contractors argued that section 7031, subdivision (d) had no application to its defense to the plaintiffs' causes of action to recover funds from an alleged unlicensed contractor under section 7031, subdivision (b). Section 7031, subdivision (d) was not limited to actions for recovery of compensation. It states:

> If licensure or proper licensure is controverted, then proof of licensure pursuant to this section shall be made by production of a verified certificate of licensure from the Contractors' State License Board which establishes that the individual or entity bringing the action was duly licensed in the proper classification of contractors at all times during the performance of any act or contract covered by the action. Nothing in this subdivision shall require any person or entity controverting licensure or proper licensure to produce a verified certificate. When licensure or proper licensure is controverted, the burden of proof to establish licensure or proper licensure shall be on the licensee.

Section 7031, subdivision (d) was held not to be limited to actions under section 7031, subdivision (a). The trial court erred in resolving the licensure issue without requiring defendants to produce a verified certificate of licensure.

The appellate court reversed the trial court's order granting summary adjudication. The appellate court ordered the case remanded for a limited retrial or other proceedings as to the second and sixth causes of action. The trial court judgment was affirmed by the appellate court in all other respects.

In *Padilla v. Pomona College*,[97.35] after being injured during a dormitory remodeling project, an employee of a subcontractor brought an action against a college and a general contractor for negligence and premises liability. The trial court entered judgment for the defendants, and the employee appealed.

The appellate court affirmed the trial court. It held that (1) any control that the college and the general contractor retained over the pressurized pipe did not affirmatively contribute to the employee's injuries; (2) a California Occupational Safety and Health (Cal-OSHA) regulation requiring that water lines be protected from damage did not impose a nondelegable duty; (3) the failure of the college and the general contractor to take steps in regulation did not affirmatively contribute to injuries; (4) the college and the general contractor did not violate a duty under a regulation supporting per se liability; and (5) the college and the general contractor did not fail to disclose a hazardous condition.

[97.35] 166 Cal. App. 4th661, 82 Cal. Rptr. 3d 869 (2008), *review denied* (Dec. 10, 2008).

In *Padilla*, the college hired a general contractor to remodel a dormitory on its college campus. Apparently, the general contractor contracted with TEG/LVI, plaintiff's employer, for the demolition of water pipes in the basement of the dormitory. The water pressure to some of the pipes in the basement area was not shut off because the pipes were needed during the remodeling process.

During the demolition, plaintiff stood on a ladder to demolish an unpressurized cast-iron metal pipe. A portion of that pipe came loose and fell, striking a pressurized PVC pipe and breaking it. Plaintiff was knocked off his ladder by the gusher of water erupting from the broken PVC pipe and sustained serious physical injuries. The parties did not dispute that the PVC pipe was not to be demolished.

Plaintiff's complaint asserted two theories, negligence and premises liability. He alleged that defendants violated their common law and statutory duties to ensure that there was no water pressure in the pipes in the area plaintiff was working.

Defendants Pomona and the general contractor moved for summary judgment, contending they had no duty to plaintiff because they did not retain control over the details of the activities causing plaintiff's injuries and did not engage in any affirmative act that contributed to plaintiff's injuries. Further, they contended that plaintiff's claim was barred because his employer, TEG/LVI, knew or should have known of the danger presented by the PVC pipe.

Defendants presented evidence that it was TEG/LVI's contractual duty to demolish pipes, asbestos, lead, and drywall, and that TEG/LVI had agreed to protect items that remained in the employees' work area. Prior to the start of the project, the general contractor worked with TEG/LVI to ensure that TEG/LVI understood the scope of the demolition, including which pipes would remain and which would be demolished. Specifically, the architect's plans for the project showed that a PVC pipe would remain in the building during demolition, and it would remain pressurized to provide water for work on the project.

The general contractor retained co-defendant Deel Mechanical to prepare the plumbing system in the dormitory for demolition, and to ensure that those pipes that were not to be demolished were cut and capped. Deel marked the pipes to be removed, and redirected temporary piping on the outside of the building. The basement was barricaded to prevent access by Deel and other subcontractors. The trial court, in a separate summary judgment motion, found Deel "had no duty to prevent the injury that occurred to plaintiff." The trial court granted Deel's motion for summary judgment. Plaintiff did not appeal from judgment in favor of Deel.

At the time of the accident, plaintiff was using TEG/LVI's tools and equipment. He was directed in his work by his TEG/LVI supervisor, Armando Takata, who according to defendant's evidence, identified to plaintiff that the PVC pipe was one of the pipes that had been left pressurized. The moving papers provided evidence that Takata expressly advised plaintiff to avoid damaging the pressurized PVC pipe. TEG/LVI's standard demolition procedures for the type of pipe that plaintiff demolished required plaintiff and a co-worker to use separate ladders, tie a rope around the midsection of the pipe to be demolished, break the pipe, and lower the pipe to the ground slowly. Plaintiff was not following this procedure at the time of the accident. Defendants, in particular Gordon & Williams, did not supervise plaintiff.

Plaintiff opposed the motion, contending that (1) the general contractor's failure to depressurize the pipe constituted negligence per se, a breach of its contractual duties, and was contrary to custom and practice; and (2) the general contractor's failure to depressurize the pipe affirmatively contributed to plaintiff's injury. Plaintiff specifically contended that the general contractor failed to follow Cal-OSHA regulations[97.36] which required utilities to be shut off, capped, or otherwise controlled during demolition, or protected if use was necessary. Plaintiff also contended the general contractor's contract with Pomona College specified that the general contractor was "responsible for initiating, maintaining and supervising all safety precautions and programs in connection with the performance of the Contract" and that the general contractor was to "take reasonable precautions for safety of, and shall provide reasonable protection to prevent damage, injury or loss to . . . employees on the Work and other persons who may be affected thereby." In addition, the general contractor was to "comply with applicable laws, ordinances, rules, regulations . . . bearing on safety of persons or property or their protection from damage, injury or loss" and designate a responsible person whose duty would be the prevention of accidents.

Hooker v. Department of Transportation,[97.37] provides the hirer can nonetheless be liable if its conduct affirmatively contributed to the injuries of the independent contractor's employees. Plaintiff in *Padilla* argued that the defendants retained control over the worksite and failed to take the necessary precautions by depressurizing the pipe, thereby contributing to his injuries.

Specifically, plaintiff contended that TEG/LVI did not have control of the water pressure in the PVC pipe, and therefore could not shut it off. The general contractor could have shut the water off to the PVC pipe while the demolition was going on in the basement. Following the accident, the general contractor had difficulty shutting the water off, and after the accident, placed a ball valve over the pipe to protect it. The plans for the project only showed that the pipe was to "remain," not that it would be pressurized. The plaintiff's supervisor did not tell him how to do his job, or that the PVC pipe would remain pressurized. His supervisor only told him that pipes marked with red paint would not be demolished, not that they were pressurized. The pipes in the area where he worked were not marked with red paint. The supervisor demolished the sewer pipe the way he had been trained to do. Plaintiff proffered expert deposition testimony that the accident was the result of the general contractor's failure to comply with custom and practice by shutting off the water before demolition began, and that damage to the PVC pipe was foreseeable.

The trial court granted defendants' motion on the basis that defendants had fully delegated the task of providing a safe work environment to TEG/LVI. Defendants had not exercised any retained control in a manner that affirmatively contributed to plaintiff's injuries. The court found that Regulation 1735(a) did not

[97.36] Cal. Code Regs. tit. 8, §§ 1735, subd. (a).

[97.37] 27 Cal. 4th 198, 115 Cal. Rptr. 2d 853, 38 P.3d 1081 (2002).

impose a duty on defendants independent of the retained control theory of liability, because plaintiff did not establish that the regulation imposed a duty on defendants as opposed to TEG/LVI, or that it was in fact necessary to relocate or shut off the PVC pipe under the circumstances. The court also sustained defendants' objection to plaintiff's expert deposition testimony on the grounds that no foundation had been laid either for the expert's qualification as an expert or for his opinion.

Plaintiffs had contended that defendants, who retained control over the PVC pipe, should have depressurized, rearranged, or relocated the pipe before the project began, or at least temporarily, while demolition was taking place in the basement. The appellate court held that the plaintiff did not successfully establish that the defendants retained control over the PVC pipe or that defendants affirmatively contributed to the accident. The appellate court in *Padilla* reviewed a series of cases on exceptions to the peculiar risk doctrine, such as *Toland v. Sunland Housing Group, Inc.*,[97.38] and *Privette v. Superior Court.*[97.39] The *Padilla* court found that under the facts of this case, the plaintiff could not establish that Regulation Section 1735(a) imposed a nondelegable duty on defendants. The *Padilla* court also found that plaintiff could not use Regulation 1735(a) to establish negligence per se, or that defendants failed to disclose a known hazardous condition of the property. The *Padilla* court held that the hazardous condition asserted by the plaintiff was the pressurized PVC pipe. TEG/LVI, the plaintiff's employer, knew of the pipe and failed to take the necessary precautions to protect its employee from harm during the demolition process. Because there was no triable issue of fact, the appellate court upheld the trial court's granting defendants' motion for summary judgment.

In *Jones v. P.S. Development Company*,[97.40] a Transportation Security Administration (TSA) employee brought an action for negligence and product liability against contractors involved in installing a machine after tripping over mounting bolts securing an explosive detection system (EDS) machine. The trial court granted summary judgment for the contractors and denied the employee's motion for reconsideration. The employee appealed.

The appellate court affirmed the trial court's grant of summary judgment, holding that: (1) the "completed and accepted" doctrine was applicable to determine whether the contractors were shielded from liability; (2) the contractors' work in installing the bolts was completed and accepted by the time appellant was injured.

In *Jones*, the injured worker filed a complaint against Invision Technologies, Inc. (Invision), based on negligence and products liability. The complaint alleged that Jones, an employee of the Transportation Security Administration (TSA) at Los AngelesInternationalAirport (LAX), had suffered injuries in the course of his duties as the result of a defect in an explosive detection system (EDS) machine. According to the complaint, Jones was injured on August 20, 2003, when he

---

[97.38] 18 Cal. 4th 253. 264, 74 Cal. Rptr. 2d 878, 955 (1998).

[97.39] 5 Cal. 4th 689, 21 Cal. Rptr. 2d 72, 854 P.2d 721 (1993).

[97.40] 166 Cal. App. 4th 707, 82 Cal. Rptr. 3d 882 (2008), *review denied* (Dec. 10, 2008).

tripped over the mounting bolts that secured the EDS machine. The complaint further alleged that Invision had "negligently or otherwise wrongfully manufactured, designed, maintained, supplied, distributed, installed, failed to warn, or . . . handled" the EDS machine.

On October 16, 2006, Boeing filed a motion for summary judgment. Lloyd joined in this motion and asserted its own motion for summary judgment. Comet filed a motion for summary judgment on October 20, 2006. In December 2006, Boeing entered into a settlement with Jones. Following a hearing, the trial court granted Lloyd's and Comet's motions for summary judgment, and it later denied Jones's motion for reconsideration. Judgment was entered in respondents' favor on March 21, 2007.

The key issues before the appellate court concerned the application of the so-called "completed and accepted" doctrine. In some circumstances, this shields contractors from liability for negligence. In granting summary judgment in this case, the trial court relied on this doctrine, as explained in *Sanchez v. Swinerton & Walberg Co.*[97.41]

In seeking summary judgment, Lloyd and Comet submitted evidence that their work on the pertinent EDS machine had been completed and accepted prior to Jones's injuries. Lloyd submitted a declaration from Doug Waldo, a former Lloyd employee who supervised the project for Lloyd from November 2002 to July 25, 2003. According to Waldo, Lloyd's limited role in the installation of the anchors was completed prior to Jones's accident on August 20, 2003. Lloyd neither designed the anchors nor provided them to Comet. Under the pertinent contracts, Comet was responsible for obtaining the seismic anchors, installing them, and obtaining approvals from the city. Waldo's duties were limited. He passed information and paperwork between Boeing and Comet, and he kept a log of Comet's activities for Boeing. He did not supervise, inspect, or direct Comet's work.

After July 25, 2003, when Lloyd's work on the site was completed, Lloyd had no access to or control over the EDS machines. Lloyd was never asked to return to the site to make changes or repairs to the anchors.

Comet submitted evidence that its role in the project was limited to installing the specified anchors on EDS machines at LAX, and that its work on the machine that Jones had identified as the source of his injuries was completed and accepted prior to his accident. In a deposition, Jones identified the pertinent machine, and the facts demonstrated that Comet completed the installation of anchor brackets and bolts on this machine in June 2003, two months before Jones's accident. The TSA accepted the machine and put it into full operation prior to the accident.

Pointing to Jones's deposition testimony, Comet also asserted that Jones and the TSA knew that the anchors on the machine posed a hazard before Jones suffered his injuries. Jones testified that a barrier shielded the machine from passengers, who were required to wait behind the barrier while TSA employees placed their luggage in the machine. Prior to the accident, he noticed protruding bolts on the anchors, and tried to steer clear of the bolts as he walked around the

[97.41] 47 Cal. App. 4th 1461, 55 Cal. Rptr. 2d 415 (1996).

machine. He discussed the hazard with his co-workers, and mentioned it to a "lead" in his chain of command. On the date of the accident, he tripped over a bolt as he carried a box around the EDS machine. According to Jones, he was aware of the bolt before he fell, but misjudged his distance from the bolt.

On appeal, Jones contended that the "completed and accepted" doctrine was abrogated in *Stewart v. Cox.*[97.42] He argued that *Stewart* and its progeny govern the issues presented in this case. The appellate court disagreed.

The appellate court stated that a subcontractor's liability would be determined by reference to the multifactored test of *Biakanja v. Irving.*[97.43] The *Biakanja* test involves balancing various factors, among which are: (1) the extent to which the transaction was intended to affect the plaintiff, (2) the foreseeability of harm to him, (3) the degree of certainty that he suffered injury, (4) the closeness of the connection between the defendant's conduct and the injury suffered, and (5) the policy of preventing future harm.

The *Jones* court found that prior to Jones's accident, the anchors had been installed on the machine, and the TSA had put the machine into service in an area reserved for TSA employees. None of the evidence before the trial court suggested that the respondents performed work on the machine after the anchors had been installed. The *Jones* court held that the completion and acceptance doctrine shielded Lloyd from liability for negligence after the TSA accepted Comet's installation of the anchors on the machine in issue. The appellate court held that there was no triable dispute as to whether the TSA had accepted Comet's completed work before Jones's accident. It affirmed the trial court's grant of the motions for summary judgment of respondents.

[97.42] 55 Cal. 2d 857, 13 Cal. Rptr. 521, 362 P.2d 345 (1961).

[97.43] 49 Cal. 2d 647, 320 P.2d 16 (1958).

Chapter 15
PAYMENT

§ 15.01 OVERVIEW OF THE PAYMENT PROCESS

Page 557, add after third paragraph :

Review and preparation of expert evidence is a crucial part of the attorney's job in preparing a construction claim. In *Stonehill-PRM WC L.L.P v. Chasco Constructors, Limited, L.L.P.*,[2.1] appellant Stonehill-PRM WC I, L.P., (Stonehill) appealed the district court's judgment in favor of appellees Chasco Constructors, Ltd., L.L.P. (Chasco) and Safeco Insurance Company of America (Safeco). Stonehill contended that the district court erred when it determined the measure of damages, when it excluded testimony from two of Stonehill's experts and one of its owners as to the value of the proposed construction, when it excluded evidence of the cost to complete the construction project, and when it refused to admit an alleged copy of the contract between the parties. The appellate court affirmed the district court's judgment holding that the district court did not err in determining the measure of damages, and that any error in the challenged evidentiary rulings was not reversible error.

In the summer of 2005, Stonehill hired Page Southerland Page Architects and Engineers (PSP) to design a student housing facility (the Project) for property that Stonehill owned in Austin, Texas. In approximately September 2005, Stonehill began negotiations with Chasco for Chasco to be the contractor for the project. The proposed scope of work included demolishing the existing structure on the property. Chasco provided several different budgets to Stonehill including a line-item budget of $16,638,030 in December 2005. The December 2005 budget was based upon design and development drawings that PSP issued in October 2005. PSP also issued permit plans for the project on February 6, 2006, and an "Addendum # 1" to the permit plans in March 2006.

Stonehill and Chasco executed a "Standard Form of Agreement Between Owner and Contractor," dated February 22, 2006 (the Contract). The standard form, titled "AIA Document A111-1997," is a form agreement from the American Institute of Architects and reflects the parties' modifications to the standard form. Section 15.1.2 of this document incorporates the standard form "AIA Document A201-1997, as modified" as the agreed "[g]eneral [c]onditions" of the contract. The contract provided that Chasco would be paid its costs for performing the work plus a fee with a guaranteed maximum price (GMP). Neither party produced an original of the contract, and the parties disagreed as to whether the contract

---

[2.1] 2009 Tex. App. LEXIS 1019, 2009 WL 349136 (Tex. App.-Austin 2009).

contained a GMP addendum and, if so, whether the GMP addendum actually contained a guaranteed maximum price. Stonehill contended that the contract contained a GMP addendum with a GMP of $16,638,030, the amount Chasco provided as the budget in December 2005.

Chasco contended that, at the time the parties executed the contract, the contract did not contain a GMP addendum and that Chasco had not completed the bidding process from the permit plans to provide final cost numbers. Based on a subsequent request from Stonehill's lender that was financing the project, two GMP addenda were prepared. According to Chasco, both addenda contained a GMP of $16,638,030 that was not final, and a sentence that the GMP "will be modified upon verification of pricing of City of Austin permit plans dated February 6, 2006."

Article 5 of the contract set forth the "basis for payment." Section 5.2.1, as modified by the parties, stated:

> The sum of the Cost of the Work and the Contractor's Fee is guaranteed by the Contractor not to exceed ($), (*see GMP addendum*) subject to additions and deductions by Change Order as provided in the Contract Documents. Such maximum sum is referred to in the Contract Documents as the Guaranteed Maximum Price.

In March 2006, Safeco issued a performance and payment bond on the project for $16,638,030, and Chasco began the demolition work on the existing structure. On April 4, 2006, Chasco notified Stonehill that construction costs based on the completion of the bidding process from the permit plans were $30,250,000. Thereafter, Chasco sent notice to Stonehill that "[b]ased upon verification of pricing of the City of Austin permit plans and specifications dated February 6, 2006 and Addendum # 1 dated March 9, 2006 along with our Final GMP budget and qualifications dated April 4, 2006," Chasco needed a written change order modifying the initial GMP to the "Final GMP budget" of $30,250,000 to "begin construction of the new structure." Stonehill would not agree to a GMP of $30,250,000, and Chasco did not begin construction.

In May 2006, Stonehill sent written notice to Safeco and Chasco that it was "formally" terminating Chasco's right to complete the project and declaring a "Contractor Default" as a result of Chasco's failure to perform its obligations, including its failure to comply with performance for the agreed GMP. In July 2006, Stonehill filed suit alleging breach of the contract and the performance bond. Attached to Stonehill's original petition was a copy of the contract that contained the version of the GMP addendum titled "Guaranteed Maximum Price Addendum to Contract."

In July 2007, Stonehill filed a second amended petition alleging additional claims and attaching a different copy of the contract, one that contained the version of the addendum titled "West Campus Student Housing" with the date "December 20, 2005." In its second amended response to appellees' request for disclosure, Stonehill disclosed that it was seeking its "expectancy damages"—the difference between the value of the project had it been constructed in accordance with the plans and specifications, "calculated using appropriate rents, expenses and prevailing capitalization rates in Austin, Texas for similar apartment structures," and the costs that Stonehill avoided. Stonehill designated Greg Hallman, Ph.D., as its damages valuation expert, disclosing that he would testify "about the value of the building that is the subject matter of this lawsuit were it constructed pursuant to the parties' Construction Contract." It was Hallman's opinion that the value of the "resulting building" would have been in excess of $36 million.

After deposing Hallman, Chasco filed a motion to exclude Hallman as Stonehill's designated expert and his testimony on several grounds, alleging that he was not qualified, because he was not licensed by the Texas Appraiser Licensing and Certification Board (TALCB), because he lacked "sufficient knowledge, skill, experience, training, or education," and that his testimony was not reliable, because his "methodology, assumptions, and processes" were not accurate and did not comply with industry standards for appraising commercial real estate. Safeco joined Chasco's motion. After a hearing in September 2007, the district court excluded Hallman.

In September 2007, the district court also granted Safeco's first motion for summary judgment, in part. It granted the motion regarding the "current model of damages sought by [Stonehill] against Safeco" and found as a matter of law that Stonehill was only entitled to actual damages under the performance bond, that "[a]ctual damages can include expectancy damages for the breach of an express contract," and that the "legal measure of damages in this case for such actual damages cannot include, either directly or indirectly, possible future rental rates, occupancy rates or similarly speculative income projections."

The district court conditionally granted Stonehill's motion for a continuance from the October 2007 trial setting, continuing the trial setting to February 2008 and extending the parties' deadlines to designate "appraiser/damages experts" and to amend their pleadings and discovery responses "to conform to the revised damages testimony and methodology[ies]." Stonehill's new deadline to designate experts was October 15, 2007, and its deadline to amend its pleadings and discovery responses was December 28, 2007.

In its third amended response to request for disclosure that it served on December 28, 2007, Stonehill disclosed that its designated damages expert, Rudy R. Robinson, III, MAI, would testify "about the value of the building that is the subject matter of this lawsuit were it constructed according to the parties' Construction Contract." Stonehill did not amend the measure of damages that it was seeking, continuing to seek its "expectancy damages" based on the difference in value of the proposed building had it been built according to the plans and specifications and the costs that it avoided, but it amended the proposed building's value. In discovery, Stonehill stated that the building "would have a value in the range of $32,000,000 to $37,000,000, calculated using appropriate rents, expenses and prevailing capitalization rates in Austin, Texas for similar apartment structures and commonly understood appraisal methods and techniques for valuation of commercial property."

In January 2008, Chasco and Safeco filed a joint motion to exclude Robinson as Stonehill's designated expert and his testimony on several grounds, including that his testimony as to the market value of the proposed building was irrelevant. The district court granted their motion to exclude Robinson on February 8, 2008. Safeco also filed a second motion for summary judgment based on Stonehill's failure to revise its damages model against Safeco. On February 8, 2008, the district court granted this motion, and because the order disposed of all claims asserted against Safeco, entered judgment dismissing Safeco with prejudice.

On the same day, the district court granted a partial summary judgment in favor of Chasco on the proper measure of damages. The district court ruled:

> The Court declares that if, *and only if,* an enforceable contract exists between the parties:
>
> i) As a matter of law, the proper measure of [Stonehill's] damages under the alleged contract is the cost to complete construction of the project to the extent the costs of completing the construction of the project exceed those costs which would have been payable to [Chasco];
> ii) As a matter of law, Stonehill's damages may not include any consequential damages, including damages for rental expenses, losses of use, income, profit, financing, and business because they are prohibited by the alleged contract; and
> iii) As a matter of law, [Stonehill] contractually waived the "benefit of the bargain" (a/k/a "expectancy") damages it seeks in this lawsuit.

The jury trial occurred February 12 to 14, 2008. The primary disputed fact was whether the parties contractually had agreed to a GMP of $16,638,000. It was Stonehill's position that the parties had, and Chasco's position that they had not. Stonehill's witnesses included Brownlow; Michael Mace, PSP's senior vice president; and Brian Selbo, the project's development coordinator for Stonehill.

Brownlow testified concerning the background of the project, communications and negotiations between the parties, and the different GMP addenda. Mace testified concerning PSP's role in the project, the plans and drawings that PSP issued, and his opinion that Chasco had adequate information based on the October 2005 plans to submit a GMP. Selbo testified to his role with the project, Stonehill's receipt of three signed copies of the contract from Chasco, and Stonehill's unsuccessful search to find an original executed contract.

Stonehill also called Curtis Cline, Chasco's corporate representative, and TempleAday, Chasco's president, as adverse witnesses. Cline testified to the negotiations between Chasco and Stonehill, the various budgets that Chasco prepared, the bidding process, the changes between the design and development plans and the permit plans and the effect of the changes on cost, the GMP addenda, and the final GMP of $30,250,000 that Chasco provided after the bidding process was completed. Aday testified that "it's practice in the construction industry" to attach a GMP addendum at a later date, that "it's customary in the construction field to sign a contract with the price to be determined at a later date," that the contract that he signed on behalf of Chasco did not have "any addendums attached," and that it was his understanding that "the addendum had not been established and would be established at a later date."

Through its witnesses, Stonehill attempted to admit the version of the contract that contained Chasco's December 2005 budget as the GMP addendum, but the district court sustained Chasco's objections and refused to admit it into evidence. No witness was able to testify to what had happened to the originals or to explain how or by whom the version that Stonehill was seeking to admit was pieced together during the litigation. Stonehill's version of the contract contained pages that had different Bates numbering identifiers. The district court admitted other versions of the contract, including the version that was attached to Stonehill's original petition.

After Stonehill rested, Chasco moved for a directed verdict on Stonehill's remaining claims for fraudulent inducement and breach of contract. The district court granted the motion, stating that there was no evidence of a "present intention not to perform" as to the fraudulent inducement claim and no evidence of damages as to the breach of contract claim. The district court entered a take-nothing judgment against Stonehill. Stonehill filed a motion for new trial, which motion the district court denied.

On appeal, Stonehill challenged the district court's determination of the proper measure of damages and its exclusion of evidence. In its first issue, Stonehill contended that the district court erred in ruling that Stonehill's measure of damages for breach of the contract was the cost to complete the project to the extent those costs exceeded the costs that would have been payable to Chasco. In its second issue, Stonehill contended that the district court erred in concluding that the consequential damages provision of the contract precluded use of an income stream to determine the value of the proposed building. In its third, fourth, and fifth issues, Stonehill contended that the district court improperly excluded the testimony of Brownlow and its experts Hallman and Robinson as to the value of the proposed building. In its sixth and seventh issues, Stonehill contended that the district court erred in sustaining Chasco's objections to evidence of cost to complete construction and in refusing to admit a copy of the contract.

Stonehill challenged the district court's ruling as to the proper measure of damages. The appellate court stated that whether the trial court erred in applying an improper measure of damages was a question of law subject to *de novo* review.[2.2]

The appellate court stated that the measure of damages in this case involved matters of contract construction. When a court concludes that contract language can be given a certain or definite legal meaning, then the language is not ambiguous, and the court will construe the contract as a matter of law. A court interprets a contract by ascertaining the true objective intentions of the parties, based on the contract language. Contract terms are given their plain, ordinary, and generally accepted meanings unless the contract itself shows them to be used in a technical or different sense. A court construes written instruments as a whole in an effort to harmonize and give effect to all the provisions of the instrument so that none will be rendered meaningless. No single provision taken alone will be

---

[2.2] TA Operating Corp. v. Solar Applications Eng'g, Inc., 191 S.W.3d 173, 183 (Tex. Ct. App.-San Antonio 2005).

given controlling effect; all the provisions must be considered with reference to the whole instrument.

Stonehill also challenged evidentiary rulings by the district court. The admission or exclusion of evidence was a matter within the trial court's discretion. A trial court abuses its discretion when it acts without reference to any guiding rules or principles. To reverse a judgment based on an error in the admission or exclusion of evidence, an appellate court must conclude that the error probably resulted in an improper judgment. Tex. R. App. P. 44.1(a)(1). To make this determination, an appellate court reviews the entire record and usually requires the complaining party to demonstrate that the judgment turns on the particular evidence admitted or excluded. In effect; all the provisions must be considered with reference to the whole instrument.

Stonehill also challenged evidentiary rulings by the district court. The admission or exclusion of evidence is a matter within the trial court's discretion. A trial court abuses its discretion when it acts without reference to any guiding rules or principles. To reverse a judgment based on an error in the admission or exclusion of evidence, an appellate court must conclude that the error probably resulted in an improper judgment. Tex. R. App. P. 44.1(a)(1). To make this determination, an appellate court reviews the entire record and usually requires the complaining party to demonstrate that the judgment turns on the particular evidence admitted or excluded.

In its first issue, Stonehill contended that the district court erred in concluding that Stonehill's measure of damages under the contract was its cost to complete the project to the extent those costs exceeded the costs that would have been payable to Chasco. Stonehill relied on section 13.4.1 of the contract that provided that contractual "rights and remedies" were in addition to "rights and remedies otherwise imposed or available by law or in equity" to contend that Stonehill was entitled to damages under the "recognized legal standard when there has not been substantial performance, that is, the difference between the value of the building as constructed and its value had it been constructed in accordance with the Construction Contract." Stonehill also contended that section 14.2.4 of the contract, which provided that Stonehill's measure of damages was its cost to complete the project that exceeded the costs that would have been payable to Safeco, only applied if Stonehill chose to complete the project. Appellees responded that, assuming that the contract was valid and enforceable, the parties agreed to Stonehill's recoverable damages as stated in section 14.2.4 of the contract.

Sections 13.4.1 and 14.2.4 as modified by the parties read:

> §§ 13.4.1 Duties and obligations imposed by the Contract Documents and rights and remedies available thereunder shall be in addition to and not a limitation of duties, obligations, rights and remedies otherwise imposed or available by law. law or in equity or by any other agreement, and any such rights and remedies shall survive the acceptance of the Work and/or any termination of the Contract Documents.

* * *

> §§ 14.2.4 To the extent the costs of completing Work, including, without limitation, compensation for additional professional services and expenses, exceed those costs which would have been payable to Contractor to complete the Work except for Contractor's default, Contractor shall pay the difference to Owner, and this obligation for payment shall survive termination of the Contract. Such costs incurred by Owner will be determined by the Owner and confirmed by the Architect.

The appellate court concluded that the contract provisions at issue were unambiguous and could be interpreted as a matter of law. Based on the plain language of the contract provisions and the applicable common law measure of damages, the appellate court concluded that the district court did not err in its determination of the measure of damages. Where there has been a "complete failure of performance" to construct a building, the common law "recognized" measure of damages for breach of contract is the "excess of the reasonable and necessary cost of completion over and above the unpaid portion of the contract price."[2.3] The parties' agreed measure of damages in the contract was consistent with the common law measure of damages for a "complete failure of performance" to build a building.[2.4]

Stonehill's interpretation of section 14.2.4 applied only if Stonehill had chosen to complete the project ignoring the section's plain language, as modified by the parties. The plain language did not condition Stonehill's recovery on a requirement that the project be completed, and courts routinely award costs to complete a construction contract without requiring that those costs be incurred. The parties could also agree contractually to the measure of damages in the event of a breach. Its interpretation of section 14.2.4 was not consistent with the contract as a whole. Section 14.2.4 is within article 14 that is titled "Termination or Suspension of the Contract." Section 14.2 is titled "Termination by the Owner for Cause," and subsection 14.2.4 expressly addressed the owner's remedies when it has terminated for cause. The parties also agreed to waive consequential damages for breach of the contract by the other party. Stonehill expressly agreed to waive any damages that it incurred for "losses of use, income, [and] profit." Binding the parties to the contractually agreed measure of damages in the event Stonehill terminated for cause was consistent with Stonehill's waiver of the types of damages expressed in the consequential damages clause.

Section 4.3.10 of the contract addressed claims for consequential damages. It read in relevant part:

[2.3] Ashley v. Bizzell, 694 S.W.2d 349, 353 (Tex.App.-San Antonio 1985, writ ref'd n.r.e.) (*quoting* Smith v. Kinslow, 598 S.W.2d 910, 913 (Tex.Civ.App.-Dallas 1980, no writ)).

[2.4] *See Bizzell*, 694 S.W.2d at 353; *see also* Fidelity & Deposit Co. v. Stool, 607 S.W.2d 17, 21 (Tex. Civ. App.-Tyler 1980), no writ. The facts and circumstances in each [breach of a building contract] case will determine whether the remedial cost or the difference in value is the proper measure of damages.

> §§ 4.3.10 Claims for Consequential Damages. The Contractor and Owner waive Claims against each other for consequential damages arising out of or relating to this Contract. This mutual waiver includes:
>
> 1. damages incurred by the Owner for rental expenses, for losses of use, income, profit, financing, business and reputation, and for loss of management or employee productivity or of the services of such persons; and
>
> 2. damages incurred by the Contractor for principal office expenses including the compensation of personnel stationed there, for losses of financing, business and reputation, and for loss of profit except anticipated profit arising directly from the Work.
>
> This mutual waiver was applicable, without limitation, to all consequential damages due to either party's termination in accordance with Article 14. . . .

The court rejected Stonehill's contention that, in any event, section 13.4.1 provided Stonehill additional remedies, including expectancy damages based on the difference-in-value measure of damages. Stonehill relied on *Turner, Collie & Braden, Inc. v. Brookhollow, Inc.*,[2.5] to support its position. In *Turner,* the Texas Supreme Court addressed when the measure of damages for the breach of a construction contract were "remedial damages"—the cost to complete construction-as opposed to the "difference-in-value measure." At issue was a dispute between the contractor and the owner after the contractor completed the construction of a sewer line that the owner alleged was defective. In the context of defective work and economic efficiencies, the Texas Supreme Court explained that the difference-in-value measure was appropriate when the contractor had not substantially complied with the contract between the parties, and the remedial measure was appropriate when the contractor had substantially performed. In contrast, Chasco had not begun construction on the new building, and Stonehill did not allege defective work.

The district court did not err in its conclusions as to the contractual measure of damages. The parties' objective intent from the plain language of section 14.2.4 and the contract as a whole was to agree that Stonehill's measure of damages in the event Chasco defaulted was the cost to complete the project to the extent those costs exceeded the costs that would have been payable to Chasco. The appellate court overruled Stonehill's first issue.

In its second issue, Stonehill contended that the district court erred in ruling that the consequential damages section of the contract precluded the use of an income stream in determining the value of the proposed building. Because the appellate court concluded that the district court did not err in determining that the measure of damages was the cost to complete the project that exceeded the costs that would have been payable to Chasco, the value of the proposed building was not relevant to an issue of material fact.[2.6] Even if the district court erred in

[2.5] 642 S.W.2d 160 (Tex. 1982).

[2.6] *See*Tex. R. Evid. 401.

precluding the use of an income stream in determining the value of the proposed building, such error did not probably cause the rendition of an improper judgment.[2.7] The appellate court overruled Stonehill's second issue.

In its third, fourth, and fifth issues, Stonehill contended that the district court erred in excluding testimony from its experts, Hallman and Robinson, and its owner, Brownlow, as to the value of the proposed building had it been completed in accordance with the plans and specifications. Since the district court did not err in determining that the measure of damages was the cost to complete the project that exceeded the costs payable to Chasco, evidence of the value of the proposed building was not relevant to an issue of material fact.[2.8] Even if the district court erred in excluding testimony from these witnesses of the value of the proposed building, the exclusion of their testimony did not probably cause the rendition of an improper judgment. *See* Tex.R.App. P. 44.1(a). The appellate court overruled Stonehill's third, fourth, and fifth issues.

In its sixth issue, Stonehill contended that, if its measure of damages was the cost to complete the project that exceeded the costs payable to Chasco, the district court should have allowed Stonehill to introduce evidence of costs. Stonehill contended that Robinson and Brownlow would have testified to the cost to complete the project and would have required a jury question on that issue. Appellees responded that the district court properly excluded evidence of the costs to complete the project, because Stonehill failed to timely designate this theory of damages. Stonehill did not dispute that it first disclosed that it would seek the cost to complete the project that exceeded the costs payable to Chasco as an alternative measure of damages in its fourth amended response to request for disclosure that it served on appellees on February 4, 2008, after the court-ordered deadline of December 28, 2007.

Texas Rule of Civil Procedure 193.6 provides for the exclusion of evidence that has not been timely disclosed and the exceptions to exclusion. Rule 193.6 provides that a party that fails to timely disclose evidence may not introduce the evidence unless the party shows that there was good cause for the failure to disclose and that the failure does not unfairly surprise or unfairly prejudice the other party. Rule 193.6(b) and (c) place the burden on the party seeking to introduce the evidence and allows a trial court to continue a trial setting even if the party seeking to admit evidence fails to carry its burden.

The appellate court held that Stonehill failed to address its burden to show good cause for its failure to disclose that it was seeking its cost to complete the project as an alternative measure of damages. Stonehill did not seek a continuance or trial postponement to amend its discovery responses, or to allow Chasco to conduct discovery regarding the costs to complete the project. Stonehill filed suit in July 2006 and, after Stonehill's initial damages expert was excluded, the district court continued the trial setting and gave Stonehill additional time to designate a new damages expert and to amend its measure of damages, specifically extending the deadline to amend the parties' pleadings and discovery responses "to conform

---

[2.7] *See* Tex. R. App. P. 44.1(a).

[2.8] *See* Tex. R. Evid. 401.

to the revised damages testimony and methodology[ies]." The contract also expressly addressed the measure of damages in the event Stonehill terminated for cause as the cost to complete the project to the extent those costs exceed the costs that would have been payable to Chasco. The appellate court held that trial court did not abuse its discretion in excluding evidence of the cost to complete the project for failure to timely disclose. The court overruled Stonehill's sixth issue.

In its seventh issue, Stonehill contended that the district court erred in refusing to admit its offered version of the contract even though it was properly authenticated and admissible. *See* Tex. R. Evid. 1003, 1004. Chasco objected that Stonehill's offered version was not an original and challenged its authenticity. Stonehill's version contained a different GMP addendum from the versions of the contract that were admitted into evidence, but the parties agreed that the contract contained the terms that were relevant to the challenged rulings on appeal. Even if the district court erred in excluding Stonehill's version of the contract, Stonehill failed to show how this exclusion probably caused the rendition of an improper judgment. *See* Tex. R. App. P. 44.1(a). The appellate court overruled Stonehill's seventh issue.

Because the court concluded that the district court did not err in its conclusions as to the measure of damages under the contract and that any error by the district court in the challenged evidentiary rulings was not reversible error, the appellate court affirmed the district court's judgment.

The contract remedy accepted by a court can make a substantial difference in the outcome of a construction case, and the admissibility of expert theories or testimony may be crucial to support a damages theory. The AIA documents waiver of consequential damages continues to be a controversial portion of the documents, and may be the sole reason that parties refuse to use AIA documents.

§ 15.04 FINANCIAL INFORMATION

Page 568, add at end of section:

Steven G.M. Stein and Ronald O. Wietecha, in their article, *A Comparison of ConsensusDOCS to the AIA Form Construction Contract Documents*,[25.1] stated that under ConsensusDOCS 200, the contractor has an ongoing, unlimited entitlement to the owner's project financing information, while A201 only provides that the owner is to provide financial information prior to the start of the work. A201-2009 Secs. 2.2.1 and 14.1.4, ConsensusDOCS 200 Para. 4.2 and Para. 11.5.2.1.

Under ConsensusDOCS 200, the contractor is entitled at any point during the project to discontinue work until the owner provides requested financial information.

[25.1] Steven G.M. Stein & Ronald O. Wietecha, *A Comparison of ConsensusDOCS to the AIA Form Construction Contract Documents*, *The Construction Lawyer*, Vol. 29, No. 1, Winter 2009.

In *Advantages of the ConsensusDOCS Construction Contracts*,[25.2] the authors describe how the obligation of the owner to provide financial information to the contractor is handled differently in ConsensusDOCS from AIA documents. A201-1997 required the owner to provide financial information, and A201-2007 reduced the owner's obligation to provide such information. A201-2007 Sec. 2.2.1. ConsensusDOCS obligate the owner to provide evidence of project financing only, as opposed to general financial information. The obligation of the owner is to provide this information under the ConsensusDOCS both when the work commences, and at any time thereafter upon written request of the contractor. ConsensusDOCS 200 Para. 4.2.

§ 15.08 PAYMENT APPLICATION: PASSAGE OF TITLE

Page 588, add after fourth full paragraph:

In *T.O. IX, et al. v. Superior Court*,[68.1] a street builder recorded nine mechanic's liens against parcels in subdivision, each of the liens for the total amount allegedly due under the developers' contract with builder. The builder moved to foreclose on the liens. The developers moved to remove the liens as being willfully overstated. The trial court denied the developers' motion to remove the liens, and also denied the developers' *ex parte* application for an order permitting the developers to release the parcels from the liens by posting a single surety bond. The developers petitioned for a writ of mandate.

The appellate court held that:

1. the liens exceeded the amount of security available under the mechanic's lien statutes; but
2. the builder did not forfeit its right to a mechanic's lien by recording nine mechanic's liens;
3. sustained the trial court's holding that it would be equitable to permit the developers to post a single bond to release parcels.

In *T.O. IX*, Asphalt Professionals, Inc. (API), the real party in interest, contracted with petitioners T.O. IX, LLC, and D and S Homes, Inc., to build a street through a nine-home subdivision developed by petitioners. API alleged that it had not been paid $79,831.18 due under the contract. It recorded a mechanic's lien against each of the nine parcels for the full amount due under the contract: nine separate liens, at $79,831.18 each, to secure API's right to be paid $79,831.18 once. After API filed this action to foreclose on the mechanics' liens, developers filed a motion to remove the liens as willfully overstated, pursuant to California Civil Code section 3118. The trial court denied the motion. Developers then applied *ex parte* for an order permitting them to release all nine parcels from the liens by posting a single surety bond in an amount equal to one and one-half

---

[25.2] Larry D. Harris & Brian M. Perlberg, *Advantages of the ConsensusDOCS Construction Contracts*, *The Construction Lawyer*, Vol. 29, No. 1, Winter 2009.

[68.1] 165 Cal. App. 4th 140, 80 Cal. Rptr. 3d 602 (2008), *review denied* (Sept. 10, 2008).

times the total amount of API's claim, as provided in section 3143. The trial court denied the application.

The developers filed a petition for a writ of mandate to direct the trial court to grant either the motion to remove the liens or to grant the *ex parte* application to post a single surety bond. The appellate court issued an order to show cause against API. API filed a return by demurrer and an answer to the writ petition. The appellate court overruled API's return by demurrer to the order to show cause, and held the developers had standing to defend the causes of action alleged against them by API.[68.2] The appellate court granted the writ petition, and held that the trial court should vacate its order denying petitioners' *ex parte* application. The trial court was ordered to enter a new order authorizing petitioners to post a single surety bond in the amount mandated by section 3143 to release the nine mechanics' liens at issue in this litigation.

The appellate court stated that California mechanic's lien statutes, California Civil Code section 3082*et seq.*, carry out the constitutional mandate by providing that contractors and other specified workers who provide labor, materials, equipment, and other services to a work of improvement, "shall have a lien" on the property on which they worked "for the value of such labor done or materials furnished. . . ."[68.3] The amount of the lien is limited to the "reasonable value of the labor, services, equipment, or materials furnished or for the price agreed upon by the claimant and the person with whom he or she contracted, whichever is less."[68.4] It is forfeited by anyone "who shall willfully include in his claim of lien labor, services, equipment or materials not furnished for the property described in such claim."[68.5]

If a single lien is recorded against multiple works of improvement that are owned or were contracted for by the same person, the claimant must designate the amount due on each work of improvement, or lose priority to other liens.[68.6] If the claimant is to be paid a lump sum for multiple works of improvement that are owned or were contracted for by the same person, and the contract does not segregate the amount due for each work of improvement separately, the claimant "may estimate an equitable distribution of the sum due the claimant over all of such works of improvement. . . ."[68.7] Finally, "if there is a single structure on more than one parcel of land owned by one or more different owners, it shall not be the duty of the claimant to segregate the proportion of material or labor entering into the structure on any one of such parcels; but upon the trial thereof the court may, where it deems it equitable so to do, distribute the lien equitably as between the several parcels involved."[68.8]

"A property owner who disputes the correctness or validity of any claim of lien may record a bond in a penal sum equal to 1½ times the amount of the claim

[68.2] Cal. Civ. Code §§ 3128, 3153.

[68.3] Cal. Civ. Code § 3110.

[68.4] Cal. Civ. Code § 3123 subd. (a).

[68.5] Cal. Civ. Code § 3118.

[68.6] Cal. Civ. Code § 3130.

[68.7] *Id.*

[68.8] *Id.*

or 1½ times the amount allocated in the claim of lien to the parcel or parcels of real property sought to be released. . . . Upon the recording of such bond the real property described in such bond is released from the lien and from any action to foreclose such lien. . . ."[68.9] The surety bond will, in many cases, be the property owner's most effective protection against an unjustified or overstated mechanics' lien. Recording a surety bond "does not deprive the lien claimant of its constitutional right to a lien and instead provides for the speedy and efficient enforcement of the lien. The recording of the release bond does not extinguish the lien; rather, the bond is substituted for the land as the object to which the lien attaches, with the lien transferred from the land to the bond."[68.10]

The appellate court was unwilling to declare API's lien rights forfeited under section 3118 based solely on API's insistence that section 3130 required it to record the duplicative liens to secure the payment of a single debt. Plaintiff was held to be entitled to a mechanics' lien because it constructed a work of improvement for which, it alleged, it had not been paid. The appellate court stated that it was equally plain that inequity resulted from requiring petitioners and other property owners to post multiple bonds to release duplicative liens, even though there was only one debt. API presented no evidence or argument indicating that it would have been prejudiced by the posting of a single bond in the statutory amount, rather than the nine bonds required by the trial court's ruling. The court stated that the balancing of equities would obviously differ in a case where the lien claimant had demonstrated that it would be prejudiced by a single bond.

The *T.O. IX* court held that the equitable result here was both to secure API's entire claim and to give petitioners a realistic opportunity to restore their property rights. Section 3130 provided for that result by allowing a trial court to divide a single lien claim among several parcels. Developers asked for a different equitable result: a single bond to release several liens recorded against several parcels reflecting a single claim. Under either scenario, API had security for the payment of its entire claim. The surety bond would not extinguish API's lien or affect its priority. It substituted the bond for the land as the object to which the lien attached. API had the degree of security mandated by the mechanics' lien statutes, and developers recovered their property rights by posting security for the entire debt they allegedly owed to API.

The appellate court ruled that a writ of mandate should issue, directing the trial court to vacate its order of September 27, 2007, denying petitioners' *ex parte* application and directing it to enter a new and different order granting the application and permitting developers to record a single bond in the amount mandated by section 3143, to release the nine mechanics' liens at issue.

[68.9] Section 3143.

[68.10] *Id.*

§ 15.10 RETAINAGE

Page 590, add after first paragraph of section:

Retainage, also called retention, is almost universally used by owners with general contractors, or general contractors with subcontractor, to provide security to the party receiving performance to ensure full and proper performance. In *McPhee Electric Limited v. Konover Construction Corp.*,[76.1] the court held that a construction contractor was not entitled to withhold release of payment in retainage to an electrical subcontractor, and the construction contractor breached its contract with the subcontractor. In *McPhee*, a town hired a contractor to build a new high school, and the contractor subcontracted out the electrical work. The town issued a "certificate of substantial completion" to the subcontractor for the work it had done, but the contractor continued to withhold release of payment of a retainage to the subcontractor, alleging that it was entitled to withhold payment because of back charges and legal fees involved in its dispute with McPhee, the subcontractor. Because the town had issued the certificate of substantial completion to McPhee, the court held that, under the general contract, Konover was not entitled to withhold release of retainage. Additionally, the subcontract did not define retainage, and it did not explicitly or implicitly permit the contractor to refuse to requisition a final payment within the terms of the general contract.

On June 19, 2003, Konover executed a construction management contract with the town. The contract was based on two standard American Institute of Architects (AIA) documents, the A121 construction management contract and the A201 General Conditions agreement. The A121 portion covered, among other things, the construction manager's responsibilities, the owner's responsibilities, compensation, changes in the work and payments to subcontractors. The A201 portion covered similar subjects including, among other things, contract administration, subcontractors, changes in the work, time, payments and completion. The town made it clear to Konover that the opening date for the new school was to be September 2005. Initially, the project was scheduled to start in early February 2004. Construction actually started on February 24, 2004. The turnover date was September 6, 2005, a period of 558 calendar days, not including the time to demolish the existing high school and construct the athletic fields.

The construction project was complex, and certain issues arose during construction regarding many facets of the work. Approximately one month before the scheduled opening date for the new NHHS, McPhee, the subcontractor, sent a lengthy letter to Tighe, seeking an equitable adjustment to its contract in the amount of $835,441.00. The letter, dated August 5, 2005, was signed by Ronald Stawecki, a vice-president of McPhee, but represented a collaborative effort on the part of Michael McPhee, Lynes, Mackie and Rasile, and was written by Michael McPhee. The purpose of the letter was to follow up after a meeting that took place sometime in June 2005, which itself was in follow-up to McPhee's April 18, 2005 letter, seeking an additional $754,295.82 to compensate it for what

[76.1] 2009 Conn. Super. LEXIS 3110, 2009 WL 4846555 (Conn. Super. Ct. Oct. 22, 2009).

it had represented to be "schedule delays, compression of work and subsequent decrease in productivity and added labor costs."

The August 5th letter itemized 13 areas of claimed damages and 13 open change orders. Konover responded to McPhee's letter on August 12, 2005, stating, in part, "given the nature of the assertions set forth in your correspondence and given KCC's contractual obligations to the Owner . . . a detailed analysis is required. We will, in good faith, review, analyze and evaluate the assertions . . . We will likely need additional information from McPhee in order to complete our analysis." Michael McPhee believed that this response was consistent with the discussions he had with Konover about McPhee's claim in June. Many delays occurred, and claims had been made during the construction by the contractor for additional compensation.

McPhee was described by the defendants as lacking "cooperation and coordination" during the project and described McPhee as "constantly at odds with Konover with respect to working as a team." The defendants claimed that McPhee interfered with the work of other subcontractors, "had significant deficiencies at various stages of the project [and] performed defective work."

The defendants claimed to a building committee that McPhee was seeking approximately $800,000 in alleged delay and interruption claims in their pending litigation. The defendants claimed that acts by McPhee were indicative of a "loathsome business practice" by McPhee as they were attempting "the same extortionate claim practice on other projects."

McPhee was given an opportunity to respond to these claims made by Konover to the building committee. He stated, "I take great offense to Mr. Dunn's representation that we have loathsome business practices, but somebody will get a chance to decide that at some other time." As to Konover, he said, "you know, they're used to bullying people around, and quite honestly, their bullying hasn't helped your job any." However, during trial McPhee candidly testified that he had no way of identifying the impact of Dunn's statement on his business nor could McPhee identify any particular job that he did not get because of Dunn's statements at the committee meeting. He agreed that bringing lawsuits against general contractors and construction managers can affect a subcontractor's ability to attract new business. Following nonpayment, McPhee sued for breach of contract on the following grounds: (1) Konover's failure to pay the contract balance it claims it was due; (2) Konover's refusal to compensate it for eleven change orders; and (3) Konover's responsibility to compensate it for a 10,887 hour labor overrun. The labor overrun claim was also at the core of McPhee's claims alleging negligence in the second count.

Konover asserted as a special defense to the first count that McPhee breached the contract as follows:

> a. failing to supply the project with a sufficient number of skilled workers;
> b. failing to perform its work consistent with the project schedule, thereby delaying their own work and the work of others;
> c. failing to properly manage its work efficiently and effectively to achieve the schedule objectives of the project;

d. failing to follow the directives of Konover as the Construction Manager;
e. making unreasonable and untimely demands for additional compensation before proceeding with the work under the subcontract;
f. failing to provide the proper materials and equipment to the project in a timely manner;
g. representing to Konover that areas of work were complete when they were not, thus requiring additional work by Konover and other subcontractors;
h. failing to coordinate its work with other trades on the project;
i. failing to timely comply with directives of the local building officials; . . .
j. failing to perform its work properly, requiring the plaintiff to troubleshoot and correct the work;
k. in failing to remobilize when directed; and
l. in engaging in direct communications with Town of North Haven officials and the architect for the Project without Konover's . . . involvement.

The *McPhee* court held that the intention of the parties to a contract is to be determined from the language used, interpreted in the light of the situation of the parties and the circumstances connected with the transaction. The court stated that it had reviewed the subcontract agreement and the contract in detail and had found both documents to be clear, unambiguous, harmonious and definitive. The appellate court further found that both parties in this case were sophisticated commercial entities with lengthy experience in the construction field. When, as here, sophisticated parties enter into commercial contracts, the court may presume that the contract language is clear and unambiguous. Further, the court held that McPhee was aware of the relevant contractual language from the beginning of the bidding process and knew that it had to accept the subcontract agreement without alteration if its bid were accepted.

McPhee claimed that Konover owed it a contract balance of $169,966.81, consisting of payments it claimed were due on two pay applications, as well as $128,368.41 in retainage. Konover maintained that it was entitled to withhold these sums under the contract as a set-off based on claims it has against McPhee.

McPhee relied, in part, on article 3 of the subcontract agreement. Article 3.a. which specified that: "Partial payment shall be due Subcontractor in the amount of 95% of the work in place for which payment has been made to Contractor by Owner." Article 3.b. spelled out the requisition procedure that was followed in this case. Under article 3.c. once Konover received payment from the town on account of McPhee's work, McPhee would be entitled to payment.

The court found in favor of McPhee Electric on the breach of contract count and awarded damages in the amount of $128,368.41, and on the defamation count awarded nominal damages of $10.00. The court, however, found for the defendant Konover Construction Corp. on the negligence count, the breach of contract count, and the breach of the covenant of good faith and fair dealing count, and the unfair competition count.

Note that many jurisdictions, including California, have enacted statutes that attempt to prevent paying parties, such as owners or general contractors, from improperly withholding payment to gain leverage in negotiating final payment. *See*Cal. Bus. & Prof. Code § 7108.5 and Cal. Civil Code § 3260.

In *Advantages of the ConsensusDOCS Construction Contracts,*[76.2] the authors describe the difference in the handling of retainage. Under the AIA documents, retainage is released upon substantial completion of the entire project, as to designated portions of the work, if there still remain portions of the work that are not substantially complete. Under the ConsensusDOCS, the owner releases retainage applicable to the work of the early completing trades and other subcontractors once their work has been accepted. After the project is 50 percent complete, the owner is not entitled to withhold any additional retainage. ConsensusDOCS 200 Para. 9.2.4. ConsensusDOCS also give the owners the option to utilize a retention bond or other form of security interest in lieu of retainage. ConsensusDOCS 200 Para. 9.2.4.3.

§ 15.11 PAYMENTS AND WITHHOLDING: PRIME CONTRACTS AND SUBCONTRACTS

Page 600, add after second paragraph:

In *Wolet Construction Corp. v. 216-20 Beach 87th Street Co., LLC.,*[102.1] the court denied the summary judgment motion of the contractors (two affiliated companies) in their action seeking to foreclose mechanic's liens, recover damages for breach of contract for nonpayment, and in quantum meruit and unjust enrichment for services rendered.The court held that the plaintiffs' submission did not satisfy their burden in proving entitlement to judgment as a matter of law. The defendants also submitted their own evidence, and there were questions of fact on many of the issues posed in this case, including whether the work was performed by the plaintiffs in accordance with the agreements, whether their delays were excused, and whether all necessary close-out documents were submitted.

The defendants (Beech, the premises owner, Suntrust, the assignee of the rents and leases for the premises, and New York City) had hired the plaintiffs to prepare the premises for occupation by Administration of Children's Services (ACS), the city's child welfare agency, which intended to use the demised premises as a child care facility pursuant to a lease between defendant Beach and the city. The work consisted of, among other things, improvements to the roof and heating, ventilation, air conditioning system, installation of doors and a fire alarm system, plumbing, electrical, painting, and exterior masonry work. The city's lease with Beach provided, among other things, that the lease terms, including ACS's obligation to pay rent, would not become effective until after the substantial completion date of the project, and that the city would reimburse the owner for part of the construction and repair cost. The lease allowed the city to dictate the timing of the project and supervise the construction, through its architects and ACS officials. The lease provided that all the work on the premises would be either "Reimbursable" work or "Landlord" work and that the

[76.2] Larry D. Harris & Brian M. Perlberg, *Advantages of the ConsensusDOCS Construction Contracts*, The Construction Lawyer, Vol. 29, No. 1, Winter 2009.

[102.1] 20 Misc.3d 1126(A), 2008 N.Y. Slip Op. 51635(U) (Queens Cty. Sup. Ct., July 24, 2008).

defendant, Beach, initially would pay for the cost of the reimbursable work, but subsequently would be reimbursed in full by the city, whereas the cost of the landlord work would be borne solely by defendant Beach.

The plaintiffs alleged that they fully completed their work and furnished material to the defendant, Beach, pursuant to the agreements, and demanded payment in full, but the defendant made only a partial payment, and there remained an outstanding sum due and owing each of them. The plaintiffs further alleged that they filed, docketed, and served notices of mechanic's liens. One of the plaintiff contractor claimed in its notice of lien that the premises owner owed it $142,462.65 for its labor performed and materials furnished, and that it owed the other plaintiff contractor, $54,532.06 for its labor performed and materials furnished.

The defendants interposed counterclaims based upon breach of contract, failure to achieve substantial completion, and willful exaggeration of the liens. They alleged that the plaintiff failed to perform the work within the time specified in the agreements and to finish the work on the project, and that the plaintiff failed to provide a 20-year warranty for the roof installed at the premises. The defendants, therefore, sought to recover damages, liquidated damages, and costs and disbursements, including reasonable attorneys' fees. The defendants also asserted that the agreements provided that time was of the essence for performance and completion of the work, and the plaintiffs failed to achieve substantial compliance on the project until August 26, 2005, when ACS issued a certificate of substantial completion. They further asserted that under the agreements, the defendant, Beach, was entitled to offset liquidated damages against any amount owed to the plaintiffs. Accordingly, Beech demanded payment of additional liquidated damages to the extent the amount of liquidated damages exceeded the amount owed the plaintiffs under the agreements.

The construction agreements at issue were standard forms of the American Institute of Architects (AIA) (Document A101-1997), and included the AIA form, "General Conditions for the Contract for Construction" (Document A201-1997). The agreement included base prices that the plaintiffs agreed to pay, which were "subject to additions and deductions as provided in the Contract Documents" (Document A101-1997). Each agreement provided for a schedule of payments, which included an initial deposit, eight progress payments, a payment for completion of the punch list, and a retainer (Document A101-1997, article 5, paragraph 5.1.5). The agreements provided that if the contractor substantially performed its contractual obligations, then it would be entitled to the payment due under the agreement, less a sum determined by the architect for incomplete work, the retainage applicable to such work ,and unsettled claims (Document A107-1997, article 5, paragraph 5.1.9). The agreements, however, also provided, at article 9, paragraph 9.10.3 (Document A201-1997) that if after substantial completion of the work, the "final completion thereof is materially delayed through no fault of the Contractor or by issuance of Change Orders affecting final completion, and the Architect so confirms, the Owner shall, upon application by the Contractor and certification by the architect, and without terminating the contract, make payment of the balance due for that portion of the Work fully completed and accepted."

In addition, the agreements provided that the final payment, constituting the entire unpaid balance of the contract sum, be made by defendant Beach upon the contractor's full performance of the contract, including but not limited to furnishing all close-out documentation, the satisfaction of other requirements, if any, which extended beyond the final payment, and the issuance of a final certificate for payment by the architect.

Article 3, paragraph 3.3 (Document A101-1997) of the Wolet agreement required Wolet to achieve substantial completion of the entire work no later than 150 days from the date of commencement. Each agreement provided, at article 3, paragraph 3.3.2 (Document A101-1997), that "[t]he Contractor recognizes that time is of the essence of this Contract and further acknowledges that the Contract Time established in this Agreement is a reasonable period for performing the Work." Each agreement further provided, at article 3, paragraph 3.4 (Document A101-1997), that:

> The Contractor recognizes that its obligations for the performance of the Work within the time provided for in this agreement and the General Conditions are of the essence of this Agreement and that the Owner will suffer financial loss if the Work is not completed within the time specified in Paragraph 3.3.... The parties also recognize the delays, expense and difficulties involved in determining and proving the actual loss suffered by Owner if the Work is not completed on time. Accordingly, instead of requiring any such determination or proof, Owner and Contractor agree that the Contractor shall be liable for and shall pay the Owner the sum of Five Hundred Dollars ($500.00) for each and every calendar day of unexcused delay, as defined in the General Conditions, past the Substantial Completion Date for the first thirty (30) consecutive days of such delay, and Eight Hundred Dollars ($800.00) for each and every calendar day of such delay thereafter, as the fair and reasonable compensation to the Owner for such losses, which compensation shall be construed as Liquidated Damages, and not as a penalty of any kind

The agreements, at article 3, paragraph 3.5, also provided:

> The Owner may deduct Liquidated Damages described in Paragraph 3.4 from any unpaid amounts then or thereafter due the Contractor under [the] Agreement. Any liquidated damages not so deducted from any unpaid amounts due the Contractor shall be payable to the Owner by the Contractor upon demand by the Owner, together with interest from the date of the demand equal to the highest lawful rate of interest.

The agreements, however, also provided, at article 9, paragraph 9 .10.3, that if after substantial completion of the work, the "final completion thereof is materially delayed through no fault of the Contractor or by issuance of Change Orders affecting final completion, and the Architect so confirms, the Owner shall, upon application by the Contractor and certification by the architect, and without terminating the contract, make payment of the balance due for that portion of the Work fully completed and accepted."

The plaintiffs claimed that they diligently performed their work and were on the job every day, and that they provided the defendant with a 20-year roof warranty. While admitting that the defendant made payments pursuant to invoices sent by them to it at the completion of each phase of the project, they asserted that notwithstanding their demands, the defendant failed to pay final invoices sent to it reflecting balances of $142,462.65, which remained due and owing to one plaintiff, Wolet, and $54,532.06, which remained due and owing the other plaintiff, N.Y. Interior.

The plaintiffs also contended that they achieved substantial completion of the project on July 15, 2005, and that ACS issued a certificate entitled "CERTIFICATE OF SUBSTANTIAL COMPLETION," indicating the project was 100 percent completed on August 26, 2005. The plaintiffs asserted that such completion must be considered to be within the time allotted under their respective agreements because they did not cause any unexcused delays. The plaintiffs claimed they submitted change orders for extensions of time, which were granted, and the delays thereafter, were not unexcused, because they were caused by events not within their control, including poor weather conditions, changes requested by the defendants' architect in the scope, specifications, and timing of the work, and interference with performance of the work by other contractors employed by the plaintiff at the job site. The plaintiffs further claimed additional costs were approved by the defendant, pursuant to change orders without objection, and that the defendant did not object to the invoices that they received. The plaintiffs also asserted that upon the defendant failure to submit full payment, they filed and docketed the verified notices of their mechanic's liens within eight months after final performance of the work, and served a copy of them upon the defendant.

In support of their motion, the plaintiffs submitted, among other things, a copy of the pleadings, the affidavit of the president of the plaintiffs (two affiliated companies), the affirmation of their counsel, and copies of the construction agreements, various correspondence and change orders, the ACS lease, notes of construction meetings, invoices, a roofing system limited warranty, contractor's applications for payments and the notices of mechanic's lien, and affidavits of service.

The court, however, held that the plaintiffs' submissions did not satisfy their burden of establishing a prima facie entitlement to judgment as a matter of law, and their own papers raised questions on that issue, including but not limited to whether the work was performed in accordance with the agreements, the delays were unexcused, and all necessary close-out documents were submitted. In addition, the plaintiffs' submissions did not include a copy of the issuance of a final certificate for payment by the architect or the unpaid final invoices.

The court also cited the evidence presented by the defendants, which included: the affidavit of Beach's principal, an affirmation of plaintiffs' counsel, copies of correspondence, including an email dated January 30, 2006, purportedly amending the date of substantial completion to July 15, 2005, and a certificate of payment dated August 25, 2005, which raised issues of fact as to whether all of the work at the premises was satisfactorily and timely performed, and whether the plaintiffs submitted all necessary close-out documents and a final certificate of payment from the architect. The principal stated that plaintiffs failed to complete all the work, to obtain substantial completion in a timely fashion, and to submit all necessary close-out documents and a final certificate of payment from the architect. He alleged the defendants walked off the job, without completing construction, and left numerous "punch list" items undone. He further averred that the defendant had incurred additional expenses for the purposes of completing and repairing the plaintiffs' work on the project. For instance, the principal cited the plaintiffs' failure to abide by the agreements' specifications regarding the replacement of air conditioning units.

After denying the plaintiffs' summary judgment motion, the court then considered the various affirmative defenses and counterclaims asserted by the defendants.

The court granted the plaintiffs' motion to dismiss the following affirmative defenses and counterclaims: (1) the first affirmative defense, which was based upon failure to state a cause of action, because it was improperly pleaded; (2) the second, fourth, fifth, and seventh affirmative defenses. The second affirmative defense that any damage sustained by plaintiffs were caused by the conduct of others, the fourth and fifth affirmative defenses based upon failure to mitigate damages, and the seventh affirmative defense based upon the doctrines of waiver and estoppel were unsupported by any factual allegations or proof; (3) the ninth affirmative defense, where the defendants asserted the statute of limitations, because the complaint was timely filed; (4) the third affirmative defense and that part of the sixth affirmative defenses, since they alleged the plaintiffs' culpable conduct, which related to tort. Since all of the causes of action related to breach of contract (including those for quantum meruit, unjust enrichment, and foreclosure of mechanic's liens), as opposed to tortious conduct, an affirmative defense based on a motion of culpable conduct was unavailable; and (5) the second counterclaim asserting failure to provide the required 20-year warranty for the roof, because the plaintiff produced a copy of a roofing system limited warranty, commencing on November 9, 2004 for a period of 20 years, for the building housing the day care center at subject premises, and naming the defendant as the building owner.

The court, however, denied the plaintiffs' motion relating to that part of the sixth affirmative defense that was based upon breach of contract. The plaintiffs had argued that the plaintiffs failed to raise, in a timely fashion, an objection to the timeliness of plaintiffs' completion of the work, alleging that the defendant was required to object to their delay in completing the agreements within 21 days of "discovery" of the delay in accordance with article 4, section 4.3.4 (Document A201-1997).

Contrary to the plaintiffs' argument, the court held that article 4, section 4.3.4 (Document A201-1997) was inapplicable to whether the defendant could assert, as an affirmative defense, a claim of breach of contract arising out of delay in completion of the work. That provision governed claims for concealed or unknown physical conditions at the work site, which were materially different from those described in the contract documents, and permitted the architect to determine whether the newly encountered conditions warranted an equitable adjustment in the contract sum or time, or both. Such provision required that any objection by the contracting parties to the architect's determination, regarding the appropriateness of such adjustment, be made within 21 days after notice of the architect's decision. Likewise, the court held that provision was inapplicable to whether the defendant could assert a defense based upon breach of contract due to delay in performance. Article 4, section 4.3.2 related to the 21-day time frame for making claims for affirmative relief under the agreements and the role of the architect in determining the acceptability and fitness of workmanship and materials. It did not preclude the defendant from raising an affirmative defense based upon breach of contract arising out of the plaintiffs' alleged failure to comply with the deadlines set forth in the agreements.

Article 13, paragraph 13.4 (Document A201-1997), also provided that "[n]o action or failure to act by the Owner, Architect or Contractor shall constitute a waiver of a right or duty afforded them under the Contract, nor shall such action or failure to act constitute approval of or acquiescence in a breach thereunder except as may be specifically agreed in writing."

The court also rejected the argument that the defendant should be estopped from raising breach of contract as an affirmative defense based on the defendant's alleged acquiescence to the delay, by continuing, after the contractual completion dates, to direct the plaintiffs regarding their work on the project. The defendant, however, was entitled to expect, even after the passage of the completion dates set in the agreements, performance of the work by plaintiffs in compliance with the agreements (article 4, paragraph 4.3.3, Document A201-1997). It also was entitled to rely upon the contractual remedy of liquidated damages in the event of unexcused delays occasioned by the plaintiffs. Nevertheless, the liquidated damages clause was only applicable to unexcused delays, and questions of fact exist as to whether any of the delays should be considered excused.

The court denied the eighth affirmative defense, and the third and sixth counterclaims pursuant to Lien Law section 39, to set aside the plaintiffs' mechanic's liens and for damages on the ground of willful exaggeration. The court held that the validity of the liens plainly turned on resolution of the dispute as to whether plaintiffs completed the work required by the agreements, or willfully or fraudulent exaggerated their liens. Such dispute could not be resolved on these papers, and had to await trial.

The court denied dismissal of the first and fourth counterclaims by the defendant seeking liquidated damages based upon breach of contract. The plaintiffs could not assert the defendants' alleged waiver of their claim to recover liquidated damages, because they failed to raise waiver as an affirmative defense in their reply. The court also rejected the plaintiffs' alternative argument that the defendant should be estopped from claiming an offset of the liquidated damages clause because of its acquiescence to the delay, by continuing, after the contractual completion dates, to direct them regarding their work on the project. The defendant was entitled to expect, even after the passage of the completion dates set in the agreements, the plaintiffs' completion of the work in accordance with the agreements. It was also entitled to rely upon the contractual remedy of liquidated damages in the event of unexcused delays occasioned by plaintiffs. Nevertheless, the liquidated damages clause was only applicable to unexcused delays, and questions of fact existed as to whether any of the delays should be considered excused.

Finally, the court denied the plaintiffs' motion seeking dismissal of the fifth counterclaim and the remainder of the second counterclaim for breach of contract, because the plaintiffs made no showing that the liquidated damages clause was the defendant's exclusive remedy or that the defendant agreed to be limited to the amount of any liquidated damages. Furthermore, questions of fact existed as to whether plaintiffs were in breach of contract.

Page 622, add at end of section:

In *Great Western Drywall v. Roel Construction,*[146.1] a subcontractor brought an action against a general contractor for breach of contract and related counts based on alleged underpayment by the general contractor. Roel, the general contractor, counterclaimed against the subcontractor for breach of contract, related counts, and negligence, based on Great Western Drywall's subcontractor's alleged failure to adequately perform, abandonment, and damage to the work of others. The trial court awarded damages to both parties, awarded prejudgment interest to subcontractor, and denied statutory interest and attorney fees to Great Western's subcontractor for the general contractor's alleged failure to timely pay in violation of the prompt payment statutes. Both parties appealed.

The appellate court, affirming in part, and reversing in part, held that the general contractor was entitled to set off its entire award for subcontractor's damage to property against the award of prejudgment interest to subcontractor on subcontractor's breach of contract claim.

The appellate court held that even if the trial court awarded property damages to the general contractor for subcontractor's damage to the work of another subcontractor, under the general contractor's negligence theory, as opposed to its breach of contract theory, the general contractor was entitled to set off its entire award against an award of prejudgment interest to the subcontractor on subcontractor's breach of contract claim, where general contractor's damages arose entirely from subcontractor's deficient performance of contract. The setoff served the interests of justice and the purposes of prejudgment interest statute since both parties had claims against each other under the subcontract. The appellate court held that any arbitrary reliance by the trial court on one theory over another should not adversely affect general contractor's setoff rights.[146.2]

Great Western Drywall, Inc. (Great Western) and Roel Construction Co., Inc. (Roel) appealed a judgment entered after a bench trial on their respective actions arising from a construction subcontract. Roel's sole contention was that the court erred by awarding Great Western prejudgment interest on its liquidated contract

[146.1] 166 Cal. App. 4th 761, 83 Cal. Rptr. 3d 235 (2008) (*certified for partial publication*).
[146.2] West's Ann.Cal. Civ. Code §§ 3287, 3528.

claims, since Roel's damages exceeded Great Western's damages and entirely offset the interest award.

Great Western challenged the sufficiency of the evidence to support certain items of damages the court awarded Roel. Great Western contended that the court erred as a matter of law by awarding Roel a cleanup contribution not directly attributable to Great Western as a subcontractor, and abused its discretion by denying Great Western prejudgment interest on unliquidated contract claims. Great Western also appealed a postjudgment order in which the court denied it penalty interest under Business and Professions Code section 7108.5 for Roel's failure to promptly make progress payments. The appellate court found in Roel's favor on its appeal, and in Great Western's favor on the cleanup contribution issue. The appellate court affirmed the judgment.

Roel was the general contractor on Renaissance, a condominium project in San Diego. The project consisted of 218 units, in two towers. In April 2001, Roel and Great Western entered into a subcontract for Great Western to install metal studs, drywall, lath and plaster, and the exterior insulation finish system at the project. Great Western worked on the project for about two years. The original amount of the subcontract was approximately $4.5 million, but numerous approved change orders increased the amount to more than $7.7 million. Roel did not approve numerous change order requests (CORs) by Great Western. In July 2003, Great Western recorded a mechanic's lien against the Renaissance property.

In September 2003, Great Western sued Roel for breach of contract and related counts, alleging Roel underpaid it on extra work. Roel cross-complained against Great Western for breach of contract and related counts, and negligence. The cross-complaint alleged Roel was damaged by Great Western's failure to adequately perform its work, by its abandonment of the project before its work was complete, and by its damage to the work of others, such as its scratching of window glass. Each breach of contract claim for damage to the work or property of others was alternatively pleaded as a tort claim.

On November 29, 2005, after a four-day bench trial, the court issued a written ruling that awarded Great Western $332,106 and awarded Roel $320,848. The award to Roel included $156,993 for glass replacement, and additional amounts to repair other property damages Great Western caused. The award did not specify whether Roel's recovery for property damages was on a contract or tort theory. The award to Great Western included $251,263 in CORs that Roel admitted in discovery were undisputed, and $57,534 in prejudgment interest on that amount. The court found there was no prevailing party for the purposes of awarding fees and costs. The ruling ordered Great Western "to prepare a judgment reflecting this decision if a Statement of Decision is not requested by either party."

On December 1, 2005, Roel moved *ex parte* for a stay of entry of judgment, arguing that the award of prejudgment interest to Great Western on the amount of undisputed CORs was improper based on the facts and established case law. No party asked for a statement of decision.

The trial judge, Thomas LaVoy, was scheduled to retire on December 8. On December 5, Judge LaVoy granted a stay pending a noticed hearing requesting a modification of the court's "tentative decision" and a showing of good cause. On

December 7, after receiving a joint letter from the parties, Judge LaVoy issued a tentative ruling to amend the trial court's original ruling to delete an amount awarded Roel for plaster repairs.

Also on December 7, Roel and Great Western jointly applied *ex parte* to the independent calendar judge, Ronald Prager, stating that because of Judge LaVoy's imminent retirement, "the parties seek guidance from this court on how it wishes them to proceed with respect to asserting objections to the tentative decision." The *ex parte* hearing was not reported, but on February 1, 2006, Judge Janis Sammartino entered a judgment that awarded Great Western $332,106 on its complaint, which included $57,534 in prejudgment interest on the sum of $251,263, and awarded Roel $315,398 on the cross-complaint.

On June 1, 2006, the parties filed a stipulation for amended judgment. The amendment corrected several computational errors in Judge LaVoy's November 29, 2005 ruling. Further, the amendment decreased the prejudgment interest award to Great Western by $20,572.86, as the parties agreed Roel was entitled to an offset of that amount for contract-based counter-claims. The stipulation reserved to Roel "its objection to the entire award of prejudgment interest."

On June 2, Judge Sammartino entered an amended judgment that awarded Great Western $328,819.69, which included prejudgment interest of $36,961.14, and awarded Roel $326,300.75. Roel filed a notice of appeal on August 4, within 60 days of Great Western's service of notice of the amended judgment.

Great Western then moved for interest and attorney fees under Business and Professions Code section 7108.5, which penalizes a contractor for violating its obligation to timely pay a subcontractor. On July 6, 2006, Judge Prager denied the motion, explaining Great Western's recovery was significantly less than it had requested. The court had previously denied fees and costs unless Great Western presented other factors at posttrial motions, which it did not do. Great Western failed to prove Roel's conduct was not in good faith. On August 21, Great Western filed its notice of appeal of the amended judgment and the postjudgment order.

The court in *Great Western Drywall* stated that prejudgment interest on liquidated damages is an element of compensatory damages. It held that the policy underlying authorization of an award of prejudgment interest is to compensate the injured party, to make that party whole for the accrual of wealth which could have been produced during the period of loss. "[I]n situations where the defendant could have timely paid [a certain] amount and has thus deprived the plaintiff of the economic benefit of those funds, the defendant should therefore compensate with appropriate interest."[146.3] "It has long been settled that [Civil Code] Section 3287 should be broadly interpreted to provide just compensation to the injured party for loss of use of money during the prejudgment period."[146.4]

The court also stated that an award of unliquidated damages to a cross-complainant is a setoff against prejudgment interest awarded a plaintiff for

[146.3] Wisper Corp. v. California Commerce Bank, 49 Cal. App. 4th 948, 962, 57 Cal. Rptr. 2d 141 (1996).

[146.4] Gourley v. State Farm Mut. Auto. Ins. Co., 53 Cal. 3d 121, 132, 3 Cal. Rptr. 2d 666, 822 P.2d 374 (1991).

liquidated damages. The *Great Western Drywall* court stated that such an offset is allowed on the theory that the contractor is entitled to interest only on such amount of the use of which he has been deprived during the period of default.

Great Western argued to the appellate court that under the above cases only unliquidated contract damages may be offset from liquidated contract damages. The cases, however, do not consider whether unliquidated tort claims may ever be offset against liquidated contract claims.

The appellate court stated that Great Western erroneously asserted that Roel could have asserted many of its tort claims as breaches of contract, but it chose not to. Roel's cross-complaint alleged property damage claims under the breach of contract and tort counts, and the court's ruling did not reveal which theory it relied on for the property damage award.

Roel cited section 9.5b of the subcontract, which allowed Roel damages for a subcontractor's default under the subcontract, and a 25 percent markup for profit and overhead. The subcontract defined the term "default" as including the failure to diligently perform the work, maintain the schedule, or provide quality workmanship. The court specifically found certain claims were default items and awarded the markup on them, but on the property damage claims the court disallowed a markup, finding they were not default items.

The appellate court ruled against Great Western's assertion that Roel did not submit both breach of contract and tort claims. The trial court could have relied on section 5.7 of the subcontract, which provided that a breach of contract includes a subcontractor's damage to the work of another subcontractor or the property of a third party, or section 15.3f, which requires a subcontractor to protect the work of others and to repair and replace damaged property at its own expense. The court found that Roel relied only on section 9.5b of the subcontract, but Roel specifically raised section 15.3f at trial, and the entire subcontract was admitted into evidence for the court's review. Roel pointed to no election by Roel to pursue a tort theory. It did not appear that a tort theory offered any advantage over a breach of contract theory. The court held that evidence that Roel did not submit property damage claims to Great Western in the form of change orders did not necessarily indicate Roel elected to proceed in tort.

The appellate court concluded that even if the trial court intended to award property damages for negligence, as opposed to breach of contract, Roel was entitled to a setoff of its entire award. It was undisputed that Roel's damages arose entirely from Great Western's deficient performance of the contract, and Roel's mere inclusion of an alternative count for negligence in its cross-complaint, and any arbitrary reliance by the trial court on one theory over another, should not adversely affect Roel's setoff rights. Both parties had claims against each other under the subcontract, thus setoff serves the interests of justice and the purposes of the prejudgment interest statute, stating that any other ruling would elevate form over substance.[146.5] Because Roel's award exceeded Great Western's

[146.5] *See* Cal. Civ. Code § 3528; *see also* Mechanical Contractors Ass'n v. Greater Bay Area Ass'n, 66 Cal. App. 4th 672, 687, n.5, 78 Cal. Rptr. 2d 225 (1998).

award, even after the adjustment to Roel's award for the cleanup contribution, the appellate court held that Great Western could not recover any prejudgment interest.

The appellate court reversed the trial court's judgment insofar as it awarded Great Western $36,961.14 in prejudgment interest on its liquidated contract claims, and it awarded Roel $26,287 for a cleanup contribution. The trial court's judgment was affirmed in all other respects. The trial court's order denying Great Western penalty interest was affirmed.

§ 15.18 FAILURE TO PAY

Page 645, add after second full paragraph:

Parties and their attorneys should carefully review the scope of an arbitration agreement to ensure that all claims that need to be presented in arbitration are put forward in a timely manner. In *Herring-Malbis I, LLC, Eastern Shore Centre I, LLC, and Eastern Shore Centre II, LLC v. Temco, Inc.*,[205.1] a contractor brought an action for breach of contract, open account, and mechanic's lien action against a developer. Following arbitration, the circuit court granted contractor's motion for attorneys' fees under the Prompt Payment Act, and developer appealed.

The appellate court held that:

> (1) the parties' arbitration agreement required the contractor to submit its claim for attorney fees under the Prompt Payment Act to arbitration;
>
> (2) *res judicata* barred the contractor from seeking attorney fees under the Prompt Payment Act in the circuit court following the arbitration hearing; and
>
> (3) the developer was not judicially estopped from asserting that *res judicata* barred contractor's claim for attorney fees. Reversed and remanded with instructions.

In *Herring-Malbis*, the owner appealed from an order of the Baldwin Circuit Court awarding an attorney fee to Temco, Inc. (TEMCO), pursuant to Ala. Code 1975, § 8-29-1 *et seq.*, usually referred to as the Prompt Payment Act. The appellate court reversed the trial court's order awarding an attorney fee to Temco.

Temco sued Herring-Malbis in May 2006, alleging that Temco was owed money "pursuant to the terms and conditions of" contract documents signed by the parties, which included a construction contract and American Institute of Architects AIA Document A201-1997 general conditions, that were incorporated into the parties' agreement by reference in the construction contract. Temco's original complaint sought damages in the amount of $486,303 plus interest and costs under several alternative theories of relief, including breach of contract, open account, account stated, work and labor done, and enforcement of mechanic's lien.

[205.1] 2009 Ala. Civ. App. LEXIS 537, 2009 WL 3517580 (Ala. Civ. App. 2009).

The circuit court granted Herring-Malbis's motion for an order compelling alternative dispute resolution under the terms of the AIA contract.

Pursuant to A201, the parties first attempted to resolve their dispute through mediation, and, when that failed, they arbitrated their dispute through the American Arbitration Association. The arbitration hearing was held on February 19 and 20, 2008. Six days before the commencement of the hearing, on February 13, 2008, Temco filed a motion to amend its original complaint. The motion sought "to amend the complaint to add a claim under the Prompt Payment Act . . . for reasonable attorneys' fees and expenses pursuant to said statute." The motion maintained that the Prompt Payment Act claim "in no way" affected the issues to be presented to the arbitrator but was a matter to be presented to court in the event that the arbitrator entered an award in favor of Temco. No action was taken on the motion prior to the arbitration hearing.

Temco presented a demand letter to AAA. Herring-Malbis presented an answering statement and counterclaim in the arbitration proceeding. In its demand letter, Temco itemized its claims for relief, which included a request for accumulated interest, but Temco omitted mention in the arbitration documents of any claim for an award of an attorney fee and any mention of particular theories of relief, including any right to relief under the Prompt Payment Act. The demand letter from Temco specified that Temco's principal claim was that it was due relief under the construction contract.

After the hearing, the arbitrator rendered a decision that Temco was owed most of what it claimed. The arbitrator also specified that each party would be responsible for its own attorney fees. The arbitration award concluded by stating that "[a]ll claims not expressly granted herein are hereby[ ] denied," thereby denying Temco its request for an award of accumulated interest on any of its claims. Temco and Herring-Malbis then filed briefs concerning whether the arbitrator's award should be modified by deleting the reference to attorney fees and by awarding Temco the accumulated interest it sought. No changes to the award were made by the arbitrator. Herring-Malbis timely tendered payment to Temco in satisfaction of the arbitration award.

In April 2008, after the arbitration hearing had been held, Herring-Malbis filed with the court a response in opposition to Temco's February 13, 2008 motion to amend its original complaint. The trial court granted Temco's motion to amend and overruled Herring-Malbis's objections. Temco then filed its amended complaint in May 2008, after which Herring-Malbis moved to dismiss that complaint. The trial court denied this motion, and, following a stipulation by the parties as to the amount of a reasonable attorney fee, and a further agreement of the parties to allow the trial court to rule on the matter without a hearing, the trial court entered an order awarding the stipulated attorney fee to Temco, "pursuant to the Prompt Payment Act," in November 2008.

The amended complaint ultimately filed by Temco pleaded the Prompt Payment Act as another alternative legal theory under which Temco sought complete relief. Under Count 10 of the amended complaint, Temco incorporated the remainder of the complaint and demanded relief as to all of its claims against all defendants, which then totaled $561,412.70, specifically including interest, costs, expenses, and attorney fees.

The demand letter written by Temco as a formality required by American Arbitration Association rules in order to initiate the arbitration process did not seek attorney fees or make claims under the Prompt Payment Act, but that omission does not conclusively establish that neither matter was discussed at the hearing.

The AIA contract incorporated into the parties' agreement provided that "any claim arising out of or related to the contract" shall be submitted first to mediation, and in the event mediation fails to resolve the dispute, as occurred here, the claim is to be submitted to arbitration. Where the contract defines "claim," it includes in that definition "other disputes and matters in question between [Herring-Malbis] and [Temco] arising out of or relating to the Contract," a sweepingly broad clause.

When parties include such a broad arbitration clause, they intend the clause to reach all aspects of the relationship. To like effect is the Alabama Supreme Court's holding that arbitration clauses, including the language "arising out of or relating to" that appears in the AIA contract, have broader application than arbitration clauses that omit "or relating to." The AIA contract further states that the party seeking relief in arbitration "must assert in the demand all Claims then known to that party on which arbitration is permitted to be demanded." Finally, the AIA contract further provides that arbitration will proceed under the Construction Industry Arbitration Rules of the American Arbitration Association, of which Rule 44(d) provides that "the award of the arbitrator may include . . . an award of attorneys' fees if all parties have requested such an award or it is authorized by law or their arbitration agreement."

The court held that Temco was required by the arbitration agreement, and by law, to submit its Prompt Payment Act claim, including the request for an award of an attorney fee, to the arbitrator. If, as Temco claimed, the parties did not submit the issue to the arbitrator, whether the arbitrator in fact made a determination concerning Temco's right to an attorney-fee award was immaterial.

In Temco's amended complaint, the Prompt Payment Act was asserted as an additional alternative theory under which Temco demanded complete relief. The entire Prompt Payment Act claim, including the request for an award of an attorney fee, was held to be within the ambit of the contract documents' definition of "claim," quoted above, and Temco was required to submit its Prompt Payment Act claim to the arbitrator, on pain of waiver, in light of the contractual provision stating that parties demanding arbitration "must assert in the demand all Claims then known to that party on which arbitration is permitted to be demanded."

Because Temco indicated its intent to assert the Prompt Payment Act claim in its motion to amend its complaint, filed in the circuit court six days before the arbitration hearing, that claim certainly was "known to" Temco at the time of the arbitration hearing.

The Prompt Payment Act claim also was a claim "on which arbitration is permitted to be demanded," contrary to Temco's assertions (a) that the contract documents provided no legal basis for requesting an award of an attorney fee and

(b) that the Prompt Payment Act provided Temco's only legal basis for seeking such an award. For a particular claim or grievance to be excluded from arbitration, the parties must expressly exclude such claim in the arbitration agreement. Temco argued that the AIA contract did not allow the recovery of attorney fees, but it cited as support for this assertion provisions in the AIA contract such as paragraph 3.18.1, under which Temco had agreed not to pursue attorney fees related to a claim "provided that such claim . . . is attributable to bodily injury, sickness, disease or death, or to injury to or destruction of tangible property (other than the Work itself), but only to the extent caused by the negligent acts or omissions of [Temco]."

That provision, as well as other provisions Temco cited, were held inapplicable to this case, which concerned contractual disputes and not claims of bodily injury or property damage. Further, the AIA contract provided at paragraph 13.4.1:

> Duties and obligations imposed by the Contract Document and rights and remedies available thereunder shall be in addition to and not a limitation of duties, obligations, rights and remedies otherwise imposed or available by law.

The appellate court also noted that contractual arbitration terms were, in effect, nothing more than agreements to submit substantive controversies to a particular forum. They did not affect the substantive rights of parties, even when those rights were provided by statute. Temco had the same legal basis for submitting the question of an attorney fee to the arbitrator that it claims to have had for submitting that question to the circuit court.

Being contractually required to assert in arbitration "all claims," and in order to avoid preclusion of claims not asserted, Temco was required to bring all legal theories of relief supported by the "same nucleus of operative facts" to the arbitrator. Otherwise, those claims would have been barred from prosecution by Temco in a separate action. Under Alabama law, the doctrine of *res judicata* applied to arbitration awards just as it applied to judgments of courts. The elements of *res judicata* are "(1) a prior judgment on the merits, (2) rendered by a court of competent jurisdiction, (3) with substantial identity of the parties, and (4) with the same cause of action presented in both actions." A party is barred from relitigating any claims that were, or that "could have been," brought in the earlier action.

The appellate court held that the arbitrator's award constituted a prior decision on the merits, because the arbitrator provided specific findings, along with underlying bases for those findings, as to liability and the monetary amounts awarded on each substantive claim Temco had presented in its demand for arbitration, and the arbitrator further specified that any relief not expressly granted was denied. It was equally clear that the parties to the arbitration and to the subsequent circuit-court proceeding were identical.

The claims also met the fourth element of *res judicata*, "the same cause of action." The established tests used to determine whether different claims present the same cause of action, whether the primary right and duty or wrong were the same, whether various theories arose from the same nucleus of operative facts, and whether the same evidence supported all the separate actions, were satisfied by both of Temco's complaints. In both the original complaint and the amended complaint, Temco stated its contended facts at the beginning, then listed each claim for relief separately in numbered counts, each of which incorporated the opening statement of facts, and then stated the requested relief under the legal theory. For example, in Temco's amended complaint, Count 10, asserting a claim under the Prompt Payment Act, incorporated the statement of facts and requested a total of $541,567 plus interest, costs, expenses, and attorney fees.

The court rejected Temco's argument that its motion to amend its original complaint, and the circuit court's ruling, amounted to, in effect, an "appeal" of the arbitrator's judgment under the Federal Arbitration Act (FAA) even though pertinent FAA guidelines were not "strictly" followed. The court stated that Temco was correct in noting that the substantive provisions of the FAA governed such issues as the enforceability of arbitration agreements, but the appellate court stated that it was Ala. Code 1975, § 6-6-15, that governed the procedural requirements for appealing from an arbitrator's decision in Alabama. Temco, in its appellate brief, essentially admitted that it did not follow any statutory procedures governing appeals of arbitration awards. Further, the appellate court noted that the AIA contract signed by the parties provided at paragraph 13.1.1 that "[t]he Contract shall be governed by the law of the place where the Project is located"—i.e., Alabama.

The pertinent provision in Alabama's arbitration statute, § 6-6-15, "contemplates a party's first seeking relief from an [arbitrator's] award in the circuit court." The court held that filing a separate motion six days before the arbitration hearing in a clear attempt to split related claims was not the equivalent of seeking judicial review of an award, as Temco asserted, and in any event recovery was barred by the parties' contract documents, as explained above. The fact that the circuit court viewed and ruled on numerous motions and briefs by the parties, and in so doing considered the same issues the parties raised on appeal, in awarding an attorney fee to Temco was found to be unavailing. The facts did not transform improper motions into a proper appeal. The trial court's failure to recognize that Temco was required to bring its Prompt Payment Act claim before the arbitrator, as reflected in its disposition of this issue, was merely an error of law.

The appellate court noted that the purposes and policies promoted by the doctrine of *res judicata* include the interests of both the public at large and the parties to a particular action in (a) finality of judgments, (b) reducing waste of private and judicial resources, and (c) avoiding inconsistent rulings. Similar results are achieved by the encouragement of arbitration in conformity to the FAA. Permitting Temco to split its claims and to try them in independent proceedings would violate its agreement with Herring-Malbis, statutory and case authority, and public policy.

Temco's final argument asserted that the *res judicata* argument advanced by Herring-Malbis was barred by judicial estoppel, because Herring-Malbis waited to respond to Temco's motion to amend its original complaint until after the arbitration hearing and allegedly failed to itself raise the issue of attorney fees at the arbitration hearing. According to Temco, those alleged omissions by Herring-Malbis amounted to the "adoption" of a "position" that Temco's motion to amend its complaint in the circuit court was a proper procedure by which Temco could seek relief under the Prompt Payment Act.

Because Temco's motion was submitted six days before the arbitration hearing, any deadline under the Rules of Civil Procedure, pursuant to which Herring-Malbis would have been required to file a response to that motion, would have occurred after the arbitration hearing. Herring-Malbis's failure to respond sooner did not amount to the assumption of a position that the circuit court could properly rule on the issue of attorney fees. Herring-Malbis had no duty to raise any of Temco's potential claims for relief before the arbitrator on Temco's behalf. The trial court rejected Temco's argument, because judicial estoppel requires first that a party assume a position in a legal proceeding, and Herring-Malbis's actions here did not amount to the assumption of a position that it later attempted to impeach.

Because the parties' contract documents required Temco to bring its Prompt Payment Act claim before the arbitrator, the appellate court held that Temco was barred under the doctrine of *res judicata* from later asserting that claim in the circuit court.

The appellate court concluded that Temco, having had "an opportunity to litigate" the claim before the arbitrator, was barred from thereafter asserting its Prompt Payment Act claim in the circuit court. The appellate court reversed the trial court's award of an attorney fee, and remanded the cause to the trial court for the entry of a judgment conforming to the arbitration award.

The AIA's reversal of its prior strong policy favoring arbitration to resolve construction disputes is a strong indicator that the earlier bias toward arbitration has shifted among those in construction. The scope of the claims subject to arbitration may not be obvious when the arbitration agreement is first reviewed, and legal research may be necessary to ensure claims omitted from arbitration are not waived.

VOLUME 2

CHAPTER 17
SUBCONTRACTORS

§ 17.02 INVOLVEMENT WITH SUBCONTRACTORS

Page 730, add after fifth full paragraph:

In *Allied-Lynn Associates, Inc. v. Alex Bro., LLC,*[25.1] the court affirmed partial summary judgment for the subcontractor in its action to foreclose a mechanic's lien on real property after the defendant-owner of the property terminated its contract with the general contractor relating to the construction of an apartment building, The subcontractor's evidence showed that the property owner was bound by contract to the architect's determination of the date of the project's substantial completion, and the owner breached the contract by not complying with its termination provisions.

The property owner was defendant Alex Bro., LLC. The general contractor was defendant Oakmont Group, Inc. The contract sum payable by Alex Bro., LLC to the general contractor, defendant Oakmont, was $2,339,650.00. The plaintiff, Allied-Lynn, provided heating and plumbing services and materials to the general contractor, defendant, Oakmont.

In the case, the plumbing and heating subcontractor, Allied-Lynn, asserted the following:

(1) Allied-Lynn sought to foreclose its mechanic's lien;
(2) Alternatively, Allied-Lynn alleged that general contractor, Oakmont, diverted $118,228.00 of Lien Law article 3A trust funds, of which Allied-Lynn was a beneficiary;
(3) Alternatively, Allied-Lynn alleged that the owner, Alex Bro., LLC, in connivance with the general contractor, Oakmont, participated in trust fund diversion;
(4) Alternatively, Allied-Lynn alleged that trust funds were wrongfully paid to parties unknown, to the detriment of Allied-Lynn; and
(5) Allied-Lynn sought recovery against Broderick Holt, principal of Oakmont, on the alleged theory that he forged a lien waiver.

The property owner, Alex Bro., LLC moved to vacate 12 liens. It relied on Lien Law section 11, contending that eight of the purported mechanic's liens were

---

[25.1] 8 A.D.3d 1198, 834 N.Y.S.2d 906 (2007), *aff'g* 18 Misc. 3d 1147A, 859 N.Y.S.2d 892 (N.Y. Sup. Ct. 2005), *aff'd* 38 A.D.3d 1198, 834 N.Y.S.2d 906 (2007), *appeal dismissed*, 9 N.Y.3d 831, 872 N.E.2d 249, 840 N.Y.S.2d 563 (2007).

not served upon the owner. The property owner also relied upon Lien Law section 17, contending that five of the purported mechanic's liens had expired and should, therefore, be vacated. In addition, relying upon Lien Law section 9(2), the owner contended that a purported mechanic's lien was invalid, for not properly identifying the owner of the premises. The owner also claimed deficiencies in the pertinent workmanship. The general contractor, Oakmont, opposed any requirement that it post additional security, and it also disputed some of the claims of the subcontractors and materialmen.

The appellate court held that the contract in this case was not ambiguous. The rights and responsibilities of the owner and the general contractor were controlled by their written agreement (AIA Document A101-1997, including the documents incorporated by reference, AIA Document A201-1997 General Conditions of Contract and Construction) (hereinafter the "written agreement"). Pursuant to the written agreement, the architect had authority to act on behalf of Alex Bro., the owner, regarding certain contract matters including interpreting and deciding matters concerning performance under, and requirements of the contract documents. Thus, the date of substantial completion was the date certified by the architect in accordance with the written agreement. The architect certified "substantial completion" of the construction project on August 28, 2002, and the owner was contractually bound by that determination of the architect relative to substantial completion.

The owner, Alex Bro., materially breached and terminated the written agreement as follows: (a) On or about September 15, 2002, Alex Bro. retained Feenaughty & Allen to complete the project; (b) Alex Bro.'s, retention of Feenaughty & Allen to complete the project less than three weeks after the date of substantial completion was not a reasonable time to allow Oakmont Group, the general contractor, to complete the project and correct the claimed faulty work; (c) Alex Bro. did not obtain pre-termination certification from its architect that sufficient cause existed to terminate the written agreement; (d) Alex Bro. failed to notify Oakmont Group of the claimed faulty work prior to termination and did not give it an opportunity to make correction of claimed faulty work within one year after the date of substantial completion; (f) pursuant to the written agreement, Alex Bro. waived any claim for breach of warranty.

Accordingly, the appellate court affirmed summary judgment on the issue of liability. The appellate court also agreed with the plaintiff that, by virtue of the language of the contract itself, Alex Bro., the owner, was deemed to have waived any remedy against the subcontractor for "consequential damages." Thus, the court precluded damages for the owner at the damages inquest.

The appellate court ordered that

1. Plaintiff Allied-Lynn Associates, Inc. was entitled to partial summary judgment, on the issue of liability, as against defendant Alex Bro., LLC;
2. In the event defendant Alex Bro., LLC was not able to furnish plaintiff Allied-Lynn with the "prior quote" document described above, Allied-Lynn may request an inference adverse to Alex Bro., LLC at the time of the inquest; and

3. That Alex Bro., LLC shall be deemed to have waived the right to assert an offset claim for consequential damages. A subcontractor that is not paid for its work can also bring suit.

In *Patel v. Shamrock Floorcovering Services,*[25.2] a subcontractor brought an adversary proceeding to except debt from discharge in a debtor's Chapter 7 case. The bankruptcy court entered judgment in favor of debtor, on the ground that it was the debtor's company, and not the debtor himself, that stood in a "fiduciary capacity" to subcontractor, as that term was used in the dischargeability exception in the Bankruptcy Code. The district court, however, reversed, and the Sixth Circuit affirmed the trial court's ruling, holding that:

1. Contractors, as result of a duty imposed on them by the Michigan Builders Trust Fund Act to account to subcontractors and materialmen for any funds received on construction project, stand in a "fiduciary capacity" to subcontractors and materialmen, as that term is used in the bankruptcy dischargeability exception;
2. Debtor who was an officer, 50 percent shareholder, and day-to-day administrator of affairs of company and hired to act as a general contractor on a construction project was himself a "contractor" under the Michigan Builders Trust Fund Act, who stood in a "fiduciary capacity" to the unpaid subcontractor; and
3. Debtor-contractor who, out of funds that he received for work on a construction project, paid his own operating expenses, including payroll, utilities, taxes, and wages to himself, before he sent any money to the subcontractor, acted in an objectively reckless manner and was guilty of "defalcation," of the kind preventing discharge of his debt to subcontractor.

Bankruptcy is designed to give debtors a "fresh start." Ordinarily, whatever assets a debtor has are allocated among his creditors and, even though they rarely cover all liabilities, the debtor emerges with no outstanding debts. But there are exceptions. Some debts are not dischargeable, and among these are debts arising from a "defalcation while acting in a fiduciary capacity."11 U.S.C. § 523(a)(4). The appeal focused on whether the defendant, Sameer Patel—corporate officer, 50 percent shareholder, and day-to-day administrator of a "contractor" under the Michigan Builders Trust Fund Act, Mich. Comp. Laws § 570.151—was a fiduciary such that § 523(a)(4) prevented him from discharging his debt, because he breached his fiduciary duty to the plaintiff, Shamrock Floorcovering. Because Patel was a fiduciary and breached his duties by "defalcation," the appellate court affirmed the district court's ruling that his debt to Shamrock, a subcontractor, was not dischargeable.

Empire Limited Partnership, owned and operated by the debtor's father, decided to build homes, and the debtor, Sameer Patel, was president and 50 percent shareholder of Empire Builders of Michigan, Inc., the general contractor

[25.2] 565 F.3d 963, 51 Bankr. Ct. Dec. 166, Bankr. L. Rep. P 81,485, (6th Cir. 2009), *reh'g denied* (June 2, 2009).

for the home construction project. In his role, the debtor handled day-to-day operations: Empire Builders contracted, worked with, and paid subcontractors according to a system the debtor established with his father's partnership. To help cover payments, the father's partnership requested funds under its line of credit from a bank, which would then turn over funds to Empire Builders, which paid the subcontractors and covered other expenses.

This arrangement began falling apart after the bank imposed additional borrowing restrictions on the partnership, and payments began to lag. As a result, the subcontractor only received partial payment for its services. Sameer Patel, the debtor, informed the subcontractor that the money owed was held in escrow, would soon be released, and the subcontractor could expect its money "ASAP." The subcontractor eventually agreed to waive the $8,400.00 owed to it in exchange for a promise that $7,048.00 would remain a continuing obligation of Empire Builders and the debtor personally. Soon thereafter, the bank pulled its line of credit, and both the father's and son's companies collapsed before completion of the construction project. The partnership sold the rest of its undeveloped lots and abandoned the remaining phases of the construction project. Shamrock was never paid what it was owed, including the $7,048.00 Patel had personally agreed to pay.

Shamrock sued both the debtor and his company, Empire Builders, in state court alleging: (1) breach of contract; (2) fraud/innocent misrepresentation; (3) account stated; (4) action on personal guarantee; and (5) fraudulent conveyance. Shamrock obtained a default judgment against Empire Builders and Patel individually for $81,171.79—$73,529.00 in damages and $7,642.79 in interest.

Patel then filed for personal Chapter 7 bankruptcy and listed Shamrock's $81,171.79 state court judgment against Empire Builders and himself as a debt to be discharged. Shamrock brought an adversary proceeding, filing a complaint to contest dischargeability. Although the bankruptcy court ruled that the debt was dischargeable holding that 11 U.S.C. § 523(a)(4) did not apply, the district court reversed, holding that Patel breached the fiduciary duties he owed Shamrock by failing to account for and pay funds, which was a "defalcation." The appellate court affirmed the district court's judgment.

Debts that are not dischargeable under the bankruptcy law include debts incurred from "fraud or defalcation while acting in a fiduciary capacity, embezzlement, or larceny." This exception for "defalcation while acting in a fiduciary capacity" follows from Congress's desire to protect trust relationships: when the bankrupt is a trustee and the creditor a trust beneficiary, § 523(a)(4) points the needle away from discharge. A debt is nondischargeable as the result of defalcation when a preponderance of the evidence establishes: (1) a pre-existing fiduciary relationship, (2) a breach of that relationship, and (3) resulting loss.[25.3] The term "fiduciary capacity" is narrower here than it is in other contexts: section 523(a)(4) covers only "express" or "technical trusts" and not trusts arising out of the very act of wrongdoing. These "constructive trusts," which arise *ex maleficio*

[25.3] Patel, *citing* Board of Trustees v. Bucci (*In re* Bucci), 493 F.3d 635, 642 (6th Cir. 2007).

(at the time the wrong is done), do not satisfy the "fiduciary capacity" requirement because the debtor was not a trustee before the wrong.

In establishing an "express" trust, the creditor must demonstrate: "(1) an intent to create a trust; (2) a trustee; (3) a trust res; and (4) a definite beneficiary." In this case, Shamrock did not allege an express trust but, instead, claimed the existence of a "technical trust" flowing from duties imposed on Patel by the Michigan Builders Trust Fund Act. The MBTFA satisfied the necessary "requirement that the trust exist separate from the act of wrongdoing" as a matter of federal law, and thus MBTFA "contractors" were fiduciaries to their subcontractors under § 523(a)(4).

The general contractor, Empire Builders of Michigan, was a corporation of which Patel was president, 50 percent shareholder, and day-to-day administrator. The bankruptcy court had held that the Patel did not owe Shamrock any fiduciary duty that could be breached based on "piercing of the corporate veil" analysis. The district court, however, disagreed and held that the "piercing the corporate veil" analysis was unnecessary, because Patel directly owed Shamrock a fiduciary duty as a "contractor" under the MBTFA. Although federal law governed the case, both the district court and the Sixth Circuit held that under the MBTFA, "contractors" were fiduciaries under MBTFA § 523(a)(4). Whether or not Patel was a "contractor" under the MBTFA, was a state-law question.

"Contractor" is not expressly defined in the Act, which states:

> In the building construction industry, the building contract fund paid by any person to a *contractor,* or by such person or contractor to a subcontractor shall be considered by this act to be a trust fund, for the benefit of the person making the payment, contractors, laborers, subcontractors, or materialmen, and the contractor or subcontractor shall be considered the trustee of all funds so paid to him for building construction purposes.

The Act requires the "contractor" "to first pay laborers, subcontractors and materialmen," and states that "appropriation by contractors," of money "paid to him for building operations before the payment by him of all moneys due or so to become due laborers, subcontractors, materialmen or others entitled to payment, shall be evidence of intent to defraud." In other words, the MBTFA makes the general contractor a trustee of project funds and imposes on him the duty to pay the beneficiaries—the subcontractors—before himself and his employees and before paying any other expenses.

The Sixth Circuit cited the Michigan Court of Appeals decision in *People v. Brown,*[25.4] in holding that it was undisputed that Patel was a "contractor" under the MBTFA. Patel was an officer and, if a defalcation did occur, Patel must have "participated" because he was the home construction project's day-to-day administrator. Thus, under Michigan law, the appellate court was confident that Patel would be an MBTFA "contractor." The court also rejected the argument that *Brown*'s holding that corporate officers of general contractors might be criminally

[25.4] 239 Mich. App. 735, 610 N.W.2d 234, 238 (2000).

liable as MBTFA "contractors" was not enough under § 523(a)(4), because any trust relationship arising under *Brown*'s reasoning would not be in effect until Patel allegedly committed the defalcation. The court, however, held that *Brown*'s finding of liability by a corporate officer rested on the officer's failure to perform a duty—i.e., not paying subcontractors first—that was imposed, because the officer was a "contractor" under the MBTFA and this duty must have pre-existed the wrongdoing. As a statutory "contractor," the corporate officer's duty to gather and disburse project funds had been in place all along—long before the defalcation.

The court also rejected the bankruptcy judge's ruling that Shamrock was required to prove a corporate "piercing the veil" or "alter ego" analysis. Although such analysis might have been relevant at some previous point to determine whether the debt at issue should have appeared on Patel's account at all, it was irrelevant in determining dischargeability of the debt under the bankruptcy code. Once Shamrock obtained a default state court judgment against Patel, the debt was his alone (and not Empire Builders Inc.). Thus, in determining whether the debt was dischargeable under the bankruptcy code, the inquiry followed the statute: Was there a fiduciary duty and a breach (defalcation)? As explained above, the fiduciary duty question turned on whether federal law recognized a pre-existing trust relationship created under state law, which, itself, turned on whether Patel was a "contractor."

After finding that Patel was a "contractor" within the meaning of the MBTFA, and, therefore, owed a fiduciary duty to the subcontractor, there remained the question whether Patel breached his duty via defalcation of money owed to Shamrock. Although the court rejected the subcontractor's attempt to show Patel's breach by claiming "defalcation per se," the court, nevertheless, applied the standard established in *In re Johnson,*[25.5] and held that Patel breached his duty when he recklessly misallocated funds and failed to pay his subcontractors first as required by the Michigan Builders Trust Fund Act (MBTFA).

In *Johnson,* the court carefully explained that defalcation in the MBTFA context occurs when evidence supports "the objective fact that monies paid into the building contract fund were used for purposes other than to pay laborers, subcontractors or materialmen first is sufficient to constitute a defalcation under section [523](a)(4) so long as the use was not the result of mere negligence or a mistake of fact." Thus, the debtor must have been objectively reckless in failing to properly account for or allocate funds.

The appellate court agreed that Patel recklessly misallocated funds and failed to pay his subcontractors first as required by the MBTFA. Although that Act (Mich. Comp. Laws § 570.153) lists the failure to pay subcontractors first as "evidence of the intent to defraud," the bankruptcy standard is a federal one, so this state law language was not dispositive. Nevertheless, Patel testified that he paid his own operating expenses—including payroll, utilities, taxes, and wages to himself for services rendered as president—before he sent any money to Shamrock.

As the district court observed, Patel's attempts at an accounting were "woefully inadequate." This provided evidence that he paid either subcontractors

[25.5] 691 F.2d 249 (6th Cir. 1982).

or general overhead (which was not permissible until the contractors were paid) which was not enough. Indeed, Patel conceded at his deposition that his "business operations were sloppy at best," that he did not know if an overall accounting was ever done, and that he did not know exactly how much was owed to Shamrock. The appellate court, therefore, agreed with the district court that Patel committed a defalcation and, thus, the debt owed to Shamrock was not dischargeable under § 523(a)(4).

Control over means and methods of construction, and respective shares of responsibility between general contractors and subcontractors for workplace accidents, which damage equipment or cause injuries, can trigger appellate cases.

In *Santos v. Ashforth, Co.*,[25.6] Connecticut superior court denied a motion for summary judgment on a project using AIA A401, the AIA form subcontract, where there was a material issue of fact whether the general contractor exercised control sufficiently over the subcontractor's work so as to be liable for a workplace injury of a subcontractor's employees. In *Santos*, the plaintiffs, Jose Santos and Oscar Pena, were injured during the course of their employment with the defendant, Jose Gomez, d/b/a Gola Roofing on November 9, 2000. On that date, Gola Roofing had hired the plaintiffs to apply roofing paper to the New CanaanTeenCenter, then under construction. Gola Roofing was hired the previous day (without a written contract or subcontract) by the roofing subcontractor, the defendant, Antonelli Roofing, to put up the roofing paper on an expedited schedule.

The plaintiffs both fell from the steeply pitched roof of the Teen Center when one or more roof brackets supporting the planks upon which they were standing collapsed, causing the planks and both plaintiffs, who were not wearing safety harnesses or any other restraining device, to fall approximately 27 feet to the edge of the roof where they hit the scaffolding which failed to stop their fall, and then fell about another 14½ feet from the eave onto a concrete slab. Both plaintiffs sustained personal injuries for which they claim moneyed damages from all defendants.

Count One of the Amended Complaint stated the negligence claim of the plaintiff, Jose Santos, against the general contractor (known as AP Construction, Inc.). Count Five stated the negligence claim of the plaintiff, Oscar Pena, against AP Construction. Count Four was derivative of Count One and stated the loss of consortium claim of the plaintiff, Lilliana Ruiz, the wife of Jose Santos. The negligence claims of the plaintiffs against AP Construction included allegations that it, as the general contractor at the job site, failed to exercise reasonable care in the selection of a roofing subcontractor; failed to provide a safe workplace; failed to implement and enforce rules for workplace safety; failed to require the roofing subcontractor to comply with the job site safety rules promulgated by AP Construction; failed to supervise and inspect the work of the roofing subcontractor; failed to comply or require the roofing subcontractor to comply with OSHA regulations including the OSHA "6 foot rule" for roofing work; and "failed, as controlling employer with general supervisory authority over the job site, to comply with all

[25.6] 2009 Conn. Super. LEXIS 353, 2009 WL 567208 (2009).

safety measures including all applicable laws, ordinances, rules, regulations and orders of public authorities for the safety of persons."

The defendant submitted a motion for summary judgment to the trial court on December 17, 2007, in which it claimed that there was no triable issue of fact, and that the undisputed record showed that it was entitled to judgment as a matter of law in that: (1) since it did not hire, employ, control, or supervise the injured workers, it owed no duty to the plaintiffs, and (2) there was no basis upon which a reasonable jury could conclude that AP Construction was negligent.

Both parties submitted extensive factual materials to the trial court. Both parties submitted excerpts from the depositions of AP Constriction job site supervisor, Thomas Coleman, Antonelli Roofing principal, John Antonelli, and Antonelli Roofing foreman Hector Comacho. In addition, the defendant, AP Construction, submitted the written subcontract (on the form of AIA Document A401) between AP Construction and Antonelli Roofing, and an affidavit of John E. Antonelli. The plaintiffs submitted copies of Thomas Coleman's job site notes, the OSHA investigative report, photographs of the accident site, photographs of the "Job Safety Rules" sign posted at the site by AP Construction, and a report and affidavit of its expert Dr. John Mroszczyk.

The primary issue raised was whether or not, or under what circumstances, a general contractor had a duty to protect and safeguard the subcontractors' employees. As to AP Construction, Gola Roofing (the employer of the injured plaintiffs) was an independent subcontractor of AP Construction's independent roofing subcontractor, Antonelli Roofing.

In Connecticut, as a general rule, "an employer is not liable for the negligence of its independent contractors." *Pelletier et al. v. Sordoni/Skansa Construction Co.*[25.7] (*Pelletier II*). The premise underlying this general rule is that "the assumption and exercise of control over the offending area is deemed to be in the independent contractor."[25.8]

The court in *Pelletier II* overruled part of the court's earlier decision in *Pelletier et al. v. Sordoni/Skansa Construction Co.*[25.9] (*Pelletier I*) which had held that, as a matter of law, an employee of an independent contractor could never pursue a common-law negligence claim against another contractor, limiting a contractor's liability to only innocent third parties. *Pelletier II* held that an employee of a subcontractor was not restricted as a matter of law from pursuing a claim against a general contractor.

The *Pelletier II* court stressed, however, that in order to succeed on its claim, the plaintiff employee had to establish a basis for the contractor's liability under the case law—i.e., show that the facts fell within one of the exceptions to the general rule of nonliability of a general contractor. The court identified four such exceptions to the general rule: (1) the work contracted for was intrinsically dangerous; (2) the independent contractor hired was incompetent or untrustworthy; (3) the general contractor had a legal duty to see that the work was

[25.7] 264 Conn. 509, 517, 825 A.2d 72 (2003).

[25.8] Darling v. Burrone Bros., Inc., 162 Conn. 187, 196 (1972).

[25.9] 262 Conn. 372 (2003).

performed properly; and (4) the general contractor exercised control over the subcontractor.[25.10]

In *Santos*, the defendant claimed that, as a matter of law, none of the *Pelletier II* exceptions applied to this case. In contrast, the plaintiffs claimed that there were genuine disputed issues of fact as to the application of all the *Pelletier II* exceptions. The court found that there were genuine disputed issues of fact as to the control issue, which prevented it from entering summary judgment in favor of AP Construction as a matter of law.

Pelletier II remanded the case for trial. The case was tried to a jury in the superior court at Waterbury on the negligence and loss of consortium counts (the very same counts outstanding against AP Construction in the case). Following a jury verdict for the plaintiffs which the trial court declined to set aside, both parties appealed and the case went to the Connecticut Supreme Court for a third time: *Pelletier et al. v. Sordoni/Skansa Construction Co.*,[25.11] (*Pelletier III*). On the plaintiffs' cross appeal, one of the issues was the trial court's refusal to instruct the jury that Sordoni, the general contractor had a duty as the general contractor to exercise reasonable care with respect to any part of the work site or inspection process over which it retained control.

Pelletier involved a claim that the general contractor had a duty to inspect the weld which failed, permitting a steel beam to fall on the plaintiff, an employee of the structural steel subcontractor who had a contract obligation to inspect all welds. The court held that the general contractor was not in control of the fabrication and inspection of welds, because "a fair and reasonable person could reach but one conclusion as to who exercised control . . ." In reaching that position, the *Pelletier II* court relied on the fact that the contract documents required the subcontractor to fabricate and inspect the welds at its own shop, thus clearly demonstrating that the general contractor did not retain control over "the area or instrumentality" that caused the plaintiff harm.[25.12] "It [Sordoni] thus had no control over the shop in which the welds were fabricated or the manner in which the inspections were to be performed . . ." The court rejected the argument that an orientation and procedures manual that Sordoni provided to the subcontractor indicating that Sordoni would conduct its own weekly inspections to ensure compliance with its safety program was evidence of an exercise of control by Sordoni. The manual was not a legally binding contract, but rather "an informational tool designed to educate the plaintiff in the protocols for the job site . . . [It was] strictly informational."[25.13]

In *Archambault v. Soneco/Northeastern, Inc.*,[25.14] the Connecticut Supreme Court addressed whether a general contractor had a nondelegable duty to the plaintiff subcontractor's employee to ensure a safe construction site, because the general contractor had allegedly exercised control over the excavation of trenches

---

[25.10] 264 Conn. 509, 519.

[25.11] 286 Conn. 563 (2008).

[25.12] 286 Conn. 563, 602.

[25.13] 287 Conn. 20, 946 A.2d 839 (2008).

[25.14] *Id.*

at the site. The court remanded the case for a new trial because of an error in ruling on evidence, but addressed the control issue because that issue "was likely to arise in the new trial."[25.15] The *Archambault* court found that the trial court had improperly instructed the jury that the general contractor had such a nondelegable duty.

There was evidence that the contract between Konover (the general contractor) and Soneco (the excavation and site work subcontractor) obligated Soneco to comply with all applicable laws and regulatory safety rules (including OSHA regulations), and to observe and comply with the Safety Project Plan. Konover had provided Soneco with a copy of its construction safety manual. This gave Konover's site superintendents the power to conduct weekly job site safety meetings, conduct safety inspections, and to issue violation notices to subcontractors. Konover also published a safety manual for excavations. Konover superintendents were authorized to halt activities that could constitute a safety violation. The Konover site supervisor testified that he was in "overall control" of the 10-acre construction site. He also testified that "the buck stopped with Konover" on overall safety and "It was my job to make sure that the contractors did the best they could with regard to safety."[25.16] In finding that under these circumstances that the nondelegable duty instruction had been improper, the appellate court found that a reasonable person could reach but one conclusion: Soneco, and not Konover, was in control and was responsible for safety at the site. The court said: "Overall responsibility for safety on the work site, however, does not necessarily translate into a nondelegable duty."[25.17]

The appellate court found that Konover's safety manual was not the source of a contractual or legal duty to provide a safe work site but was merely an informational tool.

> Although the safety manual described Konover's interest in providing safe conditions on the work site, it did not suggest that Konover would engage in daily supervision of its subcontractor's employees . . . Rather, the manual suggested that Konover would foster safety by developing site specific safety plans to identify potential hazards that might arise . . . *None of the safety concerns discussed in the manual involved control over the manner in which specific tasks would be performed by the subcontractor's employees.*[25.18]

In their post-*Pelletier III* and *Archambault* supplemental memoranda, AP Construction argued that it, like Konover, had only general overall supervision over safety at the Darien Teen Center work site, while the plaintiffs argued that there was evidence from which a reasonable juror could find that AP Construction went beyond the role of an overall supervisor and exercised control over the manner in which subcontractors performed their duties so as to ensure safety.

[25.15] 287 Conn. 20, 41.

[25.16] 287 Conn. 20, 51.

[25.17] 287 Conn. 20, 54.

[25.18] 287 Conn. 20, 55.

A juror could have concluded that the sign posted at the premises was more binding and obligatory than a mere "informational tool." For example, the sign stated:

> OSHA's 6-foot rule in proper fall protection *is to be utilized* as required.
>
> The following safety requirements are mandatory:
>
> Eye protection *must be worn* when using power tools . . .
>
> Gloves *must be* worn . . .
>
> Hard hats *must be worn* at all times . . .

Furthermore, Thomas Coleman testified at deposition that it was part of his job to "make sure that these rules were enforced," and that he had authority to stop work if he thought it was not being done in a safe manner. Yet, he testified that he saw the plaintiffs, before they fell, working on the roof (obviously more than six feet above ground) without wearing safety harnesses. There was also a notation in his job notes that, sometime prior to the date of the plaintiffs' fall, he: "[r]eviewed safety, parking and site storing requirements, w/ Panel Pro's foreman (Brian) . . . Warned Panel Pros that they *all* need to wear hart hats & [be] 'tied off.' They were tied off but not all wore hard hats. R. Marin gave out 2 for their use." This, at least suggested that AP Construction was passing out safety equipment to subcontractor employees and requiring that it be used, which could support a finding of control even under the *Pelletier III/Archambault* criteria.

This was not a case where a reasonable juror could reach no conclusion other than that AP Construction was not in control of safety at the job site. That issue was a genuine issue of material fact that could not be decided by a motion for summary judgment. For the reasons stated, the trial court denied the motion for summary judgment.

In *Staub v. William H. Lane, Inc.*,[25.19] an employee of the subcontractor brought an action against a general contractor for negligence and brought claims under New York Labor Law. The parties had used the AIA A401 Form subcontract. The general contractor sought third-party indemnification from the subcontractor for indemnification. The trial court had granted the general contractor partial summary judgment on its indemnification claim, and the subcontractor appealed.

The New York Supreme Court, Appellate Division held that a genuine issue of material fact precluded summary judgment on the indemnity claim, reversing the trial court's grant of summary judgment. There was a genuine issue of material fact as to whether the general contractor and its subcontractor agreed to be bound by the indemnification provision of the form contract incorporated by an unsigned, written proposal. Thus, an order of the supreme court was entered on November 20, 2007, partially granting the defendant's cross-motion for summary judgment seeking contractual indemnification from the third-party defendant.

[25.19] 58 A.D.3d 933, 870 N.Y.S.2d 630 (2009).

In *Staub*, the plaintiff, an employee of the subcontractor third-party defendant, was injured while installing a steel beam on a building. He commenced the underlying action against the general contractor for the project, asserting causes of action sounding in negligence and Labor Law §§ 200(1), §§ 240(1) and §§241(6). Following a joinder of issue, the defendant commenced a third-party action seeking contractual indemnification from a third-party defendant based upon an unsigned, written proposal submitted by third-party defendant.

The proposal purported to incorporate the terms of AIA Document A401 into the quote, and was accepted by the defendant orally. The parties did not, however, sign a formal, written contract containing an express agreement to indemnify. AIA Form A401, which was not transmitted to defendant along with the proposal, contains the following indemnity provision:

> To the fullest extent permitted by law, the [s]ubcontractor shall indemnify and hold harmless the [o]wner, [c]ontractor . . . from and against claims, damages, losses and expenses, including but not limited to attorney's fees, arising out of or resulting from performance of the [s]ubcontractor's Work under this [s]ubcontract . . . but only to the extent caused by the negligent acts or omissions of the [s]ubcontractor . . .

The third-party defendant moved for summary judgment dismissing the third-party complaint in its entirety, and the defendant cross-moved for summary judgment on its indemnification claim. The New York Supreme Court denied the third-party defendant's motion, and it granted the defendant's cross-motion in part, directing that the defendant be granted conditional indemnification and defense by the third-party defendant in connection with the underlying action. The third-party defendant appealed, and the appellate court modified by denying defendant's cross-motion for summary judgment in its entirety.

New York Workers' Compensation Law §§ 11 precludes third-party indemnification claims against employers unless the claim is "based upon a provision in a written contract entered into prior to the accident or occurrence by which the employer had expressly agreed to contribution to or indemnification of the claimant or person asserting the cause of action for the type of loss suffered."

Whether a written contract satisfies section 11 involves a two-part inquiry. First, the court considers whether the parties entered into a written contract containing an indemnity provision applicable to the site or job where the injury giving rise to the indemnity claim took place. Second, if so, the court examines whether the indemnity provision was sufficiently particular to meet the requirements of section 11.[25.20] The parties' dispute centered on whether the first prong of the two-part inquiry had been met.

A written agreement could be enforceable if "the course of conduct between [the parties], including their writings . . . was sufficient to spell out a binding contract, notwithstanding the failure of the parties to sign [an] integrated

[25.20] Rodrigues v. N & S Bldg. Contractors, 5 N.Y.3d 427, 432, 839 N.E.2d 357, 805 N.Y.S.2d 299 (2005).

agreement."[25.21] Thus, the parties' course of conduct must be reviewed "to determine whether there was a meeting of the minds sufficient to give rise to an enforceable contract."[25.22]

In this case, the third-party defendant included a note on its written proposal. This was the only written document governing the work performed. This document purported to incorporate the terms of AIA Contract A401. A401 includes an indemnity provision running from the employer (third-party defendant) to the contractor (defendant), as noted above. Nevertheless, third-party defendant's president, Peter Browning, indicated that the parties never used a formal AIA Contract A401 in their prior agreements. The defendant generally submitted its own written contract after receiving proposals, and Browning expected and intended that practice to be followed on this occasion.

This testimony was consistent with a statement from the defendant's senior project manager that the formal subcontract that defendant typically used was not supplied in connection with the job at issue. The court noted that while Browning admitted during his deposition that formal subcontracts were not always used, and arguably stated that he intended AIA Contract A401, including the indemnification provision, to apply to this project, the record indicated that AIA Contract A401 was never provided to the defendant. Given the failure to provide the indemnification provision of AIA Contract A401 and the absence of any evidence that the parties agreed to that provision through either past practice or their course of conduct, the New York Supreme Court concluded that questions of fact existed as to whether the parties agreed to be bound by the indemnification provisions of AIA Contract A401.[25.23]

In *Staub*, the New York court denied the defendant's cross-motion for summary judgment in its entirety, and it modified the trial court's order, with costs to third-party defendant, by reversing so much thereof as partially granted defendant's cross-motion for summary judgment.

A determination of responsibility for unsafe conditions is almost always very fact-specific, and courts are unlikely to be able to make that determination at the summary judgment level.

Page 732, add at end of section:

In *MW Erectors, Inc. v. Niederhauser Ornamental and Metal Works Co.*,[30.1] a subcontractor brought an action for breach of contract against a contractor for work performed on structural steel and ornamental metals work contracts as part

---

[25.21] Flores v. Lower E. Side Serv. Ctr., Inc., 4 N.Y.3d 363, 368, 828 N.E.2d 593, 795 N.Y.S.2d 491 (2005), *quoting* Brown Bros. Elec. Contractors v. Beam Constr. Corp., 41 N.Y.2d 397, 399, 361 N.E.2d 999, 393 N.Y.S.2d 350 (1977).

[25.22] Flores v. Lower E. Side Serv. Ctr., Inc., 4 N.Y.3d 370, 828 N.E.2d 593, 795 N.Y.S.2d 491 (2005).

[25.23] *See* Mentesana v. Bernard Janowitz Constr. Corp., 36 A.D.3d 769, 771, 828 N.Y.S.2d 522 (2007); Gilbert v. Albany Med. Ctr., 21 A.D.3d 677, 678, 799 N.Y.S.2d 685 (2005); Miller v. Mott's Inc., 5 A.D.3d 1019, 1020, 773 N.Y.S.2d 727 (2004).

[30.1] 36 Cal. 4th 412, 115 P.3d 41, 30 Cal. Rptr. 3d 755 (2005).

of a hotel project. The trial court granted summary judgment in the contractor's favor. The subcontractor appealed. The court of appeal reversed, and the contractor sought review.

The California Supreme Court held the following: (1) the doctrine of judicial estoppel was inapplicable; (2) the California statute that barred suit by unlicensed contractors from recovering payment when they are unlicensed at any time during the project prevented the subcontractor from recovering for work done prior to the time its license was issued; (3) the statutory exception for substantial compliance with licensing requirements was not available to the subcontractor under the facts of this case; and (4) the subcontractor was not barred from recovering for work solely because it was unlicensed at the time it executed the contract.

In *MW Erectors*, the California Supreme Court summarized the public policy rationale for license laws such as California Business and Professions Code section 7031. The court stated that the purpose of such laws is to protect the public. Section 7031 provides that regardless of the merits of a claim by an unpaid contractor, the contractor may not maintain any action, legal or equitable, to recover compensation for the performance of any act or contract unless the contractor was duly licensed at all times during the performance of the act or contract.

The *MW Erectors*court noted that earlier case law had softened the severity of this scheme, by allowing contractors, though technically unlicensed at the time of performance, to show they had substantially complied with licensing requirements. However, the law states that the judicial doctrine of substantial compliance shall not apply unless the contractor had been duly licensed as a contractor in California prior to performance of the act or contract for which the license was required.[30.2]

In *MW Erectors*, Disney Corporation hired Turner Construction as a general contractor. Turner hired Niederhauser to perform steel specialty work. Niederhauser hired MW Erectors to perform certain aspects of the structural and ornamental steel work on the project. MW began the work under a structural steel subcontract on approximately December 3, 1999, but it did not obtain a C-51 structural steel license until December 21, 1999. Work by MW under a second subcontract with Niederhauser began in early January 2000.

Due to payment disputes, MW sued Niederhauser and Niederhauser's payment bonds for $955,553 for work under the structural steel subcontract, and for $366,694 under the ornamental subcontract. Niederhauser moved for summary judgment, alleging that the MW claim was barred by section 7031(a) since MW was not properly licensed at all times during the performance of its contracts. Niederhauser also argued that MW could not demonstrate substantial compliance with section 7031 because MW had never held a California contractor's license before beginning work under the contracts in December 1999.

In opposing the summary judgment motion, MW admitted that the C-51 license was not technically in place when MW began work on the structural contract, and admitted that it never obtained a C-23 (ornamental steel) license.

[30.2] Cal. Bus. & Prof. Code § 7031.

MW asserted that there were triable issues that it was in substantial compliance with C-51 license requirements, and that no C-23 license was required. The trial court granted summary judgment to Niederhauser, and dismissed MW's action. MW appealed, arguing (1) it had shown substantial compliance with the C-51 license requirement, (2) it did not need a C-23 license, and (3) that Niederhauser was judicially estopped from questioning MW's licensure.

The court of appeal reversed. It held that the subcontracts were not void at the outset, despite MW's lack of a license when the subcontracts were executed. Instead, MW's right to recover depended on its licensure during performance of the contracts. The court of appeal held that MW could not recover for the work it performed before it obtained either a C-51 or C-23 license. However, section 7031 allowed MW to obtain compensation for acts it performed under the structural and ornamental subcontracts after the necessary license was in place. Although MW never obtained a C-23 license, it raised a triable issue of fact that the C-51 license was sufficient.

The California Supreme Court affirmed the court of appeal in part, and reversed in part. Niederhauser did not raise the C-23 license issue on appeal before the California Supreme Court, so the court did not address it in its opinion.

MW argued that Niederhauser was judicially estopped from raising the estoppel issue because it claimed that Niederhauser had asserted in its lawsuit against Disney, the owner, that MW was licensed, and that Niederhauser could not now use the opposite argument to defeat the MW claim. The California Supreme Court precluded MW using judicial estoppel. It held that the courts may not resort to equitable considerations in defiance of the legislative determination represented by section 7031 on the importance of deterring unlicensed persons from engaging in the contracting business. This legislative policy outweighs any harshness between the parties.

The *MW Erectors* court declined to follow what it called the court of appeal's "strained construction" of the statute's language in considering the time of lack of licensure as being during any "act or contract." The *MW Erectors* court held that the plausible meaning of the words "act or contract" is that the legislature did not intend to require contractors to perform exclusively by formal contract, but to deter them from offering or performing unlicensed services for pay. The *MW Erectors* court summarized some of the case history on the substantial compliance doctrine, and the harshness of the bar presented by section 7031. Despite arguments raised by MW about the problems presented by strict construction of section 7031, the *MW Erectors* court held that the purpose of the statute was served by such strict construction, encouraging careful adherence to the licensing laws, and deterring persons from offering or providing unlicensed contractor services for pay.

The *MW Erectors* court held that the subcontractor had not met the substantial compliance test as to the C-51 license requirement because MW never held a license prior to beginning its work under the structural steel subcontract. It would appear that the doctrine of substantial compliance was to cover an intended licensee whose license lapses due to inadvertence, such as failing to renew the license on time, and who then has a brief period in which it is unlicensed. The *MW*

Erectors court reviewed the statutory history of section 7031 to support the theory that a lapsed licensee is treated differently than one that was never licensed before beginning work or executing a contract. Because MW could not establish that it was licensed at all times, or that it held a valid license prior to beginning performance, the *MW Erectors* court reversed the court of appeal, and denied MW recovery of any money under the structural steel subcontract. The California Supreme Court held that summary judgment by the trial court was proper.

The *MW Erectors* court reviewed the argument that the subcontractor was licensed at all times during performance of the ornamental steel work, the second subcontract. The *MW Erectors* court referred to the statutory purpose of section 7031, which is to protect the public from incompetence and dishonesty in those who provide building and construction services, and to provide minimal assurance that all persons offering such services have the requisite skill and character. Holding that section 7031 and other California licensing laws did not automatically void the MW subcontract for the ornamental steel portion of the work, the *MW Erectors* court held that MW was not barred from recovering compensation for its work on the sole ground that it was unlicensed when it executed the agreement.

Steven G.M. Stein and Ronald O. Wietecha, in their article, *A Comparison of ConsensusDOCS to the AIA Form Construction Contract Documents*,[30.3] compare the effect on subcontractors of ConsensusDOCS 200 as compared to A201-2007. Under ConsensusDOCS 200 there are no provisions for issuing joint checks to the subcontractor and contractor, and there are no references to the funds received by the contractor as being in the nature of a trust obligation. A201-2007 contains these provisions at A201-2007 sections 9.5.3 and 9.6.7. Under A201-2007 section 9.3.1.2, the prime contractor is prohibited from including amounts in its payment applications that it does not intend to pay to its subcontractors. A201-2007 paragraph 9.6.2 also prohibits prime contractors from withholding a higher percentage from its payments to subcontractors than what the owner withholds from the contractor for the subcontractor's work.

§17.06 PAYMENT CLAUSES

Page 754, add after second full paragraph:

In *Universal Concrete Products v. Turner Construction Co.*,[72.1] a subcontractor brought a breach of contract action against a contractor, seeking payment for work performed on a construction (Granby Tower) project. The U.S. District Court for the Eastern District of Virginia granted the contractor's motion for summary judgment, and the appellate court affirmed the trial court. The appellate court held that unambiguous pay-when-paid clause in the parties' subcontract was not rendered ambiguous through incorporation of a prime contract provision.

[30.3] Steven G.M. Stein & Ronald O. Wietecha, *A Comparison of ConsensusDOCS to the AIA Form Construction Contract Documents*, *The Construction Lawyer*, Vol. 29, No. 1, Winter 2009.

[72.1] 595 F.3d 527 (4th Cir. 2010), applying Virginia law.

This appeal required the court to consider the applicability and enforceability of a "pay-when-paid" clause agreed to by the parties. Specifically, the appellate court stated that it had to decide whether certain provisions in a prime contract, which the general contractor and a subcontractor incorporated by reference into their subcontract, rendered an otherwise unambiguous pay-when-paid clause within that subcontract ambiguous. The district court found that they did not, which finding was affirmed by the appellate court.

In the case, the parties entered into an agreement to install precast concrete for a construction project. After Universal had substantially completed its work, the project ultimately fell through, and Turner was unable to pay Universal for any of the work performed, because Turner itself had not yet been paid by the owner. Universal sought payment of $885,507 from Turner for work performed, but Turner refused citing a pay-when-paid provision in the subcontract between Turner and Universal. Universal alleged breach of contract, specifically that when read, the subcontract was "patently ambiguous" as to when Turner was required to pay Universal for work completed. Turner argued that the subcontract was unambiguous, and the terms of the contract were consistent with, and supported the pay-when-paid clause in the subcontract. Turner was awarded summary judgment and Universal appealed, raising the issue of whether or not the district court correctly found that Universal's contract with Turner contained an unambiguous pay-when-paid clause.

The appellate court held that the district court correctly found that Universal's contract with Turner contained an unambiguous pay-when-paid clause, which conditioned any payments to Universal on Turner's first receiving payment from the owner. The court refused to follow two, out-of-jurisdiction cases, which supported Universal's reading of the contract. The court held that under Virginia law, the contract unambiguously reflected both parties' understanding that Universal would only be paid for its work after Turner was paid by the owner. The appellate court held that the pay-when-paid clause contained in the Turner-Universal subcontract was enforceable and prevented Universal from demanding payment from Turner unless and until Turner was first paid by the owner.

The parties did not dispute that the pay-when-paid clause in the Turner-Universal contract was facially unambiguous. Article IV of the agreement stated in relevant part: "The obligation of Turner to make a payment under this Agreement, whether a progress or final payment, or for extras or change orders or delays to the Work, is subject to the express condition precedent of payment therefor by the Owner."

The agreement further stated that the amount paid to Universal would be "out of funds received from the Owner." Finally, article II of the subcontract stated that the agreement was intended to supplement the agreement between Turner and the owner and that any conflict between the two agreements would be read to impose the greater obligation on the subcontractor.

Universal argued, however, that the subcontract, which incorporated Turner's contract with the owner by reference, was ambiguous when read as a whole. Universal claimed that the Turner-owner contract, which consisted of the standard American Institute of Architects (AIA) provisions, reflected an understanding that Turner would pay Universal before being paid by the owner. Specifically, Universal pointed to A121 section 6.1.3, which stated that the costs for which the owner would reimburse Turner included "[p]ayments made by the Construction Manager to Subcontractors in accordance with the requirements of the subcontracts." Universal emphasized the term "payments made," which it claimed demonstrated that Turner and the owner contemplated Turner's paying Universal before invoicing the owner.

As the district court noted, however, this interpretation ignored the remainder of the clause, which indicated that "payments made" were those payments made "in accordance with the requirements of the subcontracts." The district court was, therefore, correct to find that this clause related only to the reimbursement *amount,* not to *when* those amounts would be paid. This language did not render the pay-when-paid provision "of doubtful import" or make it capable "of being understood in more than one way." Rather, it clearly allowed the subcontracting parties freedom to contract for when those payments will be made.

Likewise, the district court correctly found that other clauses in the Turner-owner contract contemplated that Turner could pay its subcontractors after first being paid by the owner. AIA Document A201 section 9.6.2 directed Turner to pay its subcontractors "upon receipt of payment from the Owner, out of the amount paid to the Contractor on account of such Subcontractor's portion of the Work," and section 9.3.1 required Turner to submit "requisitions from Subcontractors" with its invoices. Both provisions contemplated the likelihood that the general contractor and subcontractor entered into a pay-when-paid contract. Though Universal argued that the AIA provided that provisions in A121 should control over provisions in A201 where the two conflicted, whether one of the two purportedly conflicting provisions controlled was irrelevant where, as here, the two provisions could be comfortably read together.

Despite the contract's apparent clarity, Universal pointed to two cases, one from Florida and the other from Missouri, which supported its reading of the contract. In the first case, *OBS Co. v. Pace Construction Corp.,*[72.2] the Florida Supreme Court held that almost identical provisions in a subcontract and general contract were ambiguous enough not to enforce the pay-when-paid provision. Likewise, in *MECO Sys., Inc. v. Dancing Bear Entm't,*[72.3] the Missouri Court of Appeals followed *OBS*'s reasoning to interpret another contract containing similar provisions.

The appellate court agreed that these precedents were not easily distinguishable. Nevertheless, because of how unambiguously the contractual language reflected the parties' intent that Turner pay Universal only after being paid by the owner, the appellate court stated that it believed that the Virginia Supreme Court would not follow either *OBS* or *MECO*'s reasoning.

[72.2] 558 So. 2d 404 (Fla.1990), *superseded by statute in part,* Fla. Stat. § 713.245 (2009), *as recognized in,* WMS Constr., Inc. v. Palm Springs Mile Assocs., Ltd., 762 So. 2d 973 (Fla. Ct. App. 2000).

[72.3] 42 S.W.3d 794 (Mo. Ct. App.2001).

This conclusion was reinforced by a 2009 Virginia trial court opinion, *W.O. Grubb Steel Erection, Inc. v. 515 Granby, LLC,*[72.4] which involved almost identical facts and contractual language as this case. *W.O. Grubb* dealt with a dispute between Turner and another subcontractor who, like Universal, was not paid for work performed on the Granby Tower project. Like the district court here, the trial court found the contract between Turner and the subcontractor, when viewed in light of Turner's same contract with the owner, to be unambiguous and enforced the pay-when-paid provision. Rather than attempt to distinguish *OBS* and *MECO,* the trial court simply opted not to follow their holdings after questioning their reasoning.

The appellate court stated that it was bound to follow Virginia law, and to follow the Virginia trial court's lead in the absence of any indication that the Virginia Supreme Court would disagree with its holding. And though it did not question *OBS* or *MECO*'s reasoning, the court noted that both decisions appeared to be based on policy concerns that the Virginia Supreme Court likely did not share.

The court in *OBS* made clear that its decision was largely based on what it felt to be Florida's desire to protect subcontractors relative to general contractors, while *MECO* simply adopted *OBS*'s reasoning. There is no indication that Virginia or its supreme court shared this policy preference. Quite the contrary. In *Galloway Corp. v. S.B. Ballard Construction Co.*,[72.5] the state's supreme court emphasized that its decision to recognize pay-when-paid clauses was based on its policy preference for "freedom to contract." This was an interest that directly conflicted with a paternalistic desire to protect one contracting party over the other.

Likewise, the appellate court stated that it was not even clear that the Florida legislature really favored subcontractors' rights to the extent the state supreme court thought in *OBS*. Following that decision, the Florida legislature passed a law making it easier for general contractors to enforce pay-when-paid clauses, at least where payment bonds were at stake. Where the purpose underlying one state's precedent has been so undermined by subsequent legislation and case law, the court stated that it certainly could not impute that purpose to another state whose cases and policy statements were directly contrary.

Thus, the appellate court affirmed the district court's order granting summary judgment to Turner, finding that the payment clauses were enforceable, and that Turner did not yet owe Universal payment.

[72.4] CL 08-3278 (Va. Cir. Ct. Oct. 16, 2009) (letter opinion).

[72.5] 250 Va. 493, 464 S.E.2d 349 (1995).

CHAPTER 19

CONTRACTUAL INDEMNIFICATION

§ 19.04 LEGAL CONTROLS

Page 845, add at end of section:

In *Crawford v. Weather Shield Mfg, Inc.*,[52.1] a group of homeowners in a housing development brought a construction defect action against a developer and a window subcontractor. The developer cross-complained against the subcontractor for attorneys' fees incurred in defending the suit by the homeowners, and for indemnification. The trial court entered judgment for no liability on the part of the subcontractor to the homeowners, no liability on the part of the subcontractor to the developer for the developer's causes of action for breach of contract and express indemnity, but providing, by way of declaratory relief, determination that developer was entitled to be defended by subcontractor. Subsequently, the court granted a new trial on strict product liability against the subcontractor in light of new precedent allowing such cause of action. The subcontractor appealed and the homeowners filed protective cross-appeals. The court of appeal affirmed a new trial order and judgment, and dismissed the cross-appeals as moot. The subcontractor appealed. The California Supreme Court granted review, superseding the opinion of the court of appeal.

The California Supreme Court held: (1) the subcontractor's duty to defend applied to a suit alleging a covered claim and (2) subcontractor's duty to defend arose when action was brought, affirming the appellate court.

In *Crawford*, J.M. Peters Co. (JMP) was the developer, builder, and general contractor of a large residential project. Weather Shield Manufacturing Co., Inc. (Weather Shield) contracted with JMP to manufacture and supply wood-framed windows for the project. In the contract, Weather Shield promised (1) "to indemnify and save [JMP] harmless against all claims for damages . . . loss, . . . and/or theft . . . growing out of the execution of [Weather Shield's] work," and (2) "at [its] own expense to defend any suit or action brought against [JMP] founded upon the claim of such damage[,] . . . loss or theft." (Italics added.)

In September and October 1999, 220 owners of 122 finished homes in the project sued JMP, Weather Shield, and other participants in the project's construction. The defendants included Darrow the Framing Corporation (Darrow), the project's principal subcontractor, whose responsibilities included framing the structures and installing the windows. The complaints alleged numerous construction defects, including electrical, plumbing, roofing, chimney, framing, and other

[52.1] 44 Cal. 4th 541, 187 P.3d 424, 79 Cal. Rptr. 3d 721 (2008).

structural problems. They also asserted that, because of improper design, manufacture, and installation, windows in the homes, including those supplied by Weather Shield, leaked and fogged, causing extensive damage. Theories of negligence, strict liability, breach of warranty, and breach of contract were set forth.

In April 2000, JMP cross-complained against Weather Shield, Darrow, and all the other project subcontractors sued by the homeowners. The cross-complaints asserted, among other things, that under the pertinent subcontract provisions, all of which had been drafted by JMP and were identical on the point, the subcontractors owed JMP duties of indemnity and defense against the homeowners' complaints. The cross-complaints sought declaratory relief with respect to JMP's alleged indemnity and defense rights.

JMP, and all the subcontractors except Weather Shield and Darrow, settled before trial. The "sliding scale" settlement agreement (as allowed under California Code of Civil Procedure Section 877.6 wherein settling defendants and plaintiff cooperate in a trial against non-settling defendant or defendants) provided the homeowners a minimum payment of $2.55 million, and guaranteed an additional sum of $1.45 million against any recovery from the non-settling subcontractors. The settling defendants also agreed to assist the homeowners in prosecuting their claims against the nonsettling parties. JMP and the settling subcontractors mutually released all claims, demands, and liabilities among themselves. All complaints and cross-complaints were dismissed except as to Weather Shield and Darrow.

In July 2002, during final pretrial proceedings, Weather Shield moved to dismiss the homeowners' strict liability causes of action. The motion cited then-current case law holding that a subcontractor hired by a developer, even a subcontractor that supplied a component product rather than a service, could not be strictly liable for defects in mass-produced homes, unless the subcontractor also owned or controlled the housing development.[52.2] The court granted the motion, subject to a reevaluation of prejudice in the event of an intervening change in the law.

The window leak and framing issues went to trial against Weather Shield and Darrow on the remaining theories of negligence and breach of warranty. In October 2002, the jury returned general verdicts against Darrow and in favor of Weather Shield. The jury awarded the homeowners approximately $1 million in damages against Darrow. Following the jury verdict, Darrow settled all the complaints against it.

Thereafter, in March 2003, JMP's cross-complaint against Weather Shield was separately tried to the court. JMP sought both (1) express indemnity for amounts paid to the homeowners in settlement, and (2) under the duty-to-defend provisions of Weather Shield's subcontract, attorney fees and expenses incurred by JMP in defending itself against the homeowners' suit.

[52.2] *See* Casey v. Overhead Door Corp., 74 Cal. App. 4th 112, 119-120, 87 Cal. Rptr. 2d 603 (1999); La Jolla Village Homeowners' Ass'n v. Superior Court, 212 Cal. App. 3d 1131, 1146, 261 Cal. Rptr. 146 (1989).

The trial court ruled that the subcontract's terms obliged Weather Shield to indemnify JMP for amounts paid to the homeowners only if Weather Shield was found negligent. Thus, the court determined, the jury's verdict that Weather Shield was not negligent absolved Weather Shield of indemnity liability in this case. On the other hand, the court concluded, the subcontract did give Weather Shield responsibility for JMP's legal defense against the homeowners' claims, insofar as those claims concerned the windows supplied by Weather Shield, regardless of whether Weather Shield was ultimately found negligent.

JMP presented evidence that it had incurred $375,069 in attorney fees to defend against the homeowners' claims, and that 70 percent of the homeowner settlement amount was attributable to the window problems. JMP therefore urged that, under their subcontracts, Weather Shield and Darrow were together liable for 70 percent of JMP's defense fees, or $262,548. The trial court apportioned this amount equally between Darrow and Weather Shield, and therefore awarded JMP $131,274 in damages against Weather Shield. The trial court also found Weather Shield contractually liable to JMP, as the prevailing party on JMP's cross-complaint, for $46,734 in attorney fees incurred by JMP to prosecute the cross-action.

Meanwhile, in December 2002, the California Supreme Court held in *Jimenez v. Superior Court,*[52.3] that, contrary to the teaching of such cases as *Casey* and *La Jolla* the manufacturer or supplier of a component part installed in a mass-produced home may be held strictly liable when a defect in the component causes damage to other parts of the structure.

Following entry of judgment in this case in March 2003, the homeowners moved for a judgment notwithstanding the verdict (judgment NOV)[52.4] and a new trial[52.5] against Weather Shield. Among other things, the homeowners asserted that, under *Jimenez,* they were entitled to try their previously dismissed strict liability causes of action. In May 2003, the court denied the motion for a judgment NOV, but granted a new trial against Weather Shield on the issue of strict liability.

Weather Shield appealed (1) the new trial order, and (2) the declaratory relief judgment insofar as it required Weather Shield to reimburse JMP's expense of defending the homeowners' action and prosecuting JMP's cross-complaint. Two of the groups of homeowner plaintiffs filed protective cross-appeals from the judgment against them, and in Weather Shield's favor, on the construction-defect claims. JMP did not appeal the order absolving Weather Shield from contractual indemnity liability for amounts paid by JMP to the homeowners.

In a divided decision, the California Court of Appeal affirmed the orders and judgments challenged by Weather Shield, and dismissed the cross-appeals as moot. On the issue of Weather Shield's liability for JMP's defense, regardless of its own negligence, the majority reasoned, in essence, that Weather Shield's promise "to defend" JMP against suits founded upon claims arising out of the execution of Weather Shield's work necessarily contemplated an immediate duty

[52.3] 29 Cal. 4th 473, 127 Cal. Rptr. 2d 614, 58 P.3d 450 (2002).

[52.4] Cal. Code Civ. Proc. §§ 629, 659.

[52.5] Cal. Code Civ. Proc. §§ 657, 659.

to provide a service, which duty arose at the time such a suit was brought and a defense was therefore needed. Thus, the majority concluded, the duty could not depend upon the outcome of issues to be litigated in the very action Weather Shield was obliged to defend.

The concurring and dissenting appellate opinion argued that the contract language did not compel the majority's interpretation of the duty to defend. Moreover, the concurring and dissenting opinion stated policy concerns weigh against allowing a builder or developer with superior bargaining power to impose contractual defense obligations on a nonnegligent subcontractor.

Weather Shield sought review, raising both the new-trial and defense-cost issues. The California Supreme Court granted review, limited to the following issue: Did a contract under which a subcontractor agreed "to defend any suit or action" against a developer "founded upon" any claim "growing out of the execution of the work" require the subcontractor to provide a defense to a suit against the developer even if the subcontractor was not negligent?

The *Crawford* Court stated that parties to a contract may define their duties toward one another in the event of a third-party claim against one or both arising out of their relationship. Such an agreement may require one party to indemnify the other for moneys paid or expenses incurred as a result of the claims.[52.6] The parties may also assign one party to be responsible for the other's legal defense when a third-party claim is made against the first party. In general, indemnity agreements are interpreted using the rules of contract interpretation, subject to public policy limitations. Effect is to be given to the parties' mutual intent, as ascertained from the contract's language, if it is clear and explicit, and words are to be understood in their ordinary and popular sense.

Reviewing the *Crawford* subcontract indemnity language, the Court found that it contained two promises: (1) to indemnify and save the contractor harmless against all claims for damages to persons or to property and claims for loss, damage and/or theft . . . growing out of the execution of the subcontractor's work; (2) at its own expense to defend any suit or action brought against the contractor founded upon such claim or damage, loss, or theft.

The *Crawford* Court distinguished between a duty to defend another from a duty to pay another, after the fact, for defense costs the other has incurred in defending itself. The *Crawford* Court reviewed a series of cases on this issue. Because the *Crawford* indemnity clause failed to limit or exclude the subcontractor's duty to defend, it confirmed that duty. The *Crawford* clause did not expressly condition the duty to defend on the indemnitee's request for a defense. The clause also was not strictly limited to those claims on which, in the end, the subcontractor actually owed indemnity. The clause stated that the obligation was to "defend any suit or action . . . against the contractor founded upon the claim" of such injury, damage, loss, or theft. The Court held that the duty of the subcontractor to defend in this case was for suits which alleged claims for damages growing out of the subcontractor's work, not just suits in which the claims were proven.

[52.6] *See* Cal. Civ. Code § 2772.

The *Crawford* Court stated that the subcontractor's duty to defend is distinct from, and broader than, the duty expressed in Section 2778, Subdivision 3, to reimburse an indemnitee's defense costs as part of any indemnity otherwise owed. The subcontractor's duty to defend the contractor arose when the claim was made against the general contractor, and did not depend on whether the conditions of indemnity were, or were not, later established.

The *Crawford* Court refused to accept arguments made by industry groups that raised policy concerns about an indemnity agreement which requires a subcontractor to defend a residential developer or builder in a construction defect suit, before, and regardless of whether the subcontractor itself is found to be at fault. The *Crawford* Court referred to statutory provisions in Civil Code Section 2782, which limit indemnification for sole negligence or willful misconduct, and revisions in 2005 and 2007 which make unenforceable indemnity provisions requiring a subcontractor to indemnify a builder to the extent that the claims arise out of, pertain to, or relate to the negligence of the builder or the builder's agents, and that the provisions of this statute cannot be waived or modified by contractual agreement.

Finally, the *Crawford* Court pointed out that the subcontractor did not argue that the indemnity agreement at issue was either procedurally or substantively unconscionable. It also stated that the subcontractor in this case did not argue that it was a small and relatively powerless subcontractor overwhelmed by the general contractor's superior bargaining power, and that the subcontractor did not claim it naively signed the indemnity agreement without understanding its terms. The supplier against whom the indemnity was sought described itself as an out-of-state manufacturer of wood windows, which suggests multi-state scale of operations, and a consequent sophistication, that would undermine such assertions.

Affirming the court of appeal's decision, the *Crawford* Court concluded that the duty of the subcontractor and supplier to defend the contractor against claims founded upon damage or loss caused by the subcontractor's negligent performance of its work, as set forth in the subcontract, imposed duties on the subcontractor as soon as suit was filed against the contractor asserting these claims, regardless of whether it was ultimately determined that the subcontractor was actually negligent.

In *JPI Westcoast Construction, L.P. v. RJS Associates, Inc*,[52.7] a family of a deceased construction worker settled a wrongful death lawsuit against a contractor and subcontractor, and the contractor brought an action for express contractual indemnity against the subcontractor and the subcontractor's excess insurer. The excess insurer brought a cross-complaint for equitable subrogation and equitable indemnity against the contractor's primary insurer. On cross-motions for summary judgment, the trial court entered judgment for the subcontractor and its excess insurer. The contractor and its primary insurer appealed. The appellate court held that the excess insurer was entitled to reimbursement of sums paid on behalf of contractor in settlement.

[52.7] 156 Cal. App. 4th 1448, 68 Cal. Rptr. 3d 91 (2007).

JPI was the general contractor on a large construction project, and hired RJS & Associates (RJS) as a subcontractor on a phase of the project. The construction contract between JPI and RJS contained an indemnity clause in favor of JPI. During the course of the work undertaken by RJS, a worker was killed in an accident. In the underlying action, the worker's family sued JPI, RJS, and others for wrongful death. RJS's insurers assumed defense of the action on behalf of JPI and RJS. A jury found that JPI was 20% at fault for the accident, RJS was 70% at fault, and awarded judgment in the amount of $6,853,284 in favor of the worker's family. After trial, the family settled with JPI and RJS for a total of $4.9 million.

The appeal arose from the subsequent round of litigation between JPI and its primary insurance carrier, Transcontinental Insurance Company (Transcontinental), and RJS and its excess carrier, Great American Insurance Company (Great American), over contributions to the settlement of the underlying action. On stipulated facts, the trial court ruled in favor of RJS and Great American, and against JPI and Transcontinental, on four separate motions for summary judgment. The appellate court affirmed the trial court's summary judgment rulings. In so ruling the appellate court framed the issue as follows: Assuming JPI's contractual right to indemnity by RJS was triggered under the facts presented here, did the indemnity clause control the payment obligations of the parties' respective insurers, or were such obligations determined by the language in the applicable policies of insurance?

On December 22, 1999, JPI entered into a contract with Jefferson At Bay Meadows, L.P., to serve as general contractor for the construction of Bay Meadows apartment complex. On January 18, 2000, JPI entered into subcontract number 76003-03-3001-999 with RJS, by which RJS agreed to build seven complete subterranean concrete podium structures for the contract price of $12,765,958.00, including all design engineering work.

The subcontract contained the following indemnity clause:

> To the fullest extent permitted by law, Subcontractor shall indemnify and hold harmless . . . Contractor and Contractor's agents and employees (the 'Indemnitees') from all claims, damages, losses and expenses . . . attributable to bodily injury, . . . death or injury . . . arising out of or in connection with the performance of the Work of Subcontractor performed . . . in connection with the Project, by anyone directly or indirectly employed by Subcontractor, or anyone for whose acts Subcontractor is liable even if caused jointly and concurrently by the negligence of the Indemnitees and Subcontractor. . . . The above indemnity provisions do not extend to, or cover any loss, damage, or expense arising out of the sole negligence or willful misconduct of Contractor, its employees and agents or any other Indemnitees.

The subcontract contained the following provision regarding insurance coverage:

> Prior to the commencement of the Work and periodically thereafter as required by Contractor, subcontractor shall deliver to Contractor satisfactory certificates evidencing compliance by Subcontractor with the insurance requirements set forth in Section VII of the Project Manual to these General Provisions and incorporated herein for all purposes. All policies, with the exception of Workers compensation, shall name contractor and the Owner as Additional Insured parties on a primary basis. . . . All original insurance certificates are to be sent to JPI. . . . If requested by contractor, Subcontractor shall furnish copies of insurance policies required by the Contract Documents. The requiring of any and all insurance as set forth in these paragraphs, or elsewhere, is in addition to and not in any way in substitution for all the other protection provided under the subcontract to Contractor, including Paragraph 11 (Indemnity).

JPI purchased a commercial general liability (CGL) policy from Transcontinental with a $1 million limit. RJS purchased a CGL policy from Lloyd's with aggregate coverage in the amount of $2 million, with a per occurrence limit of $1 million. JPI was named as an additional insured on the RJS Lloyd's policy. An additional rider to the RJS policy provided that it would be primary. RJS was also the sole named insured on a Great American umbrella policy with a general aggregate and per occurrence limit of $9 million. The Great American policy stated that Great American would pay sums in excess of the retained limit that the insured would become legally obligated to pay. The Great American policy defined "retained limit" as:

> [T]he greater of: 1. the total amounts stated as the applicable limits of the underlying policies listed in the Schedule of Underlying Insurance and the applicable limits of any other insurance providing coverage to the "Insured" during the Policy Period. . . .

For purposes of summary judgment, JPI and RJS stipulated that JPI qualified as an additional insured under the Great American policy.

The Great American policy also contained an "Other Insurance" clause, which stated:

> If other insurance applies to a loss that is also covered by this policy, this policy will apply excess of the other insurance. Nothing herein will be construed to make this policy subject to the terms, conditions and limitations of such other insurance. However, this provision will not apply if the other insurance is specifically written to be excess of this policy.

Sanchez was working as a "hose man" for a concrete pour at the project. A boom involved in this operation dropped down and struck him, causing his death. His estate sued JPI, RJS, and the concrete pump truck operator. JPI tendered defense to RJS and its primary carrier, Lloyd's, and Lloyd's accepted the defense of JPI as an additional insured under the RJS policy. Transcontinental noted the likelihood that the damages would likely exceed the Lloyd's policy limit, and asserted that Lloyd's and Great American owed a duty to indemnify JPI for a judgment or settlement up to the combined $10 million of those two policies. Great American rejected that assertion, and replied that all the primary coverage, including that provided by Transcontinental must exhaust prior to the excess coverage being triggered.

The case proceeded to trial against JPI, RJS, and the truck operator. The jury returned verdicts, finding all three defendants negligent, with respective fault apportioned 20% to JPI, 70% to RJS, and 10% to the truck operator. The jury award was for $1,853.284.27 for economic damages, and $5 million for non-economic damages. After reduction for previous settlements by other parties, the jury verdict was $6,839,457.50.

After the jury verdict, RJS and its insurers, Lloyd's and Great American, entered settlement negotiations with plaintiffs. Great American demanded that Transcontinental participate in the settlement, but Transcontinental refused to contribute any amount to the settlement on behalf of JPI. Nor did JPI contribute any amount to the eventual settlement. Subsequently, RJS, Lloyd's, and Great American settled with plaintiffs for $4.9 million pursuant to a Settlement Agreement and Release ("settlement agreement") signed by the parties on and around March 11, 2005. The settlement agreement stated that RJS was the named insured under the Lloyd's and Great American policies and that JPI qualified as an additional insured under those policies. Under the terms of the settlement agreement, Lloyd's paid $1 million, with $777,777.78 paid on behalf of RJS and $222,222.22 on behalf of JPI. Great American paid the remaining $3.9 million, with $3,033,333.33 paid on behalf of RJS and $866,666.67 on behalf of JPI. Great American's settlement payment on behalf of JPI was made subject to a full reservation of rights against Transcontinental. Also, JPI and Transcontinental agreed that any payment by Great American to compromise the judgment should not be deemed a voluntary payment.

On January 18, 2005, JPI filed a complaint for express contractual indemnity and declaratory relief against RJS and its insurers Great American and Lloyd's. JPI subsequently dismissed Lloyd's from the suit on March 22, 2005. In its complaint, JPI requested "that the court order RJS to indemnify JPI for the full amount of the jury verdict and any subsequent judgment in the underlying action pursuant to the terms of the express written indemnity agreement in the RJS/JPI contract." JPI also sought declaratory relief against Great American, alleging that "JPI and RJS clearly intended that RJS would be primarily responsible for fully indemnifying JPI . . . and JPI's own insurance carriers owe no obligation to pay any of the verdict entered in the underlying action."

On June 1, 2005, Great American filed a first amended cross-complaint for equitable subrogation and equitable indemnity against Transcontinental. In its cross-complaint, Great American alleged that any obligation it owed under its policy was subject to the terms and conditions of its policy. Further, Great American alleged it was entitled under equitable principles of subrogation to reimbursement from Transcontinental of its settlement payment on behalf of JPI. Great American also alleged it was entitled to equitable indemnification from Transcontinental "according to the terms of their respective policy provisions, including their 'limits of liability' and 'other insurance' clauses, as well as principles of equity," for its payment of Transcontinental's portion of the settlement.

Motions for summary judgment were filed in the trial court by various carriers. The trial court granted a motion for summary judgment by RJS on JPI's claim for express contractual indemnity. The trial court concluded that the basis of JPI's cause of actions was moot, as JPI no longer had any right of recovery against RJS. The trial court also denied summary judgment as to Great American on JPI's declaratory relief claim. The trial court concluded that there was no longer any controversy between JPI and Great American because the entire judgment/settlement had been paid by RJS's insurance carriers, including the $3.9 million paid by Great American. The declaratory relief cause of action was moot as between those parties.

Shortly thereafter, the trial resolved the coverage issue in favor of Great American. The trial court concluded that the primary carrier of the indemnitee (JPI) had to pay out before the excess carrier of the indemnitor (RJS) was obliged to contribute. The trial court therefore granted Great American's summary judgment motion on its cross-complaint against Transcontinental, ruling that Great American was entitled to reimbursement and/or contribution in the amount of $866,666.67 from Transcontinental. JPI and Transcontinental appealed.

The appellate court stated that *Rossmoor Sanitation v. Pylon, Inc.*,[52.8] stands for the proposition that an insurer's subrogation of its insured's right to contractual indemnification controls in a battle of "other insurance" clauses between co-insurers. The *JPI* court stated that key to the *Rossmoor* court's reasoning was the compelling fact that to apportion the loss between the insurers pursuant to the other insurance clauses would effectively negate the indemnity agreement and impose liability on the carrier for Rossmoor, when Rossmoor bargained with Pylon to avoid that result as a part of the consideration of the construction agreement.

The *JPI* court stated that *Reliance Nat. Indemnity Co. v. General Star Indemnity Co.*,[52.9] controlled on this issue, because it was factually analogous to the *JPI* case, and that its reasoning was highly persuasive. The *JPI* court said that *Rossmoor* did not apply. The *JPI* court stated that the duty to contribute applied to insurers that share the same level of obligation as to the same insured, but that in *Reliance*, Reliance's obligation was primary, and General Star's was excess and General Star was not liable for the loss, damage, or defense covered by the other primary insurance. Like the *Reliance* court, the *JPI* court stated that the equities favored the primary carrier, Transcontinental.

JPI contended that the trial court erred in granting summary judgment in favor of RJS on its complaint against RJS and Great American for express contractual indemnity and declaratory relief. The *JPI* court disagreed, and held that Transcontinental was not entitled to indemnification from Great American on

---

[52.8] 13 Cal. 3d 622, 119 Cal. Rptr. 449 (1975).

[52.9] 72 Cal. App. 4th 1063, 85 Cal. Rptr. 2d 627 (1999).

the basis of the indemnification clause in the construction contract between JPI and RJS. The appellate court affirmed the trial court.

As to the JPI claim for express contractual indemnity against RJS, the appellate court held that the undisputed facts showed that JPI tendered defense of the underlying action to RJS and its insurers, Lloyd's and Great American, and that Lloyd's and Great American accepted defense of the action on behalf of JPI. Lloyd's and Great American tried the case, and following an adverse jury verdict, negotiated a full and completed settlement. JPI did not pay anything toward the settlement, and therefore there was nothing for which RJS was required to indemnify JPI.

However, the *JPI* court rejected RJS's contention that the summary judgment of the trial court could be affirmed on the alternative basis that the indemnification clause was inapplicable. The *JPI* court concluded that the clause at issue in this case was not a general indemnity clause. It was a specific indemnity clause because the claim explicitly addressed the indemnitee's negligence. The clause in this case stated that loss or damage caused solely by JPI's negligence was excluded. The clause also specifically covered JPI where JPI was jointly negligent with RJS, so application of the clause in favor of JPI was not precluded by negligence attributable to JPI.

In *Greystone Homes, Inc. v. Midtec, Inc.*,[52.10] a home builder brought an action against a manufacturer of plumbing fittings for negligence and equitable indemnity. The trial court granted summary judgment for the manufacturer, and the builder appealed. The court of appeal held that:

1. The Right to Repair Act (RRA) (Cal. Civ. Code Sec. 895, et. seq., also referred to as SB 800) abrogated the economic loss rule in homeowners' actions against individual product manufacturers;
2. a builder may bring an equitable indemnity action under the RRA for reimbursement for a homeowner's economic losses;
3. RRA standards for plumbing systems apply to individual product manufacturers as well as to home builders;
4. a fact issue existed as to whether a manufacturer caused a violation of RRA standards;
5. a builder may not pursue a negligence per se action against an individual product manufacturer for violation of RRA standards; and
6. a builder had no special relationship with a manufacturer supporting recovery for economic losses.

The case was reversed and remanded to the trial court with directions.

In *Aas v. Superior Court*,[52.11] the California Supreme Court had concluded that a group of homeowners could not recover damages in negligence from the developer, contractor, or subcontractors who built their homes, for existing construction defects that had not yet caused either property damage or personal

[52.10] 168 Cal. App. 4th 1194, 86 Cal. Rptr. 3d 196 (2008).

[52.11] 24 Cal. 4th 627, 636, 101 Cal. Rptr. 2d 718, 12 P.3d 1125 (2000).

injury. In reaching this conclusion, the *Aas* Court explained that while "tort law provides a remedy for construction defects that cause property damage or personal injury,"[52.12] the "economic loss rule" precludes recovery for damages such as "the difference between price paid and value received, and deviations from standards of quality that have not resulted in property damage or personal injury."

In response to the holding in *Aas*, the Legislature enacted Civil Code Section 895 *et seq.* ("the Right to Repair Act" or "RRA"). The RRA establishes a set of building standards pertaining to new residential construction, and provides homeowners with a cause of action against, among others, builders and individual product manufacturers for violation of the standards (Secs. 896, 936). The RRA makes clear that upon a showing of violation of an applicable standard, a homeowner may recover economic losses from a builder without having to show that the violation caused property damage or personal injury (Secs. 896, 942). In such an instance, the RRA abrogates the economic loss rule, thus legislatively superseding *Aas*.

In *Greystone,* Greystone Homes, Inc. (Greystone), a home builder, brought this action against Midtec, Inc. among others. In its complaint, Greystone alleged that various homeowners had made claims against Greystone for damage caused by plumbing fittings that Midtec manufactured, and that the fittings were defective within the meaning of the RRA. Greystone claimed that it had incurred costs to replace the defective fittings, and alleged claims including negligence and equitable indemnity causes of action against Midtec.

Midtec brought a motion for summary judgment and/or summary adjudication in which it claimed that Greystone could not recover for purely economic losses that it incurred in replacing the fittings. In opposition, Greystone claimed that the RRA abolished the economic loss rule under the circumstances of this case, and argued that both builders and individual product manufacturers are liable under the RRA for the costs of repairing construction defects. In reply, Midtec contended that the RRA did not apply to Greystone's action, and that the economic loss rule precluded Greystone from prevailing against Midtec on its claims.

The trial court granted Midtec's motion for summary judgment. The trial court acknowledged that the RRA provides an exception to the economic loss rule for actions brought under the RRA by homeowners. However, the court concluded that Greystone was not entitled to pursue the statutorily created cause of action because Greystone was not a homeowner. The court ruled that the economic loss rule bars Greystone from recovering against Midtec on Greystone's common law claims.

Greystone's appeal raised two questions of first impression concerning the RRA. The first question was whether a builder may recover for economic losses caused by a product manufacturer's violations of the RRA standards, through an equitable indemnity claim against the manufacturer. The second question was whether a builder may recover its economic losses from an individual product

[52.12] *Id.* at 635, 101 Cal. Rptr. 2d 718, 12 P.3d at 1125.

manufacturer through a direct negligence claim based on the product manufacturer's violation of the RRA standards. The appellate court concluded that a builder may recover from a product manufacturer for economic losses caused by the manufacturer's violation of the standards set forth in the RRA, through an equitable indemnity action, but that a builder may not recover for these losses through a direct negligence claim against the manufacturer. The court reversed the trial court's summary judgment and remanded the matter to the trial court with directions to consider Midtec's alternative motion for summary adjudication.

In late 2000 or early 2001, Radiant Technologies, Inc. (RTI) purchased plastic plumbing fittings from Midtec. RTI used the fittings as a component part in its Plum-Pex plumbing system. RTI distributed the Plum-Pex system to plumbing wholesalers, who in turn sold the system to plumbing subcontractors.

Greystone was a merchant home builder. Beginning in approximately 2003, Greystone developed and built a new home community in Chula Vista known as Willow Bend. Willow Bend is composed of 110 condominiums/townhouses, clustered in 17 buildings. Greystone's plumbing subcontractor, Production Plus Plumbing, installed the RTI Plum-Pex system, which contained Midtec fittings, in 66 of the Willow Bend units, between 2003 and 2005.

The owners of some of the units that contained the Midtec fittings began to complain to Greystone about leaks in their plumbing systems. Twenty-two of the units experienced failures of Midtec fittings. In some instances, there were multiple failures in a single unit. The Midtec fittings failed primarily due to fatigue caused by a molding defect in the manufacturing process. Fittings continued to fail during Greystone's investigation of the homeowners' complaints. Water leaks associated with the fitting failures presented a health risk to homeowners.

There were a total of approximately 1,980 Midtec fittings in the 66 homes. Greystone determined that if it did not replace the Midtec fittings, it was highly probable that there would be additional failures. Greystone replaced all of the Midtec fittings, including those that had not yet actually failed. The total cost to replace all of the fittings was approximately $1,494,904.04. The cost for repairs related to fittings that had failed was approximately $106,000.

While Midtec had a contractual relationship with RTI, it did not have a contractual relationship with Greystone. Midtec did not provide a warranty to RTI for the fittings. The only warranty that was provided to either Greystone or to homeowners in the Willow Bend project that related to plumbing was RTI's warranty for the Plum-Pex system.

In May 2005, Greystone filed a complaint against RTI, RTI's insurance company, Zurich American Insurance Company (Zurich), and Midtec. As to Midtec, Greystone brought a claim for negligence, a separate claim for indemnity and contribution, and requested declaratory relief. Greystone subsequently reached a settlement with RTI. As part of the settlement, RTI paid Greystone $460,000, an amount that exceeded Greystone's costs to repair water damage caused by fittings that actually failed. In February 2007, the trial court found that Greystone and RTI had entered into the settlement in good faith. The court subsequently dismissed Greystone's complaint as to RTI and Zurich.

In April 2007, Midtec filed a motion for summary judgment or, in the alternative, for summary adjudication. In its motion, Midtec noted that, pursuant to the economic loss rule, a plaintiff may not recover, in tort, economic losses caused by an allegedly defective product when those losses are unrelated to either property damage or bodily injury. Midtec argued that Greystone had already recovered all of its damages that were related to property damage caused by the allegedly defective fittings, through its settlement with RTI, and maintained that the economic loss rule precluded Greystone from recovering additional damages from Midtec related to the cost of replacing fittings that had not failed or caused property damage.

Greystone opposed the motion. In its opposition, Greystone argued that the RRA had entirely abrogated the economic loss rule in construction defect litigation. Specifically, Greystone argued that the RRA imposed "cost-of-repair liability upon builders and individual product manufacturers whose products are defective, even in the absence of any specific property damage or bodily injury." Greystone claimed that Midtec was thus liable to Greystone for Greystone's costs to replace all of the fittings, including those that had not yet caused property damage. Greystone noted that its total cost to repair all of the fittings was approximately $1.5 million, which far exceeded the $460,000 it received in its settlement with RTI.

In its reply to Greystone's opposition, Midtec argued that the RRA is "completely inapplicable to the circumstances of this case." Midtec maintained that only homeowners are authorized to bring an action pursuant to the RRA. Midtec also noted that Section 936 provides in part, "Nothing in this title modifies the law pertaining to joint and several liability for builders, general contractors, subcontractors, material suppliers, individual product manufacturer[s], and design professionals that contribute to any specific violation of this title." Based on this language, Midtec argued that "[S]ection 936 alone is dispositive of the issue that [S]ections 895 et seq. do not apply to this action between the developer and a component part manufacturer."

In July 2007, the trial court held a hearing on Midtec's motion for summary judgment or summary adjudication. After oral argument, the trial court granted Midtec's motion for summary judgment. In granting the motion, the trial court reasoned in part:

> [Midtec] has met its initial burden of demonstrating each of the claims asserted by [Greystone] seeks to recover the economic losses associated with replacing defective plumbing fittings that had not yet failed, i.e. had not yet caused property damage. Per Separate Statement [of Facts] number 22, it is undisputed that the $460,000 settlement with [RTI] exceeds the cost of repairing the fittings that actually leaked prior to replacement. Therefore [Midtec] has met its burden of demonstrating that the economic loss rule bars any further recovery by [Greystone], and the burden shifts to [Greystone]. [Greystone's] only contention refuting defendant's position is that the enactment of Senate Bill 800 abolishes the economic loss rule. This contention lacks merit. Rather than abolish the economic loss rule completely, S.B. 800 created an exception to the rule where a homeowner or [homeowners']

> association brings a claim to recover damages for enumerated construction defects. [(Secs. 895, subd. (f), 896, and 942).] Arguably, the defective fittings fall within the enumerated construction defects. [(See Secs. 896, subds. (a)(14), (15)].) However, [Greystone] is not a homeowner or [homeowners' association], and as a result is not entitled to pursue the statutorily created cause of action. [Greystone's] only recourse is a common law claim, and the economic loss rule applies to bar such common law claims. In addition, [Greystone] provides no evidence demonstrating its compliance with the procedural prerequisites of S.B. 800, i.e. a pre-lawsuit notice and opportunity to repair. [(§§§§ 910, 917, 930, subd. (b).)]

The trial court subsequently entered judgment in favor of Midtec. Greystone appealed.

Greystone argued that the trial court erred in granting summary judgment as a matter of law on the common law indemnity claim. The *Greystone* court cited a series of cases allowing for equitable indemnity where both joint tortfeasors are responsible for an indivisible injury, and stated that the right to indemnity is one manner in which joint tortfeasors may apportion joint and several liability. However, the court stated that for such equitable indemnity to apply there must be some basis for tort liability against the proposed indemnitor.

The *Greystone* court cited *Aas v. Superior Court*,[52.13] for the proposition that for defective products and negligent services that have caused neither property damage nor personal injury, and have caused solely economic loss, the manufacturer is not liable to the homeowner. The California legislature enacted the RRA in response to *Aas*. The RRA sets standards for residential construction, and provides tort liability for entities which fail to meet the standards set forth in the RRA. The *Greystone* court reviewed the legislative history of the RRA, and held that the RRA abrogated the economic loss rule in actions brought under the RRA by homeowners against individual product manufacturers.

Midtec argued that the RRA preserved the economic loss rule for claims against product manufacturers that alleged a violation of the RRA standards. The *Greystone* court stated that to determine if this claim exists, the court must first determine whether the economic loss rule would preclude a homeowner from collecting damages from Midtec, since Greystone's ability to pursue an indemnity action against Midtec under the RRA is contingent upon Midtec and Greystone sharing a joint legal obligation to the homeowners for economic losses caused by violation of the RRA standards.

Section 896 provides that individual product manufacturers are liable to homeowners for violation of the RRA standards, and Sections 942 and 944 abrogate the economic loss rule and allow a homeowner to recover economic losses from a product manufacturer for a violation of the RRA standards which is caused by the manufacturer's negligence or breach of contract. Midtec argued that Greystone's equitable indemnity claim was barred because a product manufacturer was only liable to a homeowner for an unmet standard under the RRA if there is resulting damage to persons or property. Midtec claimed that since it was

[52.13] 24 Cal. 4th 627, 636, 101 Cal. Rptr. 2d 718, 12 P.3d 1125 (2000).

not obligated to the homeowners for economic losses under the RRA, there was no predicate tort upon which Greystone, as an indemnitee, may base its equitable indemnity claim. The appellate court refused to accept these arguments.

On appeal, for the first time, Midtec raised the argument that it was not an individual product manufacturer under Sections 896 and 936. The appellate court held that the failure to raise this argument either to the trial court or to the appellate court in a manner which would have allowed Greystone to respond to the argument caused Midtec to forfeit this argument. The appellate court held that Midtec was an "individual product manufacturer" as referred to in Sections 896 and 936 for the purposes of the appeal.

Although the *Greystone* court stated the rule that there was generally no duty to prevent economic loss to third parties in negligence actions at common law, the court found that the RRA had created such a duty. The *Greystone* court held that a more reasonable interpretation of Section 936 was that a product manufacturer was liable only where its negligent act or omission or a breach of contract caused a violation of the RRA standards. The court noted that although Section 942 adopted a strict liability standard by providing for liability without "showing causation or damages," Section 945.5 established a series of statutory defenses that were consistent with the principles of comparative fault. The *Greystone* court rejected Midtec's assertion that if this court were to conclude that the economic loss rule does not bar Greystone's claims, then this would "expand the law of strict product liability beyond tolerable limits."

The *Greystone* court concluded that the RRA abrogated the economic loss rule in actions brought by homeowners against individual product manufacturers for a violation of the RRA standards based upon the manufacturer's negligence or breach of contract. The matter was remanded to the trial court with directions to deny Midtec's motion for summary judgment, and for the trial court to consider Greystone's procedural objections to Midtec's alternative motion for summary adjudication.

CHAPTER 20

SUSPENSION AND TERMINATION

§ 20.04 AIA APPROACH

[A] Contractor's Power to Terminate

Page 877, add at end of subsection:

In *Advantages of the ConsensusDOCS Construction Contracts*,[37.1] by Larry D. Harris and Brian M. Perlberg, The Construction Lawyer, Vol. 29, Number 1, Winter 2009, the authors contrast how termination by the contractor differs in the ConsensusDOCS. Under the ConsensusDOCS, the contractor termination right is broader than under the AIA documents. In the event of termination by the contractor, the ConsensusDOCS allow recovery of profit on work not performed, including reasonable overhead and profit, and recovery by the contractor of certain additional costs such as demobilization. Overhead is defined in more detail in ConsensusDOCS 20 Para. 2.4.12. The ConsensusDOCS are silent about the right to recover damages other than those listed, and one interpretation would be that additional damages are not recoverable. ConsensusDOCS 200 Para. 11.5.3.

Harris and Perlberg analyze how termination for cause is handled. Under the ConsensusDOCS, the owner may act unilaterally to terminate for cause, while the AIA documents require certification by the Initial Decision Maker (IDM). The AIA documents provide for a 7-day notice. The ConsensusDOCS require two notices, with an opportunity by the contractor to cure, over a period of 21 days. ConsensusDOCS provide for notification and opportunity for a contractor to correct defective work on a project. ConsensusDOCS 200 Para. 3.9.4.

[C] Owner's Termination for Cause

Page 880, add after first paragraph:

Contractual termination procedures must be followed for effective termination for cause of a general contractor by an owner, including, if identified as a condition, architect certification of the contractor's default. In *Mike Building & Contracting, Inc. v. Just Homes, LLC*,[48.1] the plaintiff, Mike Building & Contracting, moved, pursuant to CPLR 3212, for partial summary judgment on its first cause of action against Just Homes, LLC (JH) for breach of contract for

[37.1] Larry D. Harris & Brian M. Perlberg, *Advantages of the ConsensusDOCS Construction Contracts*, The Construction Lawyer, Vol. 29, No. 1, Winter 2009.

[48.1] 2010 N.Y. Misc. LEXIS 241, 2010 WL 457303 (N.Y. Sup. 2010).

failure to comply with the termination procedures set forth in AIA A201. Sec. 14.2 of the General Conditions, to be followed in the event the owner seeks to terminate the contractor for cause.

The case involved an action for breach of a construction contract entered into by plaintiff, Mike's Building & Construction, (MBC) a general construction contractor, and defendant Just Homes, LLC (JH) a building developer owned by the individual defendant-members. New York City's Department of Housing Preservation and Development (HPD) and Community Preservation Corporation (CPC) were involved in overseeing the construction. During construction performed by MBC, a number of payment requests were submitted, and only partially paid, in part, because the owner suspected fraud by MBC. Eventually, JH attempted to terminate MBC for cause, which termination was disputed by MBC as not having been effected in accord with AIA A201, Sec. 14.2 of the General Conditions, in the contract.

The operative facts were not significantly disputed. Work commenced on the project in October, 2006, and MBC submitted a series of payment requests. On March 28, 2007, the defendant, Mr. Gutterman, attended a meeting on behalf of JH with MBC's Mike Fisher, and HPD and CPC representatives, Mr. Gaskin, and other members of JH to discuss the "huge discrepancies" between the amount requested in plaintiff's three payment requisitions and the amount approved by Mr. Streitfeld on behalf of CPC, as well as the quality of plaintiff's work and the substantial project delays. Because Mr. Streitfeld had only approved approximately $26,000 of the approximately $335,000 requested by plaintiff and certified by Mr. Gaskin in the third payment requisition, JH believed there was a "serious problem" with plaintiff and Mr. Gaskin on the project. The plaintiff's termination was discussed, and Mr. Gutterman purportedly verbally terminated the plaintiff. Neither Mr. Streitfeld nor CPC voiced objections at the time.

By letter dated April 5, 2007, Mr. Gutterman advised Ms. Foresta that JH had contacted a number of contractors to replace the plaintiff, and requested a meeting with the plaintiff to reach an amicable agreement concerning the termination. CPC did not object to this course of action. Thereafter, by letter dated April 16, 2007, JH formally terminated plaintiff's services "[p]ursuant to Section 14.2 of the contract," the owner's termination provision.

MBC alleged that JH misappropriated and diverted $58,024.50 ($19,341.50 × 3) in trust funds comprised of JH's Borrower's Equity deducted from advances by CPC and not added by JH to the payments made to MBC. The plaintiff also asserted that the defendants misappropriated $8,787.15 in trust funds (the final CPC advance) to pay for their attorney's fees ($6,000) and other unaccounted-for expenses ($2,787.15). However, the defendants submitted evidence that on or about January 4, 2007, JH made a proper trust fund payment to Ace Boring, a boring contractor which had performed test borings on the project, in the amount of $2,615 and, on or about February 8, 2007, JH made two trust fund payments to RCGA (the architect) in the amount of $5,000 each. The defendants contended that of the $135,630.45 actually disbursed to JH by CPC in loan proceeds, which they conceded were Article 3A trust funds, $130,000 was paid to the plaintiff, and the balance was exhausted in the payments made to Ace and RCGA. In contrast,

MBC insisted JH diverted $66,811.65, inclusive of $58,024.50 in Borrower's Equity and the $8,787.15, which it claimed was not applied to eligible trust purposes, but to the payment of attorney's fees and other ineligible expenses.

The parties agreed that when MBC was terminated on April 16, 2007, it had not substantially completed its work under the contract. According to MBC, JH evicted it from the project for the purpose of hiring a replacement contractor. The defendants asserted good cause for the termination alleging the plaintiff's defective and fraudulent performance.

On May 3, 2007, the plaintiff filed a mechanic's lien with the Kings County Clerk against the subject property for the sum of $7,000. CPC thereafter terminated the loan in 2007 when JH was unable to remove the lien. The instant action was commenced on August 20, 2007 and, on March 31, 2009, the note of issue was filed. In July, 2009, the plaintiff and the defendants made the motions for summary judgment discussed here.

MBC moved for partial summary judgment. It sought a judgment as to liability on its first cause of action for breach of contract, arguing that the termination was improper, because JH did not comply with Section 14.2 of AIA A201, which requires certain steps be followed by an owner seeking to terminate a contractor for cause. However, the court found that conflicting representations of fact and insufficient documentation precluded the court from granting summary judgment for MBC for JH's alleged breach of contract.

MBC had argued that JH breached the contract, because it failed to fulfill the condition precedent of Article 14.2 .1, requiring it to obtain certification from the architect that sufficient cause existed to justify its termination. MBC also argued that it was entitled to lost profits because of JH's wrongful termination.

Article 14.2.1 of the contract required the "Architect" to certify the termination of the contractor. That section provides that: "the Owner upon certification from the Architect that sufficient cause exists to justify such action, may . . . after giving the Contractor . . . seven (7) days written notice, terminate the employment of the Contractor." Inserted at the top of the first substantive page of the general conditions incorporated within the standard AIA contract was the following notation: "Where the word Architect is marked with *, it means the Architect of [sic] Engineer engaged by the owner. Where no asterisk is indicated, Architect means CPC's Engineer."

This provision was cross referenced to Article 15.1 of the General Conditions, which defined the role of "CPC's Engineer" "as an independent contractor [acting]solely on behalf of the Community Preservation Corporation." It was made clear that CPC's engineer was not the "Professional [architect or engineer] of Record," and the owner was required to retain its own architect or engineer to act on its behalf. Article 14.2.1, governing "Termination by the Owner," requires certification of cause "from the Architect," without an asterisk, and, thus, clearly required certification of cause by CPC's Engineer.

There was no evidence of certification of cause by either CPC's Engineer, Streitfeld, or by the Architect of Record, Gaskin of RCGA. The court rejected the defendant's allegation of ambiguity in the contract, upon which the defendants relied in resisting the plaintiff's motion for summary judgment on its first cause of action for breach of contract in improperly terminating JH.

Article 14.2.1 provided, in pertinent part:

> If the Contractor is adjudged a bankrupt, or if he makes a general assignment for the benefit of his creditors, or if a receiver is appointed on account of his insolvency, or if he persistently or repeatedly refuses or fails . . . to supply enough properly skilled workmen or proper materials, or if he fails to make prompt payment to subcontractors or for materials or labor, or persistently disregards laws . . . or is otherwise guilty of a substantial violation of a provision of the Contract Documents, *then the Owner upon certification from the Architect that sufficient cause exists to justify such action, may, without prejudice to any right or remedy and after giving the Contractor and his surety, if any[,] seven (7) days written notice, terminate the employment of the Contractor* and take possession of the site and all materials . . . thereon owned by the Contractor and may finish the Work by whatever method he may deem expedient. In such case the Contractor shall not be entitled to receive any further payment until the Work is finished [emphasis added].

In opposition to MBC's motion, the defendants argued that because neither Streitfeld, nor the CPC members present at the meeting of March 28, 2007, opposed JH's desire to terminate the plaintiff, compliance with "certification" should be inferred. In contrast, MBC cited the deposition of Mr. Streitfeld, who testified:

> 1. that he was not involved in MBC's termination;
> 2. that he did not have any opinion as to whether or not MBC should have been terminated from the project;
> 3. that he had never heard the reasons for the plaintiff's termination;
> 4. that he did not know if JH wanted the plaintiff terminated;
> 5. that he did not know "officially" if the plaintiff had been terminated, but had "heard rumors" to that effect; and
> 6. that he believed that the HPD did not want the plaintiff terminated, because the HPD "wanted the project to work."

In addition, MBC pointed to the deposition of Robert W. Scarpa, the architect retained as an expert by JH. Mr. Scarpa testified that when Mr. Gutterman mentioned that he was considering terminating the plaintiff, he advised Mr. Gutterman to "consult an attorney" and "have the architect certify a reason for termination."

Although Mr. Scarpa did not possess the contract at the time, and was uncertain as to the precise terms regarding termination, he testified in his deposition that "in the standard American Institute of Architect's contract, if a contractor is terminated for cause, typically the architect has to certify the reason why and that it's justified" in writing.

There was no certification of cause by either Streitfeld or Gaskin in compliance with Article 14.2.1 of the contract. Where a contract provides that a party must fulfill specific conditions precedent before it can terminate the agreement, those conditions are enforced as written and the party must comply with them.[48.2] The plaintiff made a *prima facie* showing that JH failed to terminate the contract in compliance with the contractual termination procedures. The defendants failed to successfully refute the plaintiff's proof. "[T]he termination of the contract . . . without the required previous notice [here seven days] and without a certificate from the architect in accordance with the terms of [Article 14.2.1 of] the contract was wrongful."[48.3] Article 3.4.1 of the contract required:

> If the Contractor defaults or neglects to carry out the Work in accordance with the Contract Documents and fails *within seven days after receipt of written notice from the Owner to commence and continue correction of such default or neglect with diligence and promptness, the Owner may, after seven days following receipt by the Contractor of an additional written notice and without prejudice to any other remedy he may have, make good on such deficiencies* [emphasis added].

The termination letter sent to MBC by JH merely stated "[p]ursuant to Section 14.2 of the contract dated July 12, 2005 . . . we hereby give notice of termination of your services effective seven (7) days from the receipt of this letter. Per the contract, you are not to return to the subject premises." Despite the delay of seven days in effecting the termination, MBC was given no notice of the reason for termination or the opportunity to correct any deficiency in performance. Even if the termination was based on exaggerated payment requisitions, rather than defective work, MBC was entitled, under the contract, to be afforded on opportunity to remedy the problem. It was the determination by CPC's Engineer that the work did not correspond to the claim for payment that was the provocation for JH's decision to terminate. Moreover, had JH complied with the requirement for certification by the CPC Engineer that cause for termination was present, MBC would, at least, have been on notice of the reason for termination and might have been able to remedy the problems found by Mr. Streitfeld in JH's declining to accept plaintiff's representation as to the value of work performed.

JH failed to give the plaintiff an opportunity to cure its allegedly defective or nonconforming work, and failed to provide the second written notice required by Article 3.4.1. The failure to comply with applicable notice and cure provisions in a contract bars recovery on a counterclaim based upon allegations of non-performance.[48.4]

Since the defendants failed to comply with the conditions precedent to the termination terms contained in the contract, its termination of the plaintiff breached the contract. The court found that the plaintiff was entitled to partial summary judgment as to liability on its first cause of action against JH for breach of contract and dismissal of the defendants' first counterclaim.

[48.2] Gulf Ins. Co. v. Fidelity & Deposit Co. of Md., 16 Misc. 3d 1116A, 847 N.Y.S.2d 896 (Sup. Ct., N.Y. Cty. 2007).

[48.3] General Supply & Constr. Co., 241 N.Y. 28, 34 (1925).

[48.4] Northeast Constr. Group, Inc. v Deconstruction, Inc., 16 A.D.3d 357, 793 N.Y.S.2d 17 (2005).

MBC further argued that it was entitled to $148,533, plus interest from March 16, 2007, in lost profits due to its wrongful termination, since the contract stated that this amount would have been its profit had it been permitted to fully perform. In opposition, JH argued that the plaintiff's damages were limited to the work completed and approved by the CPC's engineer under the amended terms of the contract which provided:

> If, for any reason, funding of the building construction loan from CPC for the Premises is terminated, this Contract shall be terminated simultaneously and the sole liability of the Owner shall be to pay the Contractor for Work completed and approved by CPC's engineer up to the time of such termination.

Since the CPC terminated the building construction loan in 2007, and the contract, by its terms, simultaneously terminated at that time, JH argued that MBC's damages were limited to $8,787.15, the value of the work completed as approved by Mr. Streitfeld.:

> [I]t [is] well-settled law that a plaintiff has the right of electing, on the breach of a contract, to maintain an action on the contract for the work performed and the material supplied and for the damage flowing from the failure of the defendant to permit him to complete the contract, or . . . to abandon any claim on or under the contract and to sue for *quantum meruit* for the work, labor and services and materials furnished.[48.5]

MBC's complaint contained claims for breach of contract, lien foreclosure and *quantum meruit*. The contract related to three real properties, of which the instant action related to only one. The court held that MBC's suggestion that it be awarded a sum certain, in what essentially would be liquidated damages, based upon a provision in the contract reciting anticipated profit to plaintiff for work on all three properties, was not valid. The record revealed that JH had already paid MBC $130,000 in two installments. The court held that MBC failed to establish its entitlement to damages in the amount of $148,533.

The court stated that it would be improper, in light of JH's breach of the contract, to limit the plaintiff's recovery to the $8787.15 advanced by CPC prior to the termination of the contract, particularly in light of MBC's contentions that additional work was performed that fell outside the Contract.[48.6] The assessment of damages required further factual development. The court denied that portion of the plaintiff's motion seeking summary judgment on damages.

Finally, the court denied the plaintiff's motion for judgment for attorney's fees and costs. It is well settled that legal fees are not recoverable unless provided under the terms of a contract or authorized by statute.[48.7]

[48.5] Paterno & Sons, Inc. v. Town of New Windsor, 43 A.D.2d 863, 351 N.Y.S.2d 445 (2d Dep't 1974).

[48.6] *See In re Andrew Velez Const., Inc.*, 373 B.R. 262, 279 (S.D.N.Y. 2007).

[48.7] *See* U.S. Underwriters Ins. Co. v. City Club Hotel, LLC, 3 N.Y.3d 592, 597, 822 N.E.2d 777, 789 N.Y.S.2d 470 (2004).

Termination for cause is an extreme remedy which should be used very sparingly by an owner. The cost of a substitute contractor will be borne by the owner if the termination was not considered proper.

Surety bonds usually have their own procedures, which must be followed in order to trigger liability under a payment or performance bond. Failure to follow the bond procedures could result in the failure of an owner to recover payment or receive substitute performance by the surety based on the terms of the bond.

In *Podsiadlo v. Western Insurance Co.*,[48.8] the plaintiff, Christian Podsiadlo, appealed from the summary judgment granted the defendants Western Insurance Company (Western Insurance or surety) and Bridge Bank (bank) in his action for breach of a construction loan agreement with the bank and his action to enforce performance and payment bonds issued by Western Insurance regarding the loan agreement. Bank loaned money to the plaintiff pursuant to a construction loan agreement to finance the construction of a bakery on property owned by him in South Lake Tahoe, California. The plaintiff entered into a construction contract with M.C. Neuffer Co. (Neuffer) to construct the bakery. Western Insurance issued payment and performance bonds on the construction contract.

When disputes arose between Neuffer, bank, and the plaintiff, Neuffer, sent a notice of termination to the plaintiff on June 26, 2003, and ceased construction. The plaintiff sent a letter to Neuffer terminating the contract and advised Western Insurance on August 22, 2003, that it had done so. Western Insurance replied that the plaintiff had terminated the contract without complying with the conditions of paragraph 3 of the performance bond.

On March 17, 2004 the plaintiff, Neuffer and the bank entered into an Agreement to Continue Construction that provided for a new completion date of August 17, 2004, and that required Neuffer to abide by the terms of the original construction contract. Neuffer again ceased work on May 20, 2004. The bank subsequently entered a nonjudicial foreclosure of the property.

The plaintiff then filed this action alleging that the bank breached the construction loan agreement and the covenant of good faith and fair dealing by failing to retain 10 percent of the progress payments, by exercising excessive lender control, and by advancing progress payments when the subcontractors had not performed the required work.

The trial court granted the bank's motion for summary judgment, because the plaintiff provided no evidence that the bank paid for work that was not performed, and that all disbursements were approved by the plaintiff. The plaintiff could not show that he was in any way damaged, because he had not offered evidence that payments had been made for work that had not been performed.

On appeal, the plaintiff argued that Western Insurance failed to demonstrate that he had not properly declared default by his demand on Western Insurance in August of 2003 so as to activate the notice requirements of the bond, and that, in any case, lack of notice did not justify a forfeiture of the bond. The difficulty for Podsiadlo was that he did none of the things called for in paragraph 3 of the bond, precluding any liability on the part of Western Insurance.

[48.8] 2009 WL 2901950 (Cal. Ct. App. Sept. 10, 2009).

This summary judgment proceeding arose out of an action for damages for breach of contract against the bank for making progress payments to the contractor Neuffer for work that had not been performed and for failure to obtain releases from the subcontractors relating to moneys that had been disbursed to the contractor, and against Western Insurance for damages for breach of contract, breach of the covenant of good faith and fair dealing and fraudulent misrepresentation (for failure to pay) involving performance and payment bonds issued to the plaintiff on the construction project.

In the complaint, the plaintiff, the owner of the Lorraine Bakery in South Lake Tahoe, alleged that on August 21, 2002, he entered into a loan agreement with the Small Business Bureau (SBA), evidenced by a note in the amount of $1,386,000. The defendant bank was the lender for the SBA loan, which was to finance construction of a bakery on premises owned by the plaintiff. On September 20, 2002, plaintiff entered into a construction contract with M.C. Neuffer Company ("Neuffer") as general contractor. The plaintiff assigned the construction contract to Bridge Bank, and also executed a guaranty of Completion and Performance in favor of the bank, by which Neuffer guaranteed substantial completion of its portion of construction on the project by the completion date. On March 14, 2003, defendant Western Insurance Company ("Western") issued two bonds in favor of the plaintiff: (1) a Payment Bond in the amount of $778,802.10 and (2) a Performance Bond in the amount of $578,631.91.

Thereafter, disputes arose among Neuffer, the bank, and the plaintiff, and on June 26, 2003 Neuffer sent a notice of termination to plaintiff and ceased construction. The parties negotiated and arrived at an Agreement to Continue Construction on March 17, 2004, which provided a completion date of August 17, 2004 and required Neuffer to abide by the terms of the original contract.

On May 20, 2004, Neuffer again ceased work on the project. The plaintiff made a demand on Western to pay on the bonds, which Western refused. The bank failed to retain 10 percent of the payments of the loan proceeds, as required by the agreement with plaintiff, and exercised excessive lender control, which contributed to Neuffer's default under the construction contract.

The complaint alleged: (1) breach of contract as to the bank; (2) breach of contract as to Western; (3) breach of the implied covenant of good faith and fair dealing as to both the bank and Western; and (4) fraudulent misrepresentation as to Western. The Bank and Western Insurance sought and were granted summary judgments in their favor, and the plaintiff appealed.

The plaintiff sought to recover on the performance bond issued by Western Insurance on behalf of Neuffer. Western Insurance denied recovery arguing that the plaintiff did not comply with the notice provisions of the bond prior to terminating the contract with Neuffer. The plaintiff claimed that Western Insurance failed to demonstrate that he failed to satisfy the notice provisions.

Preliminarily, the plaintiff challenged the exhibits to Western Insurance's motion for summary judgment. He claimed that certain documents were inadmissible hearsay, and that they should not have been admitted as evidence in the summary judgment proceeding. The trial judge overruled plaintiff's objections and admitted into evidence all of the exhibits except one. The appellate court found that plaintiff's arguments regarding the evidence allowed at trial were frivolous.

The plaintiff did not claim the documents set forth in the exhibits were inauthentic or that he was prejudiced by their introduction, other than that they supported the defendant's motion for summary judgment. They included documents that the plaintiff relied upon for his arguments, including the construction contract and the performance bond. The relevant part of the performance bond in fact was quoted in plaintiff's opening brief.

The trial court overruled all of the plaintiff's evidentiary objections and noted that the plaintiff's memorandum of points and authorities conceded that "[m]ost of the underlying facts in this matter are not in significant dispute." Moreover, in his opening brief on appeal, the plaintiff joined issue with Western Insurance in discussing the legal issues tendered by the documents and thereby admitted their authenticity.

The key provision of the performance bond was paragraph 3, which provided that if there was no owner default, the surety's obligation under the bond shall arise after the owner has taken the following steps:

> 1. notified the contractor and surety that he was considering declaring a contractor default;
> 2. attempted to arrange a conference with them to discuss methods of performing the contract;
> 3. thereafter declared a contractor default;
> 4. agreed to pay the balance of the contract price to the surety or to a contractor selected to perform the construction contract.

It was only if these conditions were satisfied that an obligation was imposed on Western Insurance to arrange for the contractor to finish the construction, or to undertake to do so itself, or to waive such rights and determine the amount for which the surety could be liable to the owner. It was only in the event that the surety did not proceed with reasonable promptness to do these things that the owner was "entitled to enforce any remedy available" to it.

On September 20, 2002, the plaintiff signed a contract with Neuffer, pursuant to AIA Document A111-1997, to construct a bakery. Attached to the contract was AIA Document A201-1997, which set forth the general conditions of the contract for construction. Neuffer purchased a performance bond from Western Insurance in compliance with the contract. This performance bond was the subject of this action.

The critical fact concerned the plaintiff's termination of the construction contract with Neuffer in August 2003. On August 14, 2003, the plaintiff's attorney, Jeffrey Rahbeck, sent a letter to Neuffer "to advise you that the contract with you was terminated by my client because of your breach . . . in failing to process the construction project . . . . After terminating the contract with you, my client has been in the process of hiring another contractor to complete the construction contract . . . ."

This letter was followed on August 22, 2003, by a letter from Rahbeck to Western Insurance "to advise you that my client terminated M.C. Neuffer Company as contractor . . . [for] failure to timely perform under the construction contract" and "to advise you that my client is willing to meet and confer as required by Paragraph 3.1 of the Performance Bond." On August 29, 2003, Western Insurance responded with a letter to Rahbeck stating because "your client terminated the contractor prior to any notification . . . contrary to the terms of the performance bond . . . . Western has been prejudiced by the denial [of] its contractual entitlements."

On appeal, the plaintiff responded that "there was no proper Declaration of Contractor Default . . . that would give rise to the notice requirements so as to excuse Western Insurance." By this, the plaintiff meant that such words were not used and there was no "Architect Certification of Default as required to terminate the [construction] contract." Thus, the plaintiff argued that he did not terminate the construction contract pursuant to its terms. That is not what he told Western Insurance in the letter of August 22, 2003.

Western Insurance had a right to take the plaintiff at his word and to treat the termination as a violation of paragraph 3 of the insurance contract. The purpose of paragraph 3 was to permit the insurance company to ameliorate the contractual dispute with Neuffer prior to the plaintiff's termination of the contract. That could not occur after the plaintiff terminated the contract. Rather, *on* March 17, 2004, the plaintiff, Neuffer and the Bank entered into an agreement to continue construction that provided for a new completion date of August 17, 2004, requiring Neuffer to abide by the terms of the original construction contract.

The plaintiff argued that the agreement to continue construction was nothing more than a continuation of the old contract. Under the Western Insurance agreement there was no requirement to procure a new construction bond. The plaintiff failed to invoke the procedures for recovery on the bond as set forth in paragraph 3.

The appellate court held that since the plaintiff owner did not meet the threshold notice requirements of paragraph 3, Western Insurance had no obligation to perform as set forth in paragraph 4, and the plaintiff had no remedy against Western Insurance under paragraph 5. For similar reasons, the appellate court held that the plaintiff could not claim that Western Insurance suffered no damage by his failure to exhaust the notice requirements of the bond. The property at issue had been foreclosed on. Western Insurance had been deprived of all of the procedural mechanisms by which it could have averted or, at least, minimized its liability on the bond.

Finally, the appellate court held that the plaintiff's claim that delayed notice did not exonerate the bond was ineffective, since his entitlement to enforce the bond depended upon compliance with the procedural mechanisms of paragraphs 3 and 4 of the bond. Such compliance was no longer possible.

The plaintiff argued that during the course of construction, Bridge Bank exercised excessive "lender control" which, in part, led to the cessation of work by Neuffer and the damages suffered by the plaintiff. By assuming lender control during the project, Bridge Bank assumed liability for all of the acts it undertook and had a duty to the plaintiff to act reasonably and competently. The essence of the plaintiff's claim was that the Bank wrongly paid money to Neuffer "without obtaining releases from the subcontractor[s] . . . ." damaging the plaintiff.

The bank responded that "[i]t is undisputed that Appellant approved every payment which Respondent Bank made to the General Contractor." The appellate court agreed with that statement. It was also true that the plaintiff implicitly agreed that releases were obtained from the subcontractors.

No evidence is required to support an undisputed fact. Accordingly, the appellate court looked to the statements of undisputed fact in the summary judgment papers. The appellate court also considered the evidence that supported the claims of undisputed fact. The bank supported its claim that the plaintiff authorized the payments to the general contractor, referring to facts asserted in the bank's separate statement of undisputed material facts.

Despite his approval of the payments from the bank to Neuffer, the plaintiff claimed that the bank did not obtain releases from the subcontractors as required by the agreement to continue construction, dated March 17, 2004, and that obtaining such releases had been a condition for the effectiveness of the agreement.

The court held that the plaintiff misread the agreement. It provided in relevant part:

> *Concurrently with the execution of this Agreement* and as a condition to the effectiveness thereof, Neuffer shall provide to Bridge Bank waiver and releases executed by and on behalf of itself and by and on behalf of its subcontractors whereby Neuffer and the subcontractors acknowledge payment in full for all invoices for labor and/or materials relating to the performed work [Italics added].

The appellate court stated that the italicized language "*[c]oncurrently with the execution of this Agreement*" meant that the releases were to be executed "[c]oncurrently" with the signing of the agreement. When the plaintiff signed the agreement, he either acknowledged that the subcontractor releases were executed or waived any objection to a failure to do so.

Lastly, the bank pointed out that the agreement contained a clause that discharged the bank "from any and all liabilities, causes of action, and claims which do or may exist, whether known or unknown . . . arising out of or in any way related to the Loan . . . the Project, and/or the performed work as of the date of this Agreement . . . ." The plaintiff claimed that this discharge provision never took effect because it was conditional upon the execution of releases by the subcontractors. The court, however, held that the plaintiff's claim was based on the same misreading of the release provision. The signing of the agreement admitted the execution of the releases.

The plaintiff's claims against the bank failed on the basis of his admissions. The judgment was affirmed, with defendants recovering their costs on appeal.

In *McPhee Electric Limited v. Konover Constr. Corp*,[48.9] the court held that a construction contractor was not entitled to withhold release of payment in retainage to an electrical subcontractor, and the construction contractor breached its contract with the subcontractor. In *McPhee*, a town hired a contractor to build a new high school, and the contractor subcontracted out the electrical work. The town issued a "certificate of substantial completion" to the subcontractor for the work it had done, but the contractor continued to withhold release of payment of a retainage to the subcontractor, alleging that it was entitled to withhold payment because of back charges and legal fees involved in its dispute with McPhee, the subcontractor. Because the town had issued the certificate of substantial completion to McPhee, the court held that, under the general contract, Konover was not entitled to withhold release of retainage. Additionally, the subcontract did not define retainage, and it did not explicitly or implicitly permit the contractor to refuse to requisition a final payment within the terms of the general contract.

On June 19, 2003, Konover executed a construction management contract with the town. The contract was based on two standard American Institute of Architects (AIA) documents, the A121 construction management contract and the A201 General Conditions agreement. The A121 portion covered, among other things, the construction manager's responsibilities, the owner's responsibilities, compensation, changes in the work and payments to subcontractors. The A201 portion covered similar subjects including, among other things, contract administration, subcontractors, changes in the work, time, payments and completion. The town made it clear to Konover that the opening date for the new school was to be September 2005. Initially, the project was scheduled to start in early February 2004, Construction actually started on February 24, 2004. The turnover date was September 6, 2005, a period of 558 calendar days, not including the time to demolish the existing high school and construct the athletic fields.

The construction project was complex, and certain issues arose during construction regarding many facets of the work. Approximately one month before the scheduled opening date for the new NHHS, McPhee, the subcontractor, sent a lengthy letter to Tighe, seeking an equitable adjustment to its contract in the amount of $835,441.00. The letter, dated August 5, 2005, was signed by Ronald Stawecki, a vice-president of McPhee, but represented a collaborative effort on the part of Michael McPhee, Lynes, Mackie and Rasile, and was written by Michael McPhee. The purpose of the letter was to follow up after a meeting that took place some time in June 2005, which itself was in follow-up to McPhee's April 18, 2005 letter, seeking an additional $754,295.82 to compensate it for what it had represented to be "schedule delays, compression of work and subsequent decrease in productivity and added labor costs."

The August 5th letter itemized 13 areas of claimed damages and 13 open change orders. Konover responded to McPhee's letter on August 12, 2005, stating, in part, "given the nature of the assertions set forth in your correspondence and given KCC's contractual obligations to the Owner . . . a detailed analysis is required. We will, in good faith, review, analyze and evaluate the

[48.9] 2009 Conn. Super. LEXIS 3110, 2009 WL 4846555 (Conn. Super. Ct. Oct. 22, 2009).

assertions . . . We will likely need additional information from McPhee in order to complete our analysis." Michael McPhee believed that this response was consistent with the discussions he had with Konover about McPhee's claim in June. Many delays occurred, and claims had been made during the construction by the contractor for additional compensation.

McPhee was described by the defendants as lacking "cooperation and coordination" during the project and described McPhee as "constantly at odds with Konover with respect to working as a team." The defendants claimed that McPhee interfered with the work of other subcontractors, "had significant deficiencies at various stages of the project [and] performed defective work."

The defendants claimed to a building committee that McPhee was seeking approximately $800,000 in alleged delay and interruption claims in their pending litigation. The defendants claimed that acts by McPhee were indicative of a "loathsome business practice" by McPhee as they were attempting "the same extortionate claim practice on other projects."

McPhee was given an opportunity to respond to these claims made by Konover to the building committee. He stated, "I take great offense to Mr. Dunn's representation that we have loathsome business practices, but somebody will get a chance to decide that at some other time." As to Konover, he said, "you know, they're used to bullying people around, and quite honestly, their bullying hasn't helped your job any." However, during trial McPhee candidly testified that he had no way of identifying the impact of Dunn's statement on his business nor could McPhee identify any particular job that he did not get because of Dunn's statements at the committee meeting. He agreed that bringing lawsuits against general contractors and construction managers can affect a subcontractor's ability to attract new business. Following non-payment, McPhee sued for breach of contract on the following grounds: (1) Konover's failure to pay the contract balance it claims it was due; (2) Konover's refusal to compensate it for 11 change orders; and (3) Konover's responsibility to compensate it for a 10,887 hour labor overrun. The labor overrun claim was also at the core of McPhee's claims alleging negligence in the second count.

Konover asserted as a special defense to the first count that McPhee breached the contract as follows:

> a. failing to supply the project with a sufficient number of skilled workers;
> b. failing to perform its work consistent with the project schedule, thereby delaying their own work and the work of others;
> c. failing to properly manage its work efficiently and effectively to achieve the schedule objectives of the project;
> d. failing to follow the directives of Konover as the Construction Manager;
> e. making unreasonable and untimely demands for additional compensation before proceeding with the work under the subcontract;
> f. failing to provide the proper materials and equipment to the project in a timely manner;
> g. representing to Konover that areas of work were complete when they were not, thus requiring additional work by Konover and other subcontractors;

h. failing to coordinate its work with other trades on the project;
i. failing to timely comply with directives of the local building officials; . . .
j. failing to perform its work properly, requiring the plaintiff to troubleshoot and correct the work;
k. in failing to remobilize when directed; and
l. in engaging in direct communications with Town of North Haven officials and the architect for the Project without Konover's . . . involvement.

The *McPhee* court held that the intention of the parties to a contract is to be determined from the language used, interpreted in the light of the situation of the parties and the circumstances connected with the transaction. The court stated that it had reviewed the subcontract agreement and the contract in detail and had found both documents to be clear, unambiguous, harmonious and definitive. The appellate court further found that both parties in this case were sophisticated commercial entities with lengthy experience in the construction field. When, as here, sophisticated parties enter into commercial contracts, the court may presume that the contract language is clear and unambiguous. Further, the court held that McPhee was aware of the relevant contractual language from the beginning of the bidding process and knew that it had to accept the subcontract agreement without alteration if its bid were accepted.

McPhee claimed that Konover owed it a contract balance of $169,966.81, consisting of payments it claimed were due on two pay applications, as well as $128,368.41 in retainage. Konover maintained that it was entitled to withhold these sums under the contract as a set-off based on claims it has against McPhee.

McPhee relied, in part, on Article 3 of the subcontract agreement. Article 3.a. which specified that: "Partial payment shall be due Subcontractor in the amount of 95% of the work in place for which payment has been made to Contractor by Owner." Article 3.b. spelled out the requisition procedure that was followed in this case. Under Article 3.c. once Konover received payment from the town on account of McPhee's work, McPhee would be entitled to payment.

The court found in favor of McPhee Electric on the breach of contract count and awarded damages in the amount of $128,368.41, and on the defamation count awarded nominal damages of $10.00. The court, however, found for the defendant Konover Construction Corp. on the negligence count, the breach of contract count, and the breach of the covenant of good faith and fair dealing count, and the unfair competition count.

In *Herring-Malbis I, LLC, Eastern Shore Centre I, LLC, and Eastern Shore Centre II, LLC v. Temco, Inc.*,[48.10] a contractor brought an action for breach of contract, open account, and mechanic's lien action against a developer. Following arbitration, the circuit court granted contractor's motion for attorneys fees under the Prompt Payment Act, and developer appealed.

The appellate court held that:

(1) the parties' arbitration agreement required the contractor to submit its claim for attorney fees under the Prompt Payment Act to arbitration;

[48.10] 2009 Ala. Civ. App. LEXIS 537, 2009 WL 3517580 (Ala. Civ. App. 2009).

(2) *res judicata* barred the contractor from seeking attorney fees under the Prompt Payment Act in the circuit court following the arbitration hearing; and (3) the developer was not judicially estopped from asserting that *res judicata* barred contractor's claim for attorney fees. Reversed and remanded with instructions.

In *Herring-Malbis*, the owner appealed from an order of the Baldwin Circuit Court awarding an attorney fee to Temco, Inc. ("TEMCO"), pursuant to Ala. Code 1975, § 8-29-1 *et seq.*, usually referred to as the Prompt Payment Act. The appellate court reversed the trial court's order awarding an attorney fee to Temco.

Temco sued Herring-Malbis in May 2006, alleging that Temco was owed money "pursuant to the terms and conditions of" contract documents signed by the parties, which included a construction contract and American Institute of Architects AIA Document A201-1997 general conditions, that were incorporated into the parties' agreement by reference in the construction contract. Temco's original complaint sought damages in the amount of $486,303 plus interest and costs under several alternative theories of relief, including breach of contract, open account, account stated, work and labor done, and enforcement of mechanic's lien.

The circuit court granted Herring-Malbis's motion for an order compelling alternative dispute resolution under the terms of the AIA contract.

Pursuant to A201, the parties first attempted to resolve their dispute through mediation, and, when that failed, they arbitrated their dispute through the American Arbitration Association. The arbitration hearing was held on February 19 and 20, 2008. Six days before the commencement of the hearing, on February 13, 2008, Temco filed a motion to amend its original complaint. The motion sought "to amend the complaint to add a claim under the Prompt Payment Act . . . for reasonable attorneys' fees and expenses pursuant to said statute." The motion maintained that the Prompt Payment Act claim "in no way" affected the issues to be presented to the arbitrator but was a matter to be presented to court in the event that the arbitrator entered an award in favor of Temco. No action was taken on the motion prior to the arbitration hearing.

Temco presented a demand letter to AAA. Herring-Malbis presented an answering statement and counterclaim in the arbitration proceeding. In its demand letter, Temco itemized its claims for relief, which included a request for accumulated interest, but Temco omitted mention in the arbitration documents of any claim for an award of an attorney fee and any mention of particular theories of relief, including any right to relief under the Prompt Payment Act. The demand letter from Temco specified that Temco's principal claim was that it was due relief under the construction contract.

After the hearing, the arbitrator rendered a decision that Temco was owed most of what it claimed. The arbitrator also specified that each party would be responsible for its own attorney fees. The arbitration award concluded by stating that "[a]ll claims not expressly granted herein are hereby[ ] denied," thereby denying Temco its request for an award of accumulated interest on any of its claims. Temco and Herring-Malbis then filed briefs concerning whether the arbitrator's award should be modified by deleting the reference to attorney fees and by awarding Temco the accumulated interest it sought. No changes to the award were made by the arbitrator. Herring-Malbis timely tendered payment to Temco in satisfaction of the arbitration award.

In April 2008, after the arbitration hearing had been held, Herring-Malbis filed with the court a response in opposition to Temco's February 13th, 2008 motion to amend its original complaint. The trial court granted Temco's motion to amend and overruled Herring-Malbis's objections. Temco then filed its amended complaint in May 2008, after which Herring-Malbis moved to dismiss that complaint. The trial court denied this motion, and, following a stipulation by the parties as to the amount of a reasonable attorney fee, and a further agreement of the parties to allow the trial court to rule on the matter without a hearing, the trial court entered an order awarding the stipulated attorney fee to Temco, "pursuant to the Prompt Payment Act," in November 2008.

The amended complaint ultimately filed by Temco pleaded the Prompt Payment Act as another alternative legal theory under which Temco sought complete relief. Under Count 10 of the amended complaint, Temco incorporated the remainder of the complaint and demanded relief as to all of its claims against all defendants, which then totaled $561,412.70, specifically including interest, costs, expenses, and attorney fees.

The demand letter written by Temco as a formality required by American Arbitration Association rules in order to initiate the arbitration process did not seek attorney fees or make claims under the Prompt Payment Act, but that omission does not conclusively establish that neither matter was discussed at the hearing.

The AIA contract incorporated into the parties' agreement provided that "any claim arising out of or related to the contract" shall be submitted first to mediation, and in the event mediation fails to resolve the dispute, as occurred here, the claim is to be submitted to arbitration. Where the contract defines "claim," it includes in that definition "other disputes and matters in question between [Herring-Malbis] and [Temco] arising out of or relating to the Contract," a sweepingly broad clause.

When parties include such a broad arbitration clause, they intend the clause to reach all aspects of the relationship. To like effect is the Alabama Supreme Court's holding that arbitration clauses, including the language "arising out of or relating to" that appears in the AIA contract, have broader application than arbitration clauses that omit "or relating to." The AIA contract further states that the party seeking relief in arbitration "must assert in the demand all Claims then known to that party on which arbitration is permitted to be demanded." Finally, the AIA contract further provides that arbitration will proceed under the Construction Industry Arbitration Rules of the American Arbitration Association, of which Rule 44(d) provides that "the award of the arbitrator may include . . . an award of attorneys' fees if all parties have requested such an award or it is authorized by law or their arbitration agreement."

The court held that Temco was required by the arbitration agreement, and by law, to submit its Prompt Payment Act claim, including the request for an award of an attorney fee, to the arbitrator. If, as Temco claimed, the parties did not submit the issue to the arbitrator, whether the arbitrator in fact made a determination concerning Temco's right to an attorney-fee award was immaterial.

In Temco's amended complaint, the Prompt Payment Act was asserted as an additional alternative theory under which Temco demanded complete relief. The entire Prompt Payment Act claim, including the request for an award of an attorney fee, was held to be within the ambit of the contract documents' definition of "claim," quoted above, and Temco was required to submit its Prompt Payment Act claim to the arbitrator, on pain of waiver, in light of the contractual provision stating that parties demanding arbitration "must assert in the demand all Claims then known to that party on which arbitration is permitted to be demanded."

Because Temco indicated its intent to assert the Prompt Payment Act claim in its motion to amend its complaint, filed in the circuit court six days before the arbitration hearing, that claim certainly was "known to" Temco at the time of the arbitration hearing.

The Prompt Payment Act claim also was a claim "on which arbitration is permitted to be demanded," contrary to Temco's assertions (a) that the contract documents provided no legal basis for requesting an award of an attorney fee and (b) that the Prompt Payment Act provided Temco's only legal basis for seeking such an award. For a particular claim or grievance to be excluded from arbitration, the parties must expressly exclude such claim in the arbitration agreement. Temco argued that the AIA contract did not allow the recovery of attorney fees, but it cited as support for this assertion provisions in the AIA contract such as paragraph 3.18.1, under which Temco had agreed not to pursue attorney fees related to a claim "provided that such claim . . . is attributable to bodily injury, sickness, disease or death, or to injury to or destruction of tangible property (other than the Work itself), but only to the extent caused by the negligent acts or omissions of [Temco]."

That provision, as well as other provisions Temco cited, were held inapplicable to this case, which concerned contractual disputes and not claims of bodily injury or property damage. Further, the AIA contract provided at paragraph 13.4.1 that "[d]uties and obligations imposed by the Contract Document and rights and remedies available thereunder shall be in addition to and not a limitation of duties, obligations, rights and remedies otherwise imposed or available by law."

The appellate court also noted that contractual arbitration terms were, in effect, nothing more than agreements to submit substantive controversies to a particular forum. They did not affect the substantive rights of parties, even when those rights were provided by statute. Temco had the same legal basis for submitting the question of an attorney fee to the arbitrator that it claims to have had for submitting that question to the circuit court.

Being contractually required to assert in arbitration "all claims," and in order to avoid preclusion of claims not asserted, Temco was required to bring all legal theories of relief supported by the "same nucleus of operative facts" to the arbitrator. Otherwise, those claims would have been barred from prosecution by Temco in a separate action. Under Alabama law, the doctrine of *res judicata* applied to arbitration awards just as it applied to judgments of courts. The elements of *res judicata* are "(1) a prior judgment on the merits, (2) rendered by a court of competent jurisdiction, (3) with substantial identity of the parties, and (4) with the same cause of action presented in both actions." A party is barred from relitigating any claims that were, or that "could have been," brought in the earlier action.

The appellate court held that the arbitrator's award constituted a prior decision on the merits, because the arbitrator provided specific findings, along with underlying bases for those findings, as to liability and the monetary amounts awarded on each substantive claim Temco had presented in its demand for arbitration, and the arbitrator further specified that any relief not expressly granted was denied. It was equally clear that the parties to the arbitration and to the subsequent circuit-court proceeding were identical.

The claims also met the fourth element of *res judicata*, "the same cause of action." The established tests used to determine whether different claims presented the same cause of action, whether the primary right and duty or wrong were the same, whether various theories arose from the same nucleus of operative facts, and whether the same evidence supported all the separate actions, were satisfied by both of Temco's complaints. In both the original complaint and the amended complaint, Temco stated its contended facts at the beginning, then listed each claim for relief separately in numbered counts, each of which incorporated the opening statement of facts, and then stated the requested relief under the legal theory. For example, in Temco's amended complaint, Count 10, asserting a claim under the Prompt Payment Act, incorporated the statement of facts and requested a total of $541,567 plus interest, costs, expenses, and attorney fees.

The court rejected Temco's argument that its motion to amend its original complaint, and the circuit court's ruling, amounted to, in effect, an "appeal" of the arbitrator's judgment under the Federal Arbitration Act (FAA) even though pertinent FAA guidelines were not "strictly" followed. The court stated that Temco was correct in noting that the substantive provisions of the FAA governed such issues as the enforceability of arbitration agreements, but the appellate court stated that it was Ala.Code 1975, § 6-6-15, that governed the procedural requirements for appealing from an arbitrator's decision in Alabama. Temco, in its appellate brief, essentially admitted that it did not follow any statutory procedures governing appeals of arbitration awards. Further, the appellate court noted that the AIA contract signed by the parties provided at paragraph 13.1.1 that "[t]he Contract shall be governed by the law of the place where the Project is located"—i.e., Alabama.

The pertinent provision in Alabama's arbitration statute, § 6-6-15, "contemplates a party's first seeking relief from an [arbitrator's] award in the circuit court." The court held that filing a separate motion six days before the arbitration hearing in a clear attempt to split related claims was not the equivalent of seeking judicial review of an award, as Temco asserted, and in any event recovery was barred by the parties' contract documents, as explained above. The fact that the circuit court viewed and ruled on numerous motions and briefs by the parties, and in so doing considered the same issues the parties raised on appeal, in awarding an attorney fee to Temco was found to be unavailing. The facts did not transform improper motions into a proper appeal. The trial court's failure to recognize that Temco was required to bring its Prompt Payment Act claim before the arbitrator, as reflected in its disposition of this issue, was merely an error of law.

The appellate court noted that the purposes and policies promoted by the doctrine of *res judicata* include the interests of both the public at large and the parties to a particular action in (a) finality of judgments, (b) reducing waste of private and judicial resources, and (c) avoiding inconsistent rulings. Similar results are achieved by the encouragement of arbitration in conformity to the FAA. Permitting Temco to split its claims and to try them in independent proceedings would violate its agreement with Herring-Malbis, statutory and case authority, and public policy.

Temco's final argument asserted that the *res judicata* argument advanced by Herring-Malbis was barred by judicial estoppel, because Herring-Malbis waited to respond to Temco's motion to amend its original complaint until after the arbitration hearing and allegedly failed to itself raise the issue of attorney fees at the arbitration hearing. According to Temco, those alleged omissions by Herring-Malbis amounted to the "adoption" of a "position" that Temco's motion to amend its complaint in the circuit court was a proper procedure by which Temco could seek relief under the Prompt Payment Act.

Because Temco's motion was submitted six days before the arbitration hearing, any deadline under the Rules of Civil Procedure, pursuant to which Herring-Malbis would have been required to file a response to that motion, would have occurred after the arbitration hearing. Herring-Malbis's failure to respond sooner did not amount to the assumption of a position that the circuit court could properly rule on the issue of attorney fees. Herring-Malbis had no duty to raise any of Temco's potential claims for relief before the arbitrator on Temco's behalf. The trial court rejected Temco's argument, because judicial estoppel requires first that a party assume a position in a legal proceeding, and Herring-Malbis's actions here did not amount to the assumption of a position that it later attempted to impeach.

Because the parties' contract documents required Temco to bring its Prompt Payment Act claim before the arbitrator, the appellate court held that Temco was barred under the doctrinc of *res judicata* from later asserting that claim in the circuit court.

The appellate court concluded that Temco, having had "an opportunity to litigate" the claim before the arbitrator, was barred from thereafter asserting its Prompt Payment Act claim in the circuit court. The appellate court reversed the trial court's award of an attorney fee, and remanded the cause to the trial court for the entry of a judgment conforming to the arbitration award.

Failure to timely submit all claims required to be arbitrated may preclude recovery in court or some other forum. Prior to filing a demand for arbitration, the attorney representing a claimant should review the agreement to arbitrate carefully to determine which claims must be brought in the arbitration proceeding.

[E] Owner's Power to Terminate for Convenience

Page 893, add to end of subsection:

Harris and Perlberg examine termination for convenience. The ConsensusDOCS allow a separate premium to be awarded to the contractor if terminated for convenience. The premium is to be agreed to at the time the contract is executed. ConsensusDOCS 200 Para. 11.4.2.3. Harris and Perlberg caution that care needs to be taken at arriving at and stating the basis for the premium so that it is tied to actual anticipated losses, such as lost business opportunities. If not specified adequately, it may be construed as a penalty and unenforceable under state law.[80.1]

Termination for convenience or termination without cause began in public contracting and have spread to private projects. The AIA documents provide for termination for convenience. In *DJB Building & Construction, LLC v. Parkville Plaza, LLC*,[80.2] a Connecticut court held that an owner did not breach a contract for the construction of a commercial building when it unilaterally terminated the contractor. The contract included a provision that allowed the owner to terminate the contract at its convenience. However, the owner was liable to the contractor for damages under the contract, based on its failure to make three progress payments and on its decision to unilaterally terminate the contract at its convenience.

The plaintiff, DJB Building & Construction, LLC, served the defendant, Parkville Plaza, LLC, with a six-count complaint on February 10, 2009, which were as follows:

> (1) breach of contract based on wrongful termination,
> (2) breach of contract for failure to pay contract balance,
> (3) breach of contract for failure to pay for extra work,
> (4) intentional misrepresentation,
> (5) negligent misrepresentation and
> (6) a claim under the Connecticut Unfair Trade Practices Act (CUTPA) (General Statutes §§ 42-110b *et seq.*).

The defendant filed the following special defenses on March 17, 2009:

> (1) The defendant made accord and satisfaction to the plaintiff for all time and materials actually expended on the project,
> (2) the defendant made payment to the plaintiff for all time and materials actually expended on the project,
> (3) the plaintiff is barred from recovery against the defendant due to its "unclean hands" concerning its failure to perform its duties and obligations pursuant to the contract documents, and
> (4) the parties intended to modify the "lump sum" contract to include a provision for a contingency amount of $391,008 to be used for interior finishes and/or additional changes; absent interior finishes and/or additional

---

[80.1] Restatement (Second) of Contracts § 356 (1981).

[80.2] 2009 Conn. Super. LEXIS 2621, 2009 WL 3644879 (Conn. Super. Ct. Sept. 24, 2009).

> changes performed by the plaintiff, this amount must be returned and/or credited to the defendant.

At trial, the plaintiff presented the testimony of Danny Bellman, a general contractor and president of DJB Building & Construction, LLC. Bellman stated that the plaintiff entered into a lump sum construction contract with the defendant dated March 6, 2007. The indicated lump sum of the contract was $1,380,000. Subsequently, the parties signed a contract change proposal dated March 6, 2008, which contained a contingency amount of $391,008 to be used for "interior finishes and/or additional changes." The revised contract amount, including the contingency, was $2,773,048.

Bellman indicated that payment on the lump sum contract was made through AIA form documents 702 and 703. He explained that AIA documents 702 and 703 were the industry standard application and certification for payment on a project based on the percentage of the project that has been completed at the time of the application. To obtain a progress payment, the plaintiff would make an application, using forms 702 and 703. Upon receiving this application, the architect would walk the project and sign off the percentage complete, and in 15 days the defendant would pay the plaintiff. Bellman testified that he submitted 12 applications for payment on this project. Of these 12, 11 were certified by the architect. Bellman received payment on nine of the twelve applications. Bellman did not receive payment on three other applications.

Bellman testified that the plaintiff was wrongfully terminated from the project. This termination was reflected in a letter from the defendant's attorney to Bellman dated January 13, 2009, which provided in relevant part:

> It was our trust and understanding following the meeting at USA Bank, that all issues arising between Goran Mladen [the defendant owner] and yourself would be discussed and resolved in a professional manner and in the best interests of completing the subject project.
>
> However, your recent actions violated that trust. Actions which include prohibiting the owner from communicating with any subcontractor, replacing the locks before consultation with the owner, failure to provide the owner with keys/unfettered access to the premises, and suggesting the owner was responsible for the misappropriation of building supplies stored at the subject location when after a simple investigation revealed the materials were moved to allow access to lift equipment.
>
> Therefore, it is with regret that I must inform you that the services of DJB Building & Construction, LLC as general contractor are hereby terminated.

Bellman testified that he felt the termination was wrongful in that it was not within the terms of the contract. In particular, he believed the defendant's actions violated §§ 6.1 of the contract, "Termination or Suspension," which provided: "The Contract may be terminated by the Owner or the Contractor as provided in Article 14 of AIA Document A201-1997."

Bellman responded to the January 13 termination letter, with letters to the defendant dated January 15, 2009 and January 16, 2009. In his January 15, 2009 letter he stated in relevant part:

> The purported termination is wrongful on many grounds, not the least of which is the following:
>
> Parkville Plaza, LLC ("PPL") has materially breached the contract. PPL has failed to issue payment to DJB since June. We sent PPL several non-payment notices. PPL's response was not to cure its default but to attempt to terminate DJB and to interfere with our subcontract relations. We know you have been negotiating and interfering directly with many of our subcontractors. This is improper since DJB was not terminated nor has DJB abandoned this project.
>
> Additionally, this notice of termination is wrongful because DJB has not materially breached the contract. What is completely clear is that the cause for many of these problems is your failure to issue payment since June. Other issues relate to design delays and evolving design problems, owner changes and associated delays, which have not been addressed by you. PPL has absolutely no basis in law or in fact to invoke the drastic remedy of a termination. Accordingly, for you to issue a termination notice is reckless and in bad faith.

In Bellman's subsequent January 16, 2009 letter, he stated in relevant part:

> As you know, Article 6 sets forth the procedures regarding termination, and the provisions of the Construction Standard Form AIA Document A201, Article 14 govern. Article 14 sets forth the grounds and the procedures by which Parkville Plaza is required to follow prior to termination:
>
> 14.2 TERMINATION BY THE OWNER FOR CAUSE
>
> 14.2.1 The Owner may terminate the Contract if the Contractor:
>
> > .1 persistently or repeatedly refuses or fails to supply enough properly skilled workers or proper materials;
> >
> > .2 fails to make payment to Subcontractors for materials or labor in accordance with the respective agreements between the Contractor and the Subcontractors;
> >
> > .3 persistently disregards laws, ordinances, or rules, regulations or orders of a public authority having jurisdiction; or
> >
> > .4 otherwise is guilty of substantial breach of a provision of the Contract Documents.
>
> None of the grounds listed in [the defendant's January 13, 2009] letter support termination under Article 14.2.1. Furthermore, Parkville Plaza did not issue a notice to cure as Article 14.2.2 requires. Worse yet, Parkville Plaza did not obtain an architect's certification that sufficient cause exists to justify such action.

Bellman asked for reasons as to why he was terminated, but did not receive a response.

The appellate court found that the parties formed an agreement to build a commercial building, Parkville Plaza, on March 6, 2007, and subsequently amended that agreement on March 6, 2008, through a contract change proposal. The plaintiff, general contractor, performed the agreement by substantially completing the project according to the contract's terms. The defendant owner then failed to make three progress payments. "A failure to make any payments for work in progress goes to the root of the bargain of the parties and defeats the object of the parties in making the agreement." The defendant could be considered in breach of contract when it failed to make progress payments.

At the same time, the appellate court, however, held that the defendant did not breach the contract when it made the unilateral decision to terminate the contract at its convenience. The January 13, 2009 letter from the defendant's attorney did not articulate justifiable reasons for the termination based on AIA Document A201, Article 14.2 (termination by owner for cause). Rather, the defendant's contractual basis for termination was AIA Document A201, Article 14.4, which allowed for termination by convenience of the owner. As the defendant was entitled to terminate the contract at its convenience, its termination was not a breach of contract.

Although the defendant's termination did not breach the contract, the defendant was liable for damages based on its failure to make the three progress payments and its decision to unilaterally terminate the contract at its convenience. AIA Document A201 Article 14.4.3 provided that if the owner terminates for convenience, the contractor is still entitled to be paid for work executed and costs incurred by reason of termination, along with reasonable overhead and profit on the work not executed.

The appellate court found that the plaintiff was entitled to damages. The plaintiff further claimed compensatory interest under General Statutes §§ 37-3a. The plaintiff argued that the defendant wrongfully detained the plaintiff's money, and, therefore, the plaintiff was entitled to statutory interest.

> The trier of fact may award prejudgment interest, as an element of damages, for the detention of money after it becomes payable if equitable considerations deem that such interest is warranted . . . An award of such interest is an equitable determination lying within the trier's sound discretion . . . The determination is one to be made in view of the demands of justice rather than through the application of an arbitrary rule . . . A trial court must make two determinations when awarding compensatory interest under §§ 37-3a: (1) whether the party against whom interest is sought has wrongfully detained money due the other party; and (2) the date upon which the wrongful detention began in order to determine the time from which interest should be calculated . . . A plaintiff's burden of demonstrating that the retention of money is wrongful requires more than demonstrating that the opposing party detained money when it should not have done so. The fact that an award of

> such interest is discretionary and subject to equitable considerations, rather than automatic, reflects the reality that not all improper detentions of money are wrongful.

The court declined to award compensatory interest to the plaintiff, because the plaintiff did not establish by a preponderance of the evidence that the defendant wrongfully withheld payment in the course of the project. While the defendant's failure to make the tenth, eleventh, and twelfth progress payments may have constituted a breach of contract, the trial court did not find that the payments were wrongfully withheld.

The defendant's unilateral termination for convenience did not constitute a wrongful withholding of money owed to the plaintiff, since the plaintiff did not prove that the termination was done in bad faith. Arguably, had the defendant terminated the contract on the grounds listed in AIA Document A201, Article 14.2 (termination by owner for cause), then the termination could have been deemed wrongful, because the defendant did not articulate any acceptable grounds for the termination. Rather, the defendant claimed to have terminated the contract at its convenience, under AIA Document A201, Article 14.4.1, which provides: "The Owner may, at any time, terminate the Contract for the Owner's convenience and without cause." The contractor must cease operations upon receiving written notice from the owner of this termination. AIA Document A201, Article 14.4.2. Unlike a termination for cause, an architect need not certify the grounds for terminating the contract. As it appears that a termination for the convenience of the owner was not *per se* wrongful if the termination was not in bad faith, the plaintiff could not claim compensatory interest on this ground.

The plaintiff sought damages for the defendant's alleged negligent and intentional misrepresentations concerning its ability to fund the project with proceeds from a construction loan from USA Bank. The plaintiffs claimed that the defendant falsely represented its financial condition to the plaintiff, and these misrepresentations caused the plaintiff to substantially complete the work in reliance on them. Even an innocent misrepresentation of fact may be actionable if the declarant has the means of knowing, ought to know, or has the duty of knowing the truth . . . The governing principles are set forth in similar terms in §§ 552 of the Restatement Second of Torts (1977):

> One who, in the course of his business, profession or employment . . . supplies false information for the guidance of others in their business transactions, is subject to liability for pecuniary loss caused to them by their justifiable reliance upon the information, if he fails to exercise reasonable care or competence in obtaining or communicating the information . . .

The essential elements of an action in fraud, are: (1) a false representation was made as a statement of fact; (2) it was untrue and known to be untrue by the party making it; (3) it was made to induce the other party to act on it; and (4) the latter did so act on it to his injury.

The court determined that the plaintiff did not prove by a preponderance of the evidence that the defendant either intentionally or negligently misrepresented its financial condition to the plaintiff, and that the plaintiff relied on such misrepresentations to its detriment. The court refused to award damages to the plaintiff for fraud.

Finally, the plaintiff sought damages for the defendant's alleged CUTPA (unfair trade practices) violations, which it argued included the defendant's wrongful termination, misuse and misrepresentation of funds, and intentional failure to make timely progress payments.

The CUTPA provides that "[n]o person shall engage in unfair methods of competition and unfair or deceptive acts or practices in the conduct of any trade or commerce." General Statutes §§ 42-110b(a). To enforce this prohibition, CUTPA provides a private cause of action to "[a]ny person who suffers any ascertainable loss of money or property, real or personal, as a result of the use or employment of a [prohibited] method, act or practice . . ." General Statutes §§ 42110g(a).

The purpose of CUTPA is to protect the public from unfair practices in the conduct of any trade or commerce . In determining whether certain acts constitute a violation of CUTPA, the Connecticut courts follow the criteria set out in the Federal Trade Commission's "cigarette rule": "(1)[W]hether the practice, without necessarily having been previously considered unlawful, offends public policy as it has been established by statutes, the common law, or otherwise-whether, in other words, it is within at least the penumbra of some common law, statutory, or other established concept of unfairness; (2) whether it is immoral, unethical, oppressive, or unscrupulous; (3) whether it causes substantial injury to consumers [competitors or other businessmen], *citing Sovereign Bank v. Licata*, 116 Conn. App. 483, 493, 977 A.2d 228 (2009)."

The appellate court found that the plaintiff did not prove by a preponderance of the evidence that the defendant's conduct was sufficiently offensive to meet the criteria of the cigarette rule. Therefore, the appellate court did not award damages on this count. The appellate court awarded damages to the plaintiff in the amount of $710,419.54, and declined to award compensatory damages pursuant to General Statutes §§ 37-3a, and found that the defendant was not liable to the plaintiff for negligent and intentional misrepresentation and for CUTPA violations.

Recovery by a claimant for prompt payment violations may be difficult to obtain, because proving them usually requires bad faith failure to pay, which may be hard to prove.

Chapter 21

BINDING DISPUTE RESOLUTION: LITIGATION AND ARBITRATION

§ 21.02 PLANNING DECISIONS

Page 909, add at end of section:

In *Advantages of the ConsensusDOCS Construction Contracts*,[30.1] Harris and Perlberg discuss claim resolution under the ConsensusDOCS. Under these documents, the parties initially meet and discuss the issues presented by the dispute at the project level. If that is not successful, then parties raise discussion of the issues to the senior management level. If issues are still unresolved, the parties may utilize a project neutral or dispute review board to issue non-binding findings to help resolve claims. The next step for dispute resolution is to proceed to mediation with the American Arbitration Association (AAA) Rules. If still unresolved, disputes go to binding dispute resolution. The forum to be used is selected by the parties checking a box on the forms for either litigation or arbitration. If arbitration is chosen, the AAA rules in effect at the time the claim is presented apply, rather than the rules in effect at the time the contract was signed.

§ 21.05 LEGAL CHALLENGES

[A] Validity

Page 914, add after first sentence in first full paragraph:

Because the parties must contractually agree to arbitration, courts may be reluctant to force an unwilling party to arbitrate absent strong evidence of the party's intent to be bound to arbitration. Waiver of the right to arbitrate can be found if the party acts inconsistently with seeking resolution through arbitration.

In *Illinois Concrete-I.C.I., Inc. v. Storefitters,*[35.1] after a contractor filed a demand that a subcontractor bring suit on its mechanic's lien, the subcontractor brought an action asserting three claims based on a written contract and three claims based on an alleged oral contract. The circuit court denied the contractor's motion to compel arbitration of the claims based on the written contract and its motion to dismiss the claims based on the oral contract. The appellate court

[30.1] Larry D. Harris & Brian M. Perlberg, *Advantages of the ConsensusDOCS Construction Contracts*, *The Construction Lawyer*, Vol. 29, No. 1, Winter 2009.

[35.1] 397 Ill.App.3d 798, 922 N.E.2d 542, 337 Ill. Dec. 419 (2010).

affirmed the trial court's denial of the motion to compel arbitration, and the appellate court dismissed the remainder of the appeal. The appellate court held that:(1) the appellate court could not review, on interlocutory appeal, the denial of the motion to dismiss the claims based on the oral contract;(2) the subcontractor failed to establish that the oral contract merged into the written contract; and (3) the contractor's filing of a demand that the subcontractor bring suit on its mechanic's lien waived the contractor's right to seek arbitration.

The subcontractor filed a complaint that certain concrete work the subcontractor performed for the defendants, for which the subcontractor alleged defendants did not pay, was based upon a written contract that contained an arbitration clause. The other counts pleaded a claim pertaining to the "hauling of dirt and other miscellaneous construction material" for the defendants, for which the plaintiff also alleged the defendants did not pay.

Before filing suit, the subcontractor filed mechanic's liens based upon both claims. The defendants then served upon the plaintiff a mechanic's lien notice. The subcontractor, therefore, filed the complaint, and the defendants filed a motion to compel arbitration of the first three counts.

The trial court denied the defendants' request to compel arbitration finding that the defendants waived their right to arbitration by filing the demand for the plaintiff to file suit. It also denied the defendants' motion to dismiss the latter three counts, granted the defendants 28 days to answer the complaint, and set the case for a status hearing. The defendants sought interlocutory review, citing the right of a party an appeal to review of any order granting, modifying, refusing, dissolving, or refusing to dissolve or modify an injunction. An order denying or compelling arbitration was injunctive in nature, so the trial court's denial of defendants' request to compel arbitration was within the scope of this rule. However, the defendants also relied upon Rule 307(a)(1) as the jurisdictional basis for the court to review the trial court's denial of their motion to dismiss the latter three counts of the complaint. The appellate court found that this rule did not provide it with jurisdiction over this order.

In accordance with Rule 307(a)(1), the sole issue before the appellate court on an interlocutory appeal was whether there was a sufficient showing to sustain the trial court's order denying the motion to compel arbitration. The defendants sought to invoke one of those exceptions by citing *Alfred Engineering, Inc. v. Illinois Fair Employment Practices Comm'n,*[35.2] which held:

> Upon this interlocutory appeal the appellate court stated that it did not reach the merits of the case, the single justiciable issue being whether the trial court properly granted the preliminary injunctive relief. However, upon an interlocutory appeal, the appellant was permitted to ask this court to determine not only whether the trial court had the discretionary right to issue the temporary or preliminary injunction but also to consider whether or not the complaint upon which the temporary injunction was issued was proper to sustain such injunction or to sustain a judgment.

[35.2] *Citing* 19 Ill. App. 3d 592, 599-600, 312 N.E.2d 61 (1974).

Reading this passage as broadly as the defendants advocated would eviscerate the limited scope of Rule 307(a)(1). The defendants essentially contended that, because the complaint joined the latter three counts (which have nothing to do with the propriety of arbitration) with the first three counts (which are the subject of the motion to compel arbitration), the court had jurisdiction over the ruling on the latter three counts. Beyond an identity of parties, these two claims, as pleaded, had nothing to do with each other. The propriety of compelling arbitration on the first three counts was completely independent of the propriety of dismissing the latter three counts. The *Alfred Engineering* court expressly held that Rule 307(a)(1) jurisdiction could extend to "the complaint upon which the temporary injunction was issued." The appellate court declined to read this holding as extending jurisdiction to a ruling on any otherwise unrelated counts that happened to be joined in a complaint.

Finally, the appellate court noted that the defendants asserted that the oral agreement merged with the subsequent written contract. The subcontractor responded that there was nothing in the record to indicate that the oral agreement and the written contract applied to the same work. As evidence that the agreements pertained to the same work, the defendants pointed to the mechanic's lien based on the oral contract, which stated that it was for the "trucking and hauling of dirt." The defendants then pointed to the written contract, which provided that it was for "removing and hauling concrete walls, footings and slabs in [the] subcontractor's trucks, digging a hole for a new addition and hauling away excess dirt." The defendants claimed that this showed that the scope of the work was "identical." The appellate court disagreed pointing out that the mechanic's lien did not mention demolition work, while the contract did: "Remove existing Concrete walls."

The appellate court stated that the mere fact that both agreements involved using trucks was insufficient to allow the court to conclude that the arbitration agreement applied to the oral contract and that it had jurisdiction to determine the merits of the defendants' motion to dismiss the latter three counts of the complaint. The appellate court stated that even if the latter three counts were subject to the contract's arbitration provision, by filing, and obtaining a ruling on, their motion to dismiss them, the defendants clearly waived their right to compel arbitration. The appellate court dismissed the balance of defendants' appeal for want of jurisdiction.

While recognizing that the public policy of Illinois favored arbitration, the right to compel arbitration could, nevertheless, be waived. A waiver could occur where a party's actions were inconsistent with its right to seek arbitration, thus, indicating an abandonment of the right.

The parties both cited *LaHood v. Central Illinois Construction, Inc.,*[35.3] where a contractor filed a mechanic's lien after a dispute arose with a landowner. After the contractor filed a request to have the dispute submitted to arbitration, the owner responded by filing a demand under section 34 of the Act (770 ILCS 60/34). In response to the demand, the contractor filed suit, but immediately

---

[35.3] *Citing* 335 Ill. App. 3d 363, 269 Ill. Dec. 788, 781 N.E.2d 585 (2002).

requested that court proceedings be stayed and the matter submitted to arbitration. The *LaHood* court held that the contractor had not waived its right to compel arbitration. The court first noted that filing the mechanic's lien was not inconsistent with seeking arbitration. The court then observed that the contractor filed suit only after the owner demanded that it do so and that it then promptly moved for a stay and to compel arbitration. The contractor's actions were completely responsive to the owner's demand. They did not, therefore, manifest an intent to abandon arbitration.

In this case, the key issue was whether the defendants, by filing their demand under section 34 of the Act (770 ILCS 60/34), acted in a manner inconsistent with their right to seek arbitration. The appellate court held that the defendants did act inconsistently with their right to seek arbitration. Following such a demand, a party claiming a lien must file suit within 30 days or lose the lien (770 ILCS 60/34). Nothing compelled the defendants to make this demand, and they could have simply sought arbitration. Thus, the demand was not responsive to any action taken by the plaintiff. The trial court properly determined that defendants, by making their section 34 demand, waived their right to compel arbitration, and the appellate court affirmed its decision.

The appellate court rejected the defendants' arguments as to why the trial court's holding was incorrect. First, the defendants contended that section 34 conferred a statutory right not cognizable in an arbitration proceeding. The defendants asserted that a party could not waive arbitration by invoking a remedy, which was beyond the scope of the language in the arbitration agreement. A section 34 demand did not invoke a remedy; it was a means to a remedy. What the defendants ultimately sought was clear title. They could have pursued this via section 34 and a trial or through arbitration. Both were means to the same remedy. That the defendants expressly chose a method outside the scope of the arbitration agreement bolstered the trial court's conclusion that they intended to abandon arbitration.

Second, the defendants argued that using section 34 notice could be an effective means of invalidating a lien on property without resort to litigation if the lien holder did not file suit within the statutory time. While true, it could also be effective for resolving such a matter without resort to arbitration. Moreover, the defendants ignored the fact that, by resorting to section 34, the defendants were demanding that a suit be filed. That the plaintiff might have chosen not to file a suit said nothing about the defendants' intent in serving the demand in the first place. Regarding the defendants' intent, the fact that they demanded litigation was more relevant.

Third, the defendants claimed that section 34 was simply a responsive means of dealing with a cloud on title. The defendants cited nothing indicating that they were required to respond in that manner or lose some right. Pursuant to applicable case law, that is what was meant when an action was said to be "responsive." The mere fact that the defendants were responding to a plaintiff's lien was insufficient, given that they could have simply sought arbitration instead. Indeed, filing a mechanic's lien was not inconsistent with a desire to seek arbitration so it was defendants who first manifested a desire to resort to the court system.

Fourth, the defendants claimed that the plaintiff elected the legal forum in derogation of its duty to seek arbitration. This argument begged the question in that it assumed that the defendants' demand that the plaintiff proceed to litigation was meaningless. Instead, in response to the defendants' demand, the plaintiff filed its complaint to protect its lien as section 34 of the Act required.

Fifth, the defendants pointed to a provision of the contract that incorporated a rule from the American Arbitration Association Rules for the Construction Industry. That rule provided, "[n]o judicial proceeding by a party relating to the subject matter of the arbitration shall be deemed a waiver of the party's right to arbitrate." The *ICI* court noted that in two cases, this rule and another similar one were held not to be dispositive of the issue. Instead of merely relying on the contractual provisions incorporating the rules, the courts in those cases performed full analyses of the parties' respective conduct. Such provisions provided evidence of the parties' intent at the time of contracting. The inclusion of the specific reference to the AAA Construction Industry Arbitration Rules indicated that the parties intended to favor arbitration and, as such, the appellate court declined to waive that right lightly. Nevertheless, subsequent conduct also provided evidence of intent. In this case, the defendants clearly and affirmatively demanded litigation. The plaintiff was forced to acquiesce at the pain of losing its lien. The defendants could not now rely on the right that they so clearly relinquished. Finally, the plain language of the provision cited by the defendants stated that filing a suit in itself did not constitute a waiver.

The language did not say that demanding that the other party file a suit did not constitute a waiver. The defendants' contention that making a section 34 demand did not even reach the level of filing a suit, and thus also could not constitute a waiver, was not well taken. Filing a suit can take place in various contexts, such as in response to a section 34 demand that would diminish any inference regarding an intent to abandon arbitration. Conversely, demanding that litigation be instituted pursuant to section 34 was unequivocal.

Sixth, the defendants asserted that "the subcontract itself evince[d] an intention to mediate followed by arbitration if mediation prove[d] unavailing." While true, the question was not what arbitration right the contract established. The question was whether the defendants waived that right. It was the defendants who acted in derogation of the contract's terms by demanding litigation and placing the plaintiff in a position where it was required to file a complaint or be prejudiced by its inaction.

Thus, the appellate court affirmed the circuit court's denial of the defendants' motion to compel arbitration, and the balance of the appealwas dismissed for lack of jurisdiction.

In *Shah v. Monpat Construction, Inc.*,[35.4] a property owner brought an action against a construction company, its owner, and a second construction company, seeking to permanently enjoin arbitration and to recover damages for breach of contract. The New York Supreme Court granted defendants' motion to compel arbitration. The property owner appealed.

[35.4] 65 A.D.3d 541, 884 N.Y.S.2d 116, 2009 (2009).

The New York Supreme Court, Appellate Division, held that:

> (1) The property owner and the first construction company had a valid agreement to arbitrate, but
>
> (2) The property owner, the owner of the first construction company, and the second company did not have an agreement to arbitrate. The appellate court affirmed the trial court's holding, as modified.

In *Shah*, an action to permanently enjoin arbitration and to recover damages for breach of contract, the plaintiffs appealed from the portion of an order of the New York Supreme Court, Queens County, which denied their motion to preliminarily enjoin the defendant, Monpat Construction, Inc., from proceeding with the arbitration of a claim against the plaintiff, Haresh D. Shah, under a contract dated March 15, 2001. There was also a cross-motion by the defendants, Monpat Construction, Inc., RB Construction Management Corp., and Mihir B. Patel, pursuant to CPLR 7503(c), to compel the plaintiffs to submit their claim against the defendants RB Construction Management Corp. and Mihir B. Patel to arbitration and to stay all proceedings in the action pending arbitration.

In *Shah*, a dentist (Dr. Shah), owned a property in Queens, on which he wanted to construct a building. One of Dr. Shah's patients, the individual defendant, Mihir B. Patel, owned a construction company, the defendant Monpat Construction, Inc. (Monpat). In March 2001, Shah and Patel (as the representative of Monpat) signed an agreement that provided for construction of the building. The agreement expressly incorporated by reference various other documents, one of which, "General Conditions of the Contract for Construction, AIA Document A201-1997" (Document A201-1997) contained a broad arbitration provision. Together, the agreement and the other documents formed the contract.

Construction was delayed for reasons which the parties do not agree. In early 2002, Shah and Patel agreed that the building would be constructed by the defendant RB Construction Management Corp. (RB), a construction company that had been formed by Patel's wife. The parties disagreed about whether the written contract was abandoned and replaced by an oral agreement between Shah and RB and Patel, or whether it continued in full force and effect, with the only difference being that RB would perform the work. The building was constructed and most of the contract price was paid, but there were disputes about various issues.

Monpat filed a demand for arbitration on April 28, 2008, under the written contract. In July 2008, Shah and the two other plaintiffs, Glen Oaks Medical Building, LLC, and Glen Oaks Building Corp., commenced the action to permanently enjoin the arbitration brought against Shah by Monpat, to recover damages against RB and Patel for breach of the alleged oral agreement, for a declaration that there was no agreement to arbitrate, and that Monpat had abandoned the written contract. The plaintiffs named as defendants, Patel, Monpat, and RB, as well as the American Arbitration Association (hereinafter the AAA) and an officer and a case manager of the AAA. The complaint asserted against the AAA and its officer and case manager was dismissed.

The plaintiffs moved to preliminarily enjoin the arbitration brought against Shah by Monpat. The defendants cross-moved, among other things, to compel arbitration of all claims. In the order appealed from, the court, among other things, granted that portion of the defendants' cross-motion, which was to compel arbitration of all claims, and denied that portion of the plaintiffs' motion which was for a preliminary injunction. The plaintiffs appealed.

In New York, arbitration is favored as a means of resolving disputes, and courts should interfere as little as possible with agreements to arbitrate.[35.5] There is a substantial countervailing consideration as well. "[B]y agreeing to arbitrate a party waives in large part many of his normal rights under the procedural and substantive law of the State."[35.6] For this reason, a party will not be compelled to arbitrate and, thereby, to surrender the right to resort to the courts, absent evidence that affirmatively establishes the parties' express agreement to arbitrate their disputes. Thus, the arbitration agreement must be clear, explicit, and unequivocal. Pursuant to CPLR 7502[b], once the court has determined the threshold issues of the existence of a valid agreement to arbitrate, that the party seeking arbitration has complied with the agreement, and that the claim sought to be arbitrated would not be time-barred were it asserted in state court, the remaining issues are for the arbitrator.

In this case, the written contract was clear, explicit, and unequivocal and established a valid agreement to arbitrate. The agreement expressly adopted Document A201-1997 by reference, in effect, listed it as one of the "Contract Documents" in article 1, enumerated it as one of the "Contract Documents" in article 8, and referred to it by document number throughout. Consequently, the arbitration provisions included in Document A201-1997 were part of the written contract.[35.7] Shah's contention that he never received Document A201-1997 was ineffective, and his ignorance of its provisions was attributed to "negligence or inexcusable trustfulness."

The plaintiffs did not contend in the supreme court, either in support of their motion to stay arbitration or in opposition to the defendants' motion to compel arbitration, that Monpat had not complied with conditions precedent to arbitration. Consequently, that issue was found not properly before the appellate court.

In general, where there is a broad arbitration clause, any issue with respect to changes in the substantivc provisions of a contract or its termination are to be resolved by the arbitrator, unless the modification or termination relates to the arbitration clause itself.[35.8] In this case, the plaintiffs' contention that the written contract was abandoned was not directly related to the arbitration provisions. Accordingly, the court held that the issue of abandonment should be left for the arbitrator. The issue of the statute of limitations was so intertwined with the

---

[35.5] *Citing* Matter of Smith Barney Shearson v. Sacharow, 91 N.Y.2d 39, 49, 689 N.E.2d 884, 666 N.Y.S.2d 990 (1997); *Matter of Miller*, 40 A.D.3d 861, 861-62, 835 N.Y.S.2d 728 (2007).

[35.6] *Matter of Marlene Indus. Corp. [Carnac Textiles]*, 45 N.Y.2d 327, 333-34, 408 N.Y.S.2d 410, 380 N.E.2d 239 (1978); *Matter of Miller*, 40 A.D.3d at 862, 835 N.Y.S.2d at 728.

[35.7] *See Matter of Level Export Corp. [Wolz, Aiken & Co.]*, 305 N.Y. 82, 87, 111 N.E.2d 218 (1953).

[35.8] *See Matter of Cassone*, 63 N.Y.2d 756, 759, 469 N.E.2d 835, 480 N.Y.S.2d 317 (1984).

parties' substantive contentions and the contentions regarding abandonment that the issue of the statute of limitations should be left to the arbitrator.[35.9] Issues regarding proper service of the demand for arbitration should be determined by the arbitrator.

Finally, the written contract was between Shah and Monpat. There was no clear evidence that the plaintiffs ever agreed to arbitrate any disputes with Patel and RB. Consequently, the supreme court should not have compelled the plaintiffs to arbitrate their claims against those defendants.[35.10]

Those in construction used to favor arbitration as a cost-effective and desirable method to resolve construction disputes. The perspective has changed somewhat, which is reflected by the AIA's shift reflected in A201, which now makes litigation the dispute resolution method of choice if the parties do not affirmatively elect arbitration.

[C] Jurisdiction: Preliminary Issues

Page 940, add after first paragraph:

In *Dominion Consulting and Management, Inc. v. Davis*,[104.1] the defendants' motion for a stay pending arbitration was denied on the basis of the 1997 edition of AIA Document A201 (General Conditions), which contained a carve-out provision allowing for actions on mechanic's liens to proceed despite the parties' agreement to submit disputes to arbitration. Although the parties disagreed as to the extent to which such actions may proceed while arbitration was pending, the appellate court did not reach that issue.

The appellate court, however, agreed to the defendant's motion for reconsideration of its motion to stay pending arbitration on the ground that the parties' could not incorporate the 1987 General Conditions, which did not contain the carve-out. Article 1.2 of the contract stated that "[f]or the Construction Phase, the General Conditions of the Contract shall be the 1987 Edition of AIA Document A201, General Conditions of the Contract for Construction, which is incorporated herein by reference ."

Because the dispute between these parties concerned payment for work performed during the construction phase, the 1987 General Conditions applied. This document contained neither the carve-out for mechanic's liens, nor analogous language. Instead, article 4.5.1provided simply that "[a]ny controversy or Claim arising out of or related to the Contract or the breach thereof, shall be settled by arbitration...." Article 4.5.5further provided that the "foregoing agreement to arbitrate ... shall be specifically enforceable under applicable law in any court having jurisdiction thereof."

The parties contracted, therefore, to submit all claims to arbitration, to the extent required by Virginia law. Under Virginia Code § 8.01-577, when parties

---

[35.9] *See* Matter of Corbo v. Les Chateau Assoc., 127 A.D.2d 657, 658, 511 N.Y.S.2d 883 (1987).

[35.10] *See* Estate of Castellone v. JP Morgan Chase Bank, N.A., 60 A.D.3d 621, 623, 875 N.Y.S.2d 130 (2009).

[104.1] 63 Va. Cir. 548, 2004 WL 288545 (2004).

have agreed to arbitration, submission of "any claim or controversy to arbitration pursuant to such agreement shall be a condition precedent to institution of suit or action thereon." Furthermore, "the agreement to arbitrate shall be enforceable, unless the agreement also provides that submission to arbitration shall not be a condition precedent to suit or action."

Here, the parties contracted to submit any controversy or claim to arbitration. There was no contract provision that provided that arbitration would not be a condition precedent to suit or action. Therefore, under applicable Virginia law, arbitration was a condition precedent to the complainant's suit.

In its brief, the plaintiff argued against this result on two grounds. First, it argued that the defendants should not be allowed to argue on the basis of the 1987 General Conditions, as they did not object to presentation of the 1997 edition during argument. The court, however, held that the plaintiff's reliance on *Weidman v. Babcock*[104.2] was misplaced where it argued that parties were not allowed "do overs," since that case did not support their position. In *Weidman*, the plaintiffs' attorney initially failed to timely object to the trial court's oral ruling. However, the court found that the attorney had preserved his objection by noting the objections on the written order, and timely filing a motion for reconsideration. Here, defense counsel signed the court's order as "seen and objected to," and timely asked for reconsideration. Although the defendants did not present the 1987 General Conditions during argument, the court found their presentation on the motion to be proper.

The plaintiff also argued that the 1997 General Conditions were the version generated by the defendants' architect, presented to the plaintiff when the contract was executed, and under which the parties performed. However, the parties' contract was clear and unambiguous in stating that it incorporated the 1987 General Conditions. The parties' contract clearly incorporated the 1987 General Conditions. Therefore, the court could not look outside the agreement to consider the parties' conduct.

A challenge to an arbitrator's jurisdiction is commonly brought when a demand for arbitration is filed. In *Higgins Development Partners, LLC v. Skanska U.S.A. Building, Inc.*,[104.3] a subcontractor brought an action against a construction manager and development manager for nonpayment of sheet metal roofing work on a federal project. The construction manager filed a demand for arbitration against the development manager related to two unpaid change orders that were unrelated to the sheet metal complaint. The trial court granted the development managers' motion for an injunction and enjoined the construction manager from pursuing its demand for arbitration, and the construction manager appealed. The Montana Supreme Court affirmed the trial court's decision and held that:

> (1) the district court was the proper forum for determining whether claims would be resolved by the American Arbitration Association (AAA), or pursuant to Federal Acquisition Regulations (FAR), and

---

104.2 241 Va. 44 (1991).

104.3 352 Mont. 243, 216 P.3d 199, 2009 MT 287 (2009).

(2) the evidence was sufficient to support the finding that arbitration could not proceed under the AAA.

The underlying claim arose out of the construction of an addition at the Rocky Mountain Lab in Hamilton, Montana. The National Institutes of Health (NIH) owned and operated the lab. NIH and Higgins entered into an agreement for the construction of an addition at the Rocky Mountain Lab known as the Integrative Research Facility.

On September 30, 2004, Higgins entered into a Construction Management Agreement with Skanska. The agreement designated Higgins as the development manager and Skanska as the construction manager for the Integrative Research Facility. This agreement was the subject of the dispute between Higgins and Skanska. Under the agreement, Skanska was charged with administering subcontracts for the addition. Metal Works of Montana, Inc. received a subcontract from Skanska for construction of the roof on the new addition. The subcontract between Skanska and Missoula Sheet Metal expressly incorporated by reference Skanska's contract with Higgins.

At some point after Missoula Sheet Metal installed the roof, issue arose over the quality of Missoula Sheet Metal's work. Higgins alleged that Missoula Sheet Metal's work on a section of the roof (Roof A) was defective. Higgins partially withheld payment to Skanska for that work. Missoula Sheet Metal, in turn, did not receive full payment from Skanska. Missoula Sheet Metal subsequently commenced an action against Skanska to recover approximately $50,000 under the subcontract. The subcontract contained a "pay-if-paid" clause that conditioned Skanska's obligation to pay Missoula Sheet Metal on Skanska receiving payment from Higgins.

On January 10, 2008, Skanska filed an answer, counterclaim, and third-party complaint against Missoula Sheet Metal's surety and Higgins. With respect to Higgins, Skanska alleged that Higgins failed to pay Skanska for the sums demanded by Missoula Sheet Metal and that, accordingly, Higgins was liable to Skanska to the extent it was deemed liable to Missoula Sheet Metal. Separately, Skanska also filed a demand for arbitration with the American Arbitration Association.

The unpaid amounts referenced by Skanska in the demand for arbitration involved two Change Order Requests (Change Orders) that Skanska had submitted to Higgins for payment. The Change Orders at issue related to increased cooling work and ceiling grid adjustments that were performed on the addition. Specifically, Change Order 160, in the amount of $27,999, related to revisions in the acoustical ceiling grid layout after it was 90 percent complete. Change Order 260, in the amount of $196,397, related to increased cooling costs in a mechanical room. Through Higgins, NIH approved partial payment of these requests. Skanska did not reference the dispute over Sheet Metal's work on Roof A in its demand for arbitration.

Higgins responded to Skanska's request for arbitration by filing a motion for injunction with the district court. Higgins argued that the agreement did not allow dispute resolution through arbitration with the American Arbitration Association.

Rather, Higgins claimed that any alternative dispute resolution would have to occur under the Federal Acquisition Regulations (FAR) or the Federal Contracts Disputes Act (CDA) and include NIH as a party. In support of its position, Higgins cited section 9.2.1. of the agreement, titled "Dispute Resolution for the Construction Phase." Section 9.2.1. stated:

> Any other claim, dispute or other matter in question arising out of or related to this Agreement or breach thereof that is determined to relate solely to the Development Manager's obligations during the construction phase shall be settled in accordance with Article 4 of [American Institute of Architects] Document A201 . . . unless the parties mutually agree otherwise.

Section 9.2.1. of the agreement also stated:

> Claims, disputes or other matters in question between the parties that do not relate solely to Development Manager's obligations, and involve the interests of the National Institutes of Health shall be resolved per the requirements of the FAR, as outlined in the Development Manager's Agreement. . . .

Because NIH, through Higgins, rejected the work on Roof A, Higgins argued that section 9.2.1. of the Agreement required Skanska's dispute to be resolved under the FAR and CDA. In response, Skanska argued that arbitration with the American Arbitration Association was proper, because the claim generally arose "out of [Higgins's] nonpayment of Skanska and its subcontractors for work performed at the [Rocky Mountain Lab] . . . ." Skanska drew a distinction between the underlying claim regarding the alleged defectiveness of Roof A and payment of the change orders and argued that the change orders related solely to Higgins's obligations (Skanska did not address directly whether the dispute over Roof A involved NIH's interests).

As a jurisdictional matter, Skanska also argued that any question over whether dispute resolution would occur through arbitration or under the FAR requirements was a decision for the arbitrator, not the district court. Finally, Skanska alleged that Higgins failed to properly certify the change order claims for resolution under the FAR and CDA. According to Skanska, Higgins was the only party that could initiate the FAR process, and Skanska maintained that Higgins refused or failed to do so.

The district court had granted Higgins's motion for injunction and enjoined Skanska from pursuing its demand for arbitration with the American Arbitration Association. The court concluded that NIH "was involved with [Higgins] in approving a reduced [Change Order] payment to Skanska" and that "[t]he disputes over payment of the [Change Orders did] not relate solely to Development Manager [Higgins's] obligations during the construction phase."

On a separate matter, the district court also concluded that there was no evidence that Higgins had refused or failed to properly process Skanska's change orders or "timely engage" the FAR or CDA dispute resolution procedures.

On appeal, the parties did not dispute the existence of an arbitration provision or challenge its validity. The parties recognized that section 9.2.1. of the agreement provided two alternate dispute resolution methods:

(1) binding arbitration with the American Arbitration Association or

(2) resolution under the FAR or CDA dispute resolution procedures.

The parties also agreed that the determinative question was whether the claim or dispute in the present matter related solely to Higgins's obligations as the development manager or whether it involved the interests of the NIH. If the claim or dispute related solely to Higgins's obligations as the development manager, then section 9.2.1. of the agreement provided for binding arbitration with the American Arbitration Association. Alternatively, if the claim or dispute did not relate solely to Higgins's obligations and involved the interests of the NIH, then dispute resolution was subject to the FAR requirements.

The district court determined that the interests of the NIH were involved, and that dispute resolution would have to occur under the FAR requirements. The district court concluded that the dispute at issue, full payment of the change orders, did not relate solely to Higgins's obligations during the construction phase, because Higgins discussed all disputed change orders with NIH, and, ultimately, NIH approved, disapproved, or partially approved the change orders. In reaching this decision, the district court relied heavily upon on an email message sent from Higgins to Skanska's construction manager stating that NIH and Higgins had approved a portion of the sums in question. The district court held that this email was "sufficient to support a finding that the disputes over the increased dollar payment amounts requested in the [Change Orders] involve[d] NIH's interests."

On appeal, Skanska argued that the district court erred in two primary respects by granting the order of injunction in favor of Higgins. First, Skanska claimed that if an agreement contained an arbitration provision, then the district court could not decide substantive issues pertaining to that agreement. Skanska cited *Larsen v. Western States Ins. Agency, Inc.*,[104.4] where the Montana Supreme Court noted the general proposition that once a district court determined the validity of an arbitration clause, then substantive issues under the agreement were reserved for the arbitrator. Skanska claimed that since there was no dispute over whether the agreement contained an arbitration provision, the arbitrator, instead of the district court, should have decided whether the interests of the NIH were involved. Skanska also cited § 27-5-115(2), MCA, which provided, in relevant part:

> On application, the district court may stay an arbitration proceeding commenced or threatened on a showing that there is no agreement to arbitrate. Such an issue, when in substantial and bona fide dispute, shall be immediately and summarily tried and the stay ordered if the court finds for the applying

[104.4] 339 Mont. 407, 170 P.3d 956, 2007 MT 270 (2007).

> party. If the court finds for the opposing party, it shall order the parties to proceed to arbitration.

Skanska argued that the district court erred in its application of § 27-5-115(2), MCA, because there was no "substantial and bona fide dispute" over whether the [Agreement] contained an arbitration provision.

Second, Skanska asserted that the district court erred in concluding that the interests of the NIH were involved, and that arbitration could not proceed with the American Arbitration Association. Skanska claimed that the dispute over payment of Change Orders 160 and 260 arose out of the agreement and related solely to Higgins's obligations to Skanska. Moreover, Skanska contended that its demand for arbitration sought damages for claims that could not be included in the FAR dispute resolution process. Skanska argued that because Higgins partially rejected the claims, Higgins could not submit the claims in good faith to NIH for resolution under the FAR requirements.

In response, Higgins argued that its objection to arbitration was properly raised and decided by the district court as opposed to the arbitrator. Higgins claimed that § 27-5-115, MCA, "mandates the district court to review and to determine whether the subject disputes are subject to AAA arbitration or to the FAR procedures as described in Article 9.2.1" of the Agreement and further, that arbitration proceedings only extended to those disputes that the parties actually agreed to arbitrate.

Higgins argued that for an arbitrator to determine Higgins's objection to arbitration, since "it must first be shown by clear and unmistakable evidence that [Higgins] agreed to that forum." Because section 9.2.1. stated that claims involving the interests of the NIH would be resolved pursuant to the FAR requirements, Higgins asserted that it neither intended nor agreed to arbitrate Skanska's change order claims. In addition, Higgins contended that the district court correctly concluded that the interests of the NIH were involved. Higgins pointed out that the demand for arbitration only sought payment of the two change orders, and it argued that NIH's interests were clearly involved since the demand sought specific sums of money that NIH would ultimately be required to pay.

State and federal policies generally favor arbitration when a valid arbitration agreement exists between the parties. This support is evidenced by the Federal Arbitration Act, 9 U.S.C. §§ 1-16 (2006), which establishes a strong national policy in favor of arbitration. In *AT &T Technologies, Inc. v. Communications Workers of America,*[104.5] the United States Supreme Court stated that arbitration "should not be denied unless it may be said with positive assurance that the arbitration clause is not susceptible of an interpretation that covers the asserted dispute."[104.6]

The presumption in favor of arbitration, however, is not absolute. "[A]rbitration is a matter of contract and a party cannot be required to submit to

---

[104.5] 475 U.S. 643, 650, 106 S. Ct. 1415, 1419, 89 L. Ed. 2d 648 (1986).

[104.6] *See also* Mitsubishi Motors Corp. v. Soler Chrysler-Plymouth, Inc., 473 U.S. 614, 626, 105 S. Ct. 3346, 3353, 87 L. Ed. 2d 444 (1985) (stating that doubts concerning the scope of arbitrable issues should be resolved in favor of arbitration).

arbitration any dispute which he has not agreed so to submit."[104.7] Further, unless the parties clearly and unmistakably provide otherwise, "the question of whether the parties agreed to arbitrate is to be decided by the court, not the arbitrator."[104.8] The Ninth Circuit Court clarified that: "[a]rbitrability is ordinarily for courts, not arbitrators, to decide unless the parties agree otherwise. Courts should not assume that the parties agreed to arbitrate arbitrability unless there is clear and unmistakable evidence that they did so."[104.9] While the laws generally favor arbitration, the intent of the parties remains paramount to any determination of whether an agreement will be subject to arbitration as opposed to some other dispute resolution forum.

In addition to determining whether the parties "agreed to arbitrate a certain matter, courts generally should apply ordinary state-law principles that govern the formation of contracts."[104.10] In Montana, "[a] contract must be so interpreted as to give effect to the mutual intention of the parties as it existed at the time of contracting, so far as the same is ascertainable and lawful." Section 28-3-301, MCA. Further, "[w]hen a contract is reduced to writing, the intention of the parties is to be ascertained from the writing alone if possible. . . ." Section 28-3-303, MCA.

As noted above, the dispute resolution provision set forth in the agreement stated that claims relating solely to the development manager's obligations would be settled in accordance with article4 of the American Institute of Architects—i.e., through binding arbitration with the American Arbitration Association. Claims that were determined not to relate solely to the development manager's obligations, and that involved the interests of the NIH, would be settled through the FAR requirements. However, section 9.2.1. was silent as to whether the district court or some other forum would decide whether the claim related solely to Higgins's obligations or whether the interests of the NIH were involved. In the absence of such language, the Montana Supreme Court found that it was clear that the district court was the only appropriate forum to make this determination. Since the plain language of the agreement did not designate a forum for deciding whether the interests of the NIH were involved, and further, since the parties did not clearly and unmistakably provide that an arbitrator would decide that question, the court concluded that the district court was the appropriate forum for deciding the dispute resolution forum for Skanska's claims.

The Montana Supreme Court considered whether Skanska's claim or dispute related solely to Higgins's obligations or whether it involved the interests of the NIH. While the agreement provided two alternate dispute resolution methods, there was no guidance in the agreement on how to determine if the interests of the NIH were involved. The problem arose from the use of the word "interests," which could be broadly interpreted in a variety of ways as evidenced by the

---

[104.7] United Steelworkers v. Warrior & Gulf Navigation Co., 363 U.S. 574, 582, 80 S. Ct. 1347, 1353, 4 L. Ed. 2d 1409 (1960).

[104.8] *AT & T Technologies*, 475 U.S. at 649, 106 S. Ct. at 1418.

[104.9] PowerAgent v. Electronic Data Systems, 358 F.3d 1187, 1191 (9th Cir. 2004).

[104.10] State v. Philip Morris, Inc., 352 Mont. 30, 217 P.3d 475, 2009 MT 261 (2009).

arguments set forth by the parties. Generally "interest" denotes "legal share in something."[104.11] Moreover, "legal interest" includes a pecuniary interest.

A reading of the plain language of the agreement suggested that the FAR or CDA dispute resolution procedures would be invoked when NIH possessed a right or legal share in the dispute or when its pecuniary interests were involved. However, a more straightforward approach would be to determine whether the "claims, disputes or other matters in question" between Higgins and Skanska related solely to Higgins's obligations as the Development Manager under the agreement.

As noted by the district court in its order of injunction, Skanska's demand for arbitration sought to be paid "the full amounts still owed by [Higgins]" on Change Orders 160 and 260. The evidence suggested that NIH and Higgins approved partial payment of at least one of the change orders. There was also testimony on Higgins's motion for injunction that Change Orders 160 and 260 sought additional money from NIH, and that NIH ultimately had all fiscal authority and control over increases or decreases in project costs. There was the evidence that Higgins discussed all disputed change orders with NIH, and that NIH had the final authority to approve, disapprove, or partially approve change orders. It was clear that payment of the change orders did not relate solely to Higgins's obligations as the development manager, because NIH, as the owner and financier of the Integrative Research Facility at the Rocky Mountain Lab, had a clear financial interest in the dispute over payment of the change orders.

The court stated that this conclusion was supported by substantial evidence in the record. Because Skanska's claim or dispute, as referenced in the demand for arbitration, did not relate solely to Higgins's obligations and, instead, involved the interests of the NIH, the district court did not err in ordering the parties to resolve the dispute under the FAR or CDA dispute resolution procedures, and sustained the trial court's finding that the dispute did not belong in the district court.

In *Shah v. Monpat Construction, Inc.*,[104.12] a property owner brought an action against a construction company, its owner, and a second construction company, seeking to permanently enjoin arbitration and to recover damages for breach of contract. The New York Supreme Court granted defendants' motion to compel arbitration. The property owner appealed.

The New York Supreme Court, Appellate Division, held that:

> (1) The property owner and the first construction company had a valid agreement to arbitrate, but
>
> (2) The property owner, the owner of the first construction company, and the second company did not have an agreement to arbitrate. The appellate court affirmed the trial court's holding, as modified.

In *Shah*, an action to permanently enjoin arbitration and to recover damages for breach of contract, the plaintiffs appealed from the portion of an order of the

[104.11] Blacks Law Dictionary 816 (Bryan A. Garner ed., 7th ed., West 1999).

[104.12] 65 A.D.3d 541, 884 N.Y.S.2d 116, 2009 N.Y. (2009).

New York Supreme Court, Queens County, which denied their motion to preliminarily enjoin the defendant, Monpat Construction, Inc., from proceeding with the arbitration of a claim against the plaintiff, Haresh D. Shah, under a contract dated March 15, 2001. There was also a cross-motion by the defendants, Monpat Construction, Inc., RB Construction Management Corp., and Mihir B. Patel, pursuant to CPLR 7503(c), to compel the plaintiffs to submit their claim against the defendants RB Construction Management Corp. and Mihir B. Patel to arbitration and to stay all proceedings in the action pending arbitration.

In *Shah*, a dentist (Dr. Shah), owned a property in Queens, on which he wanted to construct a building. One of Dr. Shah's patients, the individual defendant, Mihir B. Patel, owned a construction company, the defendant Monpat Construction, Inc. (Monpat). In March 2001, Shah and Patel (as the representative of Monpat) signed an agreement that provided for construction of the building. The agreement expressly incorporated by reference various other documents, one of which, "General Conditions of the Contract for Construction, AIA Document A201-1997" (Document A201-1997) contained a broad arbitration provision. Together, the agreement and the other documents formed the contract.

Construction was delayed for reasons on which the parties do not agree. In early 2002, Shah and Patel agreed that the building would be constructed by the defendant RB Construction Management Corp. (RB), a construction company that had been formed by Patel's wife. The parties disagreed about whether the written contract was abandoned and replaced by an oral agreement between Shah and RB and Patel, or whether it continued in full force and effect, with the only difference being that RB would perform the work. The building was constructed and most of the contract price was paid, but there were disputes about various issues.

Monpat filed a demand for arbitration on April 28, 2008, under the written contract. In July 2008, Shah and the two other plaintiffs, Glen Oaks Medical Building, LLC, and Glen Oaks Building Corp., commenced the action to permanently enjoin the arbitration brought against Shah by Monpat, to recover damages against RB and Patel for breach of the alleged oral agreement, for a declaration that there was no agreement to arbitrate, and that Monpat had abandoned the written contract. The plaintiffs named as defendants, Patel, Monpat, and RB, as well as the American Arbitration Association (hereinafter the AAA) and an officer and a case manager of the AAA. The complaint asserted against the AAA and its officer and case manager was dismissed.

The plaintiffs moved to preliminarily enjoin the arbitration brought against Shah by Monpat. The defendants cross-moved, among other things, to compel arbitration of all claims. In the order appealed from, the court, among other things, granted that portion of the defendants' cross-motion which was to compel arbitration of all claims, and denied that portion of the plaintiffs' motion which was for a preliminary injunction. The plaintiffs appealed.

In New York, arbitration is favored as a means of resolving disputes, and courts should interfere as little as possible with agreements to arbitrate.[104.13]

[104.13] *Citing* Matter of Smith Barney Shearson v. Sacharow, 91 N.Y.2d 39, 49, 689 N.E.2d 884, 666 N.Y.S.2d 990 (1997); *Matter of Miller*, 40 A.D.3d 861, 861-62, 835 N.Y.S.2d 728 (2007).

There is a substantial countervailing consideration as well. "[B]y agreeing to arbitrate a party waives in large part many of his normal rights under the procedural and substantive law of the State."[104.14] For this reason, a party will not be compelled to arbitrate and, thereby, to surrender the right to resort to the courts, absent evidence which affirmatively establishes that the parties expressly agreed to arbitrate their disputes. Thus, the arbitration agreement must be clear, explicit, and unequivocal. Once the court has determined the threshold issues of the existence of a valid agreement to arbitrate, that the party seeking arbitration has complied with the agreement, and that the claim sought to be arbitrated would not be time-barred were it asserted in state court, the remaining issues are for the arbitrator.[104.15]

In this case, the written contract was clear, explicit, and unequivocal and established a valid agreement to arbitrate. The agreement expressly adopted Document A201-1997 by reference, in effect, listed it as one of the "Contract Documents" in article 1, enumerated it as one of the "Contract Documents" in article 8, and referred to it by document number throughout. Consequently, the arbitration provisions included in Document A201-1997 were part of the written contract.[104.16] Shah's contention that he never received Document A201-1997 was ineffective, and his ignorance of its provisions was attributed to "negligence or inexcusable trustfulness."

The plaintiffs did not contend in the supreme court, either in support of their motion to stay arbitration or in opposition to the defendants' motion to compel arbitration, that Monpat had not complied with conditions precedent to arbitration. Consequently, that issue was found not properly before the appellate court.

In general, where there is a broad arbitration clause, any issue with respect to changes in the substantive provisions of a contract or its termination are to be resolved by the arbitrator, unless the modification or termination relates to the arbitration clause itself.[104.17] In this case, the plaintiffs' contention that the written contract was abandoned was not directly related to the arbitration provisions. Accordingly, the court held that the issue of abandonment should be left for the arbitrator. The issue of the statute of limitations was so intertwined with the parties' substantive contentions and the contentions regarding abandonment that the issue of the statute of limitations should be left to the arbitrator.[104.18] Issues regarding proper service of the demand for arbitration should be determined by the arbitrator.

Finally, the written contract was between Shah and Monpat. There was no clear evidence that the plaintiffs ever agreed to arbitrate any disputes with Patel

---

[104.14] *Matter of Marlene Indus. Corp. [Carnac Textiles]*, 45 N.Y.2d 327, 333-34, 408 N.Y.S.2d 410, 380 N.E.2d 239 (1978); *Matter of Miller*, 40 A.D.3d at 862, 835 N.Y.S.2d at 728.

[104.15] *See* CPLR 7502[b].

[104.16] *See Matter of Level Export Corp. [Wolz, Aiken & Co.]*, 305 N.Y. 82, 87, 111 N.E.2d 218 (1953).

[104.17] *See Matter of Cassone*, 63 N.Y.2d 756, 759, 469 N.E.2d 835, 480 N.Y.S.2d 317 (1984).

[104.18] *See* Matter of Corbo v. Les Chateau Assoc., 127 A.D.2d 657, 658, 511 N.Y.S.2d 883 (1987).

and RB. Consequently, the supreme court should not have compelled the plaintiffs to arbitrate their claims against those defendants.[104.19]

Page 949, add at end of subsection [C]:

In *Agri-Systems, Inc. v. Foster Poultry Farms*,[126.1] a general contractor brought a breach of contract action against a project owner. An arbitrator issued an award for the project owner. The general contractor moved for an order correcting or vacating award based on an undisclosed conflict of interest of the arbitrator. The trial court denied the motion to correct or vacate, and confirmed the arbitrator's award. The general contractor appealed.

The appellate court held that: (1) the general contractor's failure to request a statement of decision and to bring purported deficiencies in the arbitrator's award to the trial court's attention resulted in implied findings in support of the judgment; (2) on an issue of first impression, a proposed neutral arbitrator must disclose legal representation of a third party with an adversarial relationship with a party to the arbitration only if the representation raises a reasonable doubt about the arbitrator's impartiality; and (3) an arbitrator's firm's representation of third party with interests adverse to general contractor did not raise reasonable doubt about impartiality.

The appellate court affirmed the trial court's confirmation of the arbitrator's award. The general contractor challenged the trial court's decision to confirm an arbitration award, contending the award should have been vacated because the arbitrator violated his disclosure obligation. The general contractor argued that the arbitrator was required to disclose his law firm's representation of a company that owed the general contractor over $3 million. The record demonstrated that:

1. another attorney in the arbitrator's law firm represented the debtor company at the beginning of a bankruptcy proceeding;
2. the debtor company's interests were adverse to the general contractor's interests;
3. those adverse interests resulted in litigation between the debtor company and the general contractor;
4. the arbitrator's law firm had withdrawn from representing the debtor company before the litigation between the debtor company and the general contractor began; and
5. the arbitrator was appointed in the present case a year and a half after his firm's withdrawal as attorney of record for the debtor company in its bankruptcy proceeding.

[104.19] *See* Estate of Castellone v. JP Morgan Chase Bank, N.A., 60 A.D.3d 621, 623, 875 N.Y.S.2d 130 (2009).

[126.1] 168 Cal. App. 4th 1128, 85 Cal. Rptr. 3d 917 (2008), (certified for partial publication), *review denied* (Feb. 18, 2009).

Neither the California Arbitration Act[126.2] the ethics standards for contractual arbitration, nor the cases applying those provisions address specifically the disclosure of an arbitrator's legal representation of a third party who had an adversarial relationship with a party to the arbitration. The appellate court concluded that the applicable rule of law was the general requirement that a proposed neutral arbitrator "shall disclose all matters that could cause a person aware of the facts to reasonably entertain a doubt that the proposed neutral arbitrator would be able to be impartial."[126.3]

The application of this general requirement to the issue presented in this case posed a question of fact that was subject to review under the deferential substantial evidence standard. The appellate court affirmed the trial court's finding that, under the facts of this case, disclosure by the arbitrator of the prior relationship was not required, and that this finding of the trial court was supported by substantial evidence.

Agri-Systems (AS) was a California contractor. The arbitrator found that AS held itself out as a design-build contractor specializing in turnkey material handling and processing facilities. It represented itself as a major resource for the design and construction of feed mills, and claimed it had a strong performance record. Foster Farms (FF) is a California corporation. AS agreed to build FF a new grain rolling facility to produce steam-flaked grain for $2,669,800. The parties entered into a written construction agreement which included an arbitration clause calling for arbitration under the then-current Construction Industry Arbitration Rules of the American Arbitration Association. The AAA arbitration decision was to be final and binding on both parties.

Disputes arose regarding a load-out bin discharge system, as well as about the causes of the system's failure to achieve an acceptable rate of flow. FF contended the flow problems were caused by poor design, poor construction, and the breakdown of the original equipment. AS contended that the primary causes of the impeded flow were the moisture content being too high, and by FF's poor maintenance procedures. Due to this dispute, after completion, FF withheld 10 percent of the contract price. AS sued FF for breach of contract, claiming $298,668.30 due under the contract, along with prejudgment interest.

FF moved to stay the lawsuit, and to compel arbitration under paragraph 14 of the written agreement. The superior court action was stayed, and the matter was submitted to the American Arbitration Association (AAA). AAA provided the parties with a list of potential arbitrators, and eventually the parties agreed that Robert Hillison, of the law firm of Caswell, Bell & Hillison, LLP, would act as the sole arbitrator on the matter. Arbitration commenced in April 2005. In June 2005 the arbitrator issued an award in favor of FF and against AS in the amount of $178,422.40. The award included $10,000 in AAA administrative fees to be paid by AS, and $11,199 in compensation and expenses for the arbitrator.

In September 2005, AS filed a motion to correct or vacate the arbitration award, claiming that the arbitrator had an undisclosed conflict of interest. The

[126.2] Cal. Civ. Proc. Code § 1280 *et seq.*

[126.3] Cal. Civ. Proc. Code § 1281.9, subd. (a).

motion asserted that Coast Grain Company (CGC), a prior client of the arbitrator's law firm, was an adversary of AS in another matter, and that the arbitrator's law firm represented CGC in its bankruptcy proceeding, and that CGC had substantial, ongoing litigation against AS in both bankruptcy court and district court.

The trial court denied the AS motion to correct or vacate. It found no failure to disclose by the arbitrator because the relationship alleged between the arbitrator's law firm and a third party adversary was not substantial. The trial court found that the law firm's representation of CGC in bankruptcy was during a limited period in 2002, did not involve adversary proceedings against AS, and had ended before the bankruptcy trustee initiated an adversary proceeding against AS. FF filed a petition to confirm the arbitrator's award, and AS filed an opposition to confirmation of the award on the grounds that the arbitrator breached an obligation to disclose his law firm's representation of CGC. The trial court granted the petition of FF to confirm the arbitrator's award. AS appealed.

The California Arbitration Act (CAA) provides that a court may vacate an arbitration award if the arbitrator fails to disclose within the time required for disclosure a ground for disqualification for which the arbitrator was then aware.[126.4] Section 1281.9 requires disclosure of all matters that could cause a person aware of the facts to reasonably entertain a doubt that the proposed neutral arbitrator would be able to be impartial. Specific matters under section 1281.9 which must be disclosed include:

> (5) Any attorney-client relationship the proposed neutral arbitrator has or had with any party or lawyer for a party to the arbitration proceeding. (6) Any professional or significant personal relationship the proposed neutral arbitrator . . . has or has had with any party to the arbitration proceeding or lawyer for a party.[126.5]

Disclosure standards for arbitrators include the existence of any grounds specified in section 170.1 for disqualification of a judge. The *Agri-Systems*court stated that the only provisions of section 170.1 mentioned by AS in its opening appellate brief are from subdivision (a)(6)(A) which requires a judge to step aside if:

> "[f]or any reason: (i) The judge believes his or her recusal would further the interests of justice. (ii) The judge believes there is a substantial doubt as to his or her capacity to be impartial. (iii) A person aware of the facts might reasonably entertain a doubt that the judge would be able to be impartial." The latter of these three requirements is similar to the general standard contained in section 1281.9, subdivision (a).

Section 1281.85 subd. A provides that a person serving as a neutral arbitrator pursuant to an arbitration agreement shall comply with the ethics standards adopted by the Judicial Council.

[126.4] Cal. Civ. Proc. Code § 1286.4, subd. (a)(6).

[126.5] Cal. Civ. Proc. Code § 1281.9, subd. (a).

The Judicial Council adopted standards, including Standard 7, which requires a proposed arbitrator to make comprehensive disclosures regarding potential grounds for disqualification. The only paragraph of the required disclosures mentioned by AS in its opening appellate brief was 7(d)(7), which provided for disclosure by the arbitrator of any attorney-client relationship the arbitrator has or has had with a party or lawyer for a party. AS acknowledged that standard 7(d) does not mention explicitly the disclosure of an arbitrator's past or current legal representation of a third party with interests adverse to a party to the arbitration, but the comment to standard 7 includes the clarification that the specific interests, relationships, or affiliations listed in standard 7 are only examples of common matters that could cause a person aware of the facts to reasonably entertain a doubt that the arbitrator would be able to be impartial. Cal. Rules of Court, Ethics Standards for Neutral Arbitrators in Contract Arbitration, com. to std. 7.

On appeal, AS relied on standard 7(d)(7) to argue that the arbitrator should have disclosed to the parties that he was a member of a firm that represented CGC in its Chapter 11 reorganization. AS also contended that under the general disclosure standard a person aware of the facts might reasonably entertain a doubt that the arbitrator would be impartial. FF contended that there was no existing adverse relationship to disclose at the time the arbitrator was proposed and appointed, and whether disclosure was required was a factual question for the trier of fact.

A partner of the arbitrator's, Hagop Bedoyan, represented CGC in an involuntary bankruptcy proceeding in 2001. In March 2002, a Chapter 11 trustee was appointed, which engaged its own legal counsel. After March 3, 2002, Bedoyan and the arbitrator's firm played no further role in the bankruptcy.

In November 2002, CGC filed a complaint against AS alleging a construction defect, and seeking damages in excess of $9 million. AS filed a declaration which asserted that the construction defect litigation between CGC and AS asserted that FF's claim against AS helped to prove its own claim that AS's construction work was faulty. The declaration also asserted that the arbitration award in favor of FF in this case helped to support the contentions of CGC in its suit against AS.

In December 2002, CGC filed an adversary complaint against AS. The adversary complaint objected to AS's creditor claims, sought to avoid preferential transfers to AS, and requested a determination of the extent and validity of AS's liens.

In January 2004, AS filed its own Chapter 11 bankruptcy proceeding as a result of the major disputes involving accounts for which AS was not paid. The disputes involved CGC and FF. CGC and FF voted against the confirmation of the reorganization plan that AS presented to the bankruptcy court. CGC tried to convert AS's bankruptcy proceeding to a Chapter 7 liquidation in an attempt to avoid state court litigation with AS and avoid payment of the $3 million debt owed to AS. A declaration filed by the president of AS in this case stated his belief that CGC and FF were working together to prevent the confirmation of the AS plan of reorganization.

The trial court disagreed with AS's contention that any attorney-client relationship the arbitrator had had with a party required disclosure. The court stated that the provision was clear on its face and did not support AS's contention. Here, because CGC was not a party to the arbitration, the arbitration was not required by standard 7(d)(7) to disclose his law firm's representation of CGC. In applying the "reasonable person standard" on what should be disclosed by an arbitrator, another court referred to the "average person on the street" as the "reasonable person."[126.6]

In this case, the order implementing the stipulation that the lawsuit between AS and FF was stayed and the matter submitted to arbitration was filed on March 2, 2004. The arbitrator was not appointed until approximately one and one half years after the bankruptcy court granted the law firm's request to withdraw as counsel of record for CGC in the bankruptcy proceeding. The evidence showed that the arbitrator's law firm did not represent CGC during the pendency of the construction defect litigation in federal district court or in the adversary proceeding in bankruptcy court.

The *Agri-Systems* court pointed out that the arbitrator did not provide legal services or advice directly to CGC. His relationship with CGC was indirect, because a partner in his law firm acted as attorney for CGC in the bankruptcy proceedings. Using the above facts, the appellate court held that there was adequate support for the trial court's implied finding of ultimate fact that an objective person would not reasonably entertain doubts about the arbitrator's ability to be impartial.

The *Agri-Systems* court reviewed a case cited by the parties on what it identified as the one California case which addressed whether an arbitrator's legal representation of a third party, with interests adverse to a party to the arbitration, was sufficient to create an appearance of partiality.

In *Cobler*, a career consulting agency sought to vacate an arbitration award in favor of a former client. The grounds asserted by the agency included the claim that there was apparent bias on the part of the arbitrator. The claim of apparent bias was based on the fact that (1) a law partner of the arbitrator was representing a major competitor of the agency in an unfair trade practices lawsuit that the agency had filed against that competitor and (2) the arbitrator's law partner had spent five days deposing the president and sole shareholder of the agency's parent corporation, which included questions that impliedly challenged his credibility.

The *Cobler* court noted that the applicable standard provided "that an arbitrator's failure to disclose to the parties any dealings which might create an impression of possible bias is grounds for vacating the award."[126.7] The court then stated that whether a particular business relationship was required to be disclosed under this standard was a factual question.[126.8] The court concluded that there was adequate support in the record for the trial court's finding of no actual bias, based

[126.6] United Farmworkers of Am. v. Superior Court, 170 Cal. App. 3d 97, 216 Cal. Rptr. 4 (1985).
[126.7] *Cobler*, 217 Cal. App. 3d at 527, 265 Cal. Rptr. at 873.
[126.8] *Id.*

on the arbitrator's declaration that he was not aware of the potential conflict until after the arbitration decision had been made.[126.9]

According to the *Agri-Systems* court, the *Cobler* court had never decided the merits of the issue of apparent bias, which was the issue closest to the issue presented in this appeal. Instead, it had found that the agency waived that issue and was estopped from asserting it later.[126.10] The *Cobler* appellate court upheld these findings.[126.11] As a result, the factual analysis in *Cobler* provided little guidance on how the general disclosure standard contained in section 1281.9, subdivision (a) should be applied. Whether a particular relationship must be disclosed under that general standard was a question to be determined by the trier of fact.[126.12]

AS asserted that the arbitrator knew of his law firm's representation of CGC, and of CGC's adversary relationship with AS, when he made his arbitrator disclosures. AS claimed that this failure to disclose required the court to vacate the arbitrator's award. The *Agri-Systems* court failed to find this argument persuasive. It noted that the trial court made no finding that the arbitrator possessed the knowledge of potential conflict. It stated that it could not infer such knowledge existed because the doctrine of implied findings supported the court's decision. Under that doctrine, an appellate court must presume the superior court impliedly found all facts in favor of the prevailing party, so long as those implied findings are supported by substantial evidence.[126.13] In this case, there was no direct evidence of the arbitrator's state of awareness. Under the circumstances, the trial court could have inferred that the arbitrator did or did not know of the CGC representation by his law firm. The appellate court must presume, based on this legal doctrine, that the trial court found the arbitrator was not aware of the prior representation.

AS also asserted that it was not aware that the arbitrator's law firm previously represented CGC when it agreed to have him appointed to arbitrate its dispute with FF. The declaration of AS's president asserted that in August 2005 he first learned the arbitrator's law firm had represented CGC when AS's bankruptcy counsel alerted him of the fact. AS's assertion of this fact directly contradicted the trial court's statement that "the evidence supports the fact that [AS] or [AS's] counsel knew of the relationship back in 2001, and yet still chose this arbitrator." The trial court made this finding in support of its alternate rationale that AS forfeited or waived any objection to the arbitrator. The trial court appeared to have based its finding on information contained in proofs of service and other documents from CGC's bankruptcy proceeding. Relying upon the *Agri-System* court's conclusion that there was no duty to disclose, the court held that it need not address the trial court's alternate rationale, and whether findings underlying

---

[126.9] *Cobler*, 217 Cal. App. 3d at 529, 265 Cal. Rptr. at 874.

[126.10] *Id.*

[126.11] *Id.*

[126.12] *See* Advantage Medical Servs., LLC v. Hoffman, 160 Cal. App. 4th 806, 816, 72 Cal. Rptr. 3d 935 (2008).

[126.13] 121 Cal. App. 4th 452, 462, 17 Cal. Rptr. 3d 96 (2004).

that rationale were supported by sufficient evidence. The appellate court affirmed the trial court's findings, entering the arbitrator's decision as a judgment and denying AS's motion to vacate or set aside the arbitrator's award for undisclosed bias.

[D] Specific Disputes

Page 950, add after carryover paragraph:

In *Acme Arsena Co., Inc. v. J. Holden Construction Co., Ltd.*,[129.1] a subcontractor brought an action against a general contractor and a project owner, alleging breach of contract and a claim of quantum meruit, to recover payment for work done on a project. The general contractor filed counterclaims and a motion to stay proceedings pending mediation or arbitration. The trial court denied the motion and the general contractor appealed.

The court of appeals reversed and held that mandatory alternative dispute resolution provisions were incorporated into the contract, requiring the court to grant the stay. The mandatory alternative dispute resolution provisions were incorporated into the contract between the general contractor and the subcontractor, such that the general contractor was entitled to a stay of the suit brought by the subcontractor for breach of contract pending mediation and arbitration. Listed within two modified sections of the contract were specific procedures, including mandatory and binding mediation and arbitration provisions, to follow should any claims occur that arose out of or were related to the underlying contract documents.

The defendant, Mental Health Services for Homeless Persons, Inc. (MHS), had contracted with J. Holden, as general contractor, to perform construction work on its property. The general contractor then entered into a written subcontract (the subcontract) with the plaintiff-appellee, Acme Arsena Company, Inc. (Acme), wherein Acme agreed to furnish all labor and material necessary to complete all rough carpentry work, all necessary backing work, metal stud work, cold metal framing work, all insulation, all drywall work, and all acoustical ceiling work on the project.

On November 8, 2007, Acme instituted an action against J. Holden and MHS alleging breach of contract and a claim of quantum merit, maintaining that it was entitled to $73,382.20 for work performed pursuant to the subcontract and $39,262.20 for additional work. On December 17, 2007, MHS filed its answer. Thereafter, on January 18, 2008, J. Holden filed an answer and statement regarding counterclaims. Simultaneously, J. Holden filed a motion to stay proceedings pending mediation and arbitration. On April 16, 2008, the trial court denied J. Holden's motion to stay proceedings.

J. Holden claimed the trial court committed reversible error by not staying the proceedings and ordering the parties to arbitration when there was an agreement between the parties to arbitrate the issues in dispute because the

[129.1] 2008 WL 5182912 (Ohio App. 8th Dist. 2008).

subcontract between it and Acme incorporated documents that contained mandatory and binding mediation and arbitration provisions for any claim arising out of or related to the subcontract.

Before addressing the merits of this appeal, the appellate court recognized that alternative dispute resolutions (ADR) were a favored practice of both Ohio and federal courts, and there was a strong presumption in favor of avenues other than lengthy litigation to settle disputes between parties.

The appellate court found that the trial court erred in failing to stay the proceedings pending mediation and arbitration. More specifically, the appellate court found that mandatory and binding ADR provisions were incorporated into the subcontract. While the subcontract itself did not contain any ADR provisions, the subcontract expressly incorporated two other documents that were attached to the contract. The subcontract stated in relevant part:

> 1. Contract Documents. The Contract Documents consist of this Contract, the attached General Conditions and Specifications identified below, and all addenda issued prior to and all modifications issued after execution of this Contract (collectively the "Contract Documents")
>
> . . .

The trial court erroneously concluded that the "General Conditions and Specifications" documents referred to in section 1 were actually only one document, the document entitled "Specifications for Construction Contract between J. Holden Construction Company, Ltd. and Acme Arsena Company, Inc." Relying on this finding, the trial court concluded that section 24 of that document, located on page 12, governed the determination of whether ADR mechanisms were part of the contract. Accordingly, because that section made no mention of mediation or arbitration, nor was there any reference to the AIA Document, A201, the trial court held that the subcontract did not incorporate any ADR clauses.

The appellate court found the trial court's conclusion mistaken. Its review of the subcontract indicated that section 1 actually incorporated, not one, but two documents: one titled "General Conditions" and one titled "Specifications." Attached to the subcontract, and immediately following it, was a document designated as "Specifications for Construction Contract between J. Holden Construction Company, Ltd. and Acme Arsena Company, Inc." Also attached to the Subcontract was a document with the title of "General Conditions." The body of this document provided the following:

> PART 1—GENERAL
>
> 1.01 PRINTED AIA DOCUMENT
>
> A. The "General Conditions of the Contract of Construction," AIA Document A201, Fourteenth Edition, 1987, published by the American Institute of Architects, is hereby made a part of the Documents to the same extent as if herein written out in full. The General Conditions contained therein shall govern the performance of the Contract.

B. One (1) copy of AIA Document A201 shall be kept at the Project site by the Contractor.

C. Certain Articles of the AIA General Conditions have been modified, as indicated in the Supplementary Conditions and subsequent documents.

Finally, modified portions of the AIAA201 General Conditions were also attached to the subcontract. Listed within two of the modified sections, sections 4.5 and 4.6, were specific procedures, including mandatory and binding mediation and arbitration provisions, to follow should any claims occur that arise out of or are related to the underlying contract documents.

There was no dispute that Acme and J. Holden both signed the subcontract and agreed to abide by its terms. Therefore, the court held that the subcontract included an agreement between Acme and J. Holden to mediate or arbitrate any matters related to the subcontract. Consequently, the trial court erred in denying J. Holden's motion to stay proceedings pending mediation and arbitration.

In *Higgins Development Partners, LLC v. Skanska U.S.A. Building, Inc.*,[129.2] a subcontractor brought an action against a construction manager and development manager for nonpayment of sheet metal roofing work on federal project. The construction manager filed a demand for arbitration against the development manager related to two unpaid change orders that were unrelated to the sheet metal complaint. The trial court granted the development managers' motion for injunction and enjoined construction manager from pursuing its demand for arbitration, and construction manager appealed. The Montana Supreme Court affirmed the trial court's decision, and held that:

(1) the district court was the proper forum for determining whether claims would be resolved by the American Arbitration Association (AAA), or pursuant to Federal Acquisition Regulations (FAR), and

(2) the evidence was sufficient to support the finding that arbitration could not proceed under the AAA.

The underlying claim arose out of the construction of an addition at the Rocky Mountain Lab in Hamilton, Montana. The National Institutes of Health (NIH) owned and operated the lab. NIH and Higgins entered into an agreement for the construction of an addition at the Rocky Mountain Lab known as the Integrative Research Facility.

On September 30, 2004, Higgins entered into a Construction Management Agreement with Skanska. The agreement designated Higgins as the development manager and Skanska as the construction manager for the Integrative Research Facility. This agreement was the subject of the dispute between Higgins and Skanska. Under the agreement, Skanska was charged with administering subcontracts for the addition. Metal Works of Montana, Inc. received a subcontract from Skanska for construction of the roof on the new addition. The subcontract between

[129.2] 352 Mont. 243, 216 P.3d 199, 2009 MT 287 (2009).

Skanska and Missoula Sheet Metal expressly incorporated by reference Skanska's contract with Higgins.

At some point after Missoula Sheet Metal installed the roof, issue arose over the quality of Missoula Sheet Metal's work. Higgins alleged that Missoula Sheet Metal's work on a section of the roof (Roof A) was defective. Higgins partially withheld payment to Skanska for that work. Missoula Sheet Metal, in turn, did not receive full payment from Skanska. Missoula Sheet Metal subsequently commenced an action against Skanska to recover approximately $50,000 under the subcontract. The subcontract contained a "pay-if-paid" clause that conditioned Skanska's obligation to pay Missoula Sheet Metal on Skanska receiving payment from Higgins.

On January 10, 2008, Skanska filed an answer, counterclaim, and third-party complaint against Missoula Sheet Metal's surety and Higgins. With respect to Higgins, Skanska alleged that Higgins failed to pay Skanska for the sums demanded by Missoula Sheet Metal and that, accordingly, Higgins was liable to Skanska to the extent it was deemed liable to Missoula Sheet Metal. Separately, Skanska also filed a demand for arbitration with the American Arbitration Association.

The unpaid amounts referenced by Skanska in the demand for arbitration involved two Change Order Requests (Change Orders) that Skanska had submitted to Higgins for payment. The Change Orders at issue related to increased cooling work and ceiling grid adjustments that were performed on the addition. Specifically, Change Order 160, in the amount of $27,999, related to revisions in the acoustical ceiling grid layout after it was 90 percent complete. Change Order 260, in the amount of $196,397, related to increased cooling costs in a mechanical room. Through Higgins, NIH approved partial payment of these requests. Skanska did not reference the dispute over Sheet Metal's work on Roof A in its demand for arbitration.

Higgins responded to Skanska's request for arbitration by filing a Motion for Injunction with the district court. Higgins argued that the agreement did not allow dispute resolution through arbitration with the American Arbitration Association. Rather, Higgins claimed that any alternative dispute resolution would have to occur under the Federal Acquisition Regulations (FAR) or the Federal Contracts Disputes Act (CDA) and include NIH as a party. In support of its position, Higgins cited section 9.2.1. of the agreement, titled "Dispute Resolution for the Construction Phase." Section 9.2.1. stated:

> Any other claim, dispute or other matter in question arising out of or related to this Agreement or breach thereof that is determined to relate solely to the Development Manager's obligations during the construction phase shall be settled in accordance with Article 4 of [American Institute of Architects] Document A201 . . . unless the parties mutually agree otherwise.

Section 9.2.1. of the agreement also stated:

> Claims, disputes or other matters in question between the parties that do not relate solely to Development Manager's obligations, and involve the interests

of the National Institutes of Health shall be resolved per the requirements of the FAR, as outlined in the Development Manager's Agreement. . . .

Higgins argued that the dispute over the change orders (the only claims specifically noted in Skanska's demand for arbitration) did not relate solely to Higgins's obligations under the agreement, because the federal government (through NIH) owned the facility and was ultimately responsible for paying its construction costs. Further, Higgins stated that the "present litigation arose from the NIH rejection of Roof A and its refusal to pay [Higgins] for that roof." Because NIH, through Higgins, rejected the work on Roof A, Higgins argued that section 9.2.1. of the Agreement required Skanska's dispute to be resolved under the FAR and CDA.

In response, Skanska argued that arbitration with the American Arbitration Association was proper, because the claim generally arose "out of [Higgins's] nonpayment of Skanska and its subcontractors for work performed at the [Rocky Mountain Lab]. . . . " Skanska drew a distinction between the underlying claim regarding the alleged defectiveness of Roof A and payment of the change orders and argued that the change orders related solely to Higgins's obligations (Skanska did not address directly whether the dispute over Roof A involved NIH's interests).

As a jurisdictional matter, Skanska also argued that any question over whether dispute resolution would occur through arbitration or under the FAR requirements was a decision for the arbitrator, not the district court. Finally, Skanska alleged that Higgins failed to properly certify the change order claims for resolution under the FAR and CDA. According to Skanska, Higgins was the only party that could initiate the FAR process, and Skanska maintained that Higgins refused or failed to do so.

The district court had granted Higgins's motion for injunction and enjoined Skanska from pursuing its demand for arbitration with the American Arbitration Association. That court concluded that NIH "was involved with [Higgins] in approving a reduced [Change Order] payment to Skanska" and that "[t]he disputes over payment of the [Change Orders did] not relate solely to Development Manager [Higgins's] obligations during the construction phase."

On a separate matter, the district court also concluded that there was no evidence that Higgins had refused or failed to properly process Skanska's change orders or "timely engage" the FAR or CDA dispute resolution procedures.

On appeal, the parties did not dispute the existence of an arbitration provision or challenge its validity. The parties recognized that section 9.2.1. of the agreement provided two alternate dispute resolution methods:

(1) binding arbitration with the American Arbitration Association or

(2) resolution under the FAR or CDA dispute resolution procedures.

The parties also agreed that the determinative question was whether the claim or dispute in the present matter related solely to Higgins's obligations as the development manager or whether it involved the interests of the NIH. If the claim or dispute related solely to Higgins's obligations as the development manager, then section 9.2.1. of the agreement provided for binding arbitration with the American Arbitration Association. Alternatively, if the claim or dispute did not relate solely to Higgins's obligations and involved the interests of the NIH, then dispute resolution was subject to the FAR requirements.

The district court determined that the interests of the NIH were involved, and that dispute resolution would have to occur under the FAR requirements. The district court concluded that the dispute at issue, full payment of the change orders, did not relate solely to Higgins's obligations during the construction phase, because Higgins discussed all disputed change orders with NIH, and, ultimately, NIH approved, disapproved, or partially approved the change orders. In reaching this decision, the district court relied heavily upon on an email message sent from Higgins to Skanska's construction manager stating that NIH and Higgins had approved a portion of the sums in question. The district court held that this email was "sufficient to support a finding that the disputes over the increased dollar payment amounts requested in the [Change Orders] involve[d] NIH's interests."

On appeal, Skanska argued that the district court erred in two primary respects by granting the order of injunction in favor of Higgins. First, Skanska claimed that if an agreement contained an arbitration provision, then the district court could not decide substantive issues pertaining to that agreement. Skanska cited *Larsen v. Western States Ins. Agency, Inc.*, 339 Mont. 407, 170 P.3d 956, 2007 MT 270 (2007), where the Montana Supreme Court noted the general proposition that once a district court determined the validity of an arbitration clause, then substantive issues under the agreement were reserved for the arbitrator. Skanska claimed that since there was no dispute over whether the agreement contained an arbitration provision, the arbitrator, instead of the district court, should have decided whether the interests of the NIH were involved. Skanska also cited § 27-5-115(2), MCA, which provided, in relevant part, the following:

> On application, the district court may stay an arbitration proceeding commenced or threatened on a showing that there is no agreement to arbitrate. Such an issue, when in substantial and bona fide dispute, shall be immediately and summarily tried and the stay ordered if the court finds for the applying party. If the court finds for the opposing party, it shall order the parties to proceed to arbitration.

Skanska argued that the district court erred in its application of § 27-5-115(2), MCA, because there was no "substantial and bona fide dispute" over whether the [Agreement] contained an arbitration provision.

Second, Skanska broadly asserted that the district court erred in concluding that the interests of the NIH were involved, and that arbitration could not proceed with the American Arbitration Association. Skanska claimed that the dispute over payment of Change Orders 160 and 260 arose out of the agreement and related solely to Higgins's obligations to Skanska. Moreover, Skanska contended that its demand for arbitration sought damages for claims that could not be included in the

FAR dispute resolution process. Skanska argued that because Higgins partially rejected the claims, Higgins could not submit the claims in good faith to NIH for resolution under the FAR requirements.

In response, Higgins argued that its objection to arbitration was properly raised and decided by the district court as opposed to the arbitrator. Higgins claimed that § 27-5-115, MCA, "mandates the district court to review and to determine whether the subject disputes are subject to AAA arbitration or to the FAR procedures as described in Article 9.2.1" of the Agreement and further, that arbitration proceedings can only be extended to those disputes that the parties actually agreed to arbitrate.

Higgins argued that for an arbitrator to determine Higgins's objection to arbitration, "it must first be shown by clear and unmistakable evidence that [Higgins] agreed to that forum." Because section 9.2.1. stated that claims involving the interests of the NIH would be resolved pursuant to the FAR requirements, Higgins asserted that it neither intended nor agreed to arbitrate Skanska's change order claims. In addition, Higgins contended that the district court correctly concluded that the interests of the NIH were involved. Higgins pointed out that the demand for arbitration only sought payment of the two change orders, and it argued that NIH's interests were clearly involved since the demand sought specific sums of money that NIH would ultimately be required to pay.

State and federal policies generally favor arbitration when a valid arbitration agreement exists between the parties. This support is evidenced by the Federal Arbitration Act,[129.3] which establishes a strong national policy in favor of arbitration. In *AT & T Technologies, Inc., v. Communications Workers of America*,[129.4] the United States Supreme Court stated that arbitration "should not be denied unless it may be said with positive assurance that the arbitration clause is not susceptible of an interpretation that covers the asserted dispute."[129.5]

The presumption in favor of arbitration, however, is not absolute. "[A]rbitration is a matter of contract and a party cannot be required to submit to arbitration any dispute which he has not agreed so to submit."[129.6] Further, unless the parties clearly and unmistakably provide otherwise, "the question of whether the parties agreed to arbitrate is to be decided by the court, not the arbitrator."[129.7] While the laws generally favor arbitration, the intent of the parties remains

[129.3] 9 U.S.C. §§ 1-16 (2006).

[129.4] 475 U.S. 643, 650, 106 S. Ct. 1415, 1419, 89 L. Ed. 2d 648 (1986).

[129.5] *See also* Mitsubishi Motors Corp. v. Soler Chrysler-Plymouth, Inc., 473 U.S. 614, 626, 105 S. Ct. 3346, 3353, 87 L. Ed. 2d 444 (1985) (stating that doubts concerning the scope of arbitrable issues should be resolved in favor of arbitration).

[129.6] United Steelworkers v. Warrior & Gulf Navigation Co., 363 U.S. 574, 582, 80 S. Ct. 1347, 1353, 4 L. Ed. 2d 1409 (1960).

[129.7] *AT & T Technologies*, 475 U.S. at 649, 106 S. Ct. at 1418. The Ninth Circuit Court clarified that: "[a]rbitrability is ordinarily for courts, not arbitrators, to decide unless the parties agree otherwise. Courts should not assume that the parties agreed to arbitrate arbitrability unless there is clear and unmistakable evidence that they did so." PowerAgent v. Electronic Data Systems, 358 F.3d 1187, 1191 (9th Cir. 2004).

paramount to any determination of whether an agreement will be subject to arbitration as opposed to some other dispute resolution forum.

In addition to determining whether the parties "agreed to arbitrate a certain matter, courts generally should apply ordinary state-law principles that govern the formation of contracts."[129.8] In Montana, "[a] contract must be so interpreted as to give effect to the mutual intention of the parties as it existed at the time of contracting, so far as the same is ascertainable and lawful."[129.9] Further, "[w]hen a contract is reduced to writing, the intention of the parties is to be ascertained from the writing alone if possible. . . ."[129.10]

As noted above, the dispute resolution provision set forth in the agreement stated that claims relating solely to the development manager's obligations would be settled in accordance with article 4 of the American Institute of Architects—i.e., through binding arbitration with the American Arbitration Association. Claims that were determined not to relate solely to the development manager's obligations, and which involved the interests of the NIH, would be settled through the FAR requirements. However, section 9.2.1. was silent as to whether the district court or some other forum would decide whether the claim related solely to Higgins's obligations or whether the interests of the NIH were involved. In the absence of such language, the Montana Supreme Court found that it was clear that the district court was the only appropriate forum to make this determination. Since the plain language of the agreement did not designate a forum for deciding whether the interests of the NIH were involved, and further, since the parties did not clearly and unmistakably provide that an arbitrator would decide that question, the court concluded that the district court was the appropriate forum for deciding the dispute resolution forum for Skanska's claims.

The Montana Supreme Court considered whether Skanska's claim or dispute related solely to Higgins's obligations or whether it involved the interests of the NIH. While the agreement provided two alternate dispute resolution methods, it failed to define how the term "interests" should be interpreted.

There was no guidance in the agreement on how to determine if the interests of the NIH were involved. The problem arose from the use of the word "interests," which could be broadly interpreted in a variety of ways as evidenced by the arguments set forth by the parties. Generally "interest" denotes "legal share in something." Blacks Law Dictionary 816 (Bryan A. Garner ed., 7th ed., West 1999). Moreover, "legal interest" includes a pecuniary interest.

A reading of the plain language of the agreement suggested that the FAR or CDA dispute resolution procedures would be invoked when NIH possessed a right or legal share in the dispute or when its pecuniary interests were involved. However, a more straightforward approach would be to determine whether the "claims, disputes or other matters in question" between Higgins and Skanska related solely to Higgins's obligations as the Development Manager under the agreement.

[129.8] State v. Philip Morris, Inc., 352 Mont. 30, 217 P.3d 475, 2009 MT 261 (2009).

[129.9] § 28-3-301, MCA.

[129.10] § 28-3-303, MCA.

As noted by the district court in its order of injunction, Skanska's demand for arbitration sought to be paid "the full amounts still owed by [Higgins]" on Change Orders 160 and 260. The evidence suggested that NIH and Higgins approved partial payment of at least one of the change orders.

There was also testimony at the district court level on Higgins's motion for an injunction that Change Orders 160 and 260 sought additional money from NIH, and that NIH ultimately had all fiscal authority and control over increases or decreases in project costs. There was the evidence that Higgins discussed all disputed change orders with NIH, and that NIH had the final authority to approve, disapprove, or partially approve change orders. It was clear that payment of the change orders did not relate solely to Higgins's obligations as the development manager, because NIH, as the owner and financier of the Integrative Research Facility at the Rocky Mountain Lab, had a clear financial interest in the dispute over payment of the change orders.

The court stated that this conclusion was supported by substantial evidence in the record. Because Skanska's claim or dispute, as referenced in the demand for arbitration, did not relate solely to Higgins's obligations and instead involved the interests of the NIH, the district court did not err in ordering the parties to resolve the dispute under the FAR or CDA dispute resolution procedures, and sustained the trial court's finding that the dispute did not belong in the district court.

§ 21.06 AIA'S GENERAL ARBITRATION CLAUSE

[L] Subcontractor Participation

Page 982, add at end of subsection:

In *Great Western Drywall v. Roel Construction*,[196.1] a subcontractor brought an action against a general contractor for breach of contract and related counts based on alleged underpayment by the general contractor. Roel, the general contractor, counterclaimed against the subcontractor for breach of contract, related counts, and negligence, based on Great Western Drywall's subcontractor's alleged failure to adequately perform, abandonment, and damage to the work of others. The trial court awarded damages to both parties, awarded prejudgment interest to subcontractor, and denied statutory interest and attorney fees to Great Western's subcontractor for the general contractor's alleged failure to timely pay in violation of the prompt payment statutes. Both parties appealed.

The appellate court, affirming in part, and reversing in part, held that the general contractor was entitled to set off its entire award for subcontractor's damage to property against the award of prejudgment interest to subcontractor on subcontractor's breach of contract claim.

The appellate court held that even if the trial court awarded property damages to the general contractor for subcontractor's damage to the work of another subcontractor, under the general contractor's negligence theory, as

[196.1] 166 Cal. App. 4th 761, 83 Cal. Rptr. 3d 235 (2008) (certified for partial publication).

opposed to its breach of contract theory, the general contractor was entitled to set off its entire award against an award of prejudgment interest to the subcontractor on subcontractor's breach of contract claim, where general contractor's damages arose entirely from subcontractor's deficient performance of contract. The setoff served the interests of justice and the purposes of prejudgment interest statute since both parties had claims against each other under the subcontract. The appellate court held that any arbitrary reliance by the trial court on one theory over another should not adversely affect general contractor's setoff rights.[196.2]

Great Western Drywall, Inc. (Great Western) and Roel Construction Co., Inc. (Roel) appealed a judgment entered after a bench trial on their respective actions arising from a construction subcontract. Roel's sole contention was that the court erred by awarding Great Western prejudgment interest on its liquidated contract claims, since Roel's damages exceeded Great Western's damages and entirely offset the interest award.

Great Western challenged the sufficiency of the evidence to support certain items of damages the court awarded Roel. Great Western contended that the court erred as a matter of law by awarding Roel a cleanup contribution not directly attributable to Great Western as a subcontractor, and abused its discretion by denying Great Western prejudgment interest on unliquidated contract claims. Great Western also appealed a postjudgment order in which the court denied it penalty interest under Business and Professions Code section 7108.5 for Roel's failure to promptly make progress payments. The appellate court found in Roel's favor on its appeal, and in Great Western's favor on the cleanup contribution issue. The appellate court affirmed the judgment.

Roel was the general contractor on Renaissance, a condominium project in San Diego. The project consisted of 218 units in two towers. In April 2001 Roel and Great Western entered into a subcontract for Great Western to install metal studs, drywall, lath and plaster, and the exterior insulation finish system at the project. Great Western worked on the project for about two years. The original amount of the subcontract was approximately $4.5 million, but numerous approved change orders increased the amount to more than $7.7 million. Roel did not approve numerous change order requests (CORs) by Great Western. In July 2003, Great Western recorded a mechanic's lien against the Renaissance property.

In September 2003, Great Western sued Roel for breach of contract and related counts, alleging Roel underpaid it on extra work. Roel cross-complained against Great Western for breach of contract and related counts, and negligence. The cross-complaint alleged Roel was damaged by Great Western's failure to adequately perform its work, by its abandonment of the project before its work was complete, and by its damage to the work of others, such as its scratching of window glass. Each breach of contract claim for damage to the work or property of others was alternatively pleaded as a tort claim.

On November 29, 2005, after a four-day bench trial, the court issued a written ruling that awarded Great Western $332,106 and awarded Roel $320,848. The award to Roel included $156,993 for glass replacement, and additional

[196.2] West's Ann.Cal. Civ. Code §§ 3287, 3528.

amounts to repair other property damages Great Western caused. The award did not specify whether Roel's recovery for property damages was on a contract or tort theory. The award to Great Western included $251,263 in CORs that Roel admitted in discovery were undisputed, and $57,534 in prejudgment interest on that amount. The court found there was no prevailing party for the purposes of awarding fees and costs. The ruling ordered Great Western "to prepare a judgment reflecting this decision if a Statement of Decision is not requested by either party."

On December 1, 2005, Roel moved *ex parte* for a stay of entry of judgment, arguing that the award of prejudgment interest to Great Western on the amount of undisputed CORs was improper based on the facts and established case law. No party asked for a statement of decision.

The trial judge, Thomas LaVoy, was scheduled to retire on December 8. On December 5, Judge LaVoy granted a stay pending a noticed hearing requesting a modification of the court's "tentative decision" and a showing of good cause. On December 7, after receiving a joint letter from the parties, Judge LaVoy issued a tentative ruling to amend the trial court's original ruling to delete an amount awarded Roel for plaster repairs.

Also on December 7, Roel and Great Western jointly applied *ex parte* to the independent calendar judge, Ronald Prager, stating that because of Judge LaVoy's imminent retirement, "the parties seek guidance from this court on how it wishes them to proceed with respect to asserting objections to the tentative decision." The *ex parte* hearing was not reported, but on February 1, 2006, Judge Janis Sammartino entered a judgment that awarded Great Western $332,106 on its complaint, which included $57,534 in prejudgment interest on the sum of $251,263, and awarded Roel $315,398 on the cross-complaint.

On June 1, 2006, the parties filed a stipulation for amended judgment. The amendment corrected several computational errors in Judge LaVoy's November 29, 2005 ruling. Further, the amendment decreased the prejudgment interest award to Great Western by $20,572.86, as the parties agreed Roel was entitled to an offset of that amount for contract-based counter-claims. The stipulation reserved to Roel "its objection to the entire award of prejudgment interest."

On June 2, Judge Sammartino entered an amended judgment that awarded Great Western $328,819.69, which included prejudgment interest of $36,961.14, and awarded Roel $326,300.75. Roel filed a notice of appeal on August 4, within 60 days of Great Western's service of notice of the amended judgment.

Great Western then moved for interest and attorney fees under Business and Professions Code section 7108.5, which penalizes a contractor for violating its obligation to timely pay a subcontractor. On July 6, 2006, Judge Prager denied the motion, explaining Great Western's recovery was significantly less than it had requested. The court had previously denied fees and costs unless Great Western presented other factors at posttrial motions, which it did not do. Great Western failed to prove Roel's conduct was not in good faith. On August 21, Great Western filed its notice of appeal of the amended judgment and the postjudgment order.

The court in *Great Western Drywall* stated that prejudgment interest on liquidated damages is an element of compensatory damages. It held that the policy underlying authorization of an award of prejudgment interest is to compensate the injured party, to make that party whole for the accrual of wealth which could have been produced during the period of loss. "[I]n situations where the defendant could have timely paid [a certain] amount and has thus deprived the plaintiff of the economic benefit of those funds, the defendant should therefore compensate with appropriate interest."[196.3] "It has long been settled that [Civil Code] Section 3287 should be broadly interpreted to provide just compensation to the injured party for loss of use of money during the prejudgment period."[196.4]

The court also stated that an award of unliquidated damages to a cross-complainant is a setoff against prejudgment interest awarded a plaintiff for liquidated damages. The *Great Western Drywall* court stated that such an offset is allowed on the theory that the contractor is entitled to interest only on such amount of the use of which he has been deprived during the period of default.

Great Western argued to the appellate court that under the above cases only unliquidated contract damages may be offset from liquidated contract damages. The cases, however, do not consider whether unliquidated tort claims may ever be offset against liquidated contract claims.

The appellate court stated that Great Western erroneously asserted that Roel could have asserted many of its tort claims as breaches of contract, but it chose not to. Roel's cross-complaint alleged property damage claims under the breach of contract and tort counts, and the court's ruling did not reveal which theory it relied on for the property damage award.

Roel cited section 9.5b of the subcontract, which allowed Roel damages for a subcontractor's default under the subcontract, and a 25 percent markup for profit and overhead. The subcontract defined the term "default" as including the failure to diligently perform the work, maintain the schedule, or provide quality workmanship. The court specifically found certain claims were default items and awarded the markup on them, but on the property damage claims the court disallowed a markup, finding they were not default items.

The appellate court ruled against Great Western's assertion that Roel did not submit both breach of contract and tort claims. The trial court could have relied on section 5.7 of the subcontract, which provided that a breach of contract includes a subcontractor's damage to the work of another subcontractor or the property of a third party, or section 15.3f, which requires a subcontractor to protect the work of others and to repair and replace damaged property at its own expense. The court found that Roel relied only on section 9.5b of the subcontract, but Roel specifically raised section 15.3f at trial, and the entire subcontract was admitted into evidence for the court's review. Roel pointed to no election by Roel to pursue a tort theory. It did not appear that a tort theory offered any advantage over a breach of contract theory. The court held that evidence that Roel did not submit property damage claims to Great Western in the form of change orders did not necessarily indicate Roel elected to proceed in tort.

[196.3] Wisper Corp. v. California Commerce Bank, 49 Cal. App. 4th 948, 962, 57 Cal. Rptr. 2d 141 (1996).

[196.4] Gourley v. State Farm Mut. Auto. Ins. Co., 53 Cal. 3d 121, 132, 3 Cal. Rptr. 2d 666, 822 P.2d 374 (1991).

The appellate court concluded that even if the trial court intended to award property damages for negligence, as opposed to breach of contract, Roel was entitled to a setoff of its entire award. It was undisputed that Roel's damages arose entirely from Great Western's deficient performance of the contract, and Roel's mere inclusion of an alternative count for negligence in its cross-complaint, and any arbitrary reliance by the trial court on one theory over another, should not adversely affect Roel's setoff rights. Both parties had claims against each other under the subcontract, thus setoff served the interests of justice and the purposes of the prejudgment interest statute. The appellate court stated that any other ruling would elevate form over substance.[196.5] Because Roel's award exceeded Great Western's award, even after the adjustment to Roel's award for the cleanup contribution, the appellate court held that Great Western could not recover any prejudgment interest.

The appellate court reversed the trial court's judgment insofar as it awarded Great Western $36,961.14 in prejudgment interest on its liquidated contract claims, and it awarded Roel $26,287 for a cleanup contribution. The trial court's judgment was affirmed in all other respects. The trial court's order denying Great Western penalty interest was affirmed.

In *Marina Glecoe v. Neue Sentimental Film AG*,[196.6] a landlord brought an action against an alleged alter ego of a tenant for breach of a lease. While the alleged alter ego's motion for judgment was pending, the landlord filed a voluntary dismissal of the action, with prejudice. The alleged alter ego moved for attorney fees as the prevailing party, pursuant to an attorney fee provision in the lease. The trial court denied attorney fees, and the alleged alter ego appealed.

The appellate court held that: (1) dismissal with prejudice was voluntary, and thus there was no prevailing party for the purposes of recovering attorney fees, and (2) the alleged alter ego's settlement offer, which was held open well short of the period designated in the statute governing offers to compromise, was, once revoked, no longer an offer for purposes of the cost benefits of such statute. The alleged alter ego was not entitled to attorneys' fees based on that statute. The appellate court affirmed the trial court's ruling.

In *Marina Glencoe*, Neue Sentimental Film USA (NSF-USA) leased a commercial property from Marina Glencoe, L.P. The lease contained a provision for an award of attorney fees and costs to the prevailing party "if any action for breach of or to enforce the provisions of this Lease is commenced . . ." NSF-USA fell behind in paying the rent under the lease, and in May, 2003, Marina Glencoe sued NSF-USA and two related companies, Neue Sentimental Film AG (NSF-AG) and Neue Sentimental Film N.Y., Inc. (NSF-NY), for breach of the lease. Marina Glencoe's theory was that each of these related companies also owed rent as the alter egos of NSF-USA. NSF-USA filed bankruptcy in August 2003, and NSF-AG answered the complaint on September 3, 2004.

[196.5] *See* Cal. Civ. Code § 3528; *see* Mechanical Contractors Ass'n v. Greater Bay Area Ass'n, 66 Cal. App. 4th 672, 687, n.5, 78 Cal. Rptr. 2d 225 (1998).

[196.6] 168 Cal. App. 4th 874, 85 Cal. Rptr. 3d 800 (2008), *review denied* (Feb. 11, 2009).

On September 29, 2004, NSF-AG sent a letter to Marina Glencoe offering to settle the case. The offer stated it would be deemed rejected if it was not accepted in writing by October 4, 2004.

The bench trial proceeded only against NSF-AG. At Marina Glencoe's request, the court bifurcated the trial to adjudicate the issue of liability based on alter ego first, and subsequently to determine damages. After Marina Glencoe rested on the alter ego liability phase of trial, NSF-AG moved for judgment pursuant to Code of Civil Procedure section 631.8. The trial court heard arguments but did not rule on the motion that day, explaining that it wanted to review the exhibits, reread deposition testimony, and then give a tentative ruling by the end of the next day. The following day, prior to the court issuing a ruling on the pending motion, Marina Glencoe filed a voluntary dismissal of the action with prejudice.

NSF-AG moved for attorney fees as the prevailing party, pursuant to the attorney fee provision in the lease. The trial court concluded NSF-AG was not entitled to attorney fees under either California Civil Code section 1717 or Code of Civil Procedure section 998.

Civil Code section 1717 (section 1717) provides:

> (a) In any action on a contract, where the contract specifically provides that attorney's fees and costs, which are incurred to enforce that contract, shall be awarded either to one of the parties or to the prevailing party, then the party who is determined to be the party prevailing on the contract, whether he or she is the party specified in the contract or not, shall be entitled to reasonable attorney's fees in addition to other costs.

This action was for breach of a written lease which included the following attorney fee provision:

> [I]f any action for breach of or to enforce the provisions of this Lease is commenced, the court in such action shall award to the party in whose favor a judgment is entered, a reasonable sum as attorneys' fees and costs. The losing party in such action shall pay such attorneys' fees and costs.

After respondent Marina Glencoe dismissed the action, appellant NSF-AG sought attorney fees as the prevailing party under section 1717. However, section 1717 subd. (b)(2) provided that where an action has been voluntarily dismissed, or dismissed pursuant to a settlement of the case, there shall be no prevailing party for purposes of this section.

In this case, the court dismissed the action while the appellant's motion for judgment was pending. The appellant argued that this dismissal should not be deemed a voluntary dismissal. However, the *Glencoe* court stated that it was not the stage of the proceedings which distinguished a voluntary dismissal from an involuntary one, but it was the plaintiff's role in bringing about the dismissal. Because the dismissal was entered at the request of the respondent, it was voluntary, and there was no prevailing party for the purposes of recovering attorneys' fees and costs incurred in defending the contract action under section 1717.

A second ground for appellant's claim for entitlement to an award of attorneys' fees was as costs under California Code of Civil Procedure section 998, because respondent rejected appellant's offer, and failed to achieve a better result at trial. The then-current version of section 998 provided:

> Not less than 10 days prior to commencement of trial . . . , any party may serve an offer in writing upon any other party to the action to allow judgment to be taken or an award to be entered in accordance with the terms and conditions stated at that time . . . If the offer is not accepted prior to trial or arbitration, [or] within 30 days after it is made, whichever occurs first, it shall be deemed withdrawn, and cannot be given in evidence upon the trial or arbitration. If an offer made by a defendant is not accepted and the plaintiff fails to obtain a more favorable judgment or award, the plaintiff shall not recover his or her postoffer costs and shall pay the defendant's costs from the time of the offer.

Although the settlement offer from appellant stated that it was being made under section 998, the offer was written or made on September 29, 2004, and stated that the offer would be deemed rejected if not accepted in writing by October 4, 2004. The court agreed with respondent that this offer did not provide sufficient time for acceptance under section 998, and that it was well short of the statutory period. Once revoked under the terms of the offer, it was no longer an offer for the purposes of the cost benefits under section 998.

[M] Award and Attorneys' Fees

Page 983, add after first full paragraph:

Recoverability of attorneys' fees as damages may be a significant factor in whether a party may litigate, particularly with a smaller principal amount in dispute. In *Herring-Malbis I, LLC, Eastern Shore Centre I, LLC, and Eastern Shore Centre II, LLC v. Temco, Inc.*,[197.1] a contractor brought an action for breach of contract, open account, and mechanic's lien action against a developer. Following arbitration, the circuit court granted contractor's motion for attorneys' fees under the Prompt Payment Act, and developer appealed.

The appellate court held that:

> (1) the parties' arbitration agreement required the contractor to submit its claim for attorney fees under the Prompt Payment Act to arbitration;
>
> (2) *res judicata* barred the contractor from seeking attorney fees under the Prompt Payment Act in the circuit court following the arbitration hearing; and

[197.1] 2009 Ala. Civ. App. LEXIS 537, 2009 WL 3517580 (2009).

(3) the developer was not judicially estopped from asserting that *res judicata* barred contractor's claim for attorney fees. Reversed and remanded with instructions.

In *Herring-Malbis*, the owner appealed from an order of the Baldwin Circuit Court awarding an attorney fee to Temco, Inc. (TEMCO), pursuant to Ala. Code 1975, § 8-29-1 *et seq.*, usually referred to as the Prompt Payment Act. The appellate court reversed the trial court's order awarding an attorney fee to Temco.

Temco sued Herring-Malbis in May 2006, alleging that Temco was owed money "pursuant to the terms and conditions of" contract documents signed by the parties, which included a construction contract and American Institute of Architects AIA Document A201-1997 general conditions, that were incorporated into the parties' agreement by reference in the construction contract. Temco's original complaint sought damages in the amount of $486,303 plus interest and costs under several alternative theories of relief, including breach of contract, open account, account stated, work and labor done, and enforcement of mechanic's lien.

The circuit court granted Herring-Malbis's motion for an order compelling alternative dispute resolution under the terms of the AIA contract.

Pursuant to A201, the parties first attempted to resolve their dispute through mediation, and, when that failed, they arbitrated their dispute through the American Arbitration Association. The arbitration hearing was held on February 19 and 20, 2008. Six days before the hearing, on February 13, 2008, Temco filed a motion to amend its original complaint. The motion sought "to amend the complaint to add a claim under the Prompt Payment Act . . . for reasonable attorneys' fees and expenses pursuant to said statute." The motion maintained that the Prompt Payment Act claim "in no way" affected the issues to be presented to the arbitrator but was a matter to be presented to court in the event that the arbitrator entered an award in favor of Temco. No action was taken on the motion prior to the arbitration hearing.

Temco presented a demand letter to AAA. Herring-Malbis presented an answering statement and counterclaim in the arbitration proceeding. In its demand letter, Temco itemized its claims for relief, which included a request for accumulated interest, but Temco omitted mention in the arbitration documents of any claim for an award of an attorney fee and any mention of particular theories of relief, including any right to relief under the Prompt Payment Act. The demand letter from Temco specified that Temco's principal claim was that it was due relief under the construction contract.

After the hearing, the arbitrator determined that Temco was owed most of what it claimed. The arbitrator also specified that each party would be responsible for its own attorney fees. The arbitration concluded by stating that "[a]ll claims not expressly granted herein are hereby[ ] denied," thereby denying Temco its request for an award of accumulated interest on any of its claims. Temco and Herring-Malbis then filed briefs concerning whether the arbitrator's award should be modified by deleting the reference to attorney fees and by awarding Temco the accumulated interest it sought. No changes to the award were made by the arbitrator. Herring-Malbis timely tendered payment to Temco in satisfaction of the arbitration award.

In April 2008, after the arbitration hearing was held, Herring-Malbis filed with the court a response in opposition to Temco's February 13th, 2008 motion to amend its original complaint. The trial court granted Temco's motion to amend and overruled Herring-Malbis's objections. Temco then filed its amended complaint in May 2008, after which Herring-Malbis moved to dismiss that complaint. The trial court denied the motion, and, following a stipulation by the parties as to the amount of a reasonable attorney fee and a further agreement of the parties to allow the trial court to rule on the matter without a hearing, the trial court entered an order awarding the stipulated attorney fee to Temco, "pursuant to the Prompt Payment Act," in November 2008.

The amended complaint ultimately filed by Temco pleaded the Prompt Payment Act as another alternative legal theory under which Temco sought complete relief. Under Count 10 of the amended complaint, Temco incorporated the remainder of the complaint and demanded relief as to all of its claims against all defendants, which then totaled $561,412.70, specifically including interest, costs, expenses, and attorney fees.

The demand letter written by Temco as a formality required by American Arbitration Association rules in order to initiate the arbitration process did not seek attorney fees or make claims under the Prompt Payment Act, but that omission does not conclusively establish that neither matter was discussed at the hearing.

The AIA contract incorporated into the parties' agreement provided that "any claim arising out of or related to the contract" shall be submitted first to mediation, and in the event mediation fails to resolve the dispute, as occurred here, the claim is to be submitted to arbitration. Where the contract defines "claim," it includes in that definition "other disputes and matters in question between [Herring-Malbis] and [Temco] arising out of or relating to the Contract," a sweepingly broad clause.

When parties include such a broad arbitration clause, they intend the clause to reach all aspects of the relationship. To like effect is the Alabama Supreme Court's holding that arbitration clauses, including the language "arising out of or relating to" that appears in the AIA contract, have broader application than arbitration clauses that omit "or relating to." The AIA contract further states that the party seeking relief in arbitration "must assert in the demand all Claims then known to that party on which arbitration is permitted to be demanded." Finally, the AIA contract further provides that arbitration will proceed under the Construction Industry Arbitration Rules of the American Arbitration Association, of which Rule 44(d) provides that "the award of the arbitrator may include . . . an award of attorneys' fees if all parties have requested such an award or it is authorized by law or their arbitration agreement."

The court held that Temco was required by the arbitration agreement, and by law, to submit its Prompt Payment Act claim, including the request for an award of an attorney fee, to the arbitrator. If, as Temco claimed, the parties did not submit the issue to the arbitrator, whether the arbitrator in fact made a determination concerning Temco's right to an attorney-fee award was immaterial.

In Temco's amended complaint, the Prompt Payment Act was asserted as an additional alternative theory under which Temco demanded complete relief. The entire Prompt Payment Act claim, including the request for an award of an attorney fee, was held to be within the ambit of the contract documents' definition of "claim," quoted above, and Temco was required to submit its Prompt Payment Act claim to the arbitrator, on pain of waiver, in light of the contractual provision stating that parties demanding arbitration "must assert in the demand all Claims then known to that party on which arbitration is permitted to be demanded."

Because Temco indicated its intent to assert the Prompt Payment Act claim in its motion to amend its complaint, filed in the circuit court six days before the arbitration hearing, that claim certainly was "known to" Temco at the time of the arbitration hearing.

The Prompt Payment Act claim also was a claim "on which arbitration is permitted to be demanded," contrary to Temco's assertions (a) that the contract documents provided no legal basis for requesting an award of an attorney fee and (b) that the Prompt Payment Act provided Temco's only legal basis for seeking such an award. For a particular claim or grievance to be excluded from arbitration, the parties must expressly exclude such claim in the arbitration agreement. Temco argued that the AIA contract did not allow the recovery of attorney fees, but it cited as support for this assertion provisions in the AIA contract such as paragraph 3.18.1, under which Temco had agreed not to pursue attorney fees related to a claim "provided that such claim . . . is attributable to bodily injury, sickness, disease or death, or to injury to or destruction of tangible property (other than the Work itself), but only to the extent caused by the negligent acts or omissions of [Temco]."

That provision, as well as other provisions Temco cited, were held inapplicable to this case, which concerned contractual disputes and not claims of bodily injury or property damage. Further, the AIA contract provided at paragraph 13.4.1:

> Duties and obligations imposed by the Contract Document and rights and remedies available thereunder shall be in addition to and not a limitation of duties, obligations, rights and remedies otherwise imposed or available by law.

The appellate court also noted that contractual arbitration terms were, in effect, nothing more than agreements to submit substantive controversies to a particular forum. They did not affect the substantive rights of parties, even when those rights were provided by statute. Temco had the same legal basis for submitting the question of an attorney fee to the arbitrator that it claims to have had for submitting that question to the circuit court.

Being contractually required to assert in arbitration "all claims," and in order to avoid preclusion of claims not asserted, Temco was required to bring all legal theories of relief supported by the "same nucleus of operative facts" to the arbitrator. Otherwise, those claims would have been barred from prosecution by

Temco in a separate action. Under Alabama law, the doctrine of *res judicata* applied to arbitration awards just as it applied to judgments of courts. The elements of *res judicata* are "(1) a prior judgment on the merits, (2) rendered by a court of competent jurisdiction, (3) with substantial identity of the parties, and (4) with the same cause of action presented in both actions." A party is barred from relitigating any claims that were, or that "could have been," brought in the earlier action.

The appellate court held that the arbitrator's award constituted a prior decision on the merits, because the arbitrator provided specific findings, along with underlying bases for those findings, as to liability and the monetary amounts awarded on each substantive claim Temco had presented in its demand for arbitration, and the arbitrator further specified that any relief not expressly granted was denied. It was equally clear that the parties to the arbitration and to the subsequent circuit-court proceeding were identical.

The claims also met the fourth element of *res judicata*, "the same cause of action." The established tests used to determine whether different claims present the same cause of action, whether the primary right and duty or wrong were the same, whether various theories arose from the same nucleus of operative facts, and whether the same evidence supported all the separate actions, were satisfied by both of Temco's complaints. In both the original complaint and the amended complaint, Temco stated its contended facts at the beginning, then listed each claim for relief separately in numbered counts, each of which incorporated the opening statement of facts, and then stated the requested relief under the legal theory. For example, in Temco's amended complaint, Count 10, asserting a claim under the Prompt Payment Act, incorporated the statement of facts and requested a total of $541,567 plus interest, costs, expenses, and attorney fees.

The court rejected Temco's argument that its motion to amend its original complaint, and the circuit court's ruling, amounted to, in effect, an "appeal" of the arbitrator's judgment under the Federal Arbitration Act (FAA) even though pertinent FAA guidelines were not "strictly" followed. The court stated that Temco was correct in noting that the substantive provisions of the FAA governed such issues as the enforceability of arbitration agreements, but the appellate court stated that it was Alabama Code 1975, § 6-6-15, that governed the procedural requirements for appealing from an arbitrator's decision in Alabama. Temco, in its appellate brief, essentially admitted that it did not follow any statutory procedures governing appeals of arbitration awards. Further, the appellate court noted that the AIA contract signed by the parties provided at paragraph 13.1.1 that "[t]he Contract shall be governed by the law of the place where the Project is located"—i.e.,Alabama.

The pertinent provision in Alabama's arbitration statute, § 6-6-15, "contemplates a party's first seeking relief from an [arbitrator's] award in the circuit court," The court held that filing a separate motion six days before the arbitration hearing in a clear attempt to split related claims was not the equivalent of seeking judicial review of an award, as Temco asserted, and in any event recovery was barred by the parties' contract documents, as explained above. The fact that the circuit court viewed and ruled on numerous motions and briefs by the parties, and in so doing considered the same issues the parties raised on appeal, in awarding an attorney fee to Temco was found to be unavailing. The facts did not transform improper motions into a proper appeal. The trial court's failure to recognize that Temco was required to bring its Prompt Payment Act claim before the arbitrator, as reflected in its disposition of this issue, was merely an error of law.

The appellate court noted that the purposes and policies promoted by the doctrine of *res judicata* include the interests of both the public at large and the parties to a particular action in (a) finality of judgments, (b) reducing waste of private and judicial resources, and (c) avoiding inconsistent rulings. Similar results are achieved by the encouragement of arbitration in conformity to the FAA. Permitting Temco to split its claims and to try them in independent proceedings would violate its agreement with Herring-Malbis, statutory and case authority, and public policy.

Temco's final argument asserted that the *res judicata* argument advanced by Herring-Malbis was barred by judicial estoppel, because Herring-Malbis waited to respond to Temco's motion to amend its original complaint until after the arbitration hearing and allegedly failed to itself raise the issue of attorney fees at the arbitration hearing. According to Temco, those alleged omissions by Herring-Malbis amounted to the "adoption" of a "position" that Temco's motion to amend its complaint in the circuit court was a proper procedure by which Temco could seek relief under the Prompt Payment Act.

Because Temco's motion was submitted six days before the arbitration hearing, any deadline under the Rules of Civil Procedure, pursuant to which Herring-Malbis would have been required to file a response to that motion, would have occurred after the arbitration hearing. Herring-Malbis's failure to respond sooner did not amount to the assumption of a position that the circuit court could properly rule on the issue of attorney fees. Herring-Malbis had no duty to raise any of Temco's potential claims for relief before the arbitrator on Temco's behalf. The trial court rejected Temco's argument, because judicial estoppel requires first that a party assume a position in a legal proceeding, and Herring-Malbis's actions here did not amount to the assumption of a position that it later attempted to impeach.

Because the parties' contract documents required Temco to bring its Prompt Payment Act claim before the arbitrator, the appellate court held that Temco was barred under the doctrine of *res judicata* from later asserting that claim in the circuit court.

The appellate court concluded that Temco, having had "an opportunity to litigate" the claim before the arbitrator, was barred from thereafter asserting its Prompt Payment Act claim in the circuit court. The appellate court reversed the trial court's award of an attorney fee, and remanded the cause to the trial court for the entry of a judgment conforming to the arbitration award.

It usually will make sense to present a demand for attorneys' fees as a part of a claim in arbitration, if provided for by contract or statute.

[N] Finality

Page 996, add at end of subsection:

Arbitration in many states, such as California, may be resisted because of the greater finality of an arbitration award. Even where the arbitrator makes an error of law or fact in its finding, the court will generally not disturb the award. In *SouthCoronaCenter, LP v. Keaton*,[242.1] the plaintiff owners Lenny Dykstra and South Corona Center, L.P., a California limited partnership, collectively "Dykstra", hired the defendants, Bruce Keeton and Keeton Construction Co., Inc., collectively "Keeton." as a general contractor to build a gas station and retail center. Dykstra sued Keeton for fraud and other causes of action. The trial court granted Keeton's motion to compel arbitration and granted Keeton's subsequent motion to confirm the arbitration award.

Dykstra appealed contending there was no enforceable arbitration agreement, and the arbitrators erred by excluding a witness declaration. The appellate court affirmed the trial court's judgment compelling arbitration.

In late 2003 and early 2004, Keeton and Dykstra executed three Standard American Institute of Architects (AIA) form contracts. The form contracts incorporated AIA Document A201-1997, General Conditions of the Contract for Construction, which included a mandatory arbitration provision at section 4.6. Dykstra's signature is on two of the contracts. His uncle, Wayne Nielson, the construction manager and Dykstra's owner representative, signed the third contract.

The agreements stated that the basis of the contract payment was a stipulated sum.

Dykstra's complaint against Keeton alleged that Keeton misrepresented that the construction would be performed on a cost-plus basis. When Keeton filed a motion to compel arbitration, Dykstra opposed the motion, arguing that the contracts were not properly authenticated. Dykstra claimed he was not familiar with the General Conditions and its arbitration provisions, and he did not know he had agreed to arbitration. He never expressly denied signing the contracts. The trial court asked Dykstra's lawyer if there was any evidence that Dykstra did not sign the documents. The lawyer evaded the question by insisting Keeton had the burden to authenticate the documents.

The trial court compared Dykstra's signature on the contracts and on his declaration and concluded Dykstra had signed the contracts, and that they were valid. The trial court also determined the contracts incorporated and were governed by the General Conditions and its arbitration provisions. The trial court granted the motion to compel arbitration.

A panel of three arbitrators found that Dykstra, or his authorized representative, had executed the contracts, and payment was based on a stipulated sum, not a cost-plus basis. The arbitrators rejected Dykstra's claims of fraud against

---

[242.1] 2009 WL 426220 (Cal. App. 4th Dist. 2009).

Keeton. The arbitrators found that neither party was entitled to recovery and they should bear the fees and expenses of arbitration equally.

During the arbitration, Dykstra had tried to have admitted the declaration of a former Keeton employee, Melissa Tumale, to support his fraud claims. She had worked for Keeton in 2001 and 2002, before the subject contracts were executed. She contended Keeton had falsified construction bid books on other projects. Tumale could not or would not appear as a witness at the arbitration. Dykstra did not obtain Tumale's testimony by deposition instead. The arbitrators ruled against the admissibility of her declaration.

Dykstra filed a petition to vacate the arbitration award, arguing that the arbitrators erred by excluding Tumale's declaration. The trial court denied the petition on the grounds that the arbitrators had acted within their discretion.

The appellate court used a mixed standard of review to review an order granting a motion to compel arbitration: "Whether the parties formed a valid agreement to arbitrate is determined under general California contract law. Hence, when ruling on a petition to compel arbitration, the superior court may consider evidence on factual issues such as contract formation bearing on the threshold issue of arbitrability. On appeal, the court reviewed the trial court's factual ruling on arbitrability under the substantial evidence test.[242.2] The arbitration agreement itself was subject to a *de novo* review.[242.3] The appellate court stated that the record lacked substantial evidence to support the conclusion no arbitration agreement was formed under principles of general California contract law. The arbitration agreement itself was enforceable.

Dykstra strenuously argued that the contracts at issue were not properly authenticated. Keeton, however, supplied a declaration from the company comptroller about the circumstances of the legitimate formation of the construction contracts. Additionally, the court made its own comparison of Dykstra's signatures on the contracts and his declaration. Finally, Dykstra alleged in his complaint that the parties had entered into the three agreements.

For purposes of a petition to compel arbitration, the appellate court held that it was not necessary to follow the normal procedures of document authentication. "[T]he court shall order the petitioner and the respondent to arbitrate the controversy if it determines that an agreement to arbitrate the controversy exists. . . . Cal. Code of Civ. Proc. §§ 1281.2. The statute did not require the petitioner to introduce the agreement into evidence. A plain reading of the statute indicates that as a preliminary matter the court is only required to make a finding of the agreement's existence, not an evidentiary determination of its validity."[242.4]

Dykstra never seriously disputed the authenticity of the subject agreements or claimed that his signature was a forgery. Instead, he insinuated, without proving or offering to prove, that the agreements were not authentic. Additionally, Dykstra argued that the trial court erred in concluding the subject contracts incorporated

---

[242.2] City of Vista v. Sutro & Co., 52 Cal. App. 4th 401, 407, 60 Cal. Rptr. 2d 488 (1997).

[242.3] NORCAL Mutual Ins. Co. v. Newton, 84 Cal. App. 4th 64, 71, 100 Cal. Rptr. 2d 683 (2000).

[242.4] Condee v. Longwood Mgmt. Corp., 88 Cal. App. 4th 215, 218-19, 105 Cal. Rptr. 2d 597 (2001).

the General Conditions, including the arbitration provision. In *Chan v. Drexel Burnham Lambert, Inc.*,[242.5] the court cited many cases in which "the arbitration provision either appeared on the face of the document, or, was *properly* incorporated by reference. Where the arbitration provision was not set forth on the face of the contract, the contract clearly referred to and identified the incorporated document wherein the arbitration clause appeared."

All three documents executed by Dykstra incorporated the General Conditions and its arbitration provisions. Dykstra claimed that he did not know about the arbitration or understand that it applied to the agreements with Keeton. As a matter of law, however, it was well-settled that, "[a]s a general rule, a party is bound by the provisions of an agreement which he signs, even though he does not read them and signs unaware of their existence."[242.6]

Furthermore, there was evidence in the record about the easy availability of AIA form documents, which are used routinely in construction contracts. As such, substantial evidence showed the arbitration provisions had been incorporated into Dykstra's agreements with Keeton.[242.7]

The appellate court held that the trial court acted within its discretion, and substantial evidence supported its legal determination that an enforceable arbitration agreement existed between the parties.[242.8]

An arbitration award is generally subject to extremely limited review. In *Moncharsh v. Heily & Blase*, the parties' arbitration clause included no provision for an expanded scope of judicial review.[242.9] The appellate court rejected the appellant's claim that the award was, nevertheless, reviewable for error of law on its face causing substantial injustice, a proposition which had some support in case law. The appellate court reaffirmed the general rule that an arbitrator's decision is not ordinarily reviewable for error by either the trial or appellate courts and held that the statutory grounds for review were intended to implement that rule.[242.10]

An exception is provided in Code of Civil Procedure section 1286.2, subdivision (a)(1)(5).[242.11] One ground for vacating an arbitration award is "The rights of the party were substantially prejudiced . . . by the refusal of the arbitrators to hear evidence material to controversy. . . ."[242.12] The evidence must be material and its exclusion substantially prejudicial: "Where, as here, a party complains of excluded material evidence, the reviewing court should generally focus first on prejudice, not materiality. To find substantial prejudice the court

---

[242.5] 178 Cal. App. 3d 632, 641-42, 223 Cal. Rptr. 838, n.4 (1986).

[242.6] King v. Larsen Realty, Inc., 121 Cal. App. 3d 349, 358, 175 Cal. Rptr. 226 (1981), *citing* Madden v. Kaiser Foundation Hospitals, 17 Cal. 3d 699, 710, 131 Cal. Rptr. 882 (1976).

[242.7] Shaw v. Regents of University of California, 58 Cal. App. 4th 44, 54, 67 Cal. Rptr. 2d 850 (1997).

[242.8] Blank v. Kirwan, 39 Cal. 3d 311, 331, 216 Cal. Rptr. 718 (1985); Casella v. SouthWest Dealer Services, Inc., 157 Cal. App. 4th 1127, 1146, 69 Cal. Rptr. 3d 445 (2007); City of Vista v. Sutro & Co., 52 Cal. App. 4th 401, 407, 60 Cal. Rptr. 2d 488 (1997).

[242.9] Moncharsh v. Heily & Blasé, 3 Cal. 4th 1, 7, 10 Cal. Rptr. 2d 183, n.1 (1992).

[242.10] 3 Cal. 4th 1, 27-28; Cable Connection, Inc. v. DIRECTV, Inc., 44 Cal. 4th 1334, 1354-55, 190 P.3d 586 (2008).

[242.11] Formerly Code Civ. Proc.§ 1286.2, subd. (e).

[242.12] Code Civ. Proc. § 1286.2, subd. (a)(5).

must accept, for purposes of analysis, the arbitrator's legal theory and conclude that the arbitrator might well have made a different award had the evidence been allowed."[242.13] The appellate court reviews the trial court's ruling for substantial evidence.

Dykstra was unable to establish the requisite materiality or prejudice. The Tumale declaration was based on events predating the present contracts and, for that reason, had little relevance. As to the issue of prejudice, the record showed that Dykstra made an extensive offer of proof, but the arbitrators were still not persuaded in his favor. In particular, the arbitrators rejected Dykstra's theory that the contracts were to be paid on a cost-plus basis and determined the contracts were for a set fee, the stipulated sum. Therefore, Tumale's declaration that, in years past, Keeton had falsely inflated the subcontractor bids to misrepresent the cost-plus basis was not an issue which could have affected the arbitrators' decision.

The appellate court held that the trial court correctly granted Keeton's motion to compel.

Litigation has also focused on the interplay between a settlement and arbitration award. In *Wade v. Schrader*,[242.14] after a chief executive officer (CEO) was fired and his stock was revoked, he brought an action against the shareholders of the corporation for breach of fiduciary duty and conversion, seeking damages for the value of his stock. The CEO settled with the minority shareholders and engaged in binding arbitration with the majority shareholders. The arbitration decision resulted in an award less than the amount the CEO had received from the minority shareholders. The majority shareholders moved for an order compelling acknowledgment of satisfaction of judgment. The trial court granted the motion for satisfaction of judgment, except as to the portion of the judgment representing costs. The CEO appealed.

The appellate court affirmed the trial court, holding that: (1) a settlement credit could be applied to reduce liability under a judgment on an arbitration award; (2) the majority shareholders were entitled to a settlement credit for the minority shareholders' pretrial settlements with the CEO; (3) the majority shareholders were not precluded from raising the issue of a settlement credit by their failure to submit the issue to the arbitrator; (4) the order applying a settlement credit to the judgment did not result in a double credit for settlement; and (5) the motion to compel acknowledgment of satisfaction of judgment was an acceptable procedure to obtain an order applying settlement credit to judgment.

Plaintiff Thomas Wade sued defendants Donald and Jean Schrader (Schraders) and others, claiming that defendants had wrongfully deprived Wade of his stock in Enterprise Broadcasting Corporation (EBC). Wade settled his claims against several defendants, and those settlements were judicially determined to have been in good faith under Code of Civil Procedure sections 877, 877.6. Wade's claims against the Schraders were resolved through binding arbitration.

[242.13] Hall v. Superior Court, 18 Cal. App. 4th 427, 439, 22 Cal. Rptr. 2d 376 (1993).

[242.14] 168 Cal. App. 4th 1039, 85 Cal. Rptr. 3d 865 (2008).

Although the arbitrator ruled in Wade's favor, the amount of the award was less than the total Wade had received from the settling codefendants.

After the arbitrator's award was reduced to judgment, the Schraders moved in the trial court for an order compelling satisfaction of the judgment. The Schraders maintained that the proceeds from Wade's pre-arbitration settlements completely offset the judgment against them. The trial court granted the motion, in part. Wade appealed. Wade argued that the order impermissibly modified the arbitration award. The appellate court concluded that the order was an appropriate exercise of the superior court's discretion in enforcing a money judgment, and affirmed the trial court.

In *Schrader*, the Schraders were directors and majority shareholders of EBC, a start-up company planning to make high-definition theater installations for shopping malls. Wade was the company's CEO. With the business on the verge of failure, Wade was fired and his EBC stock was revoked. Wade sued the Schraders and the minority shareholders for breach of fiduciary duty and conversion, seeking damages for the value of the stock, which Wade alleged to be more than $40 million. After Wade settled with the minority shareholders, Wade and the Schraders entered into an oral agreement under California Code of Civil Procedure section 664.6 to submit the "disputes presently pending" in the superior court to binding arbitration. The parties agreed that "all rights and claims" they had as a result of the pending litigation would be resolved by the arbitration.

At the arbitration of Wade's claims against the Schraders, the arbitrator concluded that the Schraders had not breached a fiduciary duty. The stock Wade had acquired when the company was founded was given to him as a gift from the Schraders. Revocation of the stock amounted to a conversion of Wade's property. In determining the value of the stock, the arbitrator rejected the testimony of Wade's expert, who had valued the shares in the millions of dollars. The arbitrator explained:

> Under the circumstances valuation is difficult. . . . There was no real market for the shares other than the interested parties. . . . [the Schraders] believed there was some value to the company just as they had believed when it was still in its conception stage. For this reason I find the value to be what they had placed on the value of founders stock at that time. It was ".02 cents penny stock" then, as stock with little present development but great expectations; it is still ".02 cents penny stock" as stock with substantial development potential but little present value. This was a gift from the Schraders to Wade. The value of the stock was set at $75,514.04.

The arbitrator ruled:

> An award shall be entered in favor of Wade and against [the] Schrader[s] in the amount of $75,514.04 and simple interest at the rate of 7% from March 2002 to the date of the final award. . . . Wade is prevailing party and entitled to costs as against Schrader.

The award specified the procedure Wade was to use to claim costs and that, "Thereafter a final award shall be entered."

Wade moved in the trial court to confirm the award. The Schraders raised no substantive objection. The trial court granted the motion and entered judgment in favor of Wade and against the Schraders for $125,917.23. This represented the $75,514.04 arbitration award, interest on the award, and $26,175.39 in costs.

After judgment was entered, the Schraders asked Wade to file an acknowledgment of satisfaction of the judgment, based upon a credit they claimed they were owed due to Wade's pre-arbitration settlements. Wade had received a total of $170,000 through good-faith settlements with the minority shareholders. Wade did not dispute the fact of the settlement or the amount of the good-faith settlements. Nevertheless, he refused to acknowledge satisfaction of the judgment, and he opposed the Schraders' motion for an order compelling acknowledgment of satisfaction of judgment, on the ground that it was, in effect, a belated attempt to correct the arbitration award.

The trial court granted the Schraders' motion to acknowledge the satisfaction of judgment, in part. The trial court noted that in *Syverson v. Heitmann*,[242.15] "[t]he settlement completely offset the damages assessed against the nonsettling defendant, and the settlement reduced the judgment to zero by operation of law." Section 877 allows settling parties to receive a finding from the court that their settlements are in good faith, and that claims for implied indemnity by nonsettling defendants are barred.

The only difference in this case was that the judgment included an award of costs, which would not be offset by the prior good-faith settlements. Accordingly, the trial court concluded that the Schraders were entitled to a partial satisfaction of the judgment, leaving unsatisfied only the portion of the judgment attributable to costs. The court observed that:

> . . . it would have been perhaps wiser, at the time of confirmation . . . of the arbitration award to judgment, to have brought this up, rather than to wait, but in any event, that seems to be the most appropriate way to handle this.

Wade appealed.

On the issue of the section 877 good faith settlement, the appellate court stated that Wade's appeal boiled down to two questions: (1) do the arbitration statutes[242.16] prohibit the use of a section 877 settlement credit to satisfy a judgment based upon an arbitration award; and (2) does section 877 permit the nonsettling defendants to wait until after judgment to take advantage of the credit afforded them by section 877?

The *Schrader* court held that there was no case precisely on point, but that the plaintiff was entitled as a matter of right under rules of court and relevant statutes to recover costs. The prevailing party in this matter was entitled to file a

[242.15] 71 Cal. App. 3d 106, 214 Cal. Rptr. 581 (1985).

[242.16] Cal. Civ. Proc. Code §§ 1280 *et seq.*

memorandum of costs in this matter, although the arbitrator had failed to include costs in his award.

The *Schrader* court also held that nonsettling defendants were entitled, as a matter of right, to reduce their liability to plaintiff in the amount of the credit provided by section 877. This was described by the *Schrader* court as a "fundamental feature" of the good faith settlement process.

Wade argued that the arbitrator took the settlement credit into consideration when the arbitrator made the award of $75,514.4 and that applying the credit at this time modified the award and gave the Schraders a double credit. The appellate court refused to accept this argument, stating that the Schraders had no duty to ask the arbitrator to rule upon the settlement credit. Since they did not, the arbitrator's award did not take it into consideration. The appellate court found that the arbitrator's award was in the exact amount of the value of the stock, which demonstrated that the award was not reduced by the amount of the settlement credit.

Although no statute spells out how to claim a section 877 credit, such as there is for claiming costs, the appellate court in *Schrader* described the settlement credit as being like an equitable setoff, and it was to be treated as such. The appellate court found that the procedure used by the Schraders, compelling an acknowledgment of satisfaction of a judgment, was an entirely acceptable procedure for balancing offsetting judgments.

The *Schrader* court concluded that the use of the acknowledgment and satisfaction process did not modify the arbitrator's award. It was held to be an acceptable method of securing the settlement credit secured by a nonsettling defendant, under section 877. When Wade refused to acknowledge that the credit was available to satisfy the judgment, the Scharders took the next most logical step and asked the trial court to compel the acknowledgment to which they were entitled. Because the fact and amount of the settlement credit were not disputed, the appellate court found that the trial court did not abuse its discretion in compelling Wade to acknowledge partial satisfaction of the judgment.

Chapter 22

INSURANCE AND BONDS

§ 22.03 COMPREHENSIVE/COMMERCIAL GENERAL LIABILITY INSURANCE

[B] Duration: Completed Operations

Page 1031, add after first full paragraph:

Steven G.M. Stein and Ronald O. Wietecha, in their article, *A Comparison of ConsensusDOCS to the AIA Form Construction Contract Documents*,[43.1] state that the owner under the AIA documents does not enjoy completed operations coverage as part of the owner's insurance requirements, and the owner is not automatically entitled to be named an additional insured under the contractor's general liability policy. A201-2007 Sec. 11.1.4, ConsensusDOCS 200 Para. 10.5. ConsensusDOCS 200 also provides for mutual indemnification, whereas the A201 only requires the contractor to indemnify the owner for the contractor's negligence, regardless of the contributing negligence of the owner. ConsensusDOCS 2001 Para. 10.1.2. Also, under ConsensusDOCS 200 both parties have the right to be reimbursed for defense costs attributable to the negligence of the other party. A201-2007 Sec. 3.18.1, ConsensusDOCS 200 Paras. 10.1.1 and 10.1.2.

[E] Owner Insurance

Page 1041, add at end of subsection:

In *Advantages of the ConsensusDOCS Construction Contracts*,[58.1] the authors describe how project insurance is handled differently. To balance the conflicting needs of contractors and owners regarding insurance, the ConsensusDOCS give the parties options regarding additional insured coverage. An owner may decide not to require additional insurance. If the owner requires additional insurance, a menu is provided which includes additional insured status for ongoing and completed operations that is limited to the contractor's negligence. In addition, an Owners and Contractors Protective (OCP) liability insurance policy may be used for ongoing operations, alone or in combination with

---

[43.1] Steven G.M. Stein & Ronald O. Wietecha, *A Comparison of ConsensusDOCS to the AIA Form Construction Contract Documents*, *The Construction Lawyer*, Vol. 29, No. 1, Winter 2009.

[58.1] Larry D. Harris & Brian M. Perlberg, *Advantages of the ConsensusDOCS Construction Contracts*, by *The Construction Lawyer*, Vol. 29, No. 1, Winter 2009.

additional insured coverage for completed operations. The cost of additional insurance is to be paid by the owner. ConsensusDOCS 200, Para. 12.5.

In *Freedman v. State Farm Insurance Co.*,[58.2] an insured brought an action against its homeowner insurer for breach of contract, breach of the implied covenant of good faith and fair dealing, and negligence. The trial court granted summary judgment for the insurer. The insured appealed.

The appellate court affirmed the trial court's grant of summary judgment. It held that:

1. damage from corrosion and water leakage was due to a nail driven through a pipe, which was excluded from coverage;
2. the water leakage was "continuous or repeated";
3. the exclusion from coverage for leakage was not limited to normal deterioration of plumbing system; and
4. mold damage due to water leakage was held not to be covered under the homeowner's policy.

Under a homeowner's insurance policy endorsement covering losses caused by mold if such losses were "caused by or directly resulted from" either a specified peril under the personal property coverage or a peril not otherwise excluded, damage from mold caused by the excluded peril of continuous water leakage, due to a drywall contractor's negligence, was not covered.

In *Freedman*, a contractor remodeling a bathroom in the Freedmans' home drove a nail through a pipe while hanging new drywall. The nail in the pipe apparently caused no leak at the time, It went unnoticed until years later, when corrosion around the nail caused a leak and extensive water damage. The Freedmans' insurer, State Farm Insurance Company, denied their claim. The Freedmans filed suit, and the parties filed cross-motions for summary judgment on the basis of jointly stipulated facts. The superior court granted State Farm's motion, denied that of the Freedmans, and entered judgment for the defense.

The Freedmans appealed, arguing that the contractor's negligence was the efficient proximate cause of their loss and that the loss was a covered peril, so the loss was covered. The appellate court refused to accept the Freedmans' argument for coverage, stating that it was based on a form of analysis that has been superseded by the California Supreme Court's decision in *Julian v. Hartford Underwriters Insurance Co.*[58.3]

The parties submitted their cross-motions for summary judgment on the basis of the following stipulated facts. The Freedmans owned a home insured under a homeowner's policy issued by State Farm. The policy provided "all-risk" coverage for the Freedmans' dwelling (Section I, Coverage A) and "specified-peril" coverage for their personal property (Section I, Coverage B). The policy stated:

[58.2] 173 Cal. App. 4th 957, 93 Cal. Rptr. 3d 296, 2009 WL 1202559 (Cal. App. 2d Dist. 2009).
[58.3] 35 Cal. 4th 747, 27 Cal. Rptr. 3d 648 (2005).

> We insure for accidental direct physical loss to the property described in Coverage A, except as provided in SECTION I—LOSSES NOT INSURED.

Paragraph 2 of Section I—Losses Not Insured provided:

> We do not insure for any loss to the property described in Coverage A which is caused by one or more of the items below, regardless of whether the loss occurs suddenly or gradually, involves isolated or widespread damage, arises from natural or external forces, or occurs as a result of any combination of these: . . . g. wear, tear, marring, scratching, deterioration, inherent vice, latent defect or mechanical breakdown; h. corrosion, electrolysis or rust

Paragraph 4 of Section I—Losses Not Insured provided:

> We do not insure under any coverage for any loss which is caused by one or more of the items below, regardless of whether the event occurs suddenly or gradually, involves isolated or widespread damage, arises from natural or external forces, or occurs as a result of any combination of these: . . . c. Water Damage, meaning: . . . (4) continuous or repeated seepage or leakage of water or steam from (c) plumbing system . . .

Paragraph 5 of Section I—Losses Not Insured provided:

> We do not insure for loss described in paragraphs 2, 3 and 4 immediately above regardless of whether one or more of the following: (a) directly or indirectly cause, contribute to or aggravate the loss; or (b) occur before, at the same time, or after the loss or any other cause of the loss: . . . a. conduct, act, failure to act, or decision of any person, group, organization or governmental body whether intentional, wrongful, negligent, or without fault; b. defect, weakness, inadequacy, fault or unsoundness in: (2) design, specifications, workmanship, construction, grading, compaction; . . . of any property (including land, structures, or improvements of any kind) whether on or off the **residence premises** . . .

The appellate court referred to these provisions in paragraph 5 as the "third-party negligence" provisions of the Freedmans' policy.

Around 2000, the Freedmans' home was repiped, and an upstairs bathroom was remodeled, including the replacement of drywall to cover the new piping. On or about August 12, 2005, extensive water leakage was discovered in the upstairs bathroom wall. The pipe was corroded around the points of entry of the nail, and water was released through that area of corrosion.

A damage restoration company discovered mold both upstairs and downstairs. On or about August 15, 2005, the Freedmans submitted a claim to State Farm. State Farm conducted an inspection and, on or about August 25, 2005, denied the claim.

The Freedmans filed suit against State Farm, alleging claims for breach of contract, breach of the implied covenant of good faith and fair dealing, and for negligence. The parties filed cross-motions for summary judgment based on jointly stipulated facts.

The identity of the efficient proximate cause of the Freedmans' loss was not one of the stipulated facts. State Farm contended that the identity of the efficient proximate cause of the loss did not matter, because each of the possible efficient proximate causes was an excluded peril. Corrosion and seepage or leakage of water were excluded. Third-party negligence was excluded whenever it interacted with an excluded peril (such as corrosion or seepage or leakage of water). On the other hand, the Freedmans contended that the contractor's negligence in driving the nail through the pipe was a covered peril and was the efficient proximate cause of their loss.

The trial court granted State Farm's motion and denied the Freedmans', reasoning that under the stipulated facts "what [p]laintiff contends was the efficient proximate cause of the loss sued upon herein was, under the relevant State Farm policy, excluded as a [l]oss [n]ot [i]nsured." The trial court further concluded that "none of the resulting damage, such as the mold, would be covered . . . under the terms of the State Farm policy."

Under the efficient proximate cause doctrine, "[w]hen a loss is caused by a combination of a covered and specifically excluded risks, the loss is covered if the covered risk was the efficient proximate cause of the loss," but "the loss is not covered if the covered risk was only a remote cause of the loss, or the excluded risk was the efficient proximate, or predominate cause." *State Farm Fire & Casualty Co. v. Von Der Lieth.*[58.4] The efficient proximate cause of a loss is the "predominant" or "most important" cause of the loss.

The Freedmans contend that third-party negligence, the negligence of the contractor in driving the nail through the pipe, is the efficient proximate cause of their loss and is a covered peril under their policy's all-risk coverage of their dwelling. On that basis, they conclude that the loss must be covered.

In *Julian v. Hartford Underwriters Insurance Co.*,[58.5] the plaintiffs had an all-risk homeowner's policy that excluded the peril of earth movement and excluded the peril of weather conditions whenever weather conditions interacted with an excluded peril to cause the loss. Heavy rains caused a landslide that damaged the Julians' home. When the insurance carrier denied coverage, the Julians sued the insurer. The trial court granted the insurer's motion for summary judgment, concluding that "the policy excluded each of the possible efficient proximate causes of the loss."

The California Supreme Court in *Julian* affirmed. That court concluded that the exclusion of weather conditions that interact with an excluded peril was enforceable as applied to "a loss occasioned by a rain-induced landslide."

The *Freedman* court held that *Julian* applied. The third-party negligence provisions of the Freedmans' policy excluded third parties' negligent conduct and defective workmanship whenever they interacted with an excluded peril, just as the Julians' policy excluded weather conditions whenever they interacted with an excluded peril. Corrosion and continuous or repeated seepage or leakage of water were held to be excluded perils under the Freedmans' policy, just as earth

---

[58.4] 54 Cal. 3d 1123, 1131-32, 2 Cal. Rptr. 2d 183 (1991).

[58.5] 35 Cal. 4th 747, 27 Cal. Rptr. 3d 648, 110 P.3d 903 (2005).

movement was excluded under the Julians' policy. The Freedmans' policy excluded contractor-negligence-induced corrosion and contractor-negligence-induced continuous or repeated seepage or leakage of water, just as the Julians' policy excluded a rain-induced landslide. The Freedmans introduced no evidence that contractor negligence caused their loss in any way apart from the nail's role in triggering corrosion and a water leak, just as the Julians introduced no evidence that weather conditions caused their loss in any way apart from rain's role in triggering a landslide. The appellate court held that the Freedmans' loss was not covered, just as the Julians' loss was not covered.

§ 22.04 PROPERTY INSURANCE

[B] Coverage: Insured Perils

Page 1073, add at end of subsection:

In *TMW Enterprises, Inc., Shain Park Associates, L.L.C v. Federal Insurance Co.*,[116.1] an insured brought an action against a property insurer, seeking a declaratory judgment that it was entitled to insurance coverage and money damages. The district court granted summary judgment in favor of the insurer. The appellate court upheld the trial court, finding that there was no coverage under the policy, because the faulty workmanship property insurance policy exclusion applied to the water infiltration damage at issue in the case. While the faulty workmanship exclusion applied to loss or damage "caused by or resulting from" construction defect, the "ensuing loss" provision clarified that the insurance company could not use the exclusion to avoid coverage for losses remotely traceable to an excluded cause.

In the case, TMW bought a recently constructed condominium and retail building, that it insured with Federal Insurance. The insurance policy was an "all-risk" policy, which covered any "direct physical loss or damage" to the property unless "caused by or resulting from" an excluded peril. Among the policy exclusions was as follows:

> This insurance does not apply to loss or damage (including the costs of correcting or making good) caused by or resulting from any faulty, inadequate or defective:
>
> . . .
>
> > design, specifications, plans, workmanship, repair, construction, renovation, remodeling, grading, compaction;
> >
> > . . .
>
> of part or all of any property on or off the premises shown in the Declarations.
>
> This Planning, Design, Materials Or Maintenance exclusion does not apply to ensuing loss or damage caused by or resulting from a peril not otherwise excluded.

[116.1] 619 F.3d 574 (6th Cir. 2010).

Contractors that TMW hired to renovate the building's exterior discovered that the original builder had improperly constructed the exterior walls, leaving them vulnerable to water infiltration and that water had, indeed, entered the facility, "weakening the structural integrity of the building" by corroding its steel structure. After confirming that similar construction and deterioration problems plagued all four exterior walls, the contractors warned TMW that, without proper repair, the building faced "potential mold growth" and "catastrophic" structural failure due to moisture exposure. The repairs required TMW to remove the building's undamaged exterior masonry. TMW estimated that it has spent $3.9 million so far to repair the building.

TMW notified Federal Insurance of the damage to the building, but Federal Insurance denied TMW's claim. Federal Insurance attributed the damage to "construction defects" and "wear and tear," both of which the policy excluded. TMW sought a declaratory judgment that it was entitled to insurance coverage and money damages. The district court held that TMW was not entitled to coverage, and the appellate court affirmed.

The insurance policy provided that all physical loss was covered unless an exclusion applied. The key exclusion barred coverage for "loss or damage . . . caused by or resulting from . . . faulty . . . workmanship . . . [or] construction." Both parties' investigators agreed that the original builder improperly constructed the building's exterior. The faulty construction included "haphazardly installed" Tyvek building wrap, missing or improper flashing along the siding's edges and joints and a lack of "weep holes," which "allow moisture in the wall cavity to drain out." The investigators also agreed, and the parties did not dispute, that this faulty workmanship caused the water infiltration that damaged the building's structural steel, fireproofing and insulation. The undisputed facts established that the claimed damage was "caused by or resulting from . . . faulty . . . workmanship . . . [or] construction."

TMW contended that there was more to the faulty workmanship exclusion than the "caused by or resulting from . . . faulty . . . workmanship . . . [or] construction" language. At the end of that exclusion and the other three that went with it, the contract said that all four exclusions did "not apply to ensuing loss or damage caused by or resulting from a peril not otherwise excluded." It may be, as TMW acknowledged, that faulty workmanship allowed water to seep into the walls. But the intruding water, it argued, nonetheless, amounted to a "peril not otherwise excluded," because the water caused some of the damage, and water-related damage is not otherwise specifically excluded. According to TMW, this made it an "ensuing loss" and thus a covered loss.

The court, however, disagreed. Based on TMW's argument, instead of carving out an exception to this exclusion, this theory of interpretation would create a virtual, if not complete, exclusion of the exclusion. When a policy excluded "loss or damages . . . caused by or resulting from . . . faulty . . . workmanship . . . [or] construction" of a building, it should come as no surprise that the botched construction will permit the elements, such as water, air, or dirt, to enter the structure and inside of the building and eventually cause damage to both. TMW's chain of reasoning is that water technically was the final causative agent of the damage, as opposed to the faulty construction. That "water damage" was not specifically excluded from the policy. TMW's argument was that coverage accordingly applied, and essentially undid the exclusion.

As an "all-risk" policy, this insurance policy basically covered everything unless specifically excluded. That means the number of possibilities for last-in-time "but for" causes of damage were nearly unlimited. To say that the risk was not covered because other elements or natural forces were the last causative agents of the damage, though to be sure utterly foreseeable causes of the damages, was to eliminate the exclusion. It was exceedingly strange to think that a single phenomenon that was clearly an excluded risk under the policy was meant to become compensable because in a philosophical sense it could also be classified as water damage.

But if the "ensuing loss" clause did not apply, TMW asked, doesn't that make it superfluous, empty words with no independent function? No. There were two possible functions served by the clause, both sufficient to defeat TMW's argument. One was that the clause meant simply that what was not excluded was covered. The four exclusions spelled out when coverage did not apply, and the caveat at the end reminded us that if an exclusion did not apply, then coverage existed. Thus, the redundant language was not fatal when it came to insurance contracts, including this contract.

The "ensuing loss" clause also fairly could be construed as a causation-in-fact-breaking link in coverage exclusions, establishing that independent, non-foreseeable losses caused by faulty construction were covered. ("[T]he 'ensuing loss' clause [applies] in those rare cases where the reasonable damage expected to be caused by faulty workmanship leads to another peril that causes damage beyond that normally expected.")

As the district court viewed the dispute, the identification of the faulty workmanship exclusion, together with undisputed factual evidence that there was a "but for" causal relationship between the damages and this exclusion, meant that summary judgment for the insurer was in order. In view of the reality that the "ensuing loss" clause, under either way of looking at it, did not permit the insurer to deny coverage for losses not *proximately* caused by faulty workmanship, and in view of the fact that TMW did not appear to have an opportunity to seek coverage for such losses, the appellate court found that TMW should be given an opportunity to do so on remand.

The appellate court stated that the canon requiring the court to construe ambiguous insurance contracts against the drafter made no difference here for several reasons: (1) a disagreement among three judges about whether a contractual provision was ambiguous did not establish that it was ambiguous; (2) a case, arising under another state's laws, involving differing contractual provisions and, above all, not including a comparable exclusion did not establish contractual ambiguity; (3) the anti-redundancy canon by itself could not create contractual ambiguity; (4) TMW did not establish the required two reasonable, independently supportable interpretations, because the key premise of its interpretation (resolving contractual redundancies) was a false one, and a premise at any rate with which it could not comply.

In *Jalapenos, LLC v. GRC General Contractor,*[116.2] a property owner brought an action against a general contractor, asserting claims for breach of contract and negligence, asserting that an employee of the subcontractor to the general contractor caused a fire on premises, which was in the process of being remodeled by the owner for use as a restaurant. The contractor filed a motion for summary judgment, which was granted by the trial court, and the owner appealed.

The appellate court affirmed the superior court's holding that: (1) the insurance procurement provision of the contract, rather than the contract's indemnification provision, applied to determine who was liable for the loss sustained to the owner's premises;(2) a waiver of subrogation clause contained in the contract did not violate either public policy or state common law principles; and (3) there was no basis for looking to parol evidence outside the express language of contract. Thus, the appellate court affirmed the trial court's grant of summary judgment.

In the case, the owner hired a contractor to convert a former fast-food establishment into a Mexican-style restaurant. The contract was a standard form agreement generated by the American Institute of Architects (AIA) and is routinely used in remodeling and renovating construction projects throughout this country (AIA Forms A101-1997 and A201-1997). Section 11.4.1 of the contract stated the owner would purchase and maintain property insurance written on a builder's risk "all-risk" policy, the purpose of which was to insure against the peril of fire. Section 11.4.1.2 stated that if owner did not intend to purchase such insurance, the owner was to so inform the contractor in writing before the work began. If the contractor were damaged by the owner's failure to buy or maintain the insurance without notifying the contractor in writing, the owner would then bear all reasonable costs attributable to such failure to buy or maintain the insurance section 11.4.1.2. The contract further stated owner waived all rights of action against contractor for loss of the use of owner's property, including consequential losses due to fire or other hazards, however caused (section 11.4.3).

After the contractor began work on the premises there was a fire that significantly damaged the premises preventing the contractor from completing the renovations.

The record undisputedly revealed that the owner did not purchase and maintain the all-risk property insurance, and that he failed to notify the contractor in writing that he had not purchased or maintained insurance as required by the contract. The court agreed with the contractor that the owner's failure to comply with these provisions barred the owner from recovering any damages as a matter of law. The owner had argued that the applicable contractual provisions (section 11.4 *et seq.*) did not determine the assignment of liability for damages arising from the performance of the contractor's or subcontractor's work. Instead, the owner argued that section 3.18.1 pertaining to indemnification should control the outcome. The owner also argued that section 11.4 *et seq.* as interpreted by the contractor was contrary to public policy, because it purported to allow the owner to contract away

[116.2] 207 Pa. Super. 391, 939 A.2d 925 (2007).

its right to sue the contractor for its alleged negligence in starting the fire, and the owner, in signing this contract, was a party with unequal bargaining power.

Appellant's first assignment of error asserted that the lower court erred when it determined that section 11.4 of the standard AIA contract ("Property Insurance") governed the dispute, such that the contractor's claims were precluded on the basis of that section's mutual "waiver of subrogation" provision. The relevant provisions of section 11.4 of the standard AIA contract, which were not modified by the contracting parties in this litigation, read as follows:

> 11.4 PROPERTY INSURANCE
>
> 11.4.1 Unless otherwise provided, *the Owner shall purchase and maintain,* in a company or companies lawfully authorized to do business in the jurisdiction in which the Project is located, *property insurance written on a builder's risk "all-risk" or equivalent policy form in the amount of the initial Contract Sum,* plus value of subsequent Contract modifications and cost of materials supplied or installed by others, comprising total value for the entire Project at the site on a replacement cost basis without optional deductibles. Such property insurance shall be maintained, unless otherwise provided in the Contract Documents or otherwise agreed in writing by all persons and entities who are beneficiaries of such insurance, until final payment has been made as provided in Paragraph 9.10 or until no person or entity other than the Owner has an insurable interest in the property required by this Paragraph 11.4 to be covered, whichever is later. This insurance shall include interests of the Owner, the Contractor, Subcontractors and Sub-subcontractors in the Project.
>
> 11.4.1.1 *Property insurance shall be on an "all-risk" or equivalent policy form* and shall include, without limitation, insurance against the perils of fire (with extended coverage) and physical loss or damage. . . .
>
> 11.4.1.2 If the Owner does not intend to purchase such property insurance required by the Contract and with all of the coverages in the amount described above, the Owner shall so inform the Contractor in writing prior to commencement of the Work. . . . If the Contractor is damaged by the failure or neglect of the Owner to purchase or maintain insurance as described above, without so notifying the Contractor in writing, then the Owner shall bear all reasonable costs properly attributable thereto.
>
> 11.4.3 Loss of Use Insurance. The Owner, at the Owner's option, may purchase and maintain such insurance as will insure the Owner against loss of use of the Owner's property due to fire or other hazards, however caused. The Owner waives all rights of action against the Contractor for loss of use of the Owner's property, including consequential losses due to fire or other hazards however caused.
>
> . . .
>
> 11.4.7 Waivers of Subrogation. The Owner and Contractor waive all rights against (1) each other and any of their subcontractors, sub-subcontractors, agents and employees, each of the other. . . . for damages caused by fire or

> other causes of loss to the extent covered by property insurance obtained pursuant to this Paragraph 11.4 . . . except such rights as they have to proceeds of such insurance held by the Owner as fiduciary. . . . A waiver of subrogation shall be effective as to a person or entity even though that person or entity would otherwise have a duty of indemnification, contractual or otherwise, did not pay the insurance premium directly or indirectly, and whether or not the person or entity had an insurable interest in the property damaged.

The lower court determined that the clear purpose of contract provisions like those in section 11.4 "is to shift the risk of loss away from the owner and the contractor" and place it upon the "[owner's] insurer, or on the [owner] if the [owner] does not obtain insurance and fails to notify [the contractor] of this fact, a failure which deprive[s] [the contractor] of the opportunity to itself obtain such insurance." Because section 11.4 governed, the lower court concluded that section 11.4.7, the contract's "waiver of subrogation" provision, precluded the owner's claims against the contractor and, thus, the contractor was entitled to summary judgment as a matter of law.

The lower court held that the plaintiff's claims were barred by the AIA contract provisions because of the plaintiff's failure to maintain the required insurance. Acknowledging that there were few cases interpreting this section of the AIA contract, the court cited*Knob Noster R-VIII School District v. Dankenbring,*[116.3] as "on all fours" with this case. That court, in turn, cited *Valley Bank v. E.L. Crawford Construction, Inc.*,[116.4] which determined that the plain language of the clause prevented an owner from pursuing a claim against a contractor and subcontractor for damage allegedly caused by the contractor and subcontractor to the extent that the damage was covered by property insurance the contract required the owner to obtain. A contractual requirement that one party provide property insurance for all of the parties was significant in determining the intent of the parties in allocating the risk of first-party property loss. More specifically, courts have held that this type of clause signals that the parties have shifted the risk of first-party property loss from one another to the insurance company. The court stated, "Because it is economically inefficient for both parties to insure against the same risk, the parties' inclusion of an insurance procurement clause indicates that the parties intended to avoid both parties having to face potential liability for the same risk."

In this case, it was undisputed that the parties signed the standard AIA contract, leaving undisturbed and unmodified the language of the provisions of section 11.4. Understanding the language, purpose, and function of section 11.4, the appellate court agreed that it was undisputed that the owner was obliged to secure the required insurance, and if the owner did not do so, it was contractually required to advise the contractor in writing of either its decision or failure to do so. It was similarly undisputed that the owner did not secure the required

---

[116.3] *Citing* 220 S.W.3d 809 (Mo. Ct. App. 2007).

[116.4] *Citing* 126 S.W.3d 820 (Mo. App. 2004). The court also cited South Tippecanoe Sch. Bldg. Corp. v. Shambaugh & Son, Inc., 182 Ind. App. 350, 395 N.E.2d 320, 327 (1979).

insurance, nor did it advise the contractor in writing of its failure to do so. The owner's breach of section 11.4 of the standard AIA contract was, therefore, not in dispute.

The lower and appellate courts also rejected the owner's response that the AIA contract's "indemnification" provision (section 3.18) should control. The owner argued that section 11.4 entailed no more than the owner's obligation to obtain "all-coverage liability insurance for the construction coverage before the construction project began," but did not "exculpate the contractor from its own negligence." Instead, the owner argued, the contractor was responsible for the loss because section 3.18.1 clearly imposed responsibility upon the contractor for any damages caused by its own negligence or that of its subcontractors, as was alleged in the complaint.

> The courts, however, rejected this argument, concluding thatsection 3.18.1 required the contractor to hold harmless or indemnify the owner for damages occurring as a result of the contractor's or subcontractor's negligence. However, this section specifically excluded from this requirement any claims for indemnification arising from "the Work" itself and pertained to the contractor's duty to indemnify the owner for losses to third parties.

The lower court relied upon an unpublished Montana case, *Beartooth Lodge v. Yellowstone Electric Co.,*[116.5] which addressed the interplay between sections 11.4 and 3.18. In *Beartooth Lodge,* as here, the owner alleged fire damage and loss due to negligence by the general contractor or a subcontractor. The *Beartooth Lodge* court, assuming contractor negligence, set forth the relationship between the two sections of the standard AIA contract as follows:

> A101 and A201 [the standard contract forms] intentionally make provision for property damage and all risk insurance coverage to be provided by [the owner], all parties waive subrogation for the all risk property damage insurance provided by [the owner] and the only responsibilities of the contractors, if any, are for liability insurance to cover claims by third parties. Such provision is an appropriate allocation of risk and responsibilities and makes certain the obligation of the various parties under such contract documents to provide insurance.

The appellate court agreed that *Beartooth Lodge* was persuasive. It also found a California case, *Myers Building Industries, Ltd. v. Interface Technology, Inc.,*[116.6] to be instructive. In that case, the California Court of Appeal analyzed previous versions of these AIA contract provisions and held that a clause containing the words "indemnify" and "hold harmless" was an indemnity clause that generally obligated the indemnitor to reimburse the indemnitee for any damages the indemnitee became obligated to pay third persons.

[116.5] *Citing* No. DV 92-17, 1993 Mont. Dist. LEXIS 636 (Mont. Carbon Cty. 1993).

[116.6] 13 Cal. App. 4th 949, 17 Cal. Rptr. 2d 242, 254 (2d Dist.1993).

In this case, the owner presented no contrary authority that would authorize a contractor's direct liability to an owner under circumstances such as those presented here. Thus, the lower court committed no error of law in holding that section 11.4 and its "waiver of subrogation" provision controlled the factual circumstances of this matter, and that the "indemnification" provisions of section 3.18 were not applicable here. The appellate court found that this assignment of error was without merit.

The lower and appellate courts also rejected the owner's second assignment of error that even if the AIA contract placed the burden of insurance upon it as the project owner, Pennsylvania's common law and public policy concerns did not permit enforcement of a contract in which a party could contract away its potential for liability based upon its own negligence, because such contract would remove the incentive for an entity to take precautions in its business endeavors. The lower court had observed: "the purpose of section 11.4 is to protect both the owner and the contractor from the consequences of litigation and losses which might otherwise disrupt performance under the contract. Such protection encourages commercial undertakings such as the one in this case."

The appellate court cited the Connecticut case of *Best Friends Pet Care, Inc. v. Design Learned, Inc.,*[116.7] which studied a number of other states' approaches to this question and concurred with the consensus it discovered:

> Ultimately, we find persuasive . . . the distinction made by the New Hampshire Supreme Court in *Chadwick v. CSI, Ltd.*, 137 N.H. 515, 629 A.2d 820 (1993). In *Chadwick,* the court distinguished between exculpatory provisions, which were forbidden by New Hampshire common law, and allocation of risk provisions, such as the kind found in the AIA contract. These [AIA provisions] do not present the same concerns as naked exculpatory provisions. As opposed to exculpatory provisions . . . the insurance provisions of the standard AIA contract are not designed to unilaterally relieve one party from the effects of its future negligence, thereby foreclosing another party's avenue of recovery. Instead, they work to ensure that injuries or damage incurred during the construction project are covered by the appropriate types and limits of insurance, and that the costs of that coverage are appropriately allocated among the parties.
>
> The court also cited a Pennsylvania decision, *Penn Avenue Place Associates, L.P. v. Century Steel Erectors, Inc.,*[116.8] which reached a similar conclusion: "[A] waiver of subrogation clause, such as the one at issue here, does not invoke public policy concerns because it does not attempt to transfer liability for negligence away from the tortfeasor. The public policy concerns regarding indemnification for one's own negligence are therefore not an issue here. Waivers of subrogation are a matter of contract."

[116.7] 77 Conn. App. 167, 823 A.2d 329 (2003).

[116.8] 798 A.2d 256 (Pa. Super. 2002).

This analysis, which comported with the general consensus reached by other courts concerning the interpretation of the AIA's standard contract forms, led to the inescapable conclusion that the lower court correctly analyzed the contract at issue. As such, the court rejected the owner's argument that the public policy concerns did not permit enforcement.

Finally, the lower court properly rejected the owner's final assignment of error that there remained genuine issues of material fact for resolution by a jury, thereby precluding summary judgment. The owner's first contention in this regard was that the contract should not be enforced, because the owner's principal lacked bargaining power, was at a language disadvantage, and was without representation when he signed the AIA A101 and A201 contract documents presented by the contractor. The lower court rejected this argument, because it would have required the court to look beyond the unequivocal language of section 11.4 *et seq.*, when there was no indication in the record of fraud or other intentional conduct.A court may not look to extrinsic or "parol evidence" outside of the express language of a contract unless there was some showing or evidence of fraud, accident, mistake, or ambiguity in the language or making of the contract.[116.9] Here, the owner suggested that the contractor pressured him in order to obtain his signature on the AIA contracts so that work could begin on the project. The court, however, held that its review of the record, including the owner's principal's affidavit, suggested no abuse of discretion or error of law by the lower court in rejecting that contention. The record revealed that the owner was a business owner with some degree of sophistication and was a knowing and voluntary party to the contract in question. The record contained nothing to suggest that the owner was in any way prevented from obtaining counseled advice if he chose to do so. In addition, no basis existed for looking beyond the terms of the AIA contract itself.

The appellate court also rejected the owner's additional argument that both sides to the dispute presented disparate versions of the facts, which precluded summary judgment. The court, however, stated that that was not the issue. The lower court had concluded that the owner failed to obtain the insurance required by section 11.4 of the AIA standard contract form, and also failed to advise the contractor in writing of its failure to do so. As a matter of law, therefore, the lower court concluded that, pursuant to the "waiver of subrogation" provision of section 11.4, the owncr's claim was barred by the contract language and, therefore, the contractor was entitled to summary judgment. The appellate court agreed with the trial court on this point.

Finally, the appellate court rejected the owner's contention that the safety of construction work sites constituted a public interest such that the lower court should have analyzed the contract as illegally attempting to allow one party to contract away potential liability for its own negligence. The court held that the contention was not an assertion that genuine issues of material fact existed, but rather an extension of the owner's second assignment of error, which the appellate court addressed above and which it found to be without merit.

[116.9] *Citing* Ragnar Benson, Inc. v. Hempfield Twp. Mun. Auth., 916 A.2d 1183 (Pa. Super. 2007).

In *JPI Westcoast Construction, L.P. v. RJS Assocs., Inc.*,[116.10] a family of a deceased construction worker settled a wrongful death lawsuit against a contractor and subcontractor, and the contractor brought an action for express contractual indemnity against the subcontractor and the subcontractor's excess insurer. The excess insurer brought a cross-complaint for equitable subrogation and equitable indemnity against the contractor's primary insurer. On cross-motions for summary judgment, the trial court entered judgment for the subcontractor and its excess insurer. The contractor and its primary insurer appealed. The appellate court held that the excess insurer was entitled to reimbursement of sums paid on behalf of contractor in settlement.

JPI was the general contractor on a large construction project, and hired RJS & Associates (RJS) as a subcontractor on a phase of the project. The construction contract between JPI and RJS contained an indemnity clause in favor of JPI. During the course of the work undertaken by RJS, a worker was killed in an accident. In the underlying action, the worker's family sued JPI, RJS, and others for wrongful death. RJS's insurers assumed defense of the action on behalf of JPI and RJS. A jury found that JPI was 20 percent at fault for the accident, RJS was 70 percent at fault, and awarded judgment in the amount of $6,853,284 in favor of the worker's family. After trial, the family settled with JPI and RJS for a total of $4.9 million.

The appeal arose from the subsequent round of litigation between JPI and its primary insurance carrier, Transcontinental Insurance Company (Transcontinental), and RJS and its excess carrier, Great American Insurance Company (Great American), over contributions to the settlement of the underlying action. On stipulated facts, the trial court ruled in favor of RJS and Great American, and against JPI and Transcontinental, on four separate motions for summary judgment. The appellate court affirmed the trial court's summary judgment rulings. In so ruling the appellate court framed the issue as follows: Assuming JPI's contractual right to indemnity by RJS was triggered under the facts presented here, then did the indemnity clause control the payment obligations of the parties' respective insurers, or were such obligations determined by the language in the applicable policies of insurance?

On December 22, 1999, JPI entered into a contract with Jefferson At Bay Meadows, L.P., to serve as general contractor for the construction of Bay Meadows apartment complex. On January 18, 2000, JPI entered into subcontract number 76003-03-3001-999 with RJS, by which RJS agreed to build seven complete subterranean concrete podium structures for the contract price of $12,765,958.00, including all design engineering work.

The subcontract contained the following indemnity clause:

> To the fullest extent permitted by law, Subcontractor shall indemnify and hold harmless . . . Contractor and Contractor's agents and employees (the "Indemnitees") from all claims, damages, losses and expenses . . . attributable to bodily injury, . . . death or injury . . . arising out of or in connection with the

---

[116.10] 156 Cal. App. 4th 1448, 68 Cal. Rptr. 3d 91 (2007).

> performance of the Work of Subcontractor performed . . . in connection with the Project, by anyone directly or indirectly employed by Subcontractor, or anyone for whose acts Subcontractor is liable even if caused jointly and concurrently by the negligence of the Indemnitees and Subcontractor . . . The above indemnity provisions do not extend to, or cover any loss, damage, or expense arising out of the sole negligence or willful misconduct of Contractor, its employees and agents or any other Indemnitees.

The subcontract contained the following provision regarding insurance coverage:

> Prior to the commencement of the Work and periodically thereafter as required by Contractor, subcontractor shall deliver to Contractor satisfactory certificates evidencing compliance by Subcontractor with the insurance requirements set forth in Section VII of the Project Manual to these General Provisions and incorporated herein for all purposes. All policies, with the exception of Workers compensation, shall name contractor and the Owner as Additional Insured parties on a primary basis . . . . All original insurance certificates are to be sent to JPI . . . . If requested by contractor, Subcontractor shall furnish copies of insurance policies required by the Contract Documents. The requiring of any and all insurance as set forth in these paragraphs, or elsewhere, is in addition to and not in any way in substitution for all the other protection provided under the subcontract to Contractor, including Paragraph 11 (Indemnity).

JPI purchased a commercial general liability (CGL) policy from Transcontinental with a $1 million limit. RJS purchased a CGL policy from Lloyd's with aggregate coverage in the amount of $2 million, with a per occurrence limit of $1 million. JPI was named as an additional insured on the RJS Lloyd's policy. An additional rider to the RJS policy provided that it would be primary. RJS was also the sole named insured on a Great American umbrella policy with a general aggregate and per occurrence limit of $9 million. The Great American policy stated that Great American would pay sums in excess of the retained limit that the insured would become legally obligated to pay. The Great American policy defined "retained limit" as:

> [T]he greater of: 1. the total amounts stated as the applicable limits of the underlying policies listed in the Schedule of Underlying Insurance and the applicable limits of any other insurance providing coverage to the "Insured" during the Policy Period . . . .

For purposes of summary judgment, JPI and RJS stipulated that JPI qualified as an additional insured under the Great American policy.

The Great American policy also contained an "Other Insurance" clause, which stated:

> If other insurance applies to a loss that is also covered by this policy, this policy will apply excess of the other insurance. Nothing herein will be construed to make this policy subject to the terms, conditions and limitations

of such other insurance. However, this provision will not apply if the other insurance is specifically written to be excess of this policy.

Sanchez was working as a "hose man" for a concrete pour at the project. A boom involved in this operation dropped down and struck him, causing his death. His estate sued JPI, RJS, and the concrete pump truck operator. JPI tendered defense to RJS and its primary carrier, Lloyd's, and Lloyd's accepted the defense of JPI as an additional insured under the RJS policy. Coverage counsel for JPI's primary insurance, now known as Transcontinental, then known as CNA, wrote to Lloyd's and Great Western regarding indemnification. Transcontinental noted that the damages would likely exceed the Lloyd's policy limit, and asserted that Lloyd's and Great American owed a duty to indemnify JPI for a judgment or settlement up to the combined $10 million of those two policies. Great American rejected that assertion, and replied that all the primary coverage, including that provided by Transcontinental, must exhaust prior to the excess coverage being triggered.

The case proceeded to trial against JPI, RJS, and the truck operator. The jury returned verdicts, finding all three defendants negligent, with respective fault apportioned 20 percent to JPI, 70percent to RJS, and 10percent to the truck operator. The jury award was for $1,853.284.27 for economic damages, and $5 million for non-economic damages. After reduction for previous settlements by other parties, the jury verdict was $6,839,457.50.

After the jury verdict, RJS and its insurers, Lloyd's and Great American, entered settlement negotiations with plaintiffs. Great American demanded that Transcontinental participate in the settlement, but Transcontinental refused to contribute any amount to the settlement on behalf of JPI. Nor did JPI contribute any amount to the eventual settlement. Subsequently, RJS, Lloyd's, and Great American settled with plaintiffs for $4.9 million pursuant to a Settlement Agreement and Release ("settlement agreement") signed by the parties on and around March 11, 2005. The settlement agreement stated that RJS was the named insured under the Lloyd's and Great American policies and that JPI qualified as an additional insured under those policies. Under the terms of the settlement agreement, Lloyd's paid $1 million, with $777,777.78 paid on behalf of RJS and $222,222.22 on behalf of JPI. Great American paid the remaining $3.9 million, with $3,033,333.33 paid on behalf of RJS and $866,666.67 on behalf of JPI. Great American's settlement payment on behalf of JPI was made subject to a full reservation of rights against Transcontinental. Also, JPI and Transcontinental agreed that any payment by Great American to compromise the judgment should not be deemed a voluntary payment.

On January 18, 2005, JPI filed a complaint for express contractual indemnity and declaratory relief against RJS and its insurers Great American and Lloyd's. JPI subsequently dismissed Lloyd's from the suit on March 22, 2005. In its complaint, JPI requested "that the court order RJS to indemnify JPI for the full amount of the jury verdict and any subsequent judgment in the underlying action pursuant to the terms of the express written indemnity agreement in the RJS/JPI contract." JPI also sought declaratory relief against Great American, alleging that

"JPI and RJS clearly intended that RJS would be primarily responsible for fully indemnifying JPI . . . and JPI's own insurance carriers owe no obligation to pay any of the verdict entered in the underlying action."

On June 1, 2005, Great American filed a first amended cross-complaint for equitable subrogation and equitable indemnity against Transcontinental. In its cross-complaint, Great American alleged that any obligation it owed under its policy was subject to the terms and conditions of its policy. Further, Great American alleged it was entitled under equitable principles of subrogation to reimbursement from Transcontinental of its settlement payment on behalf of JPI. Great American also alleged it was entitled to equitable indemnification from Transcontinental "according to the terms of their respective policy provisions, including their 'limits of liability' and 'other insurance' clauses, as well as principles of equity," for its payment of Transcontinental's portion of the settlement.

Motions for summary judgment were filed in the trial court by various carriers. The trial court granted a motion for summary judgment by RJS on JPI's claim for express contractual indemnity. The trial court concluded that the basis of JPI's cause of actions was moot, as JPI no longer had any right of recovery against RJS. The trial court also denied summary judgment as to Great American on JPI's declaratory relief claim. The trial court concluded that there was no longer any controversy between JPI and Great American because the entire judgment/settlement had been paid by RJS's insurance carriers, including the $3.9 million paid by Great American. The declaratory relief cause of action was moot as between those parties.

Shortly thereafter, the trial resolved the coverage issue in favor of Great American. The trial court concluded that the primary carrier of the indemnitee (JPI) had to pay out before the excess carrier of the indemnitor (RJS) was obliged to contribute. The trial court therefore granted Great American's summary judgment motion on its cross-complaint against Transcontinental, ruling that Great American was entitled to reimbursement and/or contribution in the amount of $866,666.67 from Transcontinental. JPI and Transcontinental appealed.

The appellate court stated that *Rossmoor Sanitation v. Pylon, Inc.*,[116.11] stands for the proposition that an insurer's subrogation of its insured's right to contractual indemnification controls in a battle of "other insurance" clauses between co-insurers. The *JPI* court stated that key to the *Rossmoor* court's reasoning was the compelling fact that to apportion the loss between the insurers pursuant to the other insurance clauses would effectively negate the indemnity agreement and impose liability on the carrier for Rossmoor, when Rossmoor bargained with Pylon to avoid that result as a part of the consideration of the construction agreement.

The *JPI* court stated that *Reliance National Indemnity Co. v. General Star Indemnity Co.*,[116.12] controlled on this issue, because it was factually analogous to the *JPI* case, and that its reasoning was highly persuasive. The *JPI* court said that

[116.11] 13 Cal. 3d 622, 119 Cal. Rptr. 449 (1975).

[116.12] 72 Cal. App. 4th 1063, 85 Cal. Rptr. 2d 627 (1999).

Rossmoor did not apply. The *JPI* court stated that the duty to contribute applied to insurers that share the same level of obligation as to the same insured, but that in *Reliance*, Reliance's obligation was primary, and General Star's was excess and General Star was not liable for the loss, damage or defense covered by the other primary insurance. Like the *Reliance* court, the *JPI* court stated that the equities favored the primary carrier, Transcontinental.

JPI contended that the trial court erred in granting summary judgment in favor of RJS on its complaint against RJS and Great American for express contractual indemnity and declaratory relief. The *JPI* court disagreed, and held that Transcontinental was not entitled to indemnification from Great American on the basis of the indemnification clause in the construction contract between JPI and RJS, and the appellate court affirmed the trial court.

As to the JPI claim for express contractual indemnity against RJS, the appellate court held that the undisputed facts showed that JPI tendered defense of the underlying action to RJS and its insurers, Lloyd's and Great American, and that Lloyd's and Great American accepted defense of the action on behalf of JPI. Lloyd's and Great American tried the case, and following an adverse jury verdict negotiated a full and completed settlement. JPI did not pay anything toward the settlement, and therefore there was nothing for which RJS was required to indemnify JPI.

However, the *JPI* court rejected RJS's contention that the summary judgment of the trial court could be affirmed on the alternative basis that the indemnification clause was inapplicable. The *JPI* court concluded that the clause at issue in this case was not a general indemnity clause. It was a specific indemnity clause because the claim explicitly addressed the indemnitee's negligence. The clause in this case stated that loss or damage caused solely by JPI's negligence was excluded. The clause also specifically covered JPI where JPI was jointly negligent with RJS, so application of the clause in favor of JPI was not precluded by negligence attributable to JPI.

§ 22.05 SURETY BONDS

[A] Requirement of Bonds

Page 1099, add at end of subsection:

In *Financial Pacific Insurance Co. v. Northrop,*[178.1] defendant and appellant Kim Northrop challenged: (1) the trial court's order sustaining without leave to amend plaintiff and respondent Financial Pacific Insurance Company's (FPIC) demurrer to her First Amended Cross-Complaint against FPIC for breach of contract and breach of the covenant of good faith and fair dealing; and, (2) the trial court's subsequent grant of summary judgment and entry of judgment in favor of FPIC on its complaint against her for breach of contract and indemnification. The appellate court affirmed all the trial court's orders.

[178.1] Not reported in Cal. Rptr. 3d, 2009 WL 1132339 (Cal. App. 1st Dist. 2009).

Appellant's husband, John, owned Kristen Construction Company (Kristen). Kristen entered into a contract with Bridgeport Public Utility District (Bridgeport PUD) for the construction of improvements to Bridgeport's water and sewer system. The contract required that Kristen furnish a performance bond. FPIC wrote the performance bond. Under an agreement signed by both John Northrop and appellant (jointly, the Northrops), the Northrops agreed to indemnify FPIC for any losses on the performance bond.

On May 6, 2006, FPIC filed a complaint against appellant for breach of contract and indemnification, seeking damages in the amount of $849,556.13, as well as amounts for costs and attorney's fees. The complaint alleged that FPIC issued a construction performance bond on behalf of Kristen and in favor of obligee, Bridgeport PUD, in the amount of $968,638. The complaint alleged that late in 2003, a dispute arose under the contract between Bridgeport PUD and Kristen on issues of workmanship and project delays. Bridgeport PUD terminated Kristen and hired another contractor to complete the project. Kristen disputed the termination, and took the matter to arbitration as required under the terms of the contract.

The complaint alleged that on November 29, 2005, after a seven-day arbitration hearing, the arbitrator awarded Bridgeport PUD damages of $849,566.13 against Kristen. Further, the complaint alleged that on December 13, 2005, FPIC paid Bridgeport PUD the full amount of the arbitration award. FPIC then demanded reimbursement from the Northrops as co-signatories to a Continuing Agreement of Indemnity Contractor's Form (indemnity agreement) which they had executed in favor of FPIC on January 6, 2003. The Northrops refused to indemnify FPIC.

On December 12, 2006, the Northrops filed a First Amended Cross-Complaint (FACC) against FPIC on causes of action for breach of contract, breach of the covenant of good faith and fair dealing, and fraud and negligent misrepresentation. With regard to the claim for breach of contract, the FACC specifically alleged FPIC breached its contractual duty to perform its obligations as required by the terms of the performance bond, causing damages to the Northrops. With regard to the claim for breach of the covenant of good faith and fair dealing, the FACC specifically alleged FPIC failed to diligently respond to the claims of Bridgeport PUD and to take action to mitigate the Northrops' potential damages as required under the performance bond, the indemnity agreement, and the Bridgeport PUD contract.

The FACC based the above claims on the performance bond and indemnity agreement incorporated in FPIC's complaint as exhibits, as well as based upon the following allegations:

1. That on or about December 4, 2003, Bridgeport PUD notified FPIC it intended to terminate Kristen from the construction project.
2. Bridgeport PUD sent formal notice of Kristen's termination to FPIC on or about December 19.
3. In a letter dated January 22, 2004, FPIC notified Bridgeport PUD it would respond to its claim under the performance bond within 30 days.

4. Between January 22 and March 30, 2004, FPIC did not investigate or take any action to resolve Bridgeport PUD's claim.
5. On March 31, 2004, FPIC retained a contractor to inspect the Bridgeport PUD project.
6. After the inspection, FPIC took no further action to resolve Bridgeport PUD's claim.

FPIC filed a demurrer to the FACC. A hearing on FPIC's demurrer was held, and the trial court filed its order sustaining without leave to amend FPIC's demurrer as to all causes of action. The trial court ruled:

> . . . sureties are not insurers, and do not owe any non-contractual duties to their principals. In the event of a dispute between the principal and the obligee, the surety owes no duty to defend, and has no right to represent the principal's interest. In such situations, the surety may sit back and wait for the legal process to determine whether the principal is obligated to the obligee. It is at that time that its duty arises to pay the obligation. Its duty is therefore owed to the obligee, not the principal. The surety's obligations are therefore limited by the surety agreement, which is strictly construed against expansion of obligations not contained in or clearly inferable from the surety contract. The first amended cross-complaint failed to identify any specific language in the surety agreement that obligated [FPIC] to "investigate", "defend", or take any other action, until the dispute between Kristen Construction [ ] and Bridgeport was legally resolved . . . This disposes of the breach of contract and breach of implied covenant causes of action.

Having disposed of the Northrops' cross complaint, FPIC moved for summary judgment against appellant on its breach of contract and indemnification claims. Appellant opposed the motion on the basis that there was a triable issue of material fact as to whether FPIC breached duties and obligations owed to appellant under the performance bond and indemnity agreement. Appellant Northrop contended that FPIC owed her a duty to promptly determine if she was indeed in default, and if so, FPIC should have taken those steps necessary to complete the construction projects promptly, with time being of the essence. On September 18, 2007, the trial court took FPIC's summary judgment motion under submission, after hearing oral argument.

On October 17, 2007, the trial court issued its Order After Hearing on Motion for Summary Judgment. The trial court ruled that there were no triable issues as to any material fact. The indemnity agreement provided that FPIC had "sole discretion" to determine whether to pay a claim or complete construction. FPIC had established that Northrop signed the Indemnification Agreement, that pursuant thereto [FPIC] issued its performance bond on the Bridgeport [PUD] construction project, that when difficulties occurred on the project a dispute arose resulting in an arbitration award against John Northrop and John Northrop *d/b/a* Kristen Construction, and that thereafter [FPIC] paid Bridgeport [PUD] the amount of the arbitration award, $849,556.16. Despite repeated demands, Kimberley Northrop refused to pay FPIC $849,556.13. The trial court ruled that defendant Kim Northrop was obligated under the indemnity agreement to reimburse FPIC for payments made under the bond it issued pursuant to the indemnity agreement. Defendant Kim Northrop contended that FPIC should have completed the construction project. The trial court stated that Kim Northrop had not demonstrated that FPIC owed her a legal duty to complete the project. The trial court ruled that as a matter of law, defendant Kim Northrop owed FPIC $849,556.00. It granted the FPIC motion for summary judgment.

The appellate court held that the trial court properly sustained FPIC's demurrer without leave to amend on appellant's claim FPIC breached contractual duties owed to her under the performance bond. Under established principles of surety law, a performance bond is designed to protect against loss caused by the contractor's default in failing to complete the contract and pay mechanics. Under a standard construction performance bond, a surety undertakes either to promptly step in and construct the project if its principal fails to do so, or pay the obligee for its expenditures if it is forced to complete the task on its own.

The performance bond issued by FPIC guaranteed that upon default by the contractor FPIC would step in and complete the contract or obtain bids to complete the contract. None of the terms and conditions of the performance bond imposed an obligation on FPIC with respect to Kristen or on the Northrops, in the event of Kristen's default under the Bridgeport PUD contract. FPIC's contractual duties under the performance bond flowed to Bridgeport PUD as the obligee, not to Kristen Construction as the principal.

Northrop posited the novel theory that FPIC owed contractual duties to the Northrops under the performance bond to "finish the contract for [Kristen upon its default] in the most expeditious and cost efficient manner" because the indemnity agreement between the Northrops and FPIC "includes all the terms and obligations of the Performance bond and the construction contract, as each is expressly referenced and incorporated into the other."

The appellate court held that this assertion was baseless. First, the construction contract was irrelevant to the court's demurrer analysis, as it was not incorporated by reference in either the complaint or the FACC, and was not before the appellate court on appeal. Secondly, and more importantly, appellant failed to identify, either in her briefing or at oral argument, any specific terms or conditions set forth in the construction contract, the indemnity agreement, or the performance bond to support the averments in the FACC that FPIC had a contractual duty to the Northrops to promptly respond to Bridgeport PUD's notice of default and act to mitigate the Northrops' potential damages. The appellate court held that the terms of the performance bond set forth FPIC's obligations to Bridgeport PUD upon default of the contractor, but set forth no obligations owed by FPIC to the contractor upon such default. Moreover, the indemnity agreement vested in FPIC the "sole discretion" to determine its course of action when a claim is made against its performance bond upon a default by the contractor.

The appellate court held that the appellant failed to state a claim for breach of contract and failed to establish a reasonable possibility that an amendment could cure the defect. Thus, the trial court did not abuse its discretion in sustaining FPIC's demurrer without leave to amend on appellant's breach of contract claim.

Regarding the breach of covenant claim, the appellate court noted that the covenant of good faith and fair dealing, implied by law in every contract, exists merely to prevent one contracting party from unfairly frustrating the other party's right to receive the benefits of the agreement actually made. The trial court sustained the demurrer on the breach of covenant claim because appellant's FACC failed to identify any language in the performance bond showing FPIC was obligated to investigate or defend appellant against Bridgeport's claim until the dispute between Bridgeport and appellant was legally resolved. Absent the requisite contractual underpinnings, the appellate court held that the appellant could not assert an affirmative breach of covenant claim under the performance bond. The trial court properly sustained FPIC's demurrer on Northrop's second cause of action for breach of the covenant of good faith and fair dealing.

The trial court also ruled that FPIC was entitled to summary judgment on its claim for indemnification. FPIC established that Northrop signed the indemnity agreement. The indemnity agreement accorded FPIC sole discretion whether to pay Bridgeport's claim or complete the project. Kristen Construction disputed Bridgeport's claim and subsequently suffered an adverse arbitration ruling in that dispute in the amount of $849,556.16. Bridgeport demanded that FPIC pay the arbitration award under the performance bond. FPIC paid Bridgeport the amount of the arbitration award and then demanded indemnification from Northrop, which she refused. The trial court also ruled that appellant could not avoid summary judgment by asserting FPIC had a legal duty to complete the project, because she had failed to demonstrate FPIC owed her any such legal duty.

The trial court's factual findings were supported by the declaration of Edward Rocknich, FPIC's staff attorney, in support of FPIC's motion for summary judgment. In his declaration, Rocknich stated that FPIC contacted John Northrop after Bridgeport notified FPIC of its intention to terminate Kristen Construction from the project. According to Rocknich, John Northrop told FPIC that he intended to oppose Bridgeport's claim. He retained an attorney and disputed Bridgeport's claim via mandatory arbitration.

Kim Northrop agreed with allegations in Rocknich's declaration in her response to FPIC's separate statement of undisputed material facts. She agreed with FPIC's undisputed facts that she signed the indemnity agreement, that Kristen contracted with Bridgeport PUD for the purpose of a water and sewer system improvement project, that FPIC underwrote the performance bond, and that a dispute arose between Bridgeport PUD and Kristen Construction late in 2003. John Northrop and Kristen Construction took the matter to mandatory arbitration. The arbitrator awarded Bridgeport PUD $849.556.16. Northrop further concurred with FPIC's undisputed facts that Bridgeport demanded that FPIC pay the arbitration award, and that FPIC paid the arbitration award pursuant to the performance bond. Based on FPIC's undisputed material facts as agreed to by appellant, as well as on appellant's failure to raise an issue of fact that FPIC breached any obligation under the indemnity agreement, the appellate court concluded that the trial court ruled correctly that FPIC was entitled to indemnification as a matter of law.

Northrop failed to present facts that would establish that FPIC exercised its discretion under the indemnity agreement in an objectively unreasonable manner. At oral argument, Northrop's counsel contended that the trial court erred in granting summary judgment on appellant's covenant claim because her opposition conceded only the issue of termination, and made no concession regarding the reasonableness of the costs incurred in completing the construction project. The appellate court disagreed, stating that once FPIC presented evidence sufficient to shift the burden to appellant, she was obliged to present evidence sufficient to establish the specific costs that were unwarranted and/or unreasonably occurred. The appellate court held that the appellant failed to meet her burden in this regard.

FPIC established its entitlement to summary judgment on its affirmative claims for breach of contract and indemnification, and appellant failed to produce evidence sufficient to raise a triable issue of fact precluding judgment on FPIC's claims. The appellate court affirmed the trial court's summary judgment order, sustaining without leave to amend the demurrer to the claims in the FACC and the order granting FPIC summary judgment on its affirmative claims for breach of contract and indemnification.

Chapter 23

BOILERPLATE

§ 23.11 WAIVER OF SUBROGATION

Page 1149, add after second full paragraph:

A 2009 California case provides guidance on how courts view waivers of subrogation. In *State Farm General Insurance Co. v. Steigerwald-Doherty, Inc.*,[81.1] State Farm sought subrogation against Steigerwald-Dougherty, Inc. (SDI) and Sexton Company, Inc. (Sexton) to recover money it paid out on a claim involving a fire at real property owned by its insured, Larry Scaramella. SDI was the contractor Scaramella engaged to build a residence on the property, and Sexton was a subcontractor charged with installing a sprinkler system in the residence. State Farm alleged that their joint negligence during construction of the residence caused the fire. The trial court granted summary judgment on behalf of SDI and Sexton, based upon a waiver of subrogation clause incorporated by reference into the contract between Scaramella and SDI for construction of the home, which was upheld on appeal.

On appeal, State Farm had argued that the court erred in granting summary judgment asserting:

> (1) SDI and Sexton failed to meet their initial burden of proof, because the evidence they relied upon was inadmissible;
>
> (2) disputed facts as to the parties' intent in entering into the construction contract barred summary judgment;
>
> (3) there was a triable issue of fact as to whether the construction contract properly incorporated by reference the waiver of subrogation clause; and
>
> (4) there was a triable issue of fact on State Farm's defenses of waiver and estoppel. The appellate court affirmed the trial court's grant of summary judgment.

In the case, Scaramella entered into a contract with SDI to build a residence (the construction agreement). Scaramella signed the construction agreement and initialed each page. Page 1 of the construction agreement stated, "AIA Document A201-1997, General Conditions of the Contract for Construction, is adopted in this document by reference." Further, article 1 of the construction agreement, entitled "The Contract Documents," stated that

[81.1] 2009 WL 1423565 (Cal. App. 4th Dist. 2009).

> *The Contract Documents consist of this Agreement, Conditions of the Contract (General, Supplementary and other Conditions)*, Drawings, Specifications, Addenda. . . . *These listed form the Contract and are all as fully a part of the Contract as if attached to this Agreement or repeated herein* [italics added].

Article 15 of the construction agreement, entitled "Enumeration Of Contract Documents," provided:

> *The Contract Documents include:* [¶¶] .1 The agreement is this executed 2001 edition of the Standard Form of Agreement Between Owner and Contractor, AIA Document A114. [¶¶] .2 *The General Conditions are the 1997 edition of the General Conditions of the Contract for Construction, AIA Document A201* [italics added].

AIA Document A201 (Form A201), the "General Conditions" document, was referred to an additional 12 times throughout the construction agreement. Form A201 contained a provision at paragraph 11.4.7 that provided:

> Waivers of Subrogation. *The Owner and Contractor waive all rights against (1) each other and any of the subcontractors, sub-subcontractors, agents and employees, each of the other*, and (2) the Architect, Architect's consultants, separate contractors described in Article 6, if any, and any of their subcontractors, sub-subcontractors, agents and employees, *for damages caused by fire or other causes of loss to the extent covered by property insurance obtained pursuant to this Section 11.4 or other property insurance applicable to the Work*, except such rights as they have to proceeds of such insurance held by the Owner as fiduciary. . . . A waiver of subrogation shall be effective as to a person or entity even though that person or entity would otherwise have a duty of indemnification, contractual or otherwise, did not pay the insurance premium directly or indirectly, and whether or not the person or entity had an insurable interest in the property damaged [italics added].

SDI entered into a standard AIA subcontract agreement (the subcontract) with Sexton to install above-ground piping and sprinkler heads at the residence. The subcontract incorporated by reference the terms of the construction agreement.

When the residence was near completion, there was a fire that caused significant damage to the residence. According to State Farm, the cause of the fire was the spontaneous combustion of varnishing rags that were improperly disposed of by SDI's employees. Scaramella, asserted the damage was exacerbated by the failure of a sprinkler head to activate and release water as designed and intended in the room where the fire originated. State Farm paid Scaramella $1.09 million to compensate him for his losses occasioned by the fire.

State Farm brought this action against SDI and Sexton, seeking to recoup through subrogation the monies it paid to Scaramella for the fire damages. In response, SDI and Sexton brought motions for summary judgment, asserting

Form A201, as incorporated into the construction agreement, barred State Farm's subrogation action because of the waiver of subrogation clause.

In support of SDI's motion for summary judgment, it submitted the declaration of Patrick Dougherty, the chief executive officer of SDI, who stated that he negotiated the construction agreement with Scaramella. He noted that the construction agreement's terms were subject to negotiation and that Scaramella deleted paragraph 7.7.3. That paragraph provided that Scaramella would reimburse SDI for "[c]osts of repairing or correcting damaged or nonconforming Work executed by the Contractor, Subcontractors or suppliers, provided that such damaged or nonconforming Work *was not caused by the negligence or failure to fulfill a specific responsibility of the Contractor and only to the extent that the cost of repair or correction is not recovered by the Contractor from insurance, sureties, Subcontractors or suppliers*" [italics added].

Dougherty also stated he believed that he presented Scaramella with a copy of Form A201 and that, even if he did not, he "had several copies in [his] office and gladly would have presented a copy of [Form A201 to Scaramella] to review had he requested it. [He] never received a request from [Scaramella] to review [Form A201]." The construction agreement and Form A201 were lodged with the court and referenced in the declaration of B.J. Haeck, an attorney for SDI. SDI also submitted State Farm's complaint, in which State Farm admitted Scaramella "entered into a written contract with [SDI] to design, construct and build the premises."

State Farm opposed the motion, asserting first that the contract documents were not properly authenticated and were, thus, inadmissible. Specifically, State Farm asserted that because the contract exhibits were authenticated only by attorneys for SDI and Sexton, they were inadmissible. However, in opposing the summary judgment motion, State Farm submitted Scaramella's declaration, which authenticated the construction agreement, and State Farm attached the construction agreement as an exhibit. In his declaration Scaramella also admitted initialing every page of the construction agreement and signing it. Moreover, Sexton submitted excerpts from Scaramella's deposition in its reply papers, wherein he admitted entering into the contract with SDI.

State Farm argued there were triable issues of fact as to the parties' intent in entering into the construction agreement. In support of this contention, State Farm relied on Scaramella's declaration that stated it was his understanding at the time he entered the contract only the "initialed pages" of the construction agreement were part of the contract between SDI and himself. He further stated SDI never provided him with any other documents or told him that the construction contract incorporated by reference any other documents. He stated he was never provided with any "terms and conditions" document and no one told him any such document existed. He also stated that because he did not want to be liable for the contractor's mistakes, he deleted paragraph 7.7.3, because it allowed SDI to obtain reimbursement from him for the costs of repairing or correcting damaged or nonconforming work performed by SDI or its subcontractors. Finally, he declared that he "did not have readily available access to [Form A201]." Had I even known of any "terms and conditions relating to the building contract, I would not have known where to obtain a copy of such terms and conditions. [¶¶] . . . I never agreed to any of the language of the terms contained in [Form A201]."

State Farm also argued that SDI was equitably estopped from relying on the waiver of subrogation clause, because it did not raise that defense in a mediation in which the parties participated, only raising the defense for the first time when it amended its answer.

The trial court granted SDI's motion for summary judgment, finding that Form A201 was "enforceable and mandate[d] summary judgment in favor of defendant." In doing so, the trial court first found the contract documents were properly authenticated "via the declarations of Patrick Dougherty and B.J. Haeck [SDI's attorney]. In addition, the trial court held that there was no genuine dispute as to the terms of [Form A201], and that it would not be unfair to admit a copy such that it is admissible secondary evidence."

The trial court found there was no material disputed fact on the enforceability of the waiver of subrogation clause, noting Scaramella could not "avoid the binding terms of a contract simply because [he] failed to read and understand the contractual terms." The court found the construction agreement adequately incorporated by reference the waiver of subrogation clause, noting "[t]he multiple express references within the [construction agreement] to [Form A201] were clear and unequivocal. The [construction agreement] expressly called to the attention of [Scaramella] the incorporation of [Form A201] as a term of the overall agreement. These are not 'inferences' as argued by [State Farm], but instead are supported by direct evidence: the contract signed by [Scaramella]."

The trial court also found the incorporated document was enforceable, because in his declaration, Dougherty stated that copies of Form A201 were available in his office, and Scaramella's statement that he did not have access to Form A201 was "an inadmissible conclusion without foundation."

The trial court also found Scaramella's deletion of paragraph 7.7.3 did not create an inconsistency, because that section "addresses a different issue: shifting the cost of unforeseen non-negligent damages to the homeowner. This is distinct from the ability to maintain a subrogation action seeking compensation from a negligent contractor where property insurance exists to compensate for the damages claimed."

The court rejected State Farm's estoppel argument finding:

> (1) State Farm cited no authority for the proposition SDI had a duty to disclose the defense earlier than it did;
>
> (2) there was no evidence SDI knew of the waiver of subrogation defense earlier; and
>
> (3) there was no evidence State Farm relied on SDI's failure to raise the defense sooner to its detriment. The trial court granted Sexton's motion on the same basis it granted SDI's motion.

The appellate court pointed out that California Code of Civil Procedure section 437c, subdivision (d) provided that declarations filed in conjunction with summary judgment motions "shall be made by any person on personal knowledge, shall set forth admissible evidence, and shall show affirmatively that the affiant is competent to testify to the matters stated . . . ." "The requirement of this section is not that the declarant recite the conclusion that he can competently testify but that he allege facts showing his competence."[81.2]

State Farm asserted that the trial court erred in granting summary judgment, because the construction agreement was only authenticated by the attorneys for SDI and Sexton. However, State Farm did not contest the authenticity of the construction agreement submitted by SDI and Sexton. To the extent there were any deficiencies in the admissibility of the documents initially submitted by SDI and Sexton, the appellate court found that they were cured by State Farm's opposition.[81.3]

Dougherty's declaration, in which he stated he negotiated the construction agreement with Scaramella, taken together with Scaramella's own declaration, was sufficient to authenticate the document. Finally, any deficiency in the authentication of the construction agreement was cured by SDI's reply papers, which contained discovery admissions by Scaramella that he entered into the construction agreement with SDI.

The purpose of subrogation waivers in construction contracts is to allocate risks among the parties to the contract. Such agreements deter litigation and help parties avoid the cost of overlapping, multiple insurance policies. Where a contractor causes a loss covered by property insurance, the insurer who has paid for the damages has no right of subrogation against the contractor, because the waiver language waives the owner's claim.[81.4] "Viewed globally, these clauses make sense as an insurer on one project might very well be denied recovery by such a clause but benefit from the existence of such a waiver on another project."[81.5] Accordingly, subrogation waivers "are routinely upheld."

Form A201 evinced the intent to shift the risk of loss to insurance to the maximum extent possible: "The AIA has chosen . . . to put the ultimate loss on the property insurer. . . ."[81.6] "The AIA has made a strenuous effort to bar subrogation claims by having participants waive any claims the participants may have against other participants."[81.7] Whenever "loopholes" in the waiver have appeared, the AIA has changed its forms "to try to close" them and ultimately "to kill subrogation off."[81.8]

[81.2] Roy Bros. Drilling Co. v. Jones, 123 Cal. App. 3d 175, 182, 176 Cal. Rptr. 182 (1981).

[81.3] *See* Villa v. McFerren, 35 Cal. App. 4th 733, 751, 41 Cal. Rptr. 2d 719 (1995) (evidentiary gaps in moving papers may be cured by evidence submitted by opposing party as court . . . shall consider *all* of the evidence set forth in the papers submitted on a summary judgment motion).

[81.4] Lloyds Underwriters v. Craig & Rush, Inc., 26 Cal. App. 4th 1194, 1199, 32 Cal. Rptr. 2d 144 (1994).

[81.5] 4 Bruner & O'Connor, Construction Law § 11:100 (2008).

[81.6] *Citing* Text, 4th Edition, Insurance & Bonds, §§ 22.04[M], at 783.

[81.7] *Id.* at 779-80.

[81.8] *Id.* at 783; *see id.* at 780-83.

California courts have consistently upheld subrogation waivers against challenges to their enforceability.[81.9] The waiver clause in this matter is enforceable if it was properly incorporated by reference into the construction contract. Resolution of that issue requires an analysis as to what is required to effectively incorporate by reference one document into another.

A contract may include provisions that are not physically a part of the basic document, as long as those provisions are sufficiently incorporated by reference.[81.10] Incorporation by reference requires that (1) the reference to another document was clear and unequivocal; (2) the reference was called to the attention of the other party, who consented to that term; and (3) the terms of the incorporated documents were known or easily available to the contracting parties. The contract need not recite that it "incorporates another document, so long as it guide[s] the reader to the incorporated document."[81.11]

The "general conditions" in Form A201, including the waiver of subrogation clause, were clearly and specifically incorporated by reference in two separate places in the construction agreement. The construction agreement also clearly stated that Form A201 was a part of the construction agreement. The general conditions were referred to an additional 13 times in the construction agreement.

Despite this, and the fact Scaramella initialed every page of the document, he asserted in his declaration that he was unaware of the reference to Form A201, and believed only the construction agreement itself comprised his contract with SDI. However, a party to a contract is charged with knowing the terms of an agreement, even if he or she does not read it.[81.12] A party who signs a contract "cannot complain of unfamiliarity with the language of the instrument."[81.13] "[W]hen a person with the capacity of reading and understanding an instrument signs it, he is, in the absence of fraud and imposition, bound by its contents and estopped from saying that its provisions are contrary to his intentions or understanding."[81.14]

Accordingly, Scaramella's allegation he was unaware of the incorporation by reference clauses or that Form A201 was a part of the construction agreement was held to be irrelevant to the court's analysis. Because he signed the document, initialed each page, and the terms were clear, he was bound by them, and the court did not improperly resolve "inferences" in SDI and Sexton's favor. The unequivocal language of the construction agreement was direct evidence that demonstrated

[81.9] *See* Lloyd's Underwriters v. Craig & Rush, Inc., 26 Cal. App. 4th 1194, 1198-1201, 32 Cal. Rptr. 2d 144 (1994); Davlar Corp. v. Superior Court, 53 Cal. App. 4th 1121, 1124, 62 Cal. Rptr. 2d 199 (1997).

[81.10] Wolschlager v. Fidelity National Title Ins. Co., 111 Cal. App. 4th 784, 790 (2003).

[81.11] Shaw v. Regents of Univ. of California, 58 Cal. App. 4th 44, 54, 67 Cal. Rptr. 2d 850 (1997), *comparing* Baker v. Aubry, 216 Cal. App. 3d 1259, 1264, 265 Cal. Rptr. 381 (1989) *with* Chan v. Drexel Burnham Lambert, Inc., 178 Cal. App. 3d 632, 643, 223 Cal. Rptr. 838 (1986).

[81.12] Markborough California, Inc. v. Superior Court, 227 Cal. App. 3d 705, 716, 131 Cal. Rptr. 882 (1991).

[81.13] Madden v. Kaiser Foundation Hosps., 17 Cal. 3d 699, 710, 121 Cal. Rptr. 2d 391 (1976).

[81.14] Jefferson v. Department of Youth Auth., 28 Cal. 4th 299, 303 (2002).

there was no triable issue of fact on the issue of whether Form A201 was properly incorporated into the construction agreement.

State Farm asserted that because Scaramella claimed SDI never specifically told him that the construction agreement incorporated Form A201, there was a triable issue of fact as to whether he consented to Form A201. The appellate court rejected this contention.

A party to a contract does not have a duty to explain or draw attention to terms in that agreement.[81.15] Scaramella was bound by the terms of the agreement. By signing the agreement and initialing each page, he manifested an intent to consent to it, including to Form A201. Scaramella's declaration that he did not intend to agree to be bound by Form A201 did not create a triable issue of fact on this issue. "[I]t is elementary that the uncommunicated subjective belief of a contracting party is not competent evidence to prove the meaning of the contract."[81.16] The objective manifestation of an intent prevailed over Scaramella's undisclosed subjective intent.[81.17] That objective manifestation of intent was shown by his agreement to the clear terms of the construction agreement.

The fact that Scaramella struck a provision of the construction agreement concerning the allocation of risk as between Scaramella and SDI for damages not caused by SDI's negligence occurring during construction did not create a triable issue of fact on the enforceability of the waiver of subrogation clause. That clause was distinct from, and not contradictory to, the waiver of subrogation clause, which concerned what insurance would cover negligently caused damages, and barred the insured (and the insurer who covered the losses) from seeking reimbursement from the other party. There was also no triable issue of fact created by Scaramella's claim he did not receive a copy of Form A201. The law only requires that the document incorporated by reference be readily available.[81.18] The uncontroverted evidence, based upon Dougherty's declaration, was that Form A201 was available for review in SDI's office. The trial court correctly found that Scaramella's unsupported statement in his declaration claiming Form A201 was not readily available was without foundation and an improper conclusion. Scaramella did not assert he ever asked to see Form A201, nor that Dougherty refused to allow him to see it. Because the only admissible evidence established that SDI had a copy of Form A201 available for review, it was held to be binding on Scaramella and, hence, State Farm.[81.19]

State Farm contended that there was a triable issue of fact as to its estoppel defense. Specifically, State Farm asserted that SDI could not raise the waiver of subrogation clause, since it failed to raise that defense in a mediation session, only asserting the clause as a defense after State Farm filed this action and conducted discovery, and SDI and Sexton amended their answers. State Farm also asserted

---

[81.15] Brookwood v. Bank of Am., 45 Cal. App. 4th 1667, 1674, 53 Cal. Rptr. 2d 515 (1996).

[81.16] Stewart Title Co. v. Herbert, 6 Cal. App. 3d 957, 964, 96 Cal. Rptr. 631 (1970).

[81.17] Security Pac. Nat'l Bank v. Matek, 175 Cal. App. 3d 1071, 1075, 223 Cal. Rptr. 288 (1985).

[81.18] Kleveland v. Chicago Title Ins. Co., 141 Cal. App. 4th 761, 765, 46 Cal. Rptr. 314 (2006).

[81.19] *See* Slaught v. Bencomo Roofing Co., 25 Cal. App. 4th 744, 748-50, 30 Cal. Rptr. 2d 618 (1994) (arbitration clause in prime contract referenced in subcontract binding on subcontractors as subcontractors had duty to go to contractor's office to examine prime contract).

SDI and Sexton waived their right to rely on the waiver of subrogation clause. State Farm cited no authority for the proposition that a party is estopped to raise a defense if it fails to raise it in a mediation or if it amends its answer to add that defense. State Farm also briefly argued SDI and Sexton waived the right to rely on the waiver clause, because they did not seek to compel arbitration pursuant to an arbitration clause in Form A201. State Farm cited no authority for this proposition. The estoppel and waiver issues have been waived and the court did not address them further.[81.20]

The appellate court affirmed the trial court's grant of summary judgment. This decision demonstrates that the California courts still favor subrogation waivers, probably to reduce litigation in the courts between insurance companies.

§ 23.12 OMISSIONS FROM B101-2007

[E] Attorneys' Fees

Page 1166, add after first full paragraph:

Recoverability of attorneys' fees as damages may be a significant factor for a claimant determining whether to go forward with litigation. In *Herring-Malbis I, LLC, Eastern Shore Centre I, LLC, and Eastern Shore Centre II, LLC v. Temco, Inc.*,[126.1] a contractor brought an action for breach of contract, open account, and mechanic's lien action against a developer. Following arbitration, the circuit court granted contractor's motion for attorneys' fees under the Prompt Payment Act, and developer appealed.

The appellate court held that:

> (1) the parties' arbitration agreement required the contractor to submit its claim for attorney fees under the Prompt Payment Act to arbitration;
>
> (2) *res judicata* barred the contractor from seeking attorney fees under the Prompt Payment Act in the circuit court following the arbitration hearing; and
>
> (3) the developer was not judicially estopped from asserting that *res judicata* barred contractor's claim for attorney fees. Reversed and remanded with instructions.

In *Herring-Malbis*, the owner appealed from an order of the Baldwin Circuit Court awarding an attorney fee to Temco, Inc. (TEMCO), pursuant to Ala. Code 1975, § 8-29-1 *et seq.*, usually referred to as the Prompt Payment Act. The appellate court reversed the trial court's order awarding an attorney fee to Temco.

Temco sued Herring-Malbis in May 2006, alleging that Temco was owed money "pursuant to the terms and conditions of" contract documents signed by the parties, which included a construction contract and American Institute of Architects AIA Document A201-1997 general conditions, that were incorporated

---

[81.20] Associated Builders & Contractors, Inc. v. San Francisco Airports Comm'n, 21 Cal. 4th 352, 366, 87 Cal. Rptr. 2d 654 (1994).

[126.1] 2009 Ala. Civ. App. LEXIS 537, 2009 WL 3517580 (Ala. Civ. App. 2009).

into the parties' agreement by reference in the construction contract. Temco's original complaint sought damages in the amount of $486,303 plus interest and costs under several alternative theories of relief, including breach of contract, open account, account stated, work and labor done, and enforcement of mechanic's lien.

The circuit court granted Herring-Malbis's motion for an order compelling alternative dispute resolution under the terms of the AIA contract.

Pursuant to A201, the parties first attempted to resolve their dispute through mediation, and, when that failed, they arbitrated their dispute through the American Arbitration Association. The arbitration hearing was held on February 19 and 20, 2008. Six days before the commencement of the hearing, on February 13, 2008, Temco filed a motion to amend its original complaint. The motion sought "to amend the complaint to add a claim under the Prompt Payment Act . . . for reasonable attorneys' fees and expenses pursuant to said statute." The motion maintained that the Prompt Payment Act claim "in no way" affected the issues to be presented to the arbitrator but was a matter to be presented to court in the event that the arbitrator entered an award in favor of Temco. No action was taken on the motion prior to the arbitration hearing.

Temco presented a demand letter to AAA. Herring-Malbis presented an answering statement and counterclaim in the arbitration proceeding. In its demand letter, Temco itemized its claims for relief, which included a request for accumulated interest, but Temco omitted mention in the arbitration documents of any claim for an award of an attorney fee and any mention of particular theories of relief, including any right to relief under the Prompt Payment Act. The demand letter from Temco specified that Temco's principal claim was that it was due relief under the construction contract.

After the hearing, the arbitrator determined that Temco was owed most of what it claimed. The arbitrator also specified that each party would be responsible for its own attorney fees. The arbitration concluded by stating that "[a]ll claims not expressly granted herein are hereby[ ] denied," thereby denying Temco its request for an award of accumulated interest on any of its claims. Temco and Herring-Malbis then filed briefs concerning whether the arbitrator's award should be modified by deleting the reference to attorney fees and by awarding Temco the accumulated interest it sought. No changes to the award were made by the arbitrator. Herring-Malbis timely tendered payment to Temco in satisfaction of the arbitration award.

In April 2008, after the arbitration hearing, Herring-Malbis filed with the court a response in opposition to Temco's February 13, 2008 motion to amend its original complaint. The trial court granted Temco's motion to amend and overruled Herring-Malbis's objections. Temco then filed its amended complaint in May 2008, after which Herring-Malbis moved to dismiss that complaint. The trial court denied this motion, and, following a stipulation by the parties as to the amount of a reasonable attorney fee, and a further agreement of the parties to allow the trial court to rule on the matter without a hearing, the trial court entered an order awarding the stipulated attorney fee to Temco, "pursuant to the Prompt Payment Act," in November 2008.

The amended complaint ultimately filed by Temco pleaded the Prompt Payment Act as another alternative legal theory under which Temco sought complete relief. Under Count 10 of the amended complaint, Temco incorporated the remainder of the complaint and demanded relief as to all of its claims against all defendants, which then totaled $561,412.70, specifically including interest, costs, expenses, and attorney fees.

The demand letter written by Temco as a formality required by American Arbitration Association rules in order to initiate the arbitration process did not seek attorney fees or make claims under the Prompt Payment Act, but that omission does not conclusively establish that neither matter was discussed at the hearing.

The AIA contract incorporated into the parties' agreement provided that "any claim arising out of or related to the contract" shall be submitted first to mediation, and in the event mediation fails to resolve the dispute, as occurred here, the claim is to be submitted to arbitration. Where the contract defines "claim," it includes in that definition "other disputes and matters in question between [Herring-Malbis] and [Temco] arising out of or relating to the Contract," a sweepingly broad clause.

When parties include such a broad arbitration clause, they intend the clause to reach all aspects of the relationship. To like effect is the Alabama Supreme Court's holding that arbitration clauses, including the language "arising out of or relating to" that appears in the AIA contract, have broader application than arbitration clauses that omit "or relating to." The AIA contract further states that the party seeking relief in arbitration "must assert in the demand all Claims then known to that party on which arbitration is permitted to be demanded." Finally, the AIA contract further provides that arbitration will proceed under the Construction Industry Arbitration Rules of the American Arbitration Association, of which Rule 44(d) provides that "the award of the arbitrator may include . . . an award of attorneys' fees if all parties have requested such an award or it is authorized by law or their arbitration agreement."

The court held that Temco was required by the arbitration agreement, and by law, to submit its Prompt Payment Act claim, including the request for an award of an attorney fee, to the arbitrator. If, as Temco claimed, the parties did not submit the issue to the arbitrator, whether the arbitrator in fact made a determination concerning Temco's right to an attorney-fee award was immaterial.

In Temco's amended complaint, the Prompt Payment Act was asserted as an additional alternative theory under which Temco demanded complete relief. The entire Prompt Payment Act claim, including the request for an award of an attorney fee, was held to be within the ambit of the contract documents' definition of "claim," quoted above, and Temco was required to submit its Prompt Payment Act claim to the arbitrator, on pain of waiver, in light of the contractual provision stating that parties demanding arbitration "must assert in the demand all Claims then known to that party on which arbitration is permitted to be demanded."

Because Temco indicated its intent to assert the Prompt Payment Act claim in its motion to amend its complaint, filed in the circuit court six days before the arbitration hearing, that claim certainly was "known to" Temco at the time of the arbitration hearing.

The Prompt Payment Act claim also was a claim "on which arbitration is permitted to be demanded," contrary to Temco's assertions (a) that the contract documents provided no legal basis for requesting an award of an attorney fee and (b) that the Prompt Payment Act provided Temco's only legal basis for seeking such an award. For a particular claim or grievance to be excluded from arbitration, the parties must expressly exclude such claim in the arbitration agreement. Temco argued that the AIA contract did not allow the recovery of attorney fees, but it cited as support for this assertion provisions in the AIA contract such as paragraph 3.18.1, under which Temco had agreed not to pursue attorney fees related to a claim "provided that such claim . . . is attributable to bodily injury, sickness, disease or death, or to injury to or destruction of tangible property (other than the Work itself), but only to the extent caused by the negligent acts or omissions of [Temco]."

That provision, as well as other provisions Temco cited, were held inapplicable to this case, which concerned contractual disputes and not claims of bodily injury or property damage. Further, the AIA contract provided at paragraph 13.4:

> Duties and obligations imposed by the Contract Document and rights and remedies available thereunder shall be in addition to and not a limitation of duties, obligations, rights and remedies otherwise imposed or available by law.

The appellate court also noted that contractual arbitration terms were, in effect, nothing more than agreements to submit substantive controversies to a particular forum. They did not affect the substantive rights of parties, even when those rights were provided by statute. Temco had the same legal basis for submitting the question of an attorney fee to the arbitrator that it claims to have had for submitting that question to the circuit court.

Being contractually required to assert in arbitration "all claims," and in order to avoid preclusion of claims not asserted, Temco was required to bring all legal theories of relief supported by the "same nucleus of operative facts" to the arbitrator. Otherwise, those claims would have been barred from prosecution by Temco in a separate action. Under Alabama law, the doctrine of *res judicata* applied to arbitration awards just as it applied to judgments of courts. The elements of *res judicata* are "(1) a prior judgment on the merits, (2) rendered by a court of competent jurisdiction, (3) with substantial identity of the parties, and (4) with the same cause of action presented in both actions." A party is barred from relitigating any claims that were, or that "could have been," brought in the earlier action.

The appellate court held that the arbitrator's award constituted a prior decision on the merits, because the arbitrator provided specific findings, along with underlying bases for those findings, as to liability and the monetary amounts awarded on each substantive claim Temco had presented in its demand for arbitration, and the arbitrator further specified that any relief not expressly granted was denied. It was equally clear that the parties to the arbitration and to the subsequent circuit court proceeding were identical.

The claims also met the fourth element of *res judicata*, "the same cause of action." The established tests used to determine whether different claims present the same cause of action, whether the primary right and duty or wrong were the same, whether various theories arose from the same nucleus of operative facts, and whether the same evidence supported all the separate actions, were satisfied by both of Temco's complaints. In both the original complaint and the amended complaint, Temco stated its contended facts at the beginning, then listed each claim for relief separately in numbered counts, each of which incorporated the opening statement of facts, and then stated the requested relief under the legal theory. For example, in Temco's amended complaint, Count 10, asserting a claim under the Prompt Payment Act, incorporated the statement of facts and requested a total of $541,567 plus interest, costs, expenses, and attorney fees.

The court rejected Temco's argument that its motion to amend its original complaint, and the circuit court's ruling, amounted to, in effect, an "appeal" of the arbitrator's judgment under the Federal Arbitration Act (FAA) even though pertinent FAA guidelines were not "strictly" followed. The court stated that Temco was correct in noting that the substantive provisions of the FAA governed such issues as the enforceability of arbitration agreements, but the appellate court stated that it was Ala. Code 1975, § 6-6-15, that governed the procedural requirements for appealing from an arbitrator's decision in Alabama. Temco, in its appellate brief, essentially admitted that it did not follow any statutory procedures governing appeals of arbitration awards. Further, the appellate court noted that the AIA contract signed by the parties provided at paragraph 13.1.1 that "[t]he Contract shall be governed by the law of the place where the Project is located"—i.e., Alabama.

The pertinent provision in Alabama's arbitration statute, § 6-6-15, "contemplates a party's first seeking relief from an [arbitrator's] award in the circuit court." The court held that filing a separate motion six days before the arbitration hearing in a clear attempt to split related claims was not the equivalent of seeking judicial review of an award, as Temco asserted, and in any event recovery was barred by the parties' contract documents, as explained above. The fact that the circuit court viewed and ruled on numerous motions and briefs by the parties, and in so doing considered the same issues the parties raised on appeal, in awarding an attorney fee to Temco was found to be unavailing. The facts did not transform improper motions into a proper appeal. The trial court's failure to recognize that Temco was required to bring its Prompt Payment Act claim before the arbitrator, as reflected in its disposition of this issue, was merely an error of law.

The appellate court noted that the purposes and policies promoted by the doctrine of *res judicata* include the interests of both the public at large and the parties to a particular action in (a) finality of judgments, (b) reducing waste of private and judicial resources, and (c) avoiding inconsistent rulings. Similar results are achieved by the encouragement of arbitration in conformity to the FAA. Permitting Temco to split its claims and to try them in independent proceedings would violate its agreement with Herring-Malbis, statutory and case authority, and public policy.

Temco's final argument asserted that the *res judicata* argument advanced by Herring-Malbis was barred by judicial estoppel, because Herring-Malbis waited to respond to Temco's motion to amend its original complaint until after the arbitration hearing and allegedly failed to itself raise the issue of attorney fees at the arbitration hearing. According to Temco, those alleged omissions by Herring-Malbis amounted to the "adoption" of a "position" that Temco's motion to amend its complaint in the circuit court was a proper procedure by which Temco could seek relief under the Prompt Payment Act.

Because Temco's motion was submitted six days before the arbitration hearing, any deadline under the Rules of Civil Procedure, pursuant to which Herring-Malbis would have been required to file a response to that motion, would have occurred after the arbitration hearing. Herring-Malbis's failure to respond sooner did not amount to the assumption of a position that the circuit court could properly rule on the issue of attorney fees. Herring-Malbis had no duty to raise any of Temco's potential claims for relief before the arbitrator on Temco's behalf. The trial court rejected Temco's argument, because judicial estoppel requires first that a party assume a position in a legal proceeding, and Herring-Malbis's actions here did not amount to the assumption of a position that it later attempted to impeach.

Because the parties' contract documents required Temco to bring its Prompt Payment Act claim before the arbitrator, the appellate court held that Temco was barred under the doctrine of *res judicata* from later asserting that claim in the circuit court.

The appellate court concluded that Temco, having had "an opportunity to litigate" the claim before the arbitrator, was barred from, thereafter, asserting its Prompt Payment Act claim in the circuit court. The appellate court reversed the trial court's award of an attorney fee, and remanded the cause to the trial court for the entry of a judgment conforming to the arbitration award.

Failure to timely submit a claim to arbitration may bar a party later filing suit if the claim should have been brought in arbitration. Careful review by the attorney of the arbitration agreement is critical to prevent such a claim being barred if later presented in court.

Page 1169, add at end of subsection:

In *Marina Glecoe v. Neue Sentimental Film AG,*[129.1] a landlord brought an action against an alleged alter ego of a tenant for breach of a lease. While the alleged alter ego's motion for judgment was pending, the landlord filed a voluntary dismissal of the action, with prejudice. The alleged alter ego moved for attorney fees as the prevailing party, pursuant to an attorney fee provision in the lease. The trial court denied attorney fees, and the alleged alter ego appealed.

[129.1] 168 Cal. App. 4th 874, 85 Cal. Rptr. 3d 800 (2008), *review denied* (Feb. 11, 2009).

The appellate court held that: (1) dismissal with prejudice was voluntary, and thus there was no prevailing party for the purposes of recovering attorney fees, and (2) the alleged alter ego's settlement offer, which was held open well short of the period designated in the statute governing offers to compromise, was, once revoked, no longer an offer for purposes of the cost benefits of such statute. The alleged alter ego was not entitled to attorneys' fees based on that statute. The appellate court affirmed the trial court's ruling.

In *Marina Glencoe*, Neue Sentimental Film USA (NSF-USA) leased a commercial property from Marina Glencoe, L.P. The lease contained a provision for an award of attorney fees and costs to the prevailing party "if any action for breach of or to enforce the provisions of this Lease is commenced . . ." NSF-USA fell behind in paying the rent under the lease, and in May 2003, Marina Glencoe sued NSF-USA and two related companies, Neue Sentimental Film AG (NSF-AG) and Neue Sentimental Film N.Y., Inc. (NSF-NY), for breach of the lease. Marina Glencoe's theory was that each of these related companies also owed rent as the alter egos of NSF-USA. NSF-USA filed bankruptcy in August 2003, and NSF-AG answered the complaint on September 3, 2004.

On September 29, 2004, NSF-AG sent a letter to Marina Glencoe offering to settle the case. The offer stated it would be deemed rejected if it was not accepted in writing by October 4, 2004.

The bench trial proceeded only against NSF-AG. At Marina Glencoe's request, the court bifurcated the trial to adjudicate the issue of liability based on alter ego first, and subsequently to determine damages. After Marina Glencoe rested on the alter ego liability phase of trial, NSF-AG moved for judgment pursuant to Code of Civil Procedure section 631.8. The trial court heard arguments but did not rule on the motion that day, explaining that it wanted to review the exhibits, reread deposition testimony, and then give a tentative ruling by the end of the next day. The following day, prior to the court issuing a ruling on the pending motion, Marina Glencoe filed a voluntary dismissal of the action with prejudice.

NSF-AG moved for attorney fees as the prevailing party, pursuant to the attorney fee provision in the lease. The trial court concluded NSF-AG was not entitled to attorney fees under either California Civil Code section 1717 or Code of Civil Procedure section 998.

Civil Code section 1717 provides:

> (a) In any action on a contract, where the contract specifically provides that attorney's fees and costs, which are incurred to enforce that contract, shall be awarded either to one of the parties or to the prevailing party, then the party who is determined to be the party prevailing on the contract, whether he or she is the party specified in the contract or not, shall be entitled to reasonable attorney's fees in addition to other costs.

This action was for breach of a written lease which included the following attorney fee provision:

> [I]f any action for breach of or to enforce the provisions of this Lease is commenced, the court in such action shall award to the party in whose favor a judgment is entered, a reasonable sum as attorneys' fees and costs. The losing party in such action shall pay such attorneys' fees and costs.

After respondent Marina Glencoe dismissed the action, appellant NSF-AG sought attorney fees as the prevailing party under section 1717. However, section 1717 subd. (b)(2) provided that where an action has been voluntarily dismissed, or dismissed pursuant to a settlement of the case, there shall be no prevailing party for purposes of this section.

In this case, the court dismissed the action while the appellant's motion for judgment was pending. The appellant argued that this dismissal should not be deemed a voluntary dismissal. However, the *Glencoe* court stated that it was not the stage of the proceedings which distinguished a voluntary dismissal from an involuntary one, but it was the plaintiff's role in bringing about the dismissal. Because the dismissal was entered at the request of the respondent, it was voluntary, and there was no prevailing party for the purposes of recovering attorneys' fees and costs incurred in defending the contract action under section 1717.

A second ground for appellant's claim for entitlement to an award of attorneys' fees was as costs under California Code of Civil Procedure section 998, because respondent rejected appellant's offer, and failed to achieve a better result at trial. The then-current version of section 998 provided:

> Not less than 10 days prior to commencement of trial . . . , any party may serve an offer in writing upon any other party to the action to allow judgment to be taken or an award to be entered in accordance with the terms and conditions stated at that time . . . If the offer is not accepted prior to trial or arbitration, [or] within 30 days after it is made, whichever occurs first, it shall be deemed withdrawn, and cannot be given in evidence upon the trial or arbitration. If an offer made by a defendant is not accepted and the plaintiff fails to obtain a more favorable judgment or award, the plaintiff shall not recover his or her postoffer costs and shall pay the defendant's costs from the time of the offer.

Although the settlement offer from appellant stated that it was being made under section 998, the offer was written or made on September 29, 2004, and stated that the offer would be deemed rejected if not accepted in writing by October 4, 2004. The court agreed with respondent that this offer did not provide sufficient time for acceptance under section 998, and that it was well short of the statutory period. Once revoked under the terms of the offer, it was no longer an offer for the purposes of the cost benefits under section 998.

[I] Limiting Remedies

Page 1173, add after second full paragraph:

In *Advantages of the ConsensusDOCS Construction Contracts,*[140.1] the authors discuss consequential damages. The ConsensusDOCS provide for a limited waiver of consequential damages. The documents call for the owner to promptly delineate liquidated damage, and to identify items specifically excluded from the waiver of consequential damages under the documents. Harris and Perlberg claim that this sharing of information concerning the downside risk of failures of performance provides the financial incentives to achieve proper performance, which they claim is in the best interests of the project.

§ 23.23 ATTORNEYS' FEES

Page 1210, add at end of section:

In *Marina Glencoe v. Neue Sentimental Film AG,*[236.1] a landlord brought an action against an alleged alter ego of a tenant for breach of a lease. While the alleged alter ego's motion for judgment was pending, the landlord filed a voluntary dismissal of the action, with prejudice. The alleged alter ego moved for attorney fees as the prevailing party, pursuant to an attorney fee provision in the lease. The trial court denied attorney fees, and the alleged alter ego appealed.

The appellate court held that: (1) dismissal with prejudice was voluntary, and thus there was no prevailing party for the purposes of recovering attorney fees, and (2) the alleged alter ego's settlement offer, which was held open well short of the period designated in the statute governing offers to compromise, was, once revoked, no longer an offer for purposes of the cost benefits of such statute. The alleged alter ego was not entitled to attorneys' fees based on that statute. The appellate court affirmed the trial court's ruling.

In *Marina Glencoe*, Neue Sentimental Film USA (NSF-USA) leased a commercial property from Marina Glencoe, L.P. The lease contained a provision for an award of attorney fees and costs to the prevailing party "if any action for breach of or to enforce the provisions of this Lease is commenced . . ." NSF-USA fell behind in paying the rent under the lease, and in May, 2003, Marina Glencoe sued NSF-USA and two related companies, Neue Sentimental Film AG (NSF-AG) and Neue Sentimental Film N.Y., Inc. (NSF-NY), for breach of the lease. Marina Glencoe's theory was that each of these related companies also owed rent as the alter egos of NSF-USA. NSF-USA filed bankruptcy in August 2003, and NSF-AG answered the complaint on September 3, 2004.

On September 29, 2004, NSF-AG sent a letter to Marina Glencoe offering to settle the case. The offer stated it would be deemed rejected if it was not accepted in writing by October 4, 2004.

[140.1] Larry D. Harris and Brian M. Perlberg, *Advantages of the ConsensusDOCS Construction Contracts*, The Construction Lawyer, Vol. 29, No. 1, Winter 2009.

[236.1] 168 Cal. App. 4th 874, 85 Cal. Rptr. 3d 800 (2008), *review denied* (Feb. 11, 2009).

The bench trial proceeded only against NSF-AG. At Marina Glencoe's request, the court bifurcated the trial to adjudicate the issue of liability based on alter ego first, and subsequently to determine damages. After Marina Glencoe rested on the alter ego liability phase of trial, NSF-AG moved for judgment pursuant to Code of Civil Procedure section 631.8. The trial court heard arguments but did not rule on the motion that day, explaining that it wanted to review the exhibits, reread deposition testimony, and then give a tentative ruling by the end of the next day. The following day, prior to the court issuing a ruling on the pending motion, Marina Glencoe filed a voluntary dismissal of the action with prejudice.

NSF-AG moved for attorney fees as the prevailing party, pursuant to the attorney fee provision in the lease. The trial court concluded NSF-AG was not entitled to attorney fees under either California Civil Code section 1717 or Code of Civil Procedure section 998.

Civil Code section 1717 (section 1717) provides:

> (a) In any action on a contract, where the contract specifically provides that attorney's fees and costs, which are incurred to enforce that contract, shall be awarded either to one of the parties or to the prevailing party, then the party who is determined to be the party prevailing on the contract, whether he or she is the party specified in the contract or not, shall be entitled to reasonable attorney's fees in addition to other costs.

This action was for breach of a written lease which included the following attorney fee provision:

> [I]f any action for breach of or to enforce the provisions of this Lease is commenced, the court in such action shall award to the party in whose favor a judgment is entered, a reasonable sum as attorneys' fees and costs. The losing party in such action shall pay such attorneys' fees and costs.

After respondent Marina Glencoe dismissed the action, appellant NSF-AG sought attorney fees as the prevailing party under section 1717. However, section 1717 subd. (b)(2) provided that where an action has been voluntarily dismissed, or dismissed pursuant to a settlement of the case, there shall be no prevailing party for purposes of this section.

In this case, the court dismissed the action while the appellant's motion for judgment was pending. The appellant argued that this dismissal should not be deemed a voluntary dismissal. However, the *Glencoe* court stated that it was not the stage of the proceedings which distinguished a voluntary dismissal from an involuntary one, but it was the plaintiff's role in bringing about the dismissal. Because the dismissal was entered at the request of the respondent, it was voluntary, and there was no prevailing party for the purposes of recovering attorneys' fees and costs incurred in defending the contract action under section 1717.

A second ground for appellant's claim for entitlement to an award of attorneys' fees was as costs under California Code of Civil Procedure section

998, because respondent rejected appellant's offer, and failed to achieve a better result at trial. The then-current version of section 998 provided:

> Not less than 10 days prior to commencement of trial . . . , any party may serve an offer in writing upon any other party to the action to allow judgment to be taken or an award to be entered in accordance with the terms and conditions stated at that time . . . If the offer is not accepted prior to trial or arbitration, [or] within 30 days after it is made, whichever occurs first, it shall be deemed withdrawn, and cannot be given in evidence upon the trial or arbitration. If an offer made by a defendant is not accepted and the plaintiff fails to obtain a more favorable judgment or award, the plaintiff shall not recover his or her postoffer costs and shall pay the defendant's costs from the time of the offer.

Although the settlement offer from appellant stated that it was being made under section 998, the offer was written or made on September 29, 2004, and stated that the offer would be deemed rejected if not accepted in writing by October 4, 2004. The court agreed with respondent that this offer did not provide sufficient time for acceptance under section 998, and that it was well short of the statutory period. Once revoked under the terms of the offer, it was no longer an offer for the purposes of the cost benefits under section 998.

§ 23.25 PERIOD OF LIMITATIONS

Page 1216, add after carryover paragraph:

In *Heitritter v. Callahan Construction,*[247.1] homeowners brought an action against a general contractor for breach of contract to build a home and for breach of warranty. The district court granted partial summary judgment to the contractor based on the statute of limitations. The appellate court affirmed the trial court, holding that the written form agreement containing an express written warranty was not incorporated by reference into contract, and, thus, the five-year statute of limitations for unwritten contracts applied, rather than the 10-year statute of limitations for written contracts.

In the case, the Heitritters entered into a contract with the contractors, Callahan Construction Co., whereby Callahan was to provide various labor and materials for the construction of the Heitritters' new home. A construction management company, AL Lundh & Associates (Lundh) prepared the contract for the Heitritters. The Heitritters stipulated at oral argument on the motion for summary judgment that the contract was provided by them or their agent.

The contract was a standard American Institute of Architects (AIA) form and is referred to as "AIA Document A101/CM." The title on the agreement was "Standard Form of Agreement Between Owner and Contractor where the basis for payment is a STIPULATED SUM" and states it is the "1980 EDITION." The title page of the agreement also stated "THIS DOCUMENT HAS IMPORTANT

[247.1] 670 N.W.2d 430 (Table), 2003 WL 22015970 (Iowa Ct. App. 2003) (unpublished decision).

LEGAL CONSEQUENCES; CONSULTATION WITH AN ATTORNEY IS ENCOURGAGED," and that "This document is intended to be used in conjunction with AIA Documents A201/CM, 1980; B141/CM, 1980; and B801, 1980."

Article I of the parties' agreement appeared to be an incorporation clause describing those documents that can constitute part of the contract. It provided as follows:

> *ARTICLE 1*
> **THE CONTRACT DOCUMENTS**
>
> The Contract Documents consist of this Agreement, the Conditions of the Contract (General, Supplementary and other Conditions), the Drawings, the Specifications, all Addenda issued prior to and all Modifications Issued after execution of this Agreement. These form the Contract, and all are as fully a part of the Contract as if attached to this Agreement or repeated herein. An enumeration of the Contract Documents appears in Article 7.
>
> Article 7 of the agreement, entitled "Miscellaneous Provisions," includes the enumeration clause referred to in Article 1. It directs the parties to list those documents that constitute the contract. It provides as follows:
>
> 7.1 Terms used in this Agreement which are defined in the Conditions of the Contract shall have the meanings designated in those Conditions.
>
> 7.2 The Contract Documents, which constitute the entire agreement between the Owner and the Contractor, are listed in Article 1 and, except for Modifications issued after execution of this Agreement, are enumerated as follows:

The space below section 7.2 set aside for listing the contract documents was left blank by the parties. Nowhere in the agreement was there an express requirement that Callahan perform in a good and workmanlike manner. However, such express warranties are found in AIA Document A201/CM, 1980.

AIA Document A201/CM, 1980 was a 21-page document entitled "General Conditions of the Contract for Construction," which contained numerous specific contractor warranties. The document was not physically attached to the agreement when it was signed by the parties. The only documents attached to the agreement were a two-page document labeled "Proposal" and a one-page document entitled "CHANGE ORDER CONSTRUCTION MANAGEMENT EDITION AIA DOCUMENT G701/CM." It was undisputed that neither Callahan nor its agents were ever given or shown a copy of A201/CM or given a chance to review its contents. Furthermore, the parties never discussed the contents of A201/CM.

As the various contractors and subcontractors began work on the home, the Heitritters complained of various defects and problems with the home. The complaints continued through October 1994, but they did not file suit against the contractors (as well as five other entities involved in construction of their home) until December 29, 1999. The Heitritters claimed that Callahan (1) failed to follow the plans and specifications, (2) performed its services in a manner that resulted in defects and deficiencies, and (3) failed to use good workmanship in the performance of its services.

Callahan moved for partial summary judgment arguing that the second and third claims were warranty claims based upon an implied or oral provision and were, thus, barred by the five-year statute of limitations for unwritten contracts under Iowa Code section 614.1(4). Specifically, Callahan argued that its obligations to perform its work in a good and workmanlike manner, free of defects and deficiencies, were not express terms of the written contract with the Heitritters, but rather sprang from the general, implied warranties that were a part of Iowa law, and such implied warranties were subject to a five-year statute of limitation under section 614.1(4).

In contrast, the Heitritters contended that A201/CM was incorporated by reference into the parties' agreement, and their claims of breach of warranty were based on the express, written warranty set forth in Article 4.5.1 of A201/CM. Accordingly, they argued their second and third claims were not barred by the statute of limitations, because the time period to bring a suit on a written contract is 10 years under section 614.1(5).

The district court granted Callahan partial summary judgment, dismissing the Heitritters' second and third claims. It denied summary judgment on their first claim, leaving for trial only the issue of Callahan's alleged breach of contract for failure to follow the plans and specifications. The court concluded that A201/CM, and the express warranty contained therein, was not a part of the parties' agreement and, thus, the Heitritters' second and third claims were barred by the five-year statute of limitations under section 614.1(4). The Heitritters' remaining claim proceeded to trial and the jury returned a verdict in favor of Callahan. On appeal, the Heitritters challenged only the district court's grant of partial summary judgment as to the claims that were dismissed as barred by the statute of limitations.

The appellate court affirmed the trial court on this issue and rejected the contention that the A201/CM was incorporated by reference into the parties' agreement and was a part of their agreement.

Under the doctrine of incorporation by reference, one document becomes part of another separate document simply by reference as if the former is fully set out in the latter. However, clear and specific reference was required to incorporate an extrinsic document by reference.

As set forth above, nowhere in the Standard Form Agreement signed by the parties were there any express, written contractor warranties requiring Callahan to perform in a good and workmanlike manner. These written warranties were found only in A201/CM, which was not attached to the agreement, shown to Callahan, or discussed by the parties. Thus, there was no genuine issue of material fact concerning whether the General Conditions set forth in AIA Document A201/CM, 1980, were incorporated by reference into the agreement between the Heitritters and Callahan. The only place any reference to A201/CM appeared in AIADocument A101/CM was on its first, title page. A101/CM there stated, "This document is intended to be used in conjunction with AIA Documents A201/CM, 1980; B141/CM, 1980; and B801, 1980." The Heitritters relied on this language in arguing that it incorporated A201/CM into the parties' agreement by reference. The district court, however, found this phrase did not incorporate A201/CM into the agreement and make it part of the contract. The district court held and the appellate court agreed that the document in question (A101/CM) was a form designed to be used by many different people. The sentence under consideration was simply a reminder to users that there were potential documents that should be considered for use in addition to 101/CM in light of circumstances of various situations.[247.2] In concluding that the agreement executed by the parties did not include the express warranties at issue, the district court further found:

> It would be inherently unfair to burden [Callahan] with compliance with a 21 page form contract it had never seen, considered or been told about. Article 7, when executed properly, serves to make it clear what other documents the parties are intending to include as a part of the formal agreement. Failure to list AIA Document 201/CM means it isn't part of the contract.

In addition, the appellate court found that the language relied upon by the Heitritters appeared in a block of language of the first page of A101/CM, a block that set forth the title of the document, containing language noting the document had legal consequences, and was separated from the rest of the document by horizontal lines. The following, remaining portion of the document was then identified as and, thus, constituted the parties "AGREEMENT."

The court noted that preliminary recitals of an agreement do not become binding obligations unless so referred to in the operative portion of the instrument as to show a design they should form a part of it. Similarly, the introductory, instructional language appearing on the first page of the document does not become part of their "AGREEMENT" which follows unless so referred to in the operative portion as to show an intent it should form a part thereof. No language in the operative portion of A101/CM as executed by the parties incorporated A201/CM by reference, or indicated that either of the parties in fact intended to do so.

Parties using A101/CM are not required to use A201/CM as the parties' general conditions. Under Article 7, the parties in this case were directed to enumerate any general or other conditions they intended to incorporate into their agreement and they did not list A201/CM or any general, supplementary, or other conditions whatsoever.

Further, to treat the introductory language as incorporating A201/CM would produce a bizarre result. The introductory language similarly referred to AIA Documents B141/CM and B801 and, just as with A201/CM, instructed the parties that A101/CM was intended to be used with them. The appellate court stated that were it to accept the Heitritters' argument that this introductory language incorporated A201/CM by reference, the same language would of necessity by

---

[247.2] *Citing* Atlantic Mut. Ins. Co. v. Metron Eng'g & Constr. Co., 83 F.3d 897, 899 (7th Cir.1996).

reference incorporate these other documents into the parties' agreement. However, neither party suggested such an intent or result in this case, nor was there any substantial evidence in the record that would support such an intent or result. The appellate court stated that it should not read the contract in such a strained manner as to require a result the parties did not and do not intend.

In sum, the appellate court concluded that the question of incorporation by reference presented a question of law, and a clear and specific reference was required to incorporate one document into another by reference. The parties' agreement, A101/CM, did not contain a clear and specific reference incorporating A201/CM. Thus, the district court did not err in determining the Heitritters' warranty claims had to be based on implied warranties and were, thus, barred by the five-year statute of limitations in Iowa Code section 614.1(4). Accordingly, the appellate court affirmed the district court, holding that the trial court did not err in granting partial summary judgment.

TABLE OF CASES

(References are to section numbers.)

Case	***Book §***
Aas v. Superior Court, 24 Cal. 4th 627, 101 Cal. Rptr. 2d 718, 12 P.3d 1125 (2000),	12.06[C], 19.04
Acme Arsena Co., Inc. v. J. Holden Constr. Co., Ltd., 2008 WL 5182912 (Ohio App. 8 Dist., 2008),	21.05[D]
Advantage Medical Services, LLC v. Hoffman, 160 Cal. App. 4th 806, 72 Cal. Rptr. 3d 935 (2008),	21.05[C]
Agri-Systems, Inc. v. Foster Poultry Farms, 168 Cal. App. 4th 1128, 85 Cal. Rptr. 3d 917 (2008),	21.05[C]
Alatriste v. Cesar's Exterior Designs, Inc., 183 Cal. App. 4th 656, 108 Cal. Rptr. 3d 277 (2010),	9.10
Alfred Engineering, Inc. v. Illinois Fair Employment Practices Comm'n, 19 Ill. App.3d 592, 312 N.E.2d 61 (1974),	21.05[A]
Allied-Lynn Associates, Inc. v. Alex Bro., LLC, 8 A.D.3d 1198, 834 N.Y.S.2d 906 (2007), *aff'g 18 Misc.* 3d 1147A, 859 N.Y.S.2d 892 (N.Y. Sup. Ct., Aug. 12, 2005), *aff'd* 38 A.D.3d 1198, 834 N.Y.S.2d 906 (2007), *appeal dismissed*, 9 N.Y.3d 831, 872 N.E.2d 249, 840 N.Y.S.2d 563 (2007),	17.02
Amedeo Hotels Ltd. Partnership v. Zwicker Elec. Co., 291 A.D.2d 322, 739 N.Y.S.2d 10 (2002),	5.07[H], 5.09
Andrew Velez Const., Inc., *In re*, 373 B.R. 262 (S.D.N.Y. 2007),	20.04[C]
Apollo Group, Inc. v. Avnet, Inc., 58 F.3d 477 (9th Cir.1995),	5.02, 5.09
Archambault v. Soneco/Northeastern, Inc., 287 Conn. 20, 946 A.2d 839 (2008),	14.02, 14.05, 17.02
Ashley v. Bizzell, 694 S.W.2d 349 (Tex. App.-San Antonio 1985),	12.02, 15.01
Associated Builders & Contractors, Inc. v. San Francisco Airports Commission, 21 Cal. 4th 352, 87 Cal. Rptr. 2d 654 (1994),	23.11
Atlantic Mut. Ins. Co. v. Metron Eng'g & Constr. Co., 83 F.3d 897 (7th Cir.1996),	23.25
AT & T Technologies, Inc., v. Communications Workers of America, 475 U.S. 643, 106 S. Ct. 1415, 89 L. Ed. 2d 648 (1986),	21.05[C], 21.05[D]
Baker v. Aubry, 216 Cal. App. 3d 1259, 265 Cal. Rptr. 381 (1989),	23.11
Beartooth Lodge v. Yellowstone Electric Co., No. DV 92-17, 1993 Mont. Dist. LEXIS 636 (Carbon County, Mont.1993),	22.04[B]
Berschauer/Phillips Constr. Co. v. Seattle Sch. Dist. No. 1, 124 Wash. 2d 816, 881 P.2d 986 (1994),	5.02, 5.09
Best Friends Pet Care, Inc. v. Design Learned, Inc., 77 Conn. App. 167, 823 A.2d 329 (2003),	22.04[B]
Biakanja v. Irving, 49 Cal. 2d 647, 320 P.2d 16 (1958),	14.05
Blacks Law Dictionary 816 (Bryan A. Garner ed., 7th ed., West 1999),	21.05[C]

Case	*Book §*
Darling v. Burrone Bros., Inc., 162 Conn. 187 (1972),	14.02, 14.05, 17.02
Davencourt at Pilgrims Landing Homeowners Ass'n v. Davencourt at Pilgrims Landing, LC, 221 P.3d 234 (Utah 2009),	5.02, 5.09
Davlar Corp. v. Superior Court, 53 Cal. App. 4th 1121, 62 Cal. Rptr. 2d 199 (1997),	23.11
Diocese of Metuchen v.Prisco & Edwards, AIA, 374 N.J. Super. 409, 864 A.2d 1168 (App. Div. 2005),	5.09
DJB Building & Construction, LLC v. Parkville Plaza, LLC, 2009 Conn. Super. LEXIS 2621, 2009 WL 3644879 (Conn. Super. Ct., Sept. 24, 2009),	20.04[E]
Dominion Consulting and Management, Inc. v. Davis, 63 Va. Cir. 548, 2004 WL 288545 (Va. Cir. Ct.) (2004),	21.05[C]
Donnelly Construction Co. v. Oberg/Hunt/Gilleland, 139 Ariz. 184, 677 P.2d 1292 (1984),	5.02, 5.09
East River S.S. Corp. v. Transamerica Delaval, Inc., 476 U.S. 858, 106 S. Ct. 2295, 90 L. Ed. 2d 865 (1986),	5.02, 5.09
Evans v. Singer, 518 F. Supp. 2d 1134 (D.Ariz.2007),	5.02, 5.09
Ferrante Immobiliare, LLC v. Pace, 68 A.D.3d 463, 891 N.Y.S.2d 27 (2009),	5.07[H], 5.09
Fidelity & Deposit Co. v. Stool, 607 S.W.2d 17 (Tex. Civ. App.-Tyler 1980),	12.02, 15.01
Fifth Day, LLC, The v. Bolotin, 172 Cal. App. 4th 939, 91 Cal. Rptr. 3d 633 (2009)	5.07[B][1],9.05
Fillmore v. Irvine, 146 Cal. App. 3d 649, 194 Cal. Rptr. 319 (1983),	14.05
Financial Pacific Insurance Company v. Northrop, Not Reported in Cal. Rptr. 3d, 2009 WL 1132339 (Cal. App. 1 Dist.) (2009),	22.05[A]
Flagstaff Affordable Hous. Ltd. P'ship v. Design Alliance, Inc., 221 Ariz. 433, 212 P.3d 125 (App. 2009),	5.02, 5.09
Flagstaff Affordable Hous. Ltd. P'ship v. Design Alliance, Inc., 223 P.3d 664 (Ariz. 2010),	5.02, 5.09
Flores v. Lower E. Side Serv. Ctr., Inc., 4 N.Y.3d 363, 828 N.E.2d 593, 795 N.Y.S.2d 491 (2005),	14.02, 14.05, 17.02
Freedman v. State Farm Insurance Co., 173 Cal. App. 4th 957, 93 Cal. Rptr. 3d 296, 2009 WL 1202559 (Cal. App. 2 Dist.) (2009),	22.03[E]
Frisch v. International Harvester Co., 33 Ill.App.3d 507, 338 N.E.2d 90 (1975),	14.05
Galloway Cor. v. S.B. Ballard Constr. Co., 250 Va. 493, 464 S.E.2d 349 (1995),	17.06
General Supply & Constr. Co., 241 N.Y. 28 (1925),	20.04[C]
Gilbert v. Albany Med. Ctr., 21 A.D.3d 677, 799 N.Y.S.2d 685 (2005),	14.02, 14.05, 17.02
Giles v. Gen. Motors Acceptance Corp., 494 F.3d 865 (9th Cir. 2007),	5.02, 5.09
Goldstein v. Barak Constr., 164 Cal. App. 4th 845, 79 Cal. Rptr. 3d 603 (2008),	9.10
Gourley v. State Farm Mut. Auto. Ins. Co., 53 Cal. 3d 121, 3 Cal. Rptr. 2d 666, 822 P. 2d 374 (1191),	15.11, 21.06[L]
Great West Contractors v. WSS Industrial Construction, 162 Cal. App. 4th 581, 76 Cal. Rptr. 3d 8 (2008),	9.10

TABLE OF AIA DOCUMENTS

(References are to section numbers.)

INDEX

References are to chapter and section numbers.